ROBERT S. McNAMARA

In Retrospect

Robert S. McNamara was secretary of defense under Presidents
Kennedy and Johnson, president of the Ford Motor Company,
and president of the World Bank. Since leaving the World Bank
he has been active in economic development efforts across the
globe and in the arms control and non-proliferation movements.
A native of San Francisco, he lives in Washington, D.C.

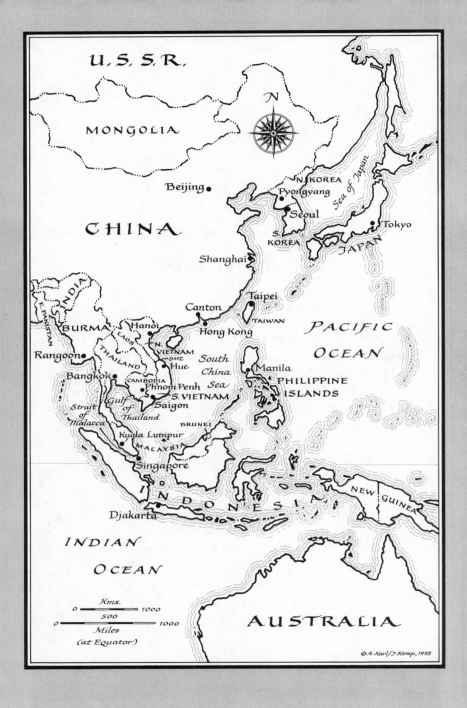

ROBERT S. MCNAMARA

In Retrospect

THE TRAGEDY AND LESSONS OF VIETNAM

with Brian VanDeMark

VINTAGE BOOKS

A Division of Random House, Inc.   New York

FIRST VINTAGE BOOKS EDITION, MARCH 1996

The Library of Congress has cataloged the Times Books edition
as follows:
McNamara, Robert S.
In retrospect : the tragedy and lessons of Vietnam / Robert S.
McNamara with Brian VanDeMark.—1st ed.
p. cm.
Includes bibliographical references and index.
ISBN 0-8129-2523-8
1. Vietnamese Conflict, 1961–1975—United States.
I. VanDeMark, Brian, 1960–. II. Title.
DS558.M44 1995
959.704´3373—dc20 94-40088
Vintage ISBN: 0-679-76749-5

Random House Web address: http://www.randomhouse.com/

Book designed by Naomi Osnos and M. Kristen Bearse

Printed in the United States of America
10 9 8 7 6 5 4 3 2 1

In Memory of Marg,

one of God's loveliest creatures.

She enriched the lives of all who knew her,

and she brought me strength and joy

as we journeyed through forty years of life together.

Contents

A brief sketch of my life from birth, June 9, 1916, to the day I became President John F. Kennedy's secretary of defense, January 20, 1961. I explain how I came to that post and the beliefs and values I brought to it.

The Kennedy administration's decisions relating to Vietnam from the time of a critical meeting with President Eisenhower the day before JFK's inauguration, through the political crisis that erupted in Saigon in the summer of 1963. The chapter outlines the assumptions behind the administration's decision to increase sharply U.S. involvement in Vietnam. It stresses the two contradictory premises that underlay that commitment: the fall of South Vietnam to Communist control would threaten the security of the West, but the U.S. military role would be limited to providing training and logistical support.

A pivotal period of U.S. involvement in Vietnam, punctuated by three important events: the overthrow and assassination of South Vietnam's president Ngo Dinh Diem; President Kennedy's decision on October 2 to begin the withdrawal of U.S. forces; and his assassination fifty days later.

The chapter opens with a statement of what I believe President Kennedy would have done in Vietnam had he lived. It then describes the subtle, incremental, but crucial slide toward deeper involvement in Vietnam during the first eight months of the Johnson Administration. After Diem's death, we confronted an unraveling political situation in Saigon, along with growing demands for more U.S. military action.

The closest the United States came to a declaration of war, the Tonkin Gulf Congressional Resolution of August 1964 generated intense controversy and enduring questions: What happened? Why? What were the consequences? What should have been done differently? This chapter addresses those questions by describing what transpired in the Tonkin Gulf; why the Johnson administration acted as it did; why Congress quickly and overwhelmingly approved the resolution: and how LBJ and his successor, President Nixon, subsequently misused it.

6. The 1964 Election and Its Aftermath:
August 8, 1964–January 27, 1965   145

As the Johnson administration's policy on Vietnam drifted during the 1964 presidential election, military and political conditions in South Vietnam rapidly worsened, heightening the dilemma between avoiding direct U.S. military involvement in the conflict and avoiding the loss of South Vietnam to communist control. Deep divisions developed within the American government, and the Pentagon itself, over what to do in the face of an increasingly difficult and dangerous problem. Events reached a critical juncture when we faced a choice among unpalatable alternatives at the beginning of 1965.

7. The Decision to Escalate:
January 28–July 28, 1965   169

The most crucial phase of America's thirty-year involvement in Indochina, the six months between January 28 and July 28, 1965, saw the United States embark on a course of massive military intervention in Vietnam, an intervention which ultimately destroyed Lyndon Johnson's presidency and polarized America like nothing since the Civil War. How did it happen? Why did we fail to foresee the implications of our actions? What hopes, fears, perceptions, and judgments—accurate and inaccurate— shaped our thinking and actions? This chapter gives answers to these and other often-asked questions.

8. The Christmas Bombing Pause, An Unsuccessful Attempt to Move to Negotiations:
July 29, 1965–January 30, 1966   207

Reality collided with expectations. Slowly and gradually the sobering, frustrating, tormenting problems and limitations dogging our military operations in Vietnam became painfully apparent. The growing realization of these difficulties led to proposals for further escalation which, in turn, increased the pressure for a diplomatic resolution of the war. This culminated in a highly controversial month-long bombing pause at the end of 1965. But

Hanoi and the Vietcong responded negatively, and 1966 began with pressures for an ever-widening war.

Between late January 1966 and mid-May 1967, the war and its casualties grew substantially; debates over ground strategy, pacification, and especially bombing intensified dramatically; and war-related pressures on the Johnson administration, my family, and me increased almost daily. Public support remained strong but dissent began to grow. Three further sporadic, amateurish, and ineffective attempts to start negotiations failed. The period ended with still another request from General Westmoreland to increase U.S. troop levels. And underlying it all was the growing gap between the president and his secretary of defense, a gap crystallized by a memorandum from me to President Johnson on May 19, 1967.

My May 19, 1967 memorandum triggered a storm of controversy. It intensified already sharp debate within the administration. It led to tense and acrimonious Senate hearings on the bombing that pitted me against the Joint Chiefs of Staff. And it accelerated the process that ultimately drove LBJ and me apart. A deluge of other crises taxed the already strained government: a Mideast war leading to the first use of the "hot line" between Moscow and Washington; racial rioting in major American cities; rising public unrest culminating in a massive attempt to shut down the Pentagon. Carrying my thoughts of May 19 further still, I gave President Johnson another memo on November 1 that brought the difference between us over Vietnam to the breaking point.

Reflections on the war: With hindsight, was the U.S. wise to intervene militarily in Vietnam? What mistakes did we make?

What lessons can be learned? And how can those lessons be applied to the present and the future?

On several occasions during the Vietnam War, the Joint Chiefs of Staff recommended actions which they stated might lead to the use of nuclear weapons. And recent disclosures have shown that during the Cuban Missile Crisis in 1962, the United States, the Soviet Union, Cuba, and indeed the world came much closer to nuclear disaster than was realized at the time. There is today both a growing recognition of the lack of military utility of nuclear weapons and a heightened understanding of the risks associated with their continued deployment. As a result, more and more security experts are urging that nuclear arsenals be reduced below the levels agreed to by Presidents Bush and Yeltsin. Some are urging we return, insofar as practicable, to a non-nuclear world.

Preface to
the Vintage Edition

The publication of *In Retrospect* in April 1995 stimulated enormous interest. The book was greeted with both harsh criticism and warm praise. I have included a sampling of both reactions in an Appendix new to this edition.

Often I am asked whether I was surprised by the controversy created by the book. My answer is no. It is clear our nation has neither fully understood nor fully come to terms with Vietnam. The wounds remain unhealed and the lessons unlearned. It was to assist in the healing process, and to accelerate the learning process, that I wrote the book. Initially I wondered whether either objective would be achieved. Later it became clearer that many of the most critical comments came from those who had simply not read the book. With the passage of time, the tone began to change from emotional reaction to constructive and thoughtful reflection. Typical of the latter were statements by three individuals who were most deeply scarred by the war:

- Anne Morrison Welsh, the widow of Norman Morrison, the Quaker who burned himself to death beneath my Pentagon window on November 2, 1965, wrote: "To heal the wounds of that war, we must forgive ourselves and each other, and help the people of Vietnam to rebuild their country. I am grateful to Robert McNamara for his courageous and honest reappraisal of the Vietnam war and his involvement in it. I hope his book will contribute to the healing process."

• Ron Kovic, the paraplegic Marine combat veteran and author of the moving story *Born on the Fourth of July,* said: "Over the long run, McNamara's book and his comments will promote healing. As Americans, we must all embrace McNamara."

• David Hackworth (Colonel, USA, retired), the most decorated American veteran of the Vietnam war, writing in *Newsweek,* April 24, 1995, quoted a fellow veteran as saying, when he first heard of the book, he "felt a sense of rage beginning to well up deep inside me, a rage I have worked hard to suppress over the last 25 years." But he ended his article with these words: "McNamara's book is an important step toward understanding what happened, and it may help some of the walking wounded to move further along the healing path of forgiveness. And that's good for America's collective soul."

The book continues to stimulate debate, not only in the U.S. but abroad. I have just returned from visits to Japan, Germany, the Netherlands, and Botswana. In each of these countries *In Retrospect* was the subject of heated discussion. More and more readers are recognizing that the lessons of Vietnam are applicable to the world of today—to Bosnia, for example—and will continue to be applicable, as well, to the world of tomorrow.

Many of the archives containing documents on the war remain closed. And many officials—both civilian and military—who participated in decisions relating to the conflict have yet to be heard from. This is true in the United States, but even more so in China, Russia, and Vietnam. Gradually, more documents will be released and more memoirs will be written. To hasten this process, I have asked the Council on Foreign Relations in New York to probe the willingness of Vietnamese scholars and former policy makers to meet with their American counterparts to identify the opportunities that each side missed—both to prevent the war in the first place and, once it started, to end it before casualties reached such tragic levels. I participated in exploratory meetings on this subject this month in Hanoi.

As the record of the Vietnam war is revealed in fuller detail, parts of *In Retrospect* may require rethinking or revision. With one exception, however, the text of this second edition remains the same as that of the first. The single change, on page 128, reflects the fact that I learned in a meeting with General Giap that the presumed second attack in the Gulf of Tonkin, on August 4, 1964, did not occur.

ROBERT S. McNAMARA
Washington, D.C.
November 15, 1995

Preface

This is the book I planned never to write.

Although pressed repeatedly for over a quarter of a century to add my views on Vietnam to the public record, I hesitated for fear that I might appear self-serving, defensive, or vindictive, which I wished to avoid at all costs. Perhaps I hesitated also because it is hard to face one's mistakes. But something changed my attitude and willingness to speak. I am responding not to a desire to get out my personal story but rather to a wish to put before the American people why their government and its leaders behaved as they did and what we may learn from that experience.

My associates in the Kennedy and Johnson administrations were an exceptional group: young, vigorous, intelligent, well-meaning, patriotic servants of the United States. How did this group—"the best and the brightest," as we eventually came to be known in an ironically pejorative phrase—get it wrong on Vietnam?

That story has not yet been told.

But why now? Why after all these years of silence am I convinced I should speak? There are many reasons; the main one is that I have grown sick at heart witnessing the cynicism and even contempt with which so many people view our political institutions and leaders.

Many factors helped lead to this: Vietnam, Watergate, scandals, corruption. But I do not believe, on balance, that America's political leaders have been incompetent or insensitive to their responsibilities and to the welfare of the people who elected them and to whom they are accountable. Nor do I believe they have been any worse than their foreign counterparts or their colleagues in the private sector. Certainly they have shown themselves to be far from perfect, but people are far from perfect. They have made mistakes, but mostly honest mistakes.

This underscores my own painful quandary about discussing Vietnam. I know that, to this day, many political leaders and scholars in the United States and abroad argue that the Vietnam War actually helped contain the spread of Communism in South and East Asia. Some argue that it hastened the end of the Cold War. But I also know that the war caused terrible damage to America. No doubt exists in my mind about that. None. I want to look at Vietnam in hindsight, not in any way to obscure my own and others' errors of judgment and their egregious costs but to show the full range of pressures and the lack of knowledge that existed at the time.

I want to put Vietnam in context.

We of the Kennedy and Johnson administrations who participated in the decisions on Vietnam acted according to what we thought were the principles and traditions of this nation. We made our decisions in light of those values.

Yet we were wrong, terribly wrong. We owe it to future generations to explain why.

I truly believe that we made an error not of values and intentions but of judgment and capabilities. I say this warily, since I know that if my comments appear to justify or rationalize what I and others did, they will lack credibility and only increase people's cynicism. It is cynicism that makes Americans reluctant to support their leaders in the actions necessary to confront and solve our problems at home and abroad.

I want Americans to understand why we made the mistakes we did, and to learn from them. I hope to say, "Here is something we can take away from Vietnam that is constructive and applicable to the world of today and tomorrow." That is the only way our nation can ever hope to leave the past behind. The ancient Greek dramatist Aeschylus wrote, "The reward of suffering is experience." Let this be the lasting legacy of Vietnam.

———

It is not easy to put people, decisions, and events in their proper places in the jigsaw puzzle that is Vietnam. In deciding how to structure this memoir, I considered trying to write a comprehensive account of my seven years as defense secretary. This would have offered readers the full context of the events and decisions I describe. I chose, instead, to write solely of Vietnam, an approach that lets me trace the development of our policies with a coherence that otherwise would be lacking.

I do so at the risk of oversimplification. One reason the Kennedy and Johnson administrations failed to take an orderly, rational approach to the basic questions underlying Vietnam was the staggering variety and complexity of other issues we faced. Simply put, we faced a blizzard of problems, there were only twenty-four hours in a day, and we often did not have time to think straight.

This predicament is not unique to the administrations in which I served or to the United States. It has existed at all times and in most countries. I have never seen a thoughtful examination of the problem. It existed then, it exists today, and it ought to be recognized and planned for when organizing a government.

———

Too often, I believe, memoirists rely on their recollections. This leads them, however honest their intent, to remember what they wish to remember—what they wish had happened—rather than what actually occurred. I have tried to minimize this real and human danger by relying on the contemporaneous record whenever possible. Rather than mechanically present the vast array of relevant documents and testimony, however, I have sought to organize the material in a way that is true to history. To those who find that I have unduly stressed one aspect or neglected another, I simply say that this account comes as close as possible to the truth as I perceive it, based on information available to me today. My aim is neither to justify errors nor to assign blame, but rather to identify the mistakes we made, understand why we made them, and consider how they can be avoided in the future.

Vietnam and my involvement in it deeply affected my family, but I will not dwell on its effect on them or me. I am not comfortable speaking in such terms; by nature, I am a private person. There are more constructive ways to address our nation's Vietnam experience than excessively to explore my own pride, accomplishments, frustrations, and failure.

In reflecting on Vietnam, I have often thought of words from a poem that Marg brought to my attention thirty years ago, in the exhilarating days when President Kennedy had just taken office. They are from T. S. Eliot's "Little Gidding":

> *We shall not cease from exploration*
> *And the end of all our exploring*
> *Will be to arrive where we started*
> *And know the place for the first time.*

I have not yet ceased from exploration, and I do not yet fully know the place, but now that I have traveled this journey of self-disclosure and self-discovery, I believe I see Vietnam far more clearly than I did in the 1960s. It is, indeed, a place to start from.

How did it happen? What lessons can be drawn from our experience?

In Retrospect

1

My Journey to Washington:

June 9, 1916–January 20, 1961

Two roads diverged in a wood, and I—
I took the one less traveled by,
And that has made all the difference.
ROBERT FROST, *"The Road Not Taken"*

The day after John F. Kennedy's inauguration was among the proudest of my life. At four o'clock that afternoon, January 21, 1961, I gathered with my nine fellow cabinet nominees in the East Room of the White House to be sworn in. We stood in a semicircle beneath the crystal chandelier facing Chief Justice Earl Warren in his black robes. I took my oath of office in unison with the others as President and Mrs. Kennedy, congressional leaders, and our families watched. Then the president stepped forward to congratulate us.

I was now the eighth, and youngest ever, secretary of defense. But even though I was just forty-four, I was not the youngest in the group. The president was forty-three; Robert Kennedy was thirty-five. Like many of these men, I had grown up in the years between the world wars and had served as a young officer in World War II. President Kennedy knew I would bring to the military techniques of management from the business world, much as my Harvard colleagues and I had done as statistical control officers in the war. I was thrilled to be called again to work for my country.

My road to the East Room had begun in San Francisco. My earliest memory is of a city exploding with joy. It was November

11, 1918—Armistice Day. I was two years old. The city was celebrating not only the end of World War I but the belief, held so strongly by President Woodrow Wilson, that the United States and its allies had won the war to end all wars.

They were wrong, of course. The twentieth century was on its way to becoming the bloodiest, by far, in human history: during it, 160 million people have been killed in wars across the globe.

I was part of a World War I baby boom that caused a classroom shortage by the time I entered first grade in 1922. My class was housed in a wooden shack. The accommodations were poor, but the teacher was superb. At the end of the month she gave us a test and reassigned our seating based on the results; the student with the highest grade would sit in the front seat in the leftmost row.

I was determined to occupy that seat. The class was predominantly WASP—white Anglo-Saxon Protestants—but my competitors for the top spot were invariably Chinese, Japanese, and Jews. After each week of hard work, I would spend Saturday and Sunday playing with my neighborhood friends while my rivals went to ethnic schools, studied their ancestral languages, absorbed ancient and complex cultures, and returned to school on Monday determined to beat their Irish classmate. I am happy to say they rarely did.

My drive for scholastic excellence reflected the fact that neither my mother nor my father had gone to college (my father never went beyond eighth grade), and they were fiercely determined that I would. Their resolve shaped my life.

Each human being looking back on his or her life—in my case, looking back on seventy-eight years—can identify defining events that influenced what they became and why they believed as they did. I want to mention three.

One was the Great Depression. I was graduated from high school in 1933. At the time, fully 25 percent of the adult males of this country were unemployed. The father of one of my classmates committed suicide because he could not feed his family. Another friend, the daughter of a wealthy family, joined the Communist Party.

Violent labor strikes were common. During the West Coast maritime strikes of 1934 and 1936, there were machine-gun emplacements on roofs along the waterfront in San Francisco to prevent fighting on the docks. Once, on Market Street I saw a long-shoreman corner a man he thought was a strikebreaker. He knocked the man down, pinned one of his knees on the curb with his ankle on the street, and stamped on the shin to shatter the bones. The violence shocked me.

I learned firsthand about the conditions that were helping to spark the violence when I went down to the union hiring hall in the summer of 1935 and applied for a job at sea to earn money for my next semester at college. I shipped out as an ordinary seaman on the freighter SS *Peter Kerr*. The pay was twenty dollars a month, there was no running fresh water in the crew's quarters, the bunks were so infested with bedbugs that one morning I counted nineteen bites on one leg, and the food was inedible—I was in superb physical shape but lost thirteen pounds during the voyage. The experience gave me sympathy for the plight of unorganized labor that still influences me. As an executive in the auto industry, I admired union leaders like Walter Reuther, and at the Pentagon I tried to recruit Jack Conway, a United Auto Workers official, as my assistant secretary for manpower.

The second and third events were related: my entry into the University of California at Berkeley and my meeting with Margaret. I went to Cal because it was the only first-rate university I could afford. Tuition was fifty-two dollars a year. Berkeley opened a totally new world to me—a world of history, ideas, ethical and moral values, scholarship, and intellectual ferment. Its president, Robert Gordon Sproul, and its provost, Monroe Deutsch, had achieved the impossible: although the university was wholly dependent on a conservative, rural-dominated state legislature for funding, Sproul and Deutsch managed to foster a liberal atmosphere of intellectual freedom and debate. My four years there exposed me to concepts of justice, freedom, and the balancing of rights and obligations that remain with me to this day.

They shaped my future in another way as well. During my first week on campus, I met Margaret McKinstry Craig, a bright, attractive, vivacious young woman from Alameda, California. Seven years later, we married. Marg brought balance, strength, and joy to my life. She complemented me in every way that mattered. Marg was born wise; she was warm, open, gentle, extroverted, and beloved by all. Without her, I would have been diminished.

I chose economics as my major, and philosophy and mathematics as minors, with no particular career in mind. (Given the historic circumstances, it is easy to see why economics seemed fascinating.) The defining moments in my education, though, came in my philosophy and mathematics curricula. The ethics courses forced me to begin to shape my values; studying logic exposed me to rigor and precision in thinking. And my mathematics professors taught me to see math as a process of thought—a language in which to express much, but certainly not all, of human activity.

It was a revelation. To this day, I see quantification as a language to add precision to reasoning about the world. Of course, it cannot deal with issues of morality, beauty, and love, but it is a powerful tool too often neglected when we seek to overcome poverty, fiscal deficits, or the failure of our national health programs.

Another experience that was to have a great impact on my life, although I scarcely realized it at the time, was the Reserve Officers Training Corps (ROTC). Because Berkeley was a land-grant college that operated at public expense, every male student in those days was required to take at least two years of military training. I applied for the optional four-year navy program, but the navy rejected me because I had poor eyesight. So I served two years in Army ROTC.

What I learned was that nobody took the military seriously. My classmates and I saw it as a pointless ritual, irrelevant to our world. On the day of our final parade, when we had to march before the president of the university, we threw down our rifles as soon as we were done—the hell with it! Within a few years, of course, we had ample reason to marvel that a generation of career military officers like George Marshall, Hap Arnold, Max Taylor, and Dwight Eisenhower had stuck it out during that period when nobody cared. Depression or no, men like Max Taylor could have gone out and made a fortune before World War II. Yet they chose to serve their nation. And when the time came, they saved it. We will be eternally indebted to them.

———

After Berkeley, I attended the Harvard Graduate School of Business Administration, soaking up nuts-and-bolts skills I figured I would need to land a job. Many on the faculty appeared to believe that the purpose of business was solely to make money. But a handful of people, including Ross G. Walker, my financial controls professor, and Edmund P. Learned, my marketing professor, took a broader view. They taught that business leaders had a duty to serve society as well as their shareholders, and that a company could drive for profits and at the same time meet social responsibilities. I think of this in a phrase Walker and Learned might have liked: "There is no contradiction between a soft heart and a hard head." That has been a guiding principle in my life.

Much as I liked Harvard, I felt homesick for California. As soon as I graduated in 1939, I went back to San Francisco and took a job at $125 a month. The next summer, Dean Wallace Donham of the business school asked me to return as a very junior faculty member.

The dean needed an answer immediately—the start of the academic year was only six weeks off—but I told him the decision was not entirely mine. I explained I had been courting a young lady. If I could persuade her to marry me, I would move back to Harvard; otherwise, the answer was no. At the time, Marg was on vacation, driving with her mother and aunt across the country. I tracked them down at the YWCA in Baltimore. There, at a pay phone, she received—and accepted—my marriage proposal. On the way back to California, she realized there was little time to prepare for the wedding, so from Red Wing, Minnesota, she wired: "MUST

ORDER ENGRAVED WEDDING INVITATIONS NOW—WHAT IS YOUR MIDDLE NAME?" "STRANGE" I wired back; it was my mother's maiden name. "NO MATTER IF IT IS STRANGE," she answered. "WHAT IS IT?"

We took a one-room apartment in Cambridge—we washed the dishes in the bathtub—and for more than a year lived more happily than we had ever dreamed possible. Our first child was born on October 31, 1941.

Japan's surprise attack on Pearl Harbor came five weeks later. In early 1942 the business school signed a contract with the U.S. Army Air Corps to train statistical control officers. The air corps was exploding in size. It had had fewer than 1,800 airplanes and 500 pilots when the blitzkrieg began in Europe; when Hitler invaded France in May 1940, President Roosevelt called for the production of at least 50,000 planes a year. Practically overnight the army found itself trying to manage one of the largest and most complex enterprises in the nation, and it looked to Harvard for help.

The head of the air corps statistical control program was a brash, extraordinarily talented young officer by the name of Charles B. "Tex" Thornton. He worked closely with Robert A. Lovett, the assistant secretary of war for air. Lovett was almost at wit's end. He had been a prominent investment banker in New York and understood how crucial the flow of information is to good management. But the air corps he had inherited was tiny, gung ho, and so informal that he had almost no data with which to plan and control operations.

Thornton quickly put in place a rudimentary control system. Before long, wherever U.S. air forces flew, clerks attached to the units would record things like the status of planes (ready for combat, repairable, out of action), the condition of the men (types of training, casualties, replacement needs), and the state of operations (number of missions flown, type of mission, targets attacked, degree of success, losses of men and equipment, and so on). By assembling such reports, commanders could get an up-to-date picture of the operations—and shortcomings—of American airpower all over the world. Thornton had no interest in building an empire of clerks. His vision was much more sophisticated. He thought the system and the data, if used intelligently, could help win the war. That was the guiding principle of statistical control and what made it exciting to be part of this team.

Wanting to help in the war effort, several of my colleagues and I accepted Dean Donham's invitation to teach in the program. In early 1943 the War Department asked me and another young professor, Myles Mace, to work directly with the U.S. Eighth Air Force, which was just being established in England. Although we were to start out as civilian consultants to the War Department, there was a clear indication we would later be asked to accept commissions as army officers.

Myles and I were exempt from the draft on two grounds—we were teaching in an army school and we both had young families— but we agreed to go. I never would have or could have volunteered without Marg's support, which she gave enthusiastically despite the sacrifices involved. If I were killed, her financial position would be tenuous at best. That was an immediate concern: I was scheduled to fly to London on the Pan American Clipper, and my colleagues urged me to buy life insurance because of the flight's risk (in fact, the plane I flew on crashed in Lisbon on its next trip). I had to borrow the $100 from the business school dean to pay the premium on a $10,000 policy.

During the next three years, I served in England, Kansas, India, China, Washington, D.C., the Pacific, and Ohio. Although Thornton's methods were not applied very consistently, there were occasions when they made a major difference, and I was awarded the Legion of Merit by General Arnold, the chief of staff of the air corps, for my part in the program when I left the service in January 1946 as a lieutenant colonel.

———

On V-J Day in August 1945, Marg and I were both in the Army Air Corps Regional Hospital in Dayton, Ohio, stricken with polio. My case was very mild, and I was released in six weeks or so. Marg's was so serious that at one point the doctors said she would never lift an arm or leg off the bed again. That fall, the dean of the Harvard Medical School helped me arrange to move Marg to one of the top orthopedic clinics, Children's Hospital in Baltimore. The care she received over the following months—and Marg's own vitality and powerful will—saved her. But it was very, very expensive.

Meanwhile Tex Thornton had a new project: assembling a team of veterans from his office to work together in civilian life. The idea was to find a big company in need of reorganization and modernization that would hire him and his team in a package deal. It was the kind of audacious plan that was typical of Tex. When he asked me to join the group as second-in-command, I gave an unequivocal no. I told him Marg and I wanted to go back to our life at Harvard.

Tex kept after me. He finally got my attention by bluntly pointing out, "Bob, you know you can't go back to Harvard. You'll never be able to pay Margaret's medical bills." By this time he believed he had found a taker—Henry Ford II, who had just succeeded his grandfather, the founder, as president of Ford Motor Company. I still thought Tex's scheme was quixotic, but I told him I would consider it if we went to Ford headquarters in Michigan, met with the young Ford, and heard from his lips that he wanted us and had plans to use us effectively.

A few weeks later, in November 1945, still in our army uniforms, several of us drove all the way to Dearborn, Michigan. We met Henry and his vice president for industrial relations, John Bugas. John was a former FBI agent who had been in charge of the bureau's Detroit office. Ford Sr. had hired him in the early 1940s to protect his grandchildren—Henry Ford II and his siblings. (Like many wealthy people, Ford had been deeply shaken by the kidnapping of the Lindbergh baby several years before.)

The company was a pretty rough place. John later told a story about Harry Bennett, a navy prizefighter who had also started as the grandchildren's bodyguard but had risen in power to where he had a big office in the basement of the main administration building. But that did not change his style. He liked to keep a loaded gun in his desk drawer and, sometimes, when a visitor came to meet with him, he would shoot into the wall over the visitor's shoulder. In 1943 young Henry decided he wanted Bennett out of the company and asked John to fire him. John thought about that. Before going down to Bennett's office, he strapped on his FBI shoulder-holster and pistol in case Bennett decided to shoot it out. The departure was peaceful.

When the war ended, John believed he would have little competition in his rise to the top of the company. There were then not more than a handful of college graduates among the 1,000 most senior Ford executives. So when our group showed up, he saw us as competition. He was far from thrilled. During our meeting with Henry, he sat silent for a while, then began, "Well, Henry, if you want to hire these fellows—"

Henry cut him off. "John, how many times do I have to tell you I want to hire them? It's a done deal."

As far as John was concerned, it was not a done deal. When we reported for work at the Dearborn headquarters in late January 1946, he had us sent to the employment offices at Ford's giant River Rouge Plant, a mile or so away. There we learned we would be required to take two days of tests. We were exposed to every type of test I had ever heard of: intelligence tests, achievement tests, personality tests, leadership tests—the list went on and on. It was obvious that John was looking for flaws he could use to convince Henry that he had made a mistake.

After we completed the tests, I figured we had done well—my own scores, which were explained to me by one of the industrial psychologists, were quite high, and the company put all of us to work in executive positions. But it was only recently that I learned how well the group as a whole had done. Four of us scored in the one-hundredth percentile for our ability to reason and to think, and all ten scored in the one hundredth percentile in an exam measuring practical judgment. That took care of John's attempt at sabotage.[1]

Because of our cerebral approach to making decisions and our youth, we became known as the Whiz Kids. We were as much a shock to Ford's parochial culture as the automotive culture was to us. Most of our group avoided the Detroit social scene. Senior automobile executives always lived in the wealthy suburbs of Grosse Point or Bloomfield Hills, but two of us chose Ann Arbor, home of the University of Michigan, so that we could raise our children in a university environment.

Our political views were not typical of motor company executives, either. One of John Bugas's jobs, I soon discovered, was to go around to top Ford executives and collect money for the Republican Party. I refused to contribute. After I became head of the Ford Division, the company's biggest unit, in the early 1950s, I also refused when he asked me to solicit contributions for the Republicans from the 1,100 or so highest-paid executives in my division.

Instead, I sent each man a letter saying we lived in a democracy, our political system was based on a vigorous two-party system that depended on private financial contributions, and I hoped they—like I—would donate to one or the other party. If they wished to give to the Democrats, the letter went on, they could do so by sending their contribution to Mr. So-and-so; contributions to the Republicans could be sent to Mr. Bugas. No one would know which party they supported, but I hoped they would support one or the other. Things like this did not endear me to many of my fellow executives.

The friction made no difference. I had a kind of unwritten contract with Henry Ford II: if I produced profits for the company, I could live any damned way I pleased. The Whiz Kids accomplished what he had hired us to do. Over the next fifteen years, six of us rose to become senior executives (including two presidents). During that time the company grew rapidly and won back a big chunk of market share it had lost to General Motors. The value of the stock increased dramatically.

Tex Thornton did not stay with the group—he lasted less than two years before getting himself fired in a run-in with Lewis Crusoe, the vice president for finance. I might have gotten fired at any point too, particularly because my views were at variance with those of most people in the company and the industry on increasingly controversial issues like safety, the use of functional design, economy of operation, and pollution reduction. But I found ways to work with my associates, and I received a series of promotions because I produced results.

In the summer of 1960, Ernest Breech, second in command under Henry Ford II, was getting ready to retire from Ford. In July, Henry, John Bugas, and I went to Cologne, West Germany, to visit our German company, which was headquartered there. We returned to our hotel about 2:00 A.M. after one of Henry's nights on the town. The elevator stopped at the floor where John and I had rooms, and we started to get off. Henry, whose suite was one floor above, said, "Bob, come on up for a nightcap."

"I don't want a nightcap," I said. "I'm going to bed."

"Henry, I'll join you," said John.

"I didn't ask you," Henry told him. "I invited Bob."

I went on up, and it was then that Henry asked me to become president of the company. I told him I would think about it, talk to Marg, and give him an answer within a week. A week later I accepted. I was formally elected by the board in late October.

———

On Thursday, December 8, 1960, seven weeks after I became president of Ford, I left my home in Ann Arbor early in the morning to drive to my office in Dearborn. I made a stop at the River Rouge Plant on the way, and when I finally reached headquarters at about 10:30 A.M., my secretary, Virginia Marshall, handed me a long list of phone messages. I had directed her to force me to return every call that came in—including complaints—so, without looking at the list, I handed it back and said, "Start down it."

About half an hour later, she announced, "Robert Kennedy is on the line." I had never met him (seven and a half years later I was to help carry his casket to the grave site in Arlington National

Cemetery) and had no idea why he had called, but he soon made it clear. "The president-elect would be grateful if you would meet with our brother-in-law, Sargent Shriver," he said.

I told him I would be happy to do so—although I did not know Sarge or have the faintest idea why he wanted to meet. I suggested the following Tuesday.

"No, no," said Robert Kennedy. "He wants to see you today."

I pointed out it was already nearly 11:00 A.M.

He replied, "You set the time and he'll be there."

So I said, "Four o'clock."

At four sharp, Sarge Shriver entered my office. He began the conversation by saying, "The president-elect has instructed me to offer you the position of secretary of the treasury."

"You're out of your mind," I said. "I'm not qualified for that."

"If you hold to that position," said Sarge, "I am authorized to say Jack Kennedy wishes you to serve as secretary of defense."

"This is absurd!" I said. "I'm not qualified."

"Well, the president-elect at least hopes you will give him the courtesy of agreeing to meet with him tomorrow in Washington," Sarge countered. I could not say no.

Henry Ford's office adjoined mine. After Sarge left, I walked in to tell him of the conversation, planning to assure him that nothing would come of it. But it turned out Henry had just left for New York. I called for a company plane to take me there so that I could brief him before I met the president-elect the next day. Henry was stunned when we spoke, but I stressed that nothing would change as a result of my Washington visit.

The next day, I met President-elect Kennedy at his home on N Street in Georgetown. Photographers, radio broadcasters, and television cameramen jammed the street in front of the three-story red-brick town house. The Secret Service was bringing visitors into the house undisclosed through a back alley.

We met and shook hands. When the president-elect asked if I would serve as his secretary of defense, I told him what I had told Sarge: "I am not qualified."

"Who is?" he asked.

I did not realize he meant the question rhetorically. I suggested Thomas Gates, the current defense secretary. On the way to Georgetown that morning, I had actually stopped at the Pentagon to find out whether Tom, whom I knew from Scott Paper Company, where we had both been directors at different times, was willing to stay on in the new administration. He had indicated he was.

The president-elect let that pass without comment. He rejected my claim that I was not qualified, pointing out dryly that there were no schools for defense secretaries, as far as he knew, and no schools for presidents either. He asked me to consider his proposal at least and meet again the following Monday.

I agreed but said I was confident the answer would be the same.

How did President-elect Kennedy come to offer me a cabinet post? I am not certain, but I believe two people were primarily responsible: Bob Lovett, who knew my reputation at Ford and my work in the army; and John Kenneth Galbraith, the liberal Harvard economist. I met Ken, who is now a close friend, during one of his field trips to Detroit in the mid-1950s. He was researching corporate governance and sought me out because he had heard of a motor company executive who seemed an oddball for Detroit. I had long admired his writing and still chuckle when I think of his phrase from *The Affluent Society:* "The bland leading the bland."

Ken later said he had suggested my name because he thought the president needed a businessman with innovative ideas. Party affiliation had almost nothing to do with it. Like many people, Ken probably thought I was a Republican. The press had identified me as one from time to time because when I had registered to vote in California at age twenty-one, I had registered Republican for no other reason than that my father was.

Marg and I spent the weekend discussing the matter. We talked with our three children, explaining that, if I left Ford, our financial future would be totally different. My net worth was not large, but I had huge unexercised stock options and a total annual income exceeding $400,000 (the equivalent of about $2 million in today's dollars). If I accepted the president-elect's offer, I would be moving to an annual salary of $25,000.

The children cared not a whit. Marg wanted only what I wanted. So on Sunday we sat in our study and agreed I should accept the offer as long as I felt I could do the job well.

We talked awhile about what that would entail. Two things: I had to have authority to staff the Defense Department's upper echelons with the ablest individuals in the nation—regardless of party affiliation—to offset my own inexperience. It would also have to be understood that I would not take time from my job to participate in Washington's social circuit. I had not the faintest idea how I was going to make those two conditions clear. After all, one does not negotiate a contract with a president-elect.

As we talked, I noticed it was snowing heavily outside. Suddenly it hit me. I thought, "Why don't I call the president-elect, tell him the weather will delay my return to Washington for a day or two, and say that, in the meantime, I'll send a letter explaining my position?" .

I called a number he had given me, but he was not in Washington. I finally tracked him down in Palm Beach. The president-elect was quite relaxed about the delay in our meeting, saying it was also snowing in Washington and he could not get back there tomorrow either.

How I imagined the letter would reach him, I do not know. I ended up carrying it in my pocket when I went to see him on Tuesday. I again entered the N Street house from the back. The president-elect and Robert Kennedy were seated on a love seat. I took the chair opposite them and opened the conversation by saying I had put my thoughts in writing and perhaps the quickest way to get into the matter would be for the president-elect to read the letter.

He did so and, without comment, handed it to his brother, who glanced at it and passed it back. The president-elect said, "What do you think?"

"I think it's great," said Robert Kennedy.

"So do I," the president-elect said. "Let's announce it." He took out a yellow pad and drafted a statement. We then walked out onto his front stoop and addressed the cameras and the press. Thus did Marg and the children learn we were moving to Washington.

Henry and his mother, Mrs. Edsel Ford, were shocked to learn of my decision. I explained that while I felt a deep loyalty to them and to Ford Motor Company, I could not let their interests outweigh my obligation to serve the nation when called upon. They accepted that, but Mrs. Ford was particularly upset. She was convinced that her father-in-law, Henry Ford, had caused the death of her husband by placing him in a business environment so stressful it was certain to kill him. It did. She was determined that her son would not suffer a similar fate and had looked to me to shield him.

A few days after agreeing to take the job, I returned to Washington and set about recruiting senior staff for my department. With no residence, no office, no secretary, no staff—we received no transition allowance—I moved into Ford Motor Company's suite at the Shoreham Hotel. I started by drawing up a list of people who might meet my standards of intelligence, education, and experience. I began by calling people for recommendations: Lovett, Galbraith, and John McCloy, a New York lawyer and a prominent member of the Eastern Establishment. For each name they and others recommended, I set up a three-by-five note card and entered on it all the information I could learn about the individual.

After numerous cross-checks and with much assistance from Sarge Shriver and his associate, Adam Yarmolinsky (who later became my special assistant at the Pentagon), I chose the ones I would interview. After the interviews I decided whom to recommend to the president-elect for nomination to Congress. President Kennedy did not turn down a single one of my nominees.

Out of this process emerged the most outstanding group ever to serve in a cabinet department. It included, among many others, five men who subsequently achieved cabinet status of their own: Harold Brown, Joseph Califano, John Connally, Paul Nitze, and Cyrus Vance.

The recruitment process reveals something about me: I had hay in my hair. It also reveals something about President-elect Kennedy, because he kept his word that the key appointments would be mine and would be made solely on the basis of merit.

Soon after I arrived in Washington, I heard reports that Franklin Roosevelt, Jr., was to be named secretary of the navy. I had never met the man, but what I had heard about him did not make me think him qualified for such a post, so I paid no attention to the reports. It never occurred to me that FDR Jr., wanting to follow in his father's footsteps, had arranged this with President-elect Kennedy and then he or one of his friends leaked it to the press to set it in concrete.

Four or five days later, after the president-elect had accepted a number of my appointments, he called and said, "Bob, you haven't recommended anyone for secretary of the navy. What progress are you making?"

"You're right," I replied. "I just can't find the right person."

"Have you thought of Franklin Roosevelt, Jr.?"

"I have heard his name mentioned," I answered, "but he's a playboy and totally unqualified."

"Well, have you met him?"

When I answered no, the president-elect said: "Don't you think you should meet him before coming to a final judgment?" I agreed to do so.

I remembered having read that Roosevelt was a Fiat dealer, so I looked up Fiat in the yellow pages of the telephone directory, called him, introduced myself, and asked to come by. I think he nearly dropped the receiver. After we met, I called the president-elect.

With great anticipation in his voice, Kennedy said, "What do you think?"

"I think he's a playboy and totally unqualified for the job," I replied.

There was a long pause. "Bob," the president-elect said, "did you follow the West Virginia Democratic primary?"

I told him that, having been in Detroit at the time, I had only a superficial knowledge of the campaign, but I recognized, of course, that his primary victory in West Virginia had been a turning point in his path to the White House. It was there, by beating Hubert Humphrey, a Protestant, that he had put to rest the belief that a Catholic could not win the presidency.

"Yes," he said quickly, "and do you know how it came about?" When I told him no, he said, "Franklin Roosevelt, Jr., played a major role in my victory." (I later learned that Roosevelt allegedly spread the rumor that Humphrey had evaded the draft during World War II.)

"Well," I said, "he's still not qualified to be secretary of the navy."

A silence ensued that I thought would never end. Finally, the president-elect sighed and said, "I guess I'll have to take care of him some other way." (He later appointed Roosevelt undersecretary of commerce.) Exchanges like this were what caused me to love Kennedy as I did.

I still had not decided on a secretary of the navy when I took my family skiing that Christmas. But I was getting close. Finally, in Aspen, I made up my mind and called the president-elect. He was in Florida again. I announced that, after thorough investigation, I had decided on John B. Connally, Jr.

"Well, that's interesting," he said. "It's not a name I would have thought of. But there are two men here who probably know Connally better than I. Tell them your views, get theirs, and then I'll come back on the line."

I asked who they were, and he replied: "Vice President—elect Johnson and Speaker Rayburn."

I was so green I did not realize Kennedy was playing a joke. Johnson and Rayburn were Texans like Connally and were as close to him as his own father. In fact, Connally had managed Johnson's floor campaign at the 1960 Los Angeles Democratic Convention when he tried to beat Kennedy to the nomination. Some believed it was Connally who had spread the rumor that JFK suffered from Addison's disease.

When Johnson and Rayburn picked up the phone, they did not let on. They heard my story, gave me their views, and returned the receiver to the president-elect. He said, "Bob, I am delighted." It was not until afterward that I figured it out.

The president never had cause to complain about my choice. Connally became one of his and my strongest supporters. We regretted his departure two years later when he resigned to run successfully for the governorship of Texas.

It still amazes me that my naïveté never seemed to annoy President Kennedy, even when it expressed itself in an embarrassing way. A major issue in the 1960 campaign had been the so-called missile gap. Kennedy charged that President Eisenhower had neglected our nuclear defenses and that, as a result, the Soviet Union had achieved numerical superiority in the most modern of offensive weapons: nuclear-equipped intercontinental ballistic missiles (ICBMs). The accusation derived from an air force intelligence report that had been leaked to Kennedy by way of Sen. Stuart Symington (D-Mo.), a former air force secretary. Unbeknownst to them, the Central Intelligence Agency disagreed with the air force's conclusion. (No procedure existed then for reconciling such divergent assessments.)

As soon as I entered the Pentagon, I made it my top priority to determine the size of the gap and the remedial action required to close it. My deputy Roswell Gilpatric and I spent days with the air force's assistant chief of staff for intelligence, personally reviewing hundreds of photographs of Soviet missile sites that had been the basis for the air force report. Interpretation was difficult, but we finally concluded that the CIA was right and the air force was wrong. There was a gap—but it was in our favor!

Right then, on February 6, 1961, my press secretary, Arthur Sylvester, said, "Bob, you haven't met the Pentagon press yet, and you have to do that." I told him I knew nothing about the Washington press and was totally unprepared to meet them.

"Don't worry," he said. "They're a fine bunch and will treat you well." Actually, as they themselves would have admitted, they were sharks.

I gave in and agreed to meet with them early that afternoon in the conference room adjoining my office. The reporters crowded in, the doors were closed, and Arthur established the ground rules. I understood the meeting to be off the record, but Arthur had evidently said it was "on background"—meaning that the reporters could publish what they heard as long as they did not attribute it directly to me. At the time I didn't know the difference.

The first question was "Mr. Secretary, you have been here now for three weeks. What do you have to say about the missile gap?"

I replied that I had made the issue my first order of business and had concluded that if there was a gap, it was in our favor.

The reporters nearly broke down the door in their rush to get to the phones. I can still remember the inflammatory headlines in that afternoon's *Washington Evening Star*. The next morning, *The New York Times* highlighted the story on page one. Republicans in Congress and all across the country made a huge protest; Senate Minority Leader Everett Dirksen (R-Ill.) called for my resignation and, perhaps with tongue in cheek, demanded a rerun of the presidential election.

I went to see President Kennedy. "Mr. President," I said, "I came down here to help you, and all I've done is stimulate demands for your resignation. I'm fully prepared to resign."

"Oh, come on, Bob, forget it," said Kennedy without the slightest hint of anger. "We're in a helluva mess, but we all put our foot in our mouth once in a while. Just forget it. It'll blow over." It eventually did, but I never forgot the generous way he forgave my stupidity.

———

By then I had laid out a list of over a hundred topics on which I wanted studies made and papers prepared. Within the department it was nicknamed "Ninety-nine Trombones." It covered the entire range of the Defense Department's activities, including the threats we faced, the force structure necessary to counter them, the major weapons systems required, and an evaluation of our nuclear strike plan.

Among other things, the "Ninety-nine Trombones" list helped send the message that we were serious about getting control of the department. By 1961, a decade and a half into the Cold War, it had grown into a behemoth. Some 4.5 million people worked for Defense—3.5 million in uniform and another million civilians—which made the Pentagon bigger than America's top twenty-five or thirty corporations combined. The annual budget, $280 billion (in 1994 dollars), was bigger than the national budgets of any one of our main NATO allies. The Pentagon operated huge complexes of transportation, telecommunications, logistical support, and maintenance, as well as armies, naval fleets, and air forces, including, of course, the nuclear arsenal.

The Constitution says that the U.S. military is under civilian control, meaning that the president and the secretary of defense are responsible for directing the entire range of Defense Department activities. But the fact was that most of my predecessors had gone into the job with big ambitions only to find that heading that vast bureaucracy kept them too busy to think. They ended up deferring to the old-line bureaucrats and to generals and admirals on matters of budgeting, procurement, strategy, and sometimes even policy—without understanding the issues—because the military establishment had grown so complex.

I had no patience with the myth that the Defense Department could not be managed. It was an extraordinarily large organization, but the notion that it was some sort of ungovernable force was absurd. I had spent fifteen years as a manager identifying problems and forcing organizations—often against their will—to think deeply and realistically about alternative courses of action and their consequences. My team and I were determined to guide the department in such a way as to achieve the objective the president had set: security for the nation at the lowest possible cost.

As I told a TV interviewer a month after starting the job: "The role of a public manager is very similar to the role of a private manager; in each case he has the option of following one of two major alternative courses of action. He can either act as a judge or a leader. . . . I have always believed in and endeavored to follow the active leadership role as opposed to the passive judicial role."

Privately, I spoke much more bluntly about intending to shake things up. I made it clear that I was determined to subordinate the powerful institutional interests of the various armed services and the defense contractors to a broad conception of the national interest. I wanted to challenge the Pentagon's resistance to change, and I intended that the big decisions would be made on the basis of study and analysis and not simply by perpetuating the practice of allocating blocs of funds to the various services and letting them use the money as they saw fit.

We had to make sweeping changes to achieve these goals. It meant moving the senior civilian officials much deeper into the management of defense programs. As part of the process, we shifted from a one-year to a five-year planning period, a revolutionary change that has now spread across the government. And we instituted the Planning, Programming, Budgeting System to clarify procurement choices. This system worked by forcing long-term cost and effectiveness comparisons across service lines for weapons systems, force structures, and strategies. Even the tenor of top-level meetings in the Pentagon had to change. They became far less routine and far more policy oriented.

One of the most important things we did was to change substantially what were called posture statements, the formal yearly reports to Congress by the secretary of defense. We began each with a statement of America's foreign policy objectives and then derived from those an analysis of the threats we would face in pursuing the objectives, the military strategy to be followed in the face of the threats, the force structure we would need to accomplish it, and the budgets required to support the force structure. This integration of foreign policy and the defense budget was absolutely fundamental. It is the only sound way to proceed. At the time there was much opposition to our approach. Many in the State Department, for example, believed we were usurping their function by preparing the written statement of U.S. foreign policy. But there was no other such statement. And what they did not know was that I asked Dean Rusk to review every word of it before I used it as the foundation of our military strategy and defense programs.·

This all reflected an approach to organizing human activities that I had developed at Harvard and applied in the army during the war and later at Ford, and in the World Bank. Put very simply, it was to define a clear objective for whatever organization I was associated with, develop a plan to achieve that objective, and systematically monitor progress against the plan. Then, if progress was deficient, one could either adjust the plan or introduce corrective action to accelerate progress. The objective of the Defense Department was clear to me from the start: to defend the nation at minimal risk and minimal cost, and, whenever we got into combat, with minimal loss of life.

We immediately tackled a most urgent task—reexamining and redefining our nuclear strategy. The impetus grew out of a long-standing strategic debate. In the 1950s, contrary to the advice of some senior military leaders—for example, Army Chief of Staff Gen. Maxwell Taylor—the Eisenhower administration had relied increasingly on nuclear weapons for the national defense. Secretary of State John Foster Dulles had summarized this doctrine of massive retaliation when he declared that the United States aimed to deter aggression by relying "primarily upon a great capacity to retaliate [with nuclear weapons] instantly, by means and at places of our own choosing."

The Kennedy administration worried that this reliance on nuclear weapons gave us no way to respond to large nonnuclear attacks without committing suicide. President Kennedy said we had put ourselves in the position of having to choose in a crisis between "inglorious retreat or unlimited retaliation." We decided to broaden the range of options by strengthening and modernizing the military's ability to fight a nonnuclear war. This involved a shift in doctrine from massive retaliation to what came to be known as flexible response, a strategy intended to reduce the risk of nuclear war. We were only partially successful in raising the nuclear "threshold." Our proposals were debated for five years by NATO, then accepted with substantial modifications.

In any event, in the early days of the administration we worked long hours developing plans to strengthen our forces. At the end of March, President Kennedy presented our blueprint in a special defense message to Congress. He asked for an additional $650 million for the Pentagon so we could put in place an array of measures to increase our ability to deter or resist nonnuclear aggression.

———

For three months after President Kennedy's inauguration, we felt as though we were on a roll. But only a few days after he presented the defense blueprint to Congress, we faced a decision that showed that our judgment—and our luck—had severe limitations.

Early in 1960 the Eisenhower administration had authorized the CIA to organize, arm, and train secretly in Central America a brigade of 1,400 Cuban exiles to invade Cuba and overthrow the regime of Fidel Castro. Castro had seized power on the island the year before and appeared to be leading Cuba into the Soviet orbit. The Kennedy administration inherited the scheme and allowed planning for the invasion to continue.

Now, less than ninety days after his inauguration, Kennedy had to decide whether to go ahead with the operation. He called his advisers—perhaps twenty of us in all—to a meeting at the State Department and asked what to do. He went around the table and asked each person's opinion. With one exception—Sen. J. William Fulbright (D-Ark.), who dissented vigorously—everyone in the room supported the action. It was a CIA operation, but all the Joint Chiefs of Staff endorsed it. Secretary of State Dean Rusk and I, though not enthusiastic, also said yes, as did National Security Adviser McGeorge Bundy and all other members of the National Security Council (NSC).

The invasion took place on April 17, 1961, at the Bay of Pigs, on Cuba's southwestern coast. It quickly proved, as one historian put it, "a perfect failure": Castro's agents had thoroughly infiltrated the brigade; contrary to CIA predictions, the Cuban people did not rally in support of the invasion; Castro marshaled forces in the area more quickly and in greater numbers than anticipated; air cover for the landings had not been properly planned; the "escape hatch" into the mountains lay across eighty miles of impassable swamp; Washington's hand in the operation, once exposed, aroused global indignation—the list of blunders went on and on.

President Kennedy went on national television and took full responsibility for the debacle.

Watching him do this taught me a bitter lesson. I had entered the Pentagon with a limited grasp of military affairs and even less grasp of covert operations. This lack of understanding, coupled with my preoccupation with other matters and my deference to the CIA on what I considered an agency operation, led me to accept the plan uncritically. I had listened to the briefings leading up to the invasion. I had even passed along to the president, without comment, an ambiguous assessment by the Joint Chiefs that the invasion would probably contribute to Castro's overthrow even if it did not succeed right away. The truth is I did not understand the plan very well and did not know the facts. I had let myself become a passive bystander.

The next day, I went to the Oval Office and said, "Mr. President, I know where I was when you made the decision to launch the invasion. I was in a room where, with one exception, all of your advisers—including me—recommended you proceed. I am fully prepared to go on TV and say so."

Kennedy heard me out. "Bob," he said, "I'm grateful to you for your willingness to assume part of the responsibility. But I am the president. I did not have to do what all of you recommended. I did it. I am responsible, and I will not try to put part of the blame on you, or Eisenhower, or anyone else."

I admired him for that, and the incident brought us closer. I made up my mind not to let him down again.

2

The Early Years:

January 19, 1961–August 23, 1963

We must be clear-sighted in beginnings, for, as in their
budding we discern not the danger, so in their full growth we
perceive not the remedy.
—MONTAIGNE, *Essays*

The beginnings of all things are small, and the story of my
involvement with Vietnam is no different. When John F.
Kennedy became president, we faced a complex and growing crisis
in Southeast Asia with sparse knowledge, scant experience, and
simplistic assumptions. As time passed, we came to recognize
that the problems plaguing South Vietnam and its embattled
leader, Ngo Dinh Diem, were far more complicated than we had
initially perceived. And we remained divided over how to deal with
them.

Throughout the Kennedy years, we operated on two premises
that ultimately proved contradictory. One was that the fall of South
Vietnam to Communism would threaten the security of the United
States and the Western world. The other was that only the South
Vietnamese could defend their nation, and that America should limit
its role to providing training and logistical support. In line with that
latter view, we actually began planning for the phased withdrawal of
U.S. forces in 1963, a step adamantly opposed by those who
believed it could lead to the loss of South Vietnam and, very likely,
all of Asia.

My thinking about Southeast Asia in 1961 differed little from that of many Americans of my generation who had served in World War II and followed foreign affairs by reading the newspapers but lacked expertise in geopolitics and Asian affairs. Having spent three years helping turn back German and Japanese aggression only to witness the Soviet takeover of Eastern Europe following the war, I accepted the idea advanced by George F. Kennan, in his famous July 1947 "X" article in *Foreign Affairs*, that the West, led by the United States, must guard against Communist expansion through a policy of containment. I considered this a sensible basis for decisions about national security and the application of Western military force.

Like most Americans, I saw Communism as monolithic. I believed the Soviets and Chinese were cooperating in trying to extend their hegemony. In hindsight, of course, it is clear that they had no unified strategy after the late 1950s. But their split grew slowly and only gradually became apparent. At the time, Communism still seemed on the march. Mao Zedong and his followers had controlled China since 1949 and had fought with North Korea against the West; Nikita Khrushchev had predicted Communist victory through "wars of national liberation" in the Third World and had told the West, "We will bury you." His threat gained credibility when the USSR launched *Sputnik* in 1957, demonstrating its lead in space technology. The next year Khrushchev started turning up the heat on West Berlin. And now Castro had transformed Cuba into a Communist beachhead in our hemisphere. We felt beset and at risk. This fear underlay our involvement in Vietnam.

I did not see the Communist danger as overwhelming, as did many people on the right. It was a threat I was certain could be dealt with, and I shared President Kennedy's sentiment when he called on America and the West to bear the burden of a long twilight struggle. "Let every nation know," he said in his inaugural address, "whether it wishes us well or ill, that we shall pay any price, bear any burden, meet any hardship, support any friend, oppose any foe to assure the survival and the success of liberty."[1]

I knew some things about the recent history of Indochina, particularly Vietnam. I knew that Ho Chi Minh, a Communist, had begun efforts to free the country from French rule after World War I. I knew that Japan had occupied the country during World War II; I knew that Ho Chi Minh had declared Vietnam's independence after Japan's surrender but that the United States had acquiesced to France's return to Indochina for fear that a Franco-American split would make it harder to contain Soviet expansion in Europe. In fact, during the decade just past, we had subsidized French military action against Ho's forces, which were in turn supported by the Chinese. And I knew that the United States viewed Indochina as a necessary part of our containment policy—an important bulwark in the Cold War.

It seemed obvious that the Communist movement in Vietnam was closely related to guerrilla insurgencies in Burma, Indonesia, Malaya, and the Philippines during the 1950s. We viewed these conflicts not as nationalistic movements—as they largely appear in hindsight—but as signs of a unified Communist drive for hegemony in Asia. This way of thinking had led Dean Acheson, President Truman's secretary of state, to call Ho Chi Minh "the mortal enemy of native independence in Indochina."[2]

I also knew that the Eisenhower administration had accepted the Truman administration's view that Indochina's fall to Communism would threaten U.S. security. Although it had appeared unwilling to commit U.S. combat forces in the region, it had sounded the warning of the Communist threat there clearly and often. In April 1954, President Eisenhower made his famous prediction that if Indochina fell, the rest of Southeast Asia would "go over very quickly" like a "row of dominoes." He had added, "The possible consequences of the loss are just incalculable to the free world."[3] That year our country assumed responsibility from France for protecting Vietnam south of the 1954 partition line. We had also negotiated the Southeast Asia Treaty (SEATO), conditionally pledging the United States to protect Indochina. And we had pumped more than $7 billion in economic and military aid into South Vietnam from 1955 to 1961.

I was aware, finally, that during his years in the Senate, John F. Kennedy had echoed Eisenhower's assessment of Southeast Asia. "Vietnam represents the cornerstone of the Free World in Southeast Asia," he had said in a widely publicized speech in 1956. "It is our offspring. We cannot abandon it, we cannot ignore its needs."[4]

Two developments after I became secretary of defense reinforced my way of thinking about Vietnam: the intensification of relations between Cuba and the Soviets, and a new wave of Soviet provocations in Berlin. Both seemed to underscore the aggressive intent of Communist policy. In that context, the danger of Vietnam's loss and, through falling dominoes, the loss of all Southeast Asia made it seemed reasonable to consider expanding the U.S. effort in Vietnam.

None of this made me anything close to an East Asian expert, however. I had never visited Indochina, nor did I understand or appreciate its history, language, culture, or values. The same must be said, to varying degrees, about President Kennedy, Secretary of State Dean Rusk, National Security Adviser McGeorge Bundy, military adviser Maxwell Taylor, and many others. When it came to Vietnam, we found ourselves setting policy for a region that was terra incognita.

Worse, our government lacked experts for us to consult to compensate for our ignorance. When the Berlin crisis occurred in 1961 and during the Cuban Missile Crisis in 1962, President Kennedy was able to turn to senior people like Llewellyn Thompson, Charles Bohlen, and George Kennan, who knew the Soviets intimately. There were no senior officials in the Pentagon or State Department with comparable knowledge of Southeast Asia. I knew of only one Pentagon officer with counterinsurgency experience in the region— Col. Edward Lansdale, who had served as an adviser to Ramon Magsaysay in the Philippines and Diem in South Vietnam. But Lansdale was relatively junior and lacked broad geopolitical expertise.

The irony of this gap was that it existed largely because the top

East Asian and China experts in the State Department—John Paton Davies, Jr., John Stewart Service, and John Carter Vincent—had been purged during the McCarthy hysteria of the 1950s. Without men like these to provide sophisticated, nuanced insights, we—certainly I—badly misread China's objectives and mistook its bellicose rhetoric to imply a drive for regional hegemony. We also totally underestimated the nationalist aspect of Ho Chi Minh's movement. We saw him first as a Communist and only second as a Vietnamese nationalist.

Why did we fail to consider China and Vietnam in the same light as we did Yugoslavia—a Communist nation independent of Moscow? For several reasons, I believe. Tito seemed unique; he and Stalin had openly fallen out. China's and North Vietnam's heated rhetoric made us think they sought regional hegemony. And Cuba's recent tilt toward the Soviet Union seemed illustrative of how ostensibly independent Third World movements quickly placed themselves within the Communist orbit. Thus, we equated Ho Chi Minh not with Marshal Tito but with Fidel Castro.

Such ill-founded judgments were accepted without debate by the Kennedy administration, as they had been by its Democratic and Republican predecessors. We failed to analyze our assumptions critically, then or later. The foundations of our decision making were gravely flawed.

There were other mistakes as well. I will seek to identify them and to illuminate and distill from them lessons applicable to the future. Scores of books have been written on Vietnam. They describe the conflict in great detail. I see no need to duplicate their work. Instead, I will concentrate on eleven key events or decisions and discuss the implications or decision-making process related to each:

- A January 19, 1961, meeting between President Eisenhower and President-elect Kennedy.
- President Kennedy's decision in late 1961 to eventually send

16,000 U.S. military advisers to South Vietnam to help train the South Vietnamese to defend themselves against pressure from the North.

- President Kennedy's announcement on October 2, 1963, that he expected the training mission to be completed by 1965 and that he would begin withdrawing U.S. training forces within ninety days of that time (i.e., by December 31, 1963).
- The November 1, 1963, coup, which resulted in the assassination of President Diem.
- Political disintegration in South Vietnam during the first twelve months of Lyndon Johnson's presidency, and the administration's reaction to it.
- Events in the Tonkin Gulf in August 1964, the president's response, and the subsequent congressional resolution.
- A watershed memo from McGeorge Bundy and me to President Johnson in late January 1965. It was followed within a few weeks by the start of the U.S. bombing of North Vietnam.
- A fateful decision in July 1965 to send 175,000 U.S. combat troops by the end of the year to defend South Vietnam, while recognizing that still more forces might subsequently be required.
- Repeated attempts, beginning in late 1965 and continuing through 1967, to end the war by initiating negotiations, given our inability to end it militarily.
- The decision in the spring of 1966 to send an additional 200,000 troops to Vietnam by year's end, while recognizing that there was no likelihood of bringing the war to a conclusion soon.
- Acrimonious debate in 1967 over the war's conduct and the requirements for further U.S. reinforcements—controversy that ultimately led to my departure from the government on February 29, 1968.

It has been alleged that false reports of progress by military and political leaders, including me, affected both the government's decisions and the public's reaction to events in Vietnam throughout this period. I will comment on these allegations as the story progresses.

I first confronted the Indochina problem in a relatively brief meeting between President Eisenhower and President-elect Kennedy. It was January 19, 1961, President Eisenhower's last full day in office. He and his closest associates—Secretary of State Christian Herter, Secretary of Defense Thomas Gates, Treasury Secretary Robert Anderson, and staff aide Gen. Wilton Persons—met with President-elect Kennedy, Secretary of State designate Dean Rusk, Treasury Secretary designate Douglas Dillon, transition adviser Clark Clifford, and me to lay out pressing national issues we would have to face.*

We covered an immense number of subjects that afternoon, but the emphasis was on Indochina. I would never trust my memory of what was said; however, several of the participants, including me, wrote memoranda for the record shortly after. These and subsequent memoirs of the meeting reflect differing views of what Eisenhower advised Kennedy about the crucial issue of military intervention in Southeast Asia.

Eisenhower's focus in that part of the discussion was actually on Laos, not Vietnam. The Communist Pathet Lao had intensified their struggle against the U.S.-backed forces of Phoumi Nosavan for control of the country. Here is what Clark Clifford wrote: "President Eisenhower stated that Laos is the present key to the entire area of South East Asia. If Laos were lost to the Communists, it would bring an unbelievable pressure to bear on Thailand, Cambodia and South Vietnam. President Eisenhower stated that he considered Laos [and, by implication, Vietnam] of such importance

---

*The meeting illustrates a weakness in our form of government—the lack of an effective way to transfer knowledge and experience from one administration to another—and suggests the heavy price we pay. In parliamentary systems, a new government's ministers have usually served as opposition shadow ministers for several years before they take office. I recall, for example, dealing with Denis Healey of Great Britain and Helmut Schmidt of West Germany when they became defense ministers of their countries. Both had been trained, in effect, for their responsibilities by serving as opposition party leaders and studying their country's security issues for many years. I, in contrast, came to Washington from having served as president of Ford Motor Company. The meeting between the Eisenhower and Kennedy teams was a poor substitute for such training. John Locke was correct when he wrote: "No man's knowledge can go beyond his experience."

that if it reached the stage where we could not persuade others to act with us, then he would be willing, *'as a last desperate hope, to intervene unilaterally'* [emphasis in original]."[5]

Dean Rusk remembered the meeting largely as Clifford reported it. He thought he had heard Eisenhower recommend unilateral action in Laos if that were the only alternative to losing Laos to Communism.[6]

But my memorandum, prepared at President Kennedy's request from notes I took at the meeting, suggested that Eisenhower was actually giving a mixed message. I had the impression he was deeply uncertain about the proper course of action. I wrote: "President Eisenhower advised against unilateral action by the United States in connection with Laos," and I noted that Eisenhower did not answer Kennedy's direct question "What action can be taken to keep the Chinese Communists out of Laos?" I concluded by writing, "President Eisenhower stated without qualification, 'If Laos is lost to the Free World, in the long run we will lose all of Southeast Asia.' "[7]

Douglas Dillon's recollection jibed completely with my memo, he later told a scholar. Dillon even went a step further, adding his impression that "Eisenhower and [Secretary of State] Herter both got a certain inner satisfaction from laying a potentially intractable problem in Kennedy's lap."[8]

Doug's impression was absolutely correct, in my opinion: Eisenhower did not know what to do in Southeast Asia and was glad to leave it to the Democrats. Still, I cannot fault him for handing us a problem with no solution. The Indochina problem *was* intractable, the way both Eisenhower and we defined it. Just how intractable, our nation would learn painfully over the next fourteen years.

There is other evidence that Eisenhower felt stumped. It was later reported that he had told his staff three weeks before the Kennedy briefing, "We must not allow Laos to fall to the Communists, even if it involves war."[9] Yet that statement contrasts starkly with the stand he had taken during the Dien Bien Phu crisis six years before, when he had decided against U.S. intervention. Perhaps Eisenhower had adjusted his views as world events unfolded, but I cannot reconcile the two. Would Eisenhower ultimately have gone to war in Vietnam as we did? I do not know.

What I do know is that we received no thoughtful analysis of the problem and no pros and cons regarding alternative ways to deal with it. We were left only with the ominous prediction that if Laos were lost, all of Southeast Asia would fall. By implication, the West would have to do whatever was necessary to prevent that outcome. The meeting made a deep impression on Kennedy and us all. It heavily influenced our subsequent approach to Southeast Asia.

———

Within a few weeks it became evident that trouble was developing in South Vietnam in addition to Laos, and faster than we had anticipated. In March, President Kennedy set up a task force of sub-cabinet officials headed by Ros Gilpatric to explore alternative courses of action and make recommendations. Its report, presented on May 8, called for what seemed to us a massive increase in the number of U.S. military personnel in South Vietnam, from a few hundred to several thousand. President Kennedy scaled back the plan substantially, authorizing a modest increase of 100 advisers and 400 Special Forces troops to train the South Vietnamese in counterinsurgency techniques.

Meanwhile, conditions deteriorated in Laos. By August, Dean Rusk recommended at a White House meeting that we should continue diplomatic negotiations but be ready to take military action to defend Indochina under a plan prepared by SEATO. It called for the dispatch of some 30,000 combat troops, to be supplied by the signatories of the treaty, including Great Britain, France, and the United States. But the British and French had already made it clear that they had no intention of sending troops. And Dean's proposal presented another problem as well. I told President Kennedy that, before making any military commitment in Indochina, he should weigh Laos against other world problems.

Berlin, in particular, was on my mind: tension had increased to the point where we were contemplating moving six divisions (approximately 90,000 combat troops) to Europe. I argued that it was inconceivable that we would be able to do that and fight a war in Southeast Asia with anything short of total mobilization. The president concluded—and Dean agreed—that we should not commit ourselves to the SEATO plan without regard to whatever else might happen in the world.[10]

By the fall of 1961, guerrilla infiltration from North Vietnam into South Vietnam had increased substantially, and the Vietcong had intensified their attacks on Diem's government. President Kennedy decided to send Max Taylor and Walt Rostow of the NSC staff to South Vietnam to assess conditions and suggest what to do. In their report, Max and Walt urged that we substantially boost our support to South Vietnam, by sending more advisers, equipment, and even small numbers of combat troops. Such steps, they noted, would mean a fundamental "transition from advice to partnership" in the war.[11]

On November 8, 1961, I submitted a brief, hastily prepared memorandum to President Kennedy addressing these recommendations. It reflected my initial reaction, along with those of the Joint Chiefs of Staff and my deputy secretary, Ros Gilpatric. I observed that the Taylor-Rostow Report raised two fundamental questions: Would the United States commit itself to the objective of preventing the fall of South Vietnam to Communism? And would we support this commitment by moving more military personnel to South Vietnam immediately while preparing to add reinforcements later, should they prove necessary? I concluded by saying we were "inclined to recommend" we should accept both the objective and the means of pursuing it.[12]

As soon as I sent the memo to the White House, I started worrying that we had been too hasty in our advice to the President. For the next couple of days, I dug deeper into the Vietnam problem. The more I probed, the more the complexity of the situation and the uncertainties of our ability to deal with it by military means became apparent. I realized that seconding the Taylor-Rostow memo had been a bad idea.

Dean Rusk and his advisers at the State Department came to the same conclusion. On November 11, he and I, after more thought and discussion, submitted a joint memorandum to the president advising against sending combat forces in the way Max and Walt had recommended. While acknowledging that such forces might be necessary someday, we pointed out that we were facing a dilemma: "If there is a strong South Vietnamese effort, [U.S. combat troops] may not be needed; if there is not such an effort, U.S. forces could not accomplish their mission in the midst of an apathetic or hostile population."[13]

President Kennedy took up both memos in a meeting at the White House later that day. He made clear he did not wish to make an unconditional commitment to prevent the loss of South Vietnam and flatly refused to endorse the introduction of U.S. combat forces.[14]

The dilemma Dean and I defined was going to haunt us for years. Looking back at the record of those meetings, it is clear our analysis was nowhere near adequate. We failed to ask the five most basic questions: Was it true that the fall of South Vietnam would trigger the fall of all Southeast Asia? Would that constitute a grave threat to the West's security? What kind of war—conventional or guerrilla—might develop? Could we win it with U.S. troops fighting alongside the South Vietnamese? Should we not know the answers to all these questions before deciding whether to commit troops?

It seems beyond understanding, incredible, that we did not force ourselves to confront such issues head-on. But then, it is very hard, today, to recapture the innocence and confidence with which we approached Vietnam in the early days of the Kennedy administration. We knew very little about the region. We lacked experience dealing with crises. Other pressing international matters clamored for our attention during that first year: Cuba, Berlin, and the Congo to name but three. Finally, and perhaps most important, we were confronting problems for which there were no ready, or good, answers. I fear that, in such circumstances, governments—and, indeed, most people—tend to stick their heads in the sand. It may help to explain, but it certainly does not excuse, our behavior.

The president repeated his doubts about our military involvement in South Vietnam to the National Security Council a few days later, on November 15. He said he was afraid of becoming engaged simultaneously on two fronts on opposite sides of the world and pointed out how starkly the situation in Vietnam contrasted with the Korean War. In Korea enemy aggression had been quite clear; here the situation was ambiguous. He felt a strong case could actually be made *against* intervening 10,000 miles away to help a native army of 200,000 fight 16,000 guerrillas; we had already spent billions of dollars in Vietnam with little, if any, success. He doubted the United States would ever receive military support from our SEATO allies. It was pretty clear he did not like the situation. But the meeting ended inconclusively.[15]

In spite of the incoherence of our approach to South Vietnam during those early months, many of us—including the president and me—came to believe that the problem was such that only the South Vietnamese could deal with it. We could try to help them through training and logistical support, but we could not fight their war. That was our view then. Had we held to it, the whole history of the period would have been different.

I took great care to communicate the president's thoughts to the military chiefs—both those at the Pentagon and the commanders directly responsible for our Vietnam operations. In a November 28 telegram, I told Adm. Harry Felt, the commander in chief of the Pacific fleet, and Gen. Lionel McGarr, the senior U.S. military man in South Vietnam: "We must adjust ourselves to a perennially unclear political framework and to . . . limits on military action." I reiterated these points to Admiral Felt and General McGarr at our first conference in Hawaii the following month, telling them that U.S. combat troops would not be sent to South Vietnam.[16]

But because the basic issues had not been confronted squarely or explained clearly, they continued to be debated within the government until the president's death two years later. On January 13, 1962, the Joint Chiefs of Staff gave me a memorandum that they asked me to pass along to the president. In it they argued that American combat forces would be effective in preventing South Vietnam's loss, and they urged President Kennedy to authorize a deployment. The chiefs believed such a move would be absolutely consistent with American policy. "The United States has clearly stated . . . that one of its unalterable objectives is the prevention of South Vietnam falling to communist aggression." But they were wrong: it was exactly that basic decision that had not been made.

I forwarded their memorandum to President Kennedy on January 27 with a terse comment: "I am not prepared to endorse the views of the Chiefs until we have had more experience with our present [training] program in South Vietnam."[17]

———

Vietnam was far from the biggest problem in those early months of 1962 as we continued to get the Defense Department into shape. But unlike many issues that I delegated to Ros Gilpatric, I increasingly made Vietnam my personal responsibility. That was only right: it was the one place where Americans were in a shooting war, albeit as advisers. I felt a very heavy responsibility for it, and I got involved as deeply as I felt I could and be effective. That is what ultimately led people to call Vietnam McNamara's War.

As I came into closer contact with South Vietnam during 1962, I came to know its leader, President Ngo Dinh Diem. I participated in several long conferences with him beneath the whirring ceiling fans and gilded cornices of his office in Gia Long Palace. We thought that Diem aimed to move his people toward freedom and democracy. That he had studied at a Catholic seminary in New Jersey in the early 1950s seemed evidence that he shared Western values. As we got closer and closer to the situation, however, we came to learn otherwise. Diem, those around him, and the political structures that he built lacked a connection to the South Vietnamese

people; he never developed a bond with them. We totally misjudged that.

Because he was uncommunicative and from such a different
cultural background, Diem was an enigma to me and, indeed, to
virtually every American who met him. I did not understand him.
He appeared autocratic, suspicious, secretive, and insulated from his
people.

It was said that Diem was unaccustomed to the company of
women: he had never married and was believed never to have had
sexual relations. But one of his closest confidants was his sister-in-
law, Madame Nhu. She was married to Diem's conspiratorial and
very influential brother, Ngo Dinh Nhu, but also, in effect, served
as Diem's wife. Madame Nhu comforted Diem after the day's work
was done, relieved his tensions, argued with him often, and clearly
played a major role in shaping his thinking. What that thinking was
remained a mystery to me, however. Even today, I do not know
what long-term objectives Diem envisioned for his nation and his
people.[18] Like most Americans who visited the country and, I
suspect, many Vietnamese, I saw Madame Nhu as bright, forceful,
and beautiful, but also diabolical and scheming—a true sorceress.

Although we recognized these limitations, many of us
nonetheless accepted the conventional view of Diem expressed, for
instance, by *Newsweek* in 1959, when it labeled him "one of the
ablest free Asian leaders." Informed people in government,
including Sen. Mike Mansfield, an ex-professor of East Asian
history, expressed great admiration for Diem because of his
achievements during the transition to independence in 1954 and
1955. "In that period," Mansfield stated in 1963, "his personal
courage, integrity, determination, and authentic nationalism were
essential forces in forestalling a total collapse in South Vietnam and
in bringing a measure of order and hope out of the chaos, intrigue,
and widespread corruption."[19]

We rightly credited Diem with confronting an extraordinarily
difficult task in trying to build a nation deeply divided by religious

and political differences, and doing so in the face of North Vietnam's determination to force its control. Whatever his faults, and they were many, I and others believed that the prospect of getting anyone better than Diem was chancy at best.

But was our judgment of President Diem correct? Were our views of the problems we faced realistic? Would our plans to deal with them succeed? How were we to know, when we were moving in an alien environment, alongside a people whose language and culture we did not understand and whose history, values, and political traditions differed profoundly from our own? There was no easy way to answer those and a host of similar questions.

None of us—not me, not the president, not Mac, nor Dean, nor Max—was ever satisfied with the information we received from Vietnam. Of course, we asked for and got factual reports on military operations. And we avidly read the flood of narrative analyses from our embassy in Saigon. But very early on we decided there was a need for regular meetings among the senior U.S. officials in Saigon and Washington dealing with these issues. This led to my frequent trips to Hawaii and South Vietnam, beginning in late 1961.

The Hawaii meetings took place at the headquarters of the U.S. military commander in the Pacific (CINCPAC), overlooking Pearl Harbor. Fifty or sixty people—military and civilian, from Washington, Saigon, and Hawaii—would gather in a cavernous conference room, where we would listen to long series of briefings. The crowded atmosphere and agenda often made it hard to focus on the issues at hand and ensure we were receiving candid reports and thoughtful recommendations.

Much the same was true of our conferences in Vietnam. They were held at the U.S. military headquarters, first in a converted colonial-era hotel on Pasteur Street in downtown Saigon and later at Tan Son Nhut air base on the city's western outskirts. Because the locations were well known to the Vietcong, they often sought to disrupt the meetings. On one occasion, in May 1964, they tried to assassinate me by rigging mines beneath a bridge on a road they knew I would take into Saigon. South Vietnamese police discovered and defused the explosives shortly before my car passed over the bridge.

Critics have subsequently faulted us for holding such meetings, not recognizing that they constituted only one source of our information. While they were far from perfect, the meetings in Hawaii and Vietnam permitted those of us from Washington to convey the president's thinking and objectives to our colleagues in Vietnam, and gave them the opportunity to offer reports and make recommendations for further action. I believe we would have been far worse off if the meetings had not been held.

From Washington we traveled to these conferences aboard what came to be known as the Poor Man's 707. One of my first actions after becoming secretary had been to cancel unnecessary and wasteful orders for a third Air Force One and a number of small but expensive Lockheed jets for use by Defense Department executives. In their place, I suggested to Brig. Gen. George S. Brown (my military assistant, who later became air force chief of staff and subsequently chairman of the Joint Chiefs) that we spend no more than $20,000 to design a few seats that could be temporarily buttoned into an air force cargo plane when senior personnel needed to travel on special missions.

The cargo plane, a version of the KC–135 tanker outfitted with wing fuel tanks, possessed nearly enough range to fly nonstop from any one point in the world to any other. Long before the advent of 747s, it could fly nonstop from Paris to Saigon and, with only one stop, from Saigon to Washington.

The aircraft had one disadvantage: it lacked soundproofing, and I refused to spend the money to install it. As a result, conversation was difficult. But Max Taylor and Assistant Secretary of State W. Averell Harriman, two of my frequent traveling companions, suffered partial deafness and had trouble conversing even with soundproofing. So they welcomed the excuse to stay silent.

Eventually, I relaxed the expenditure limits somewhat, and we spent enough to add a few bunks and a secretary's desk to the kit. We could then take off from Saigon or Honolulu in the evening, dine, write our report to the president, have it typed en route while we slept, and present it to him when we returned to Washington the next day.

The traveling schedule was rough. For the Hawaiian meetings, I would leave Washington on Sunday afternoon, arrive in Honolulu before midnight local time after a nine- or ten-hour flight, meet with CINCPAC and the commander of the Military Assistance Command, Vietnam (COMUSMACV) all day Monday, depart Monday evening, sleep en route, and report to the president Tuesday morning.

Bobby Kennedy told his brother that this schedule was going to kill me. So the president urged me to allow an extra day once in a while, take Marg along, use his Air Force One, and stay in a luxurious bungalow maintained by the army for top personnel and high-ranking guests at Fort DeRussy on Waikiki Beach. I did so just once. The result was a Drew Pearson column, in *The Washington Post* and syndicated around the nation, blasting a scandalous diversion and misuse of government property for the personal pleasure of Secretary McNamara! We went back to the Poor Man's 707.

As I have said, the trips to Hawaii and South Vietnam permitted my associates and me to hear directly from large numbers of our U.S. and South Vietnamese colleagues. We always supplemented those meetings with consultations with independent observers. I particularly sought the military advice of the Israeli military hero Gen. Moshe Dayan and the British counterinsurgency expert Sir Robert Thompson. Thompson had led the successful campaign against guerrillas in Malaya during the 1950s; now he was head of the British Advisory Mission in South Vietnam.

Based on what we learned from all these sources, Dean and I, and our associates, gave frequent reports to Congress and the press. Were they accurate? They were meant to be. But with hindsight, the answer must be that the reports—including my own—on the military situation were often too optimistic. My reports on the stability of political institutions—which I always stressed as a precondition for military success—were far more accurate, however.

For example, in March 1962, I told a meeting of the Advertising Council in Washington that "success in opposing guerrilla warfare will depend at least as much and probably more upon the political and economic actions and programs than upon the military programs." In an interview published eleven days later in *The Washington Post*, I said: "Southeast Asia is vital to the security of the Pacific and the Pacific is vital to the security of the United States, but the application of military force alone will not automatically defeat the Communists unless there is internal economic and social reform."

However, typical of my reports on U.S. military operations were these:

February 5, 1962:

The actions which the South Vietnamese Government has taken to counter the very serious threat of subversion and aggression, covert aggression, in that nation, are beginning to be effective. . . . The combination of the actions they have initiated themselves and the actions which they have requested from us, I think, is leading to an improvement in the situation, but it is far too early to predict the eventual outcome.[20]

July 23, 1962:

Our military assistance to Vietnam is paying off. The South Vietnamese are beginning to hit the Viet Cong insurgents where it hurts most—in winning the people to the side of the government. . . . The Vietnamese armed forces are carrying the war to the Viet Cong with greater initiative and frequency. . . . The sign posts are encouraging and we are looking now to sustaining this momentum.[21]

October 9, 1962:

> I think it is too early to say that the tide has turned or to predict the final outcome, but a tremendous amount of progress had been made during the past year. . . . We are delighted at the progress that was reported to us. Whether it is measured in terms of the relative ratio of casualties suffered by the South Vietnamese forces versus the Communist aggressors or any other measure we looked at, progress is quite apparent.[22]

Why were my comments about the political situation in South Vietnam realistic while, in retrospect, those about military progress were overly optimistic?

The military reports reflected the picture presented by our military leaders at the conferences in Hawaii and South Vietnam. At each, I met with COMUSMACV Gen. Paul D. Harkins. Harkins was tall, handsome, and articulate; he looked and spoke exactly as a general should. He was a protégé of the scholarly Max Taylor, and while he lacked his mentor's intellectual caliber, he was very straightforward and persuasive.

General Harkins and his staff reported that South Vietnamese forces were pushing back the Vietcong and loosening their grip on the countryside. For example, at Honolulu on July 23, 1962, Harkins told me: "There is no doubt we are on the winning side. If our programs continue we can expect Vietcong actions to decline."[23] I did not then and do not now believe that he or other officers consciously misled me. It went against their training and tradition. Besides, there were other reporting channels I could use to cross-check what the military told me—the CIA, the State Department, and the media, to cite only three.

The reasons for their mistaken optimism lay elsewhere. It is now clear they were receiving very inaccurate information from the South Vietnamese, who tended to report what they believed Americans wanted to hear. As CIA Director John McCone later wrote,

> Information furnished to us from MACV and the Embassy con-
> cerning . . . Viet Cong activities in a number of provinces and the
> relative position of the SVN [South Vietnam] Government vs. the
> Viet Cong Forces was incorrect, due to the fact that the field
> officers . . . had been grossly misinformed by the South Viet-
> namese province and district chiefs. . . . The province and district
> chiefs felt obliged to "create statistics" which would meet the
> approbation of the Central Government.[24]

Like many people, the U.S. commanders also indulged, to some
extent, in wishful thinking. Moreover, they—as did I—misunderstood the nature of the conflict. They viewed it primarily as a
military operation when in fact it was a highly complex nationalistic
and internecine struggle.

I always pressed our commanders very hard for estimates of
progress—or lack of it. The monitoring of progress—which I still
consider a bedrock principle of good management—was very poorly
handled in Vietnam. Both the chiefs and I bear responsibility for that
failure. Uncertain how to evaluate results in a war without battle
lines, the military tried to gauge its progress with quantitative mea-
surements such as enemy casualties (which became infamous as body
counts), weapons seized, prisoners taken, sorties flown, and so on.
We later learned that many of these measures were misleading or
erroneous. I tempered the military's optimism about progress in the
war in my public comments, but not nearly enough.

———

By mid-1962 the clear and frequently stated objective of the
Kennedy administration in Vietnam was to train the South Vietnamese to defend themselves. To me, that implied we ought to set
a time limit on U.S. training support. I reasoned that either the
training would prove successful—in which case we would be able to
withdraw—or enough time would elapse to indicate it would fail—
in which case our withdrawal would also be justified.

Thinking ahead, I asked General Harkins in Honolulu on July
23, 1962, how long he thought it would take to eliminate the

military potential of the Vietcong. His estimate was something like this: one year after the South Vietnamese military and civil guard forces become fully operational and begin pressing the Vietcong in all areas.

Putting that together with other assessments, I ordered long-range planning for a phased withdrawal of U.S. advisers based on the assumption that it would take three years to subdue the Vietcong. We then had approximately 16,000 advisers in South Vietnam.[25]

The following spring, on March 29, 1963, I asked Sir Robert Thompson whether he thought it advisable to reduce the number of advisers. He replied that if progress continued and the Vietcong could be cleared from a particular area of South Vietnam during the summer, it might be possible to reduce our strength by 1,000 men.[26]

At my next meeting with General Harkins, in Honolulu on May 6, 1963, he told me we were continuing to make progress in the war. I therefore directed the military to prepare a plan for phasing out U.S. forces beginning with the withdrawal of 1,000 advisers by year's end.[27]

About that time a political and religious crisis erupted across South Vietnam. Buddhists angry at the Diem regime's curbs on religious freedom launched protests that led to violent retaliation by Diem's security forces. This brutal response provoked more protests, including horrifying self-immolations by Buddhist monks. These events shocked and appalled me and others in Washington, and made Diem's rule appear more troubled than ever.

The situation was still chaotic in late August, when the Joint Chiefs delivered the withdrawal plan I had asked for. They stated their own belief, however, that no U.S. forces should be withdrawn until the crisis subsided. They suggested no decision be made to implement the withdrawal plan until late October.[28]

The chiefs' wish to put off the decision underscored an important difference between two camps within the administration. Both saw our mission as training the South Vietnamese to defend themselves. But one believed we should stay until the South Vietnamese possessed that capability, no matter how long it took. The other thought we should limit our training to a finite period and then pull out. If the South Vietnamese had not learned to defend themselves by then, it would mean they were untrainable. The issue lurked beneath the surface and was never fully discussed or resolved. It was to have an important influence on a major decision by the president on October 2, 1963.

3

The Fateful Fall of 1963:

August 24–November 22, 1963

Conflict smoldered all summer between the Buddhists and the South Vietnamese government. Suddenly, on August 21, the government cracked down. With Diem's approval, Nhu ordered an elite military unit to raid the Buddhist pagodas in the early hours. They smashed down doors barricaded against them and roughed up monks who resisted. Several hundred were hauled off to jail.

Diem acted despite having personally assured Frederick E. Nolting, Jr., the departing U.S. ambassador, that he would take no further repressive steps against the Buddhists. This galling about-face came on top of another puzzling development, involving Charles de Gaulle in Paris. Earlier in the summer, we had gotten word that Diem, through his brother, Nhu, had secretly established contact with Hanoi. De Gaulle, eager to reassert French influence in Indochina, had picked up the same news from his own sources in North and South Vietnam and saw it as an opportunity. He quickly issued a call for Vietnam's reunification and neutralization. We were not certain whether the rumor was true, but we wondered if Diem was attempting to blackmail the United States for pressuring him to be less harsh in his treatment of dissident groups.[1]

Diem could not have timed the pagoda raid more poorly. That week, all of our key decision makers on Vietnam—President Kennedy, Dean Rusk, McGeorge Bundy, John McCone, and I—were out of Washington simultaneously for the first and only time I can remember. The president was in Hyannis Port, and Marg and I were in the Tetons in Wyoming for a brief but much needed vacation. Although there were telephones where we were staying, I was out much of the time and had given full authority to my deputy as I always did when away from Washington.

As reports of the violence flowed into Washington on August 24, several of the officials we had left behind saw an opportunity to move against the Diem regime. Before the day was out, the United States had set in motion a military coup, which I believe was one of the truly pivotal decisions concerning Vietnam made during the Kennedy and Johnson administrations.

The man who took the initiative was Roger Hilsman, Jr., who had succeeded Averell Harriman as assistant secretary of state for Far Eastern affairs. Hilsman was a smart, abrasive, talkative West Point graduate who had been involved in guerrilla combat in World War II and had subsequently become an academic. He and his associates believed we could not win with Diem and, therefore, Diem should be removed.

Hilsman began the action by drafting a cable to our brand-new ambassador in Saigon, Henry Cabot Lodge, Jr. The cable started with a condemnation of Nhu's actions:

> It is now clear that whether the military proposed martial law or whether Nhu tricked them into it, Nhu took advantage of its imposition to smash pagodas. . . . Also clear that Nhu has maneuvered himself into commanding position.
>
> U.S. Government cannot tolerate situation in which power lies in Nhu's hands. Diem must be given chance to rid himself of Nhu and his coterie and replace them with best military and political personalities available.
>
> If, in spite of all your efforts, Diem remains obdurate and refuses, then we must face the possibility that Diem himself cannot be preserved.

. . . We must at same time also tell key military leaders that U.S. would find it impossible to continue support GVN [government of Vietnam] militarily and economically unless . . . steps [to release the arrested monks] are taken immediately which we recognize requires removal of the Nhus from the scene. We wish to give Diem reasonable opportunity to remove Nhus, but if he remains obdurate, then we are prepared to accept the obvious implication that we can no longer support Diem. You may also tell appropriate military commanders we will give them direct support in any interim period of breakdown central government mechanism.

. . . Concurrently with above, Ambassador and country team should urgently examine all possible alternative leadership and make detailed plans as to how we might bring about Diem's replacement if this should become necessary.[2]

After Hilsman completed the cable, on August 24, Averell Harriman, who had just become undersecretary of state for political affairs, approved it. Michael Forrestal, son of the first secretary of defense and a member of the NSC staff, immediately sent the cable to President Kennedy in Hyannis Port, stating, "Clearances are being obtained from [Undersecretary of State George] Ball and Defense. . . . Suggest you let me know if you wish . . . to hold up action.[3]

The cable's sponsors were determined to transmit it to Saigon that very day. They found George Ball on the golf course and asked him to call the president on Cape Cod. He did, and President Kennedy said he would agree to the cable's transmission if his senior advisers concurred. George immediately telephoned Dean Rusk in New York and told him the president agreed. Dean endorsed it, though he was unenthusiastic. Averell, meanwhile, sought clearance from the CIA. Since John McCone was absent, he talked to Richard Helms, the deputy director for plans. Helms was reluctant, but, like Rusk, went along because the president had already done so.

Forrestal, meanwhile, called Ros Gilpatric at home and told him the same story: the president and secretary of state had seen the cable and concurred.

Ros felt as I did: we were both distressed at the Diem government's increasing repressiveness, but we did not see how we could replace it with a more satisfactory regime. We thought our best course was to try to persuade Diem to change. The advisers, equipment, and money we were supplying to his military gave us considerable leverage, and it seemed to us that was the key to stability in South Vietnam. By threatening to reduce U.S. help or even actually reducing it, we thought we could, over time, convince him to modify his destructive behavior.

Despite such feelings, with the approval process so far along, Ros gave his approval as well. But he became so worried about the thrust of the message that, even as the cable went out to Saigon on Saturday night, he sent a copy to Max Taylor, the president's military adviser.

Max was the wisest uniformed geopolitician and security adviser I ever met. He belonged to that generation of military officers who had started their careers in the 1920s and 1930s—the period when, as I have said, our nation believed it had no need for the military and looked on men in uniform with indifference if not outright contempt. Max was a war hero, having commanded the 101st Airborne Division during World War II and parachuted into Normandy in the early hours of D day. He was also a scholar who spoke six or seven languages, including Japanese and Korean, and he had written two notable books on military issues.

Hilsman's cable shocked him—especially the fact that it had already been approved and sent. Max knew it represented a major change in our Vietnam policy; what is more, it was totally at variance with what he believed was the proper course. He later stated the cable would never have been approved had not the anti-Diem faction in Washington made what he called an "egregious end run" during the absence of high-level officials.[4]

The president soon regretted the cable. In an oral history interview the following year, Bobby Kennedy recalled that his brother viewed the decision as a major mistake. Bobby explained: "He passed it off too quickly over the weekend at the Cape—he had thought it was cleared by McNamara and Taylor and everyone at State. In fact, it was Harriman, Hilsman, and Mike Forrestal at the White House and they were the ones who were strongly for a coup."[5]

I do not share Max's view that the cable represented an egregious end run. We all knew that Hilsman sometimes went outside official channels to increase the chances his views would prevail. The fault lay as much with those who failed to rein him in as it did with Hilsman himself. But it shocks and saddens me today to realize that action which eventually led to the overthrow and murder of Diem began while U.S. officials in both Washington and Saigon remained deeply divided over the wisdom of his removal; no careful examination and evaluation of alternatives to Diem had been made by me or others; no high-level approach to Diem—with appropriate carrots and sticks—had been attempted to persuade him to mend his ways. Moreover, we allowed the controversy concerning the status of Diem to overshadow de Gaulle's proposal. We never did give it the consideration it deserved. Neutralization had been the solution in Laos the year before—suppose Nhu and the French were able to achieve it in Vietnam? We discussed the issue in only a cursory way. It remained unresolved.

—————

Events cascaded one upon another after the cable reached Saigon. The day after Lodge received it, he called a meeting to consider how to organize a coup. He decided that the official American hand should not show, and so put the CIA station, which had been instructed to take its policy orders from the ambassador, in charge of the operation. Lodge understood the August 24 cable as instructing him to initiate action to remove Diem as leader of South Vietnam.*[6]

_____

*Years later, however, Lodge professed he had been "thunderstruck" by the cable and had thought it "very ill-advised." But he had indicated otherwise at the time. On August 28, four days after receiving the telegram, he cabled Dean: "I am personally in full agreement with the policy which I was instructed to carry out by last Sunday's telegram."

At that point Lodge had been at his post exactly two days. He was a former Republican senator and vice presidential candidate, and I admired his bipartisan willingness to serve the administration of a bitter Massachusetts political adversary in a difficult and dangerous diplomatic assignment. But I also thought he was patrician and self-confident to the point of arrogance.

When he arrived in Saigon, he had voiced disgust at what he considered the regime's inhumane repression of its own people, illustrated in particular by its crackdown on the Buddhists. Lodge appeared to be equally upset by the rumors about Diem's secret overtures to the North Vietnamese to move the country away from the United States toward neutrality. When the cable arrived, he interpreted it exactly as its author had intended: as an order from President Kennedy to encourage the South Vietnamese military to launch a coup. (In fact, as we have seen, the cable did not *explicitly* instruct him to do this.)

At Lodge's behest, the CIA station chief wasted no time in sending agents to Gen. Tran Thien Khiem in Saigon and Gen. Nguyen Khanh in Pleiku. They told the generals the Nhus had to go but left the question of retaining Diem up to them.[7]

Meanwhile, in Washington, we belatedly got around to debating whether to support a military plot against Diem. It was not a fight between hawks and doves but a debate over the importance of political stability in South Vietnam and how to achieve it. The arguments seethed for months behind the scenes. Oddly, although the press corps in Saigon repeatedly had filed stories critical of Diem and increasingly questioned administration policy in Vietnam, reporters in Washington never picked up our struggles.

Kennedy was extraordinarily sensitive to the media. It was one of the things that differentiated him from his predecessors. He liked journalists. He enjoyed their open, imaginative, stimulating minds and sometimes bawdy humor. He respected their intelligence and knowledge, and thought he should take account of it. And he wanted to influence them because he recognized and understood their importance in society.*

The press accounts of the pagoda raids were the first thing Kennedy talked about at a White House meeting on August 26, the first after the cable was sent. He said he thought Diem and Nhu, however repugnant in some ways, had actually done a great deal along the lines we desired. Therefore we should not move to eliminate them simply because of "media pressure." Max said he opposed a military coup. He pointed out that the South Vietnamese military split different ways over Diem, and, in any event, we should not turn over the job of choosing a head of state to the military.

Then I shifted the focus to Ambassador Lodge, who was so new to Saigon that his meetings with Diem and Nhu had been mere courtesy calls. I raised two fundamental questions:

What Ambassador Lodge should say to Diem—that is, what we expected him to do if we "allowed" him to remain in power and

---

*Often, he socialized with journalists. This led to an incident that reveals much about JFK the man. One Monday morning, Dean and I were scheduled to meet with the president at nine o'clock following his return from a weekend with Jackie at her mother's home in Newport, Rhode Island. As was my custom, I arrived in the office at seven, leafed through the advance copy of *Newsweek* on my desk, and to my horror discovered it contained a report of the worst news leak one could imagine. Today, I cannot even remember what the story was about, but then only a handful of people in the administration—the president, Dean, I, and two or three of our subordinates—were privy to what was considered highly sensitive information. I quickly checked my associates and learned none of them had leaked it.

When I arrived in the Cabinet Room at nine o'clock, Dean was already there. I said, "My God, Dean, what do you think happened?" He said, "Bob, I checked those of my colleagues who had knowledge of the facts and they clearly were not the source of the leak."

At that moment, the president walked in. He said, "Damn it, Dean, I put you over there to run that department and what do I find? The worst leak that's occurred in the U.S. government in years."

"Well, Mr. President," replied Dean, "Bob and I were just discussing that. We each checked our departments this morning and found the same thing: no one in our departments leaked it."

"I don't believe it," Kennedy said with rising impatience. "That's what I have you there for—to introduce some discipline into that department."

Dean calmly replied, "During my examination of the problem this morning, Mr. President, I learned that Ben Bradlee [then *Newsweek*'s Washington bureau chief and a close Kennedy friend] left Newport Thursday night, before *Newsweek* went to press on Friday."

Any president other than Kennedy would have snapped, "What in God's name are you trying to tell me? That I leaked it?" Instead, "Oh, my God" was all he said.

That is why I was drawn to the man.

what pressures or inducements might obtain his acquiescence to our request.

Who Lodge believed could replace Diem, pointing out that if we stood by and let a weak man get the presidency, "we're going to be in *real* trouble" [emphasis in original].[8]

Neither question received an adequate answer, and Lodge was not given instructions to meet with Diem.

Hilsman stressed the imperative to act now. But the president told him he wanted another meeting the next day and asked that former Ambassador Nolting be present. Hilsman did not like that. He complained that Nolting's views had become colored and that he had become emotionally involved in the situation. The president replied acidly, "Maybe logically."[9]

The August 27 meeting opened with a report from the CIA's Vietnam expert, William E. Colby, who described the situation in Saigon as quiet and said unrest had not spread to the countryside. In answer to a question from the president, Marine Corps Maj. Gen. Victor H. Krulak, Jr., of the Joint Staff said the effect of civil disturbances on the military campaign against the Vietcong had been minimal and there had been no dramatic degradation of South Vietnamese military capability. Dean noted Lodge had yet to talk to Diem and Nhu about the problems in Vietnam. Nolting echoed Max's judgment of the previous day that the generals lacked unity and real leadership.

This led the president to say he saw no point in attempting a coup unless it seemed likely to succeed, and he asked what military support existed for one. Nolting said he saw no such support, but he thought it might materialize now that the CIA had put out the word that the United States wanted to remove Diem and Nhu.

The president said we had not gone so far that a coup could not be delayed. I proposed we ask Lodge and General Harkins in Saigon to evaluate whether a military coup could succeed, and that in the meantime we tell the CIA to leave the generals alone. That set off

Hilsman again. The longer we waited, he said, the harder it would be to remove Diem. The president let that pass and asked Max what Harkins thought about a coup. Max replied he had never been asked. The president concluded the meeting by directing that a cable be sent asking Lodge and Harkins for their advice on whether to proceed with the coup or pull back.[10]

Our deliberations were taking on an increasingly urgent character and tone. The following day—August 28—we again met with the president, first at midday and then in the evening. At the noon meeting, I recommended we firmly decide whether we wished to support the generals' effort to topple Diem and Nhu. George Ball said we had no choice but to support a coup, to which I replied that we should not proceed as if propelled by momentum. The president agreed we should not go ahead simply because we had gone so far already.

Nolting expressed grave doubts about moving against Diem. He said we could not assume a new government would be any easier to deal with or provide a stronger base on which to prosecute the war. George dismissed that, arguing we could not win the war with Diem in power and, therefore, must throw him out. Averell Harriman agreed, saying we had lost the fight in Vietnam and would have to withdraw if a coup did not occur. Hilsman added there was no stopping the generals now.

Nolting then repeated a fundamental question we had raised before but never fully explored or answered. What condition would South Vietnam be in if a coup succeeded? Hilsman admitted we had little insight into how the generals planned to run the country if they took control. Nolting said only Diem could hold that fragmented country together.

In the face of such divided opinion, it seemed no wonder the president asked the group to reconvene that evening.[11]

At 6:00 P.M., we went at it again. The president met first with Dean, Mac, Max, and me, and then with a larger group. He ordered three messages sent to Saigon: one from Max to General Harkins, asking for his assessment of the situation and the generals' plans, and a second from the president to Lodge, seeking his assessment too. A third cable to both men would report our discussion at noon and make clear that Kennedy wanted their personal views about what to do—not their reactions to what they thought may have been decided in Washington.[12]

Dean had answers from Lodge and Harkins by the time we met again the next day. They agreed that the war could not be won under the Diem regime. But Harkins wanted to try to detach the Nhus from Diem, and Nolting agreed. He recommended "one last try with Diem." Dean urged we decide whether to instruct Harkins to back up the CIA approaches to the generals. The president asked if anyone else had reservations about the course of action under way.

I did. I recommended we ask Harkins to try to persuade Diem to fire his brother. Ros agreed with me. I explained my position by saying, "I see no good alternative on the horizon. The military leaders are now thinking of a military junta, and yet from what little I know of them—and I think I know them well—they aren't capable of running the government for long."[13]

Mac relayed John McCone's belief that we should make another attempt to persuade Nhu to leave. Nolting pointed out that Lodge still had not had a substantive talk with Diem. What Nolting did not say—but I suspect knew—was that Lodge did not want such a meeting and that his superiors at the State Department had not ordered him to arrange it.

The president authorized a cable to Lodge stating two things: Harkins should assure the generals that the CIA messages represented U.S. policy, but the United States must know the generals' plan before they took specific action; and a last approach to Diem remained undecided.

As an indication of the uncertainty the president felt, he, Dean, Mac, and I agreed this cable to Lodge should be followed by a second one—to be seen by no one else in the government. In this secret cable, President Kennedy told Lodge, "There is one point on my own constitutional responsibilities as President and Commander in Chief which I wish to state to you: . . . Until the very moment of the go signal for the operation by the Generals, I must reserve a contingent right to change course and reverse previous instructions." He added, "While fully aware . . . of the consequences of such a reversal, I know from experience that failure is more destructive than an appearance of indecision. I would, of course, accept full responsibility for any such change."[14]

That others shared President Kennedy's uncertainty became clear at a where-do-we-go-from-here meeting in Dean Rusk's conference room at the State Department on August 31. Dean opened the discussion by observing that our thinking seemed to have come full circle. We were back to our posture before the August 24 cable indicating U.S. support for a coup.

He suggested that we have Lodge tell Diem his repressions threatened continued U.S. support and proposed we ask the ambassador what concessions he thought Diem would make regarding the Buddhists' safety and Madame Nhu's departure. I fully agreed and emphasized the importance of reestablishing communication among Lodge, Harkins, and the South Vietnamese government. Obviously it would have been wiser to have done that before, not after, the August 24 cable. Yet the meeting ended without further consideration of my points and without any instructions to Lodge and his staff to act on them.[15]

Amid this turmoil, on September 2, CBS-TV marked the expansion of its evening news program from fifteen to thirty minutes by assigning Walter Cronkite to interview President Kennedy in the backyard of his family's compound at Hyannis Port. Cronkite said, "Mr. President, the only hot war we've got running at the moment is of course the one in Vietnam, and we have our difficulties there, quite obviously." The president replied: "I don't think that unless a greater effort is made by the [South Vietnamese] Government to win popular support that the war can be won out there. In the final analysis, it is their war. They are the ones who have to win it or lose it. We can help them, we can give them equipment, we can send our men out there as *advisers,* but they have to win it, the people of Vietnam, against the Communists [emphasis added]. . . . All we can do is help, and we are making it very clear, but I don't agree with those who say we should withdraw. That would be a great mistake."[16]

The president could not have been clearer in stating his belief that the war could only be won by the South Vietnamese, and he certainly gave no indication of sending U.S. combat troops to augment or substitute for South Vietnamese troops (nor had Diem given any indication he would welcome such action).

I quote President Kennedy's words because I believe they reflect his deeply felt conclusions regarding the U.S. role in the war.

———

At a meeting on September 3, the president speculated that France sought for Vietnam what the recent international negotiations had established for neighboring Laos—neutralization, which involved forming a coalition of the three warring factions. He was convinced neutralization had not worked in Laos and doubted it would work next door. But neither then nor at any later time did we carefully debate how a neutral South Vietnam—if this could be achieved—might affect the United States geopolitically. This was because we assumed that South Vietnam would never be truly neutral, that it would be controlled by the North, and that this would, in effect, trigger the domino effect Eisenhower had envisioned.

In retrospect, we erred seriously in not even exploring the neutralization option. If a sophisticated statesman like de Gaulle thought it desirable, it at least deserved our close attention. Our position was replete with inconsistencies and incongruities. We (particularly Dean Rusk) feared our NATO status would be weakened if we failed to honor what he interpreted as our SEATO obligations to South Vietnam. But SEATO, which consisted of the United States, the United Kingdom, France, Australia, New Zealand, Thailand, the Philippines, and Pakistan, bound its member nations only to "meet common danger" in accordance with their own "constitutional processes" and to "consult" with one another. A separate protocol designated Cambodia, Laos, and South Vietnam as areas that, if threatened, would "endanger" the "peace and security" of the signatory powers. But one of these signatory powers, France, not only believed it had no obligation under the treaty but seemed to be suggesting that U.S. intervention went against our common interests. If France—a charter member of SEATO and a prime beneficiary of America's security guarantee to NATO—thought a neutralized Vietnam would not seriously weaken NATO or Western security, then we should, at a minimum, have fully debated the issue. We did not.

The meeting ended with agreement that Lodge should see Diem at the earliest opportunity to discuss the subjects raised at our August 31 State Department conference.[17]

But when we met again on September 6, Lodge, inexplicably, had still not seen Diem. At this point Bobby Kennedy, who had taken a greater interest in Vietnam since the controversy over the August 24 cable, began to get actively involved. He wondered aloud why, if we had concluded we would lose the war with Diem, "we not grasp the nettle now"—by which he meant threaten to pull out.

That alarmed Dean. He replied it would be "very serious" to threaten to pull out, saying if the Vietcong took over South Vietnam, we would be in "real trouble." Max seconded him, reminding us that just three weeks earlier we had still believed we could win the war with Diem, and that the Joint Chiefs had shared that view. Then Dean continued, describing our present position—talking to Diem—as Stage One. He noted there would be no Stage Two if we pulled out. "Prior to pulling out," he said, "we might want to consider promoting a coup"—as if we were not already in the process of initiating one! Ironically, amid all the debate, we still failed to analyze the pros and cons of withdrawal.[18]

Further insight into President Kennedy's thinking in the midst of this crisis came in his September 9 interview with NBC-TV evening news anchors Chet Huntley and David Brinkley. "Mr.

President," Brinkley asked, "have you had any reason to doubt this so-called 'domino theory' that if South Vietnam falls, the rest of Southeast Asia will go behind it?" Perhaps recalling Eisenhower's warning, the president replied, "No, I believe it. . . . China is so large, looms so high just beyond the frontiers, that if South Vietnam went, it would not only give them an improved geographic position for a guerrilla assault on Malaya, but would also give the impression that the wave of the future in Southeast Asia was China and the Communists. So I believe it."[19]

On September 10, our deliberations resumed. Bobby said we should discuss specific actions relating to Diem and Nhu. In reply, I said our approach did not seem viable: "We have been trying to overthrow Diem, but we have no alternatives I am aware of. Therefore, we are making it impossible to continue working with Diem on the one hand and, on the other, we are not developing an alternative solution. We should go back to what we were doing three weeks ago."

Averell heatedly disagreed. A man whom I admired immensely, Averell was one of that breed, represented also by Nelson Rockefeller and Douglas Dillon, who were born to wealth but drawn to public service. He had served as ambassador to the Soviet Union during World War II, as special assistant to President Truman, and as governor of New York in the mid-1950s. Yet he so wanted to return to Washington and help the young president after his defeat in New York's gubernatorial election, that, at age sixty-nine, he accepted the relatively insignificant position of roving ambassador in an administration populated by men young enough to have been his sons. Averell's vigor and counsel quickly won him the confidence of the president, who appointed him chief of the U.S. delegation to the Geneva Conference on Laos, then assistant secretary of state for Far Eastern affairs, and later undersecretary of state for political affairs.

Averell never muffled his opinions. He flatly disputed me on the issue of Diem's removal. He said Diem had created a situation such that we could never achieve our objectives in Vietnam with him in control. Max and John McCone agreed with me. The meeting ended with the disagreement unresolved.[20]

The next day, Lodge cabled his estimate of the current situation in South Vietnam. He reported: "It is worsening rapidly . . . and the time has arrived for the U.S. to use what effective sanctions it has to bring about the fall of the existing government and the installation of another." Mac, in conversation with Dean, said the president was inclined to think Lodge's assessment the most powerful he had seen on the situation, while Dean replied it bothered him that Lodge had still not laid it out for Diem.[21]

A few days later, at yet another State Department conference— this one attended by John McCone and two CIA agents recently returned from South Vietnam—McCone asked what ideas underlay current coup planning. The agents described the generals' ideas, adding: "The substance which they all lack is a comprehensive follow-on plan." We then discussed two approaches to Diem: one conciliatory and one confrontational. I proposed a cable to Lodge embodying the conciliatory approach and requesting his views on it. Dean agreed and directed such a cable be drafted for the president's consideration.[22]

After meeting with his closest advisers on September 17, the president sent Lodge the "conciliatory" cable. It read, in part:

CAP 63516. Eyes only personal for Ambassador Lodge. Dept pass immediately. Deliver only copy. No other distribution in Dept whatever. From the President.

1. Highest level meeting today has approved broad outline of an action . . . program designed to obtain from GVN [government of South Vietnam], if possible, reforms and changes in personnel necessary to maintain support of Vietnamese and U.S. opinion in war against Viet Cong. This cable reports this program and our thinking for your comment before a final decision. . . .

2. We see no good opportunity for action to remove present government in immediate future. Therefore, as your most

recent messages suggest, we must for the present apply such pressures as are available. . . . We think it likely that such improvement can make a difference, at least in the short run. Such a course, moreover, is consistent with more drastic effort as and when means become available. . . .

3. We share your view . . '. that best available reinforcement to your bargaining position in this interim period is clear evidence that all U.S. assistance is granted only on your say-so. . . . You are authorized to delay any delivery of supplies or transfer of funds by any agency until you are satisfied that delivery is in U.S. interest, bearing in mind that it is not our current policy to cut off aid entirely. . . . We think it may be particularly desirable for you to use this authority in limiting or rerouting any and all forms of assistance and support which now go to or through Nhu or individuals . . . associated with him. . . .

4. Subject to your comment and amendment our own list of possible helpful actions by government runs as follows in approximate order of importance:

a. Clear the air—Diem should get everyone back to work and get them to focus on winning the war. He should be broad-minded and compassionate in his attitude toward those who have, for understandable reasons, found it difficult under recent circumstances fully to support him.

A real spirit of reconciliation could work wonders on the people he leads; a punitive, harsh or autocratic attitude could only lead to further resistance.

b. Buddhists and students—Let them out and leave them unmolested. This more than anything else would demonstrate the return of a better day and the refocussing on the main job at hand, the war.

c. Press—The press should be allowed full latitude of expression. Diem will be criticized, but leniency and cooperation with the domestic and foreign press at this time would bring praise for his leadership in due course. While tendentious reporting is irritating, suppression of news leads to much more serious trouble.

d. Secret and combat police—Confine its role to operations against the VC [Vietcong] and abandon operations against non-Communist opposition groups thereby indicating clearly that a period of reconciliation and political stability has returned.

e. Cabinet changes to inject new untainted blood, remove targets of popular discontent.

f. Elections—These should be held, should be free, and should be widely observed.

g. Assembly—Assembly should be convoked soon after the elections. The government should submit its policies to it and should receive its confidence. . . .

6. Specific reforms are apt to have little impact without dramatic, symbolic move which convinces Vietnamese that reforms are real. As practical matter we share your view that this can best be achieved by some visible reduction in influence of Nhus, who are symbol to disaffected of all that they dislike in GVN. This we think would require Nhus' departure from Saigon and preferably Vietnam at least for extended vacation. We recognize the strong possibility that these and other pressures may not produce this result, but we are convinced that it is necessary to try. . . .

8. We note your reluctance to continue dialogue with Diem until you have more to say, but we continue to believe that discussions with him are at a minimum an important source of intelligence and may conceivably be a means of exerting some persuasive effect even in his present state of mind. . . . We ourselves can see much virtue in effort to reason even with an unreasonable man when he is on a collision course. . . .

9. Meanwhile, there is increasing concern here with strictly military aspects of the problem, both in terms of actual progress of operations and of need to make effective case with Congress for continued prosecution of the effort. To meet these needs, President has decided to send Secretary of Defense and General Taylor to Vietnam, arriving early next week. It will be emphasized here that it is a military mission and that all political decisions are being handled through you as President's senior representative. . . .[23]

The same day, before the cable went out, Averell telephoned Mike Forrestal to say he and Hilsman were "very much disappointed with the draft cable." He went on to describe the proposed visit as "a disaster" because, he said, "it is sending two men opposed to our policy [McNamara and Taylor], plus one [Deputy Undersecretary of State U. Alexis Johnson] who wouldn't stand up to carry out policy." Forrestal agreed.[24]

After receiving the president's message, Lodge weighed in the following day, saying he opposed our visit. He feared our trip would signal Diem we had decided to "forgive and forget" and would put a "wet blanket" on efforts to change the government. Lodge favored a policy of stony silence toward Diem, believed it had begun to have an effect, and felt our mission jeopardized it.[25]

In order to meet his objections, I suggested to the president that Max and I meet Lodge and Harkins, in Hawaii rather than Saigon. But, as Mac told Dean, "the President thinks you have to look at it [i.e., McNamara should examine the problem on the spot] to see it." Kennedy explained this in another cable to Lodge that afternoon. "I quite understand the problem you see in visit of McNamara and Taylor. At the same time my need for this visit is very great indeed, and I believe we can work out an arrangement which takes care of your basic concerns. . . . In any visit McNamara makes to Diem he will want to speak some hard truths on the military consequences of the current difficulties."[26]

On September 23, the president signed the following written instructions to me:

It may be useful to put on paper our understanding of the purpose of your visit to South Vietnam. I am asking you to go because of my desire to have the best possible on-the-spot appraisal of the military and paramilitary effort to defeat the Viet Cong. The program developed after General Taylor's mission and carried forward under your close supervision has brought heartening results, at least until recently. The events in South Vietnam since May have now raised serious questions both about the present prospects for success against the Viet Cong and still more about the future effectiveness of this effort unless there can be important political improvement in the country. It is in this context that I now need your appraisal of the situation. If the prognosis in your judgment is not hopeful, I would like your views on what action must be taken by the South Vietnamese Government and what steps our Government should take to lead the Vietnamese to the action.

Ambassador Lodge has joined heartily in supporting this mission[!] and I will rely on you both for the closest exchange of views. It is obvious that the overall political situation and the military and paramilitary effort are closely interconnected in all sorts of ways, and in executing your responsibility for appraisal of the military and paramilitary problem I expect that you will consult fully with Ambassador Lodge on related political and social questions. I will also expect you to examine with Ambassador Lodge ways and means of fashioning all forms of our assistance to South Vietnam so that it will support our foreign policy objectives more precisely.

I am providing you separately with a letter from me to President Diem which Ambassador Lodge and you should discuss and which the Ambassador should deliver on the occasion of a call on President Diem if after discussion and reference to me I conclude that such a letter is desirable.

In my judgment the question of the progress of the contest in South Vietnam is of the first importance and in executing this mission you should take as much time as is necessary for a thorough examination both in Saigon and in the field.

As he handed me these instructions, the president added he thought it would be necessary for me to see Diem twice, and if Max and I judged the need for reform and change essential to winning the war, I should press this conclusion strongly with him.[27]

Kennedy saw the letter as a guidance to me but also as a document that I could show to others and say: "This is what the president desires." But the anti–Diem activists in Washington continued their rearguard action. Unbeknownst to Mac and me, Hilsman sent Lodge a letter after reading the president's instructions to me. It said:

Dear Cabot: I am taking advantage of Mike Forrestal's safe hands to deliver this message.

. . . I have the feeling that more and more of the town is coming around to our view [i.e., that Diem must be removed by a coup] and that if you in Saigon and we in the Department stick to our guns the rest will also come around. As Mike will tell you, a determined group here will back you all the way. . . .[28]

President Kennedy's written instructions to me and Hilsman's back-channel letter to Lodge capped a month of indecision by the administration as it confronted an important problem that worsened each day and demanded decisive action. Before authorizing the coup against Diem, we had failed to confront the basic issues in Vietnam that ultimately led to his overthrow, and we continued to ignore them after his removal. Looking back, I believe we were each at fault:

- I should have forced examination, debate, and discussion on such basic questions as Could we win with Diem? If not, could he be replaced by someone with whom we could do better? If not, should we have considered working with Nhu and France for neutralization? Or, alternatively, withdrawing on the grounds that South Vietnam's political disorder made it impossible for the United States to remain there?
- Max did not push to resolve the continuing reporting differences surrounding military progress—or the lack thereof—in South Vietnam.
- Dean—one of the most selfless, dedicated individuals ever to serve the United States—failed utterly to manage the State Department and to supervise Lodge. Nor did he participate forcefully in presidential meetings.
- And President Kennedy—whom I fault least, facing as he did a host of other problems ranging from conflict over civil rights to securing congressional support for the Nuclear Atmospheric Test Ban Treaty—failed to pull together a divided U.S. government. Confronted with a choice among evils, he remained indecisive far too long.

I should add that the pros and cons of neutralization and withdrawal had begun to be debated in the press, if not within the administration. In the summer and fall of 1963, columnists Walter Lippmann and James Reston suggested consideration be given to neutralization. But journalist David Halberstam, who reported for *The New York Times* from South Vietnam during the early 1960s and forcefully criticized the administration's policy, opposed both alternatives. He wrote in 1965:

The basic alternatives for Vietnam are the same now as they were in 1961; they are no different, no more palatable, no less of a nightmare.

First, there is a great deal of talk about the possibility of a neutral Vietnam. But under present conditions this is out of the question. There is not the remotest possibility of neutrality in the sense that Switzerland, Austria, India, or even Laos, are neutral—which is these countries' way of saying that they wish to be neither a battlefield nor a participant of either side in the Cold War. The first step toward a neutral Vietnam would undoubtedly be the withdrawal of all U.S. forces in the country and a cutback in American military aid; this would create a vacuum so that the Communists, the only truly organized force in the South, could subvert the country at their leisure—perhaps in six months, perhaps in two years. There would simply be no force to resist them, and if Hanoi offered us and the South Vietnamese a neutral solution, it would only mean a way of saving face for the United States.

What *about* withdrawal? Few Americans who have served in Vietnam can stomach this idea. It means that those Vietnamese who committed themselves fully to the United States will suffer the most under a Communist government, while we lucky few with blue passports retire unharmed; it means a drab, lifeless and controlled society for a people who deserve better. Withdrawal also means that the United States' prestige will be lowered throughout the world, and it means that the pressure of Communism on the rest of Southeast Asia will intensify. Lastly, withdrawal means that throughout the world the enemies of the West will be encouraged to try insurgencies like the one in Vietnam.

Just as our commitment in Korea in 1950 has served to discourage overt Communist border crossings ever since, an anti-Communist victory in Vietnam would serve to discourage so-called wars of liberation.[29]

To be fair to Halberstam, the hawkish views he was expressing reflected the opinion of the majority of journalists at the time.

———

On September 25, on the eve of my departure for Saigon, Harry Reasoner of *CBS Reports* asked me if the South Vietnamese "with our assistance . . . might win the war on the battlefield and lose it in Saigon?" I replied:

> The current period is a difficult one to appraise. Certainly, instability has been accentuated in the last several weeks by the actions of the government. It is entirely possible that they have alienated important elements of the population, and unless the government and the population can work together in a unified effort to defeat the Viet Cong, they won't be defeated.

I went on to say:

> It is important to recognize it's a South Vietnamese war. It will be won or lost depending upon what they do. We can advise and help, but they are responsible for the final results, and it remains to be seen how they will continue to conduct that war.[30]

These words proved hauntingly prophetic.

———

While en route to Saigon, I reminded my traveling party of our mission's goal: to appraise the effectiveness of South Vietnam's fight against the Vietcong and to evaluate its prospects for success. If the prognosis appeared poor, we needed to ask what action South

Vietnam must take, and how the United States might lead South Vietnam to that action.

I told them I believed we needed to answer some specific questions before we could make recommendations:

- What explained the conflicting reports about military progress and political stability? Which were correct?
- How significant had opposition to Diem become among students, the military, the bureaucracy, the general population? Would it increase?
- Who exercised political control in the rural hamlets and villages? Did we know how to gauge this, and were we confident of our judgments?
- Had Diem's and Nhu's physical and mental health changed? How did their present relationship compare with their past relationship?
- Could Diem retain effective political power? Had key elements of South Vietnam's power base moved away from him?
- If Diem retained power, would the military effort succeed or deteriorate?
- If we concluded Diem should change course, what levers— economic, military, political—did we possess to induce him to do so

To answer these, I believed we should canvass the broadest possible spectrum of opinion: South Vietnamese military at all levels; U.S. military at all levels; press; foreign ambassadors; South Vietnamese, French, and American businessmen and labor leaders; International Control Commission members; academicians; and Catholic clergy. I directed that we meet each morning to exchange views and that there be only one reporting system to Washington; any differences of opinion would be cited in the daily group cable, and dissenting views, if any, noted in my report to the president.[31]

During our ten-day stay, we toured virtually every operational area in South Vietnam and held dozens of meetings. I found three of my own interviews particularly illuminating and disturbing.

On September 26, I met with P. J. Honey, a lecturer on Viet-namese affairs at the University of London's School of Oriental and African Studies who spoke Vietnamese fluently and maintained close contacts with leaders of both North and South Vietnam. His comments carried special weight with me because of his strong background and because he had previously supported Diem.

During our discussion, Honey stated that when he had arrived in Saigon a few weeks before, he had believed the United States could somehow manage to live with Diem and it would be dangerous to change. But he had now changed his mind. Diem had aged terribly over the last three years and had slowed mentally. Criticism of Diem now came openly, from military as well as civilian quarters. Diem's attacks on Buddhists had particularly shocked the population. All these factors convinced Honey that it was impossible to liberalize the regime or change Diem. The United States therefore had to decide, he said, whether it could win with the regime. In Honey's opinion, it could not, even though he asserted the strategic hamlet program had proved its workability and the Vietcong had failed to exploit Saigon's political instability.

But did that mean we should replace Diem? Honey was equivocal: he said that any movement away from the regime was risky, and in the event of a military coup or assassination, he judged the chance of getting something better as fifty-fifty.

In closing, Honey predicted that if the Communists took control of South Vietnam, no political leader in all of Asia would put any confidence in the word of the West. Indeed, he said, the loss of confidence would not be limited to Asia.[32]

On September 30, I interviewed the papal delegate, Monsignor Asta. He began by telling me that beneath South Vietnam's surface calm was a "turning of the screw." The regime had established a police state and perpetrated widespread torture. Intellectuals and students saw all government adversaries being eliminated. Some turned toward the Vietcong, many more toward neutralism. Honey had confirmed Hanoi's approach through the French to Nhu, and Monsignor Asta added that if Nhu grasped power, first he would ask the United States to leave and then he would cut a deal with the Communists. The monsignor closed with a criticism I fully shared: the U.S. government had not been speaking with one voice in Saigon, and this had blurred American policy and confused the South Vietnamese people.[33]

I held the third interview on September 27 with John Richardson, who had been the CIA's Saigon station chief since 1962. Richardson told me the Buddhist crisis had crystallized wider discontent, which had lain dormant for some time. The night arrests of students and the climate of suspicion particularly troubled him. He described Diem as patriotic and respected for his moral qualities, but his associates—particularly Nhu—damaged his reputation and threatened to ruin him. It was a tragedy.

Richardson reported that Diem's close personal assistant feared the budding crisis would lead to a coup by high-ranking military officers, although Richardson saw no one on the horizon with sufficient moral authority to replace Diem. To save South Vietnam, he concluded, the United States must pressure Diem to stop the repressions and force Nhu to leave. Otherwise, a coup would occur, and this would be disastrous. He saw no other way. He said, "I ask you, Mr. Secretary, to be very firm with Diem."[34]

———

Finally, on September 29, Max and I went to Gia Long Palace on Cong Ly Street, just a few blocks from the U.S. embassy, for a three-hour meeting with Diem, followed by a formal dinner. Lodge and Harkins accompanied us. Nhu did not appear.

Purring French in somnolent tones and chain-smoking cigarettes, Diem spent the first two and a half hours delivering a monologue about the wisdom of his policies and the progress of the war, frequently springing up and referring to maps to make his case. His serene self-assurance disconcerted me.

During a pause in the monologue, I finally spoke. I told Diem the United States sincerely wished to help South Vietnam defeat the Vietcong. I emphasized this was basically a Vietnamese war and all the United States could do was help. While agreeing with him that reasonable military progress had been made, I deliberately and forcefully conveyed U.S. concern over South Vietnam's political unrest. I emphasized that the unrest and the repression it had triggered endangered the war effort and America's support. Therefore the repression must stop and the unrest be resolved.

Diem flatly rejected my assertions. He said vicious press attacks against his government and his family accounted for a U.S. misunderstanding of the real situation in South Vietnam. Although I acknowledged some press accounts might be erroneous, I said there was no escaping the serious crisis of confidence in the Diem government in both South Vietnam and the United States. He again disagreed. He blamed "immature, untrained, and irresponsible" students for the recent wave of arrests. Chillingly, he added that he bore a certain responsibility for the Buddhists' unrest: he had been "too kind" to them.

I also pressed him on the subject of Madame Nhu, telling Diem that no small part of his government's difficulties with U.S. public opinion derived from her ill-advised and unfortunate declarations. I drew from my pocket a newspaper clipping quoting her remark that American junior officers in South Vietnam were "acting like little soldiers of fortune." Such outbursts, I told Diem, deeply offended U.S. public opinion.

His glances and manners suggested that for the first time he understood my point, but he rose to Madame Nhu's defense. "This is not satisfactory," I said. The problems were real and serious. They had to be solved before the war could be won.

Max recapitulated my points. He stressed the need for Diem to respond to widespread and legitimate anxiety in the United States concerning recent events in South Vietnam. In a follow-up letter to Diem two days later, Max wrote: "After talking to scores of officers, Vietnamese and American, I am convinced that the Viet Cong insurgency in the north and center can be reduced to little more than sporadic elements by the end of 1964. The Delta will take longer but should be completed by the end of 1965. But for these predictions to be valid, certain conditions [i.e., those Secretary McNamara indicated] must be met."[35]

But Diem did not answer. He offered absolutely no assurance that he would take any steps in response to the points we had made to him. As the U.S. note taker at our meeting wrote: "His manner was one of at least outward serenity and of a man who had patiently explained a great deal and who hoped he had thus corrected a number of misapprehensions."[36]

———

Flying back to Washington, Max and I drafted our report to the president, with the help of Assistant Secretary of Defense for International Security Affairs William P. Bundy. Because of its importance and the events that followed, I draw extensively from the report. The following excerpts stand as a better summary of our conclusions and recommendations than any restatement could:*

Conclusions
- The military campaign has made great progress and continues to progress.
- There are serious political tensions in Saigon (and perhaps elsewhere in South Vietnam) where the Diem-Nhu government is becoming increasingly unpopular.
- Further repressive actions by Diem and Nhu could change the present favorable military trends. On the other hand, a return to more moderate methods of control and administration, unlikely though it may be, would substantially mitigate the political crisis.
- It is not clear that pressures exerted by the U.S. will move Diem and Nhu toward moderation. Indeed, pressures may increase their obduracy. But unless such pressures are exerted, they are almost certain to continue past patterns of behavior.
- The prospects that a replacement regime would be an improve-

---

*I informed the president that all members of our mission concurred in the report, with one important exception: Bill Sullivan, Averell Harriman's assistant, indicated his belief that "a replacement regime which does not suffer from the overriding danger of Nhu's ambition to establish a totalitarian state . . . would be inevitably better than the current regime."

ment appear to be about 50-50. Initially, only a strongly author-itarian regime would be able to pull the government together and maintain order. In view of the preeminent role of the military in Vietnam today, it is probable that this role would be filled by a military officer, perhaps taking power after the selective process of a junta dispute. Such an authoritarian military regime, perhaps after an initial period of euphoria at the departure of Diem/Nhu, would be apt to entail a resumption of the repression at least of Diem, the corruption of the Viet-namese Establishment before Diem, and an emphasis on con-ventional military rather than social, economic and political considerations, with at least an equivalent degree of xenophobic nationalism.

Recommendations

We recommend that:

- General Harkins review with Diem the military changes nec-essary to complete the military campaign in the Northern and Central areas by the end of 1964, and in the Delta by the end of 1965.

- A program be established to train Vietnamese so that essential functions now performed by U.S. military personnel can be carried out by Vietnamese by the end of 1965. It should be possible to withdraw the bulk of U.S. personnel by that time.

- In accordance with the program to train progressively Viet-namese to take over military functions, the Defense Department should announce in the very near future presently prepared plans to withdraw 1000 U.S. military personnel by the end of 1963.

- To impress upon Diem our disapproval of his political program we:
  - Withhold important financial support of his development programs.
  - Maintain the present purely "correct" relations with the top of the South Vietnamese government.
  - Monitor the situation closely to see what steps Diem takes to reduce repressive practices and to improve the effec-tiveness of the military effort. We should recognize we may have to decide in two to four months to move to more drastic action.

- We not take any initiative to encourage actively a change in government.

We particularly emphasized we did not believe action to organize a coup should be taken at that time.[37]

———

We reached Washington early on October 2. Later that morning Max and I went to the White House and briefed the president for an hour on our trip. A major subject of discussion was the recommendation to remove 1,000 of our advisers. "I think, Mr. President, we must have a means of disengaging from this area, and we must show our country that means," I said.[38]

President Kennedy convened the National Security Council that evening to discuss our report. With the preceding weeks' sharp divisions in his mind, the president summarized where he believed we stood. He said we needed to find effective ways of persuading Diem to change the political atmosphere in Saigon, but he stressed the administration's unity at last on Vietnam. He said we now had a policy and a report endorsed by all.

Everyone agreed that it was South Vietnam's war, that we were there only as advisers to help the South Vietnamese defend themselves, and that if they were incapable of defending themselves, the war could not be won. But there was heated debate about our recommendation that the Defense Department announce plans to withdraw U.S. military forces by the end of 1965, starting with the withdrawal of 1,000 men by the end of the year. Although all mission members had agreed to the language in the report, once discussion began, we battled over the recommendation. The debate reflected a total lack of consensus over where we stood in *meeting* our objectives.

One faction believed military progress had been good and training had progressed to the point where we could begin to withdraw. A second faction did not see the war as progressing well and did not see the South Vietnamese showing evidence of successful training. But they, too, agreed we should begin to withdraw, because if the South Vietnamese were "trainable" we had been there long enough to achieve results, and if results were not apparent they were unachievable because of political instability. The third faction—representing the view of the majority—considered the South Vietnamese trainable but believed our training had not been in place long enough to achieve results and, therefore, should continue at current levels.

After much debate, the president endorsed our recommendation to withdraw 1,000 men by December 31, 1963. He did so, as I recall, without indicating his reasoning. In any event, because objections had been so intense and because I suspected others might try to get him to reverse the decision, I urged him to announce it publicly. That would set it in concrete.

This, not surprisingly, proved controversial. But the president finally agreed, although he objected to including the phrase "by the end of the year." He felt if we made the announcement and could not take such action within ninety days, we would be accused of being overly optimistic. I said, "The advantage to taking them out is that we can say to the Congress and the people that we *do* have a plan for reducing the exposure of U.S. combat personnel to the guerrilla actions in South Vietnam—actions that the people of South Vietnam should gradually develop a capability to suppress themselves. And I think this will be of great value to us in meeting the very strong views of Fulbright and others that we're bogged down in Asia and will be there for decades [emphasis in original]."[39]

The president finally agreed, and the announcement was released by Press Secretary Pierre Salinger after the meeting. The White House press release included this statement:

> Secretary McNamara and General Taylor . . . reported that by the end of this year, the U.S. program for training Vietnamese should have progressed to the point where 1,000 U.S. military personnel assigned to South Viet Nam can be withdrawn. The political situation in South Viet Nam remains deeply serious. . . . While

[repressive] actions [in that country] have not yet significantly affected the war effort, they could do so in the future.[40]

The debate about our report to the president resumed on the morning of October 5. There was more heated argument, but in the end the president clearly stated his approval of the section of our report that related to coup planning. We had written: "At this time, no initiative should be taken to encourage actively a change in government. Our policy should be to seek urgently to identify and build contacts with an alternative leadership if and when it appears." The president ordered instructions to that effect sent to Saigon through CIA channels.[41]

———

The president's decision that the United States "not take any initiative to encourage actively a change in government" began unraveling within weeks. In a cable to Mac on October 25, Lodge urged that, as plotting among South Vietnam's generals was now far advanced, "we should not thwart a coup." His rationale was that "it seems at least an even bet that the next government would not bungle and stumble as much as the present one has." Speaking for the president, Mac replied that short of thwarting a coup, we should retain the prerogative of reviewing the generals' plans and discouraging any attempt with poor prospects of success.[42]

At a meeting with the president four days later, I asked who among our officials in Saigon headed coup planning and observed Harkins might not know what the embassy and CIA were doing. Bobby, acknowledging he had not seen all the cables, said the present situation made no sense to him. Supporting a coup meant putting the future of South Vietnam—indeed, the future of all Southeast Asia—in the hands of someone whose identity and intentions remained unknown to us. Max agreed, saying even a successful coup would hamper the war effort as a new, inexperienced government learned its way. McCone concurred. Earlier, he had said: "Mr. President, if I was manager of a baseball team, and I had one pitcher, I'd keep him in the box whether he was a good pitcher or not." Dean felt in the long run, if the Diem government continued, the war effort would deteriorate. The meeting ended indecisively, and the president asked us to reconvene that evening.[43]

At the 6:00 P.M. meeting, the president, who had never shared Lodge's certainty or enthusiasm for a coup against Diem, felt the burden should be on the generals to show a substantial likelihood of quick success. After the meeting, Mac sent Lodge a message to this effect and instructed him to show the cables about the Vietnamese generals' plot to Harkins and seek his and the CIA station's assessment of what action to take.[44]

After reading the cables, Harkins fired off an angry message to Max in Washington. He complained bitterly about Lodge's failure to keep him informed of coup planning, reiterated his opposition to a coup, and said he saw no alternative leader with Diem's strength of character—particularly among the generals, whom he knew well. Harkins suggested that "we not try to change horses too quickly but that we continue to take persuasive actions that will make the horses change their course and methods of action."

Lodge, appalled by the thought of a U.S. attempt to thwart a coup, replied with evident exasperation: "Do not think we have the power to delay or discourage a coup." I seriously questioned whether the South Vietnamese generals would proceed with a coup if they believed the American government opposed it. Mac apparently shared my thinking. Later that same day, he cabled Lodge: "We do not accept as a basis for U.S. policy that we have no power to delay or discourage a coup. . . . We believe . . . you should take action and persuade coup leaders to stop or delay any operation which . . . does not clearly give high prospect of success."[45]

———

Lodge was scheduled to leave Saigon for consultations in Washington on November 1. Just before getting on the plane, he joined Admiral Felt in a courtesy call on Diem. Earlier Diem had sent a note saying he wished Lodge to stay fifteen minutes after Felt left.

Lodge did so. Later, he cabled Washington: "When I got up to go, he said: Please tell President Kennedy that I am a good and a frank ally, that I would rather be frank and settle questions now than talk about them after we have lost everything. . . . Tell President Kennedy that I take all his suggestions very seriously and wish to carry them out but it is a question of timing." Lodge added this comment: "I feel that this is another step in the dialogue which . . . Diem had begun at our meeting in Dalat on Sunday [October 27]. *If U.S. wants to make a package deal. I would think we were in a position to do it. . . . In effect he said: Tell us what you want and we'll do it.* Hope to discuss this in Washington [emphasis added]."[46]

The cable went through normal channels and finally reached the State Department at 9:18 A.M. (Washington time) November 1. It arrived at 9:37 A.M. at the White House, where we were meeting with the president to resume our discussion of events in Saigon. By then it was too late; the coup had begun.

———

At 9:30 A.M. on November 2, we met again with the president to resume our discussions of events in Saigon. When the meeting began, Diem's and Nhu's fate remained unknown. Midway through the meeting, Mike Forrestal burst into the room with a flash message from the Situation Room. The CIA station in Saigon reported it had been informed by its South Vietnamese counterparts that the brothers had committed suicide "en route from city to Joint General Staff headquarters."[47]

In fact, after expressing a willingness to surrender, Diem and Nhu had waited in a Catholic church in Cholon, the Chinese district south of downtown Saigon. General Minh, who later became president, dispatched two jeeps and an armored personnel carrier to pick them up. They were pushed into the personnel carrier and had their hands tied behind their backs. When the convoy arrived at Joint General Staff headquarters and the carrier's doors were opened, Diem and Nhu were dead. Both had been shot; Nhu had been knifed several times as well.

"Why are they dead?" General Don, one of the coup leaders, is said to have asked Minh.

"What does it matter?" Minh replied.

He told an American months after their death: "We had no alternative. They had to be killed. Diem could not be allowed to live because he was too much respected among simple, gullible people in the countryside." A civilian, Tran Van Huong, who had been a critic of Diem and had been imprisoned for his opposition to the regime, said: "The top generals who decided to murder Diem and his brother were scared to death. The generals knew very well that having no talent, no moral virtues, no political support what-soever, they could not prevent a spectacular comeback of the president and Mr. Nhu if they were alive."[48]

When President Kennedy received the news, he literally blanched. I had never seen him so moved. The deaths "shook him personally," Forrestal later recalled, "bothered him as a moral and religious matter . . . shook his confidence . . . in the kind of advice he was getting about South Vietnam." Arthur Schlesinger, Jr., noted that the president was "somber and shaken" and seemed more depressed than at any time since the Bay of Pigs.[49]

As the president absorbed the news, he commented on the serious effect he thought the deaths would have both here and abroad. He doubted that, as Catholics, the two men had killed themselves. Hilsman countered that it was not difficult to conceive Diem and Nhu taking their own lives despite their Catholicism—in a spirit of "This is Armageddon." Mac later commented dryly that it seemed uncommon for individuals to shoot and knife themselves with their hands tied behind their backs.[50]

The president clearly believed that after twenty years' service to Vietnam, Diem's life should not have ended as it did. His judgment of Diem was apparently shared by Mao Zedong, who in an early 1965 interview with journalist Edgar Snow suggested that the Americans had not listened to Diem. Mao went on to say that both Ho Chi Minh and he [Mao] thought Ngo Dinh Diem was not so bad. After all, he said, following his assassination, was everything between Heaven and Earth more peaceful? The full implications of Mao's remark for events in Vietnam had Diem lived cannot be known until China and Vietnam open their archives, but it raises a host of questions.[51]

Diem's killing shook President Kennedy, but that was not the most shocking thing. In retrospect, the most shocking thing was that we faced an utter political vacuum in South Vietnam and had no basis for proceeding on any course compatible with U.S. objectives.

———

Diem's death brought no end to the deep differences within the administration over Vietnam. In a masterpiece of understatement, Lodge told Washington on November 4 there appeared to be

> some divergence between ourselves and yourselves on the signif-
> icance and merit of the coup. Here is how it looks to us:
> a. To whomever has ever been involved in either a military or a
>   political campaign, this coup appears to have been a remark-
>   ably able performance in both respects. . . .
> b. Experts who have all along been hostile to the coup and who
>   said "win with Diem" now say that *this coup means that the war
>   can be drastically shortened* [emphasis added].

Lodge concluded by saying that he too believed the coup would shorten the war and speed the time when Americans could return home.[52] Max and I were skeptical. Before the coup, we had seen little prospect of a strong and effective government emerging to replace Diem, and we did not see one materializing after it.

To try to get at the truth, the president asked me to chair a meeting of all parties in Honolulu on November 20. It was to be our last meeting on Vietnam before we met with Lyndon Johnson, at the start of his Presidency, four days later.

This conference was like all its predecessors, and I have no specific memory of it. But it made a big impression on Mac Bundy, who had never attended a Hawaii briefing before. He told a staff meeting upon our return: "The briefings of McNamara tend to be sessions where people try to fool him, and he tries to convince them they cannot." Perhaps this was unfair to the military, but it did reflect the difficulty we faced in getting a clear picture of the situation and our prospects in Vietnam.

Mac had extracted quite an accurate assessment from the conference, as it turned out. Speaking of the political picture in South Vietnam, he told the staff that while it was too early to see what course the junta would follow, the coalition of generals clearly might not last. How prophetic he was! The military government was a revolving door that spun at dizzying speed for the next eighteen months, with one set of leaders after another.[53]

President Kennedy's last public comments on Vietnam came at a news conference on November 14, when he asked rhetorically, "Are we going to give up in South Vietnam?" He answered his own question by saying, "The most important program, of course, is our national security, but I don't want the United States to have to put troops there."

Earlier, at the same press conference, in answer to the question "Would you give us your appraisal of the situation in South Vietnam now, since the coup, and the purposes for the Honolulu conference?" he replied: "The purpose of the meeting at Honolulu . . . is to attempt to assess the situation: what American policy should be, and what our aid policy should be, how we can intensify the struggle, how we can bring Americans out of there. Now, that is our object, *to bring Americans home, permit the South Vietnamese to maintain themselves* as a free and independent country [emphasis added]."[54]

Both comments echoed the answer he had given to Walter Cronkite ten weeks earlier, when he said that in the final analysis, it was their war—they were the ones who would have to win it or lose it. Kennedy had not been unequivocal on the subject, however; he had told Chet Huntley and David Brinkley one week later: "I think we should stay. We should use our influence in as effective a way as we can . . . we should not withdraw."[55] But the great preponderance of President Kennedy's remarks—both before and after this interview, in public and in private—was that, in the end, the South Vietnamese must carry the war themselves; the United States could not do it for them.

4

A Time of Transition:

November 23, 1963–July 29, 1964

Transitions often bring uncertainty, confusion, and error, and this was never more the case than in the six months that followed President Kennedy's assassination. President Johnson, who approached Vietnam differently than did his predecessor, inherited a host of unanswered questions and unsolved problems. These became more and more evident and more and more troublesome as we slid toward deeper involvement in Vietnam.

On Friday afternoon, November 22, 1963, as President Kennedy rode to a speaking engagement in Dallas, I met in a conference room adjoining my Pentagon office with my senior associates, Mac Bundy, Kermit Gordon of the Budget Bureau, and science adviser Jerome Wiesner. We were reviewing the defense budget that the White House planned to submit to Congress in January. This budget review was part of my effort to define department objectives and make certain that they would be coordinated with the president's foreign policy goals. After the meeting, I planned to fly up to Hyannis Port with Joint Chiefs Chairman Max Taylor to present my proposals to the president over the Thanksgiving weekend.

In the midst of our discussion—at about 2:00 P.M.—my secretary informed me of an urgent, personal telephone call. I left the conference room and took it alone in my office. It was Bobby Kennedy, even more lonely and distant than usual. He told me simply and quietly that the president had been shot.

I was stunned. Slowly, I walked back to the conference room and, barely controlling my voice, reported the news to the group. Strange as it may sound, we did not disperse: we were in such shock that we simply did not know what to do. So, as best as we could, we resumed our deliberations.

A second call from Bobby came about forty-five minutes later. The president was dead. Our meeting immediately adjourned amid tears and stunned silence.

Not knowing what had prompted the assassination or what might follow, I met immediately with the Joint Chiefs. We agreed U.S. military forces worldwide should be placed on alert, a standard procedure in times of crisis. A few minutes later, Bobby called again. He asked Max and me to accompany him, later in the afternoon, to nearby Andrews Air Force Base to meet the plane returning his brother's body.

Once Bobby arrived at the Pentagon, the three of us boarded a helicopter and headed toward Andrews. We crossed the Potomac and looked silently out the windows. We were already remembering. There was nothing that could be said.

Shortly after we arrived at Andrews, the blue and white presidential jet slowly taxied up to the terminal, its landing lights still on. Bobby turned and asked me to board the plane with him. It so clearly seemed a moment of intimacy and privacy for a family in shock and sorrow that I refused.

After the body was unloaded, I returned home, thinking about what had happened and unsure of what would follow. The

Kennedys and I had started as strangers but had grown very close. Unlike many subsequent administrations, they drew in some of their associates, transforming them from colleagues to friends. We could laugh with one another. And we could cry with one another. It had been that way with me, and that made the president's death even more devastating.

At home I struggled through dinner with Marg. As I was finishing, Bobby called from Bethesda Naval Hospital to say that Jackie wanted me to join her while she awaited completion of the autopsy. I drove immediately to the hospital and sat with Jackie, Bobby, and other family members and friends. In the early morning hours, we accompanied the president's body back to the White House, where the casket was placed on a bier in the elegant East Room, draped by the flag he had served and loved and lit softly by candles.

At that moment, disagreement emerged about where the president should be buried. Some insisted it be in his home state of Massachusetts. I said he had not been president of Massachusetts but, rather, of the fifty United States, and therefore should be laid to rest in the nation's capital.

I set about to find the proper place. Arlington National Cemetery was administered by the Defense Department, and I began there. It was a gray and rainy morning, and the cemetery was shrouded in a faint mist. The superintendent met me, and we walked side by side across the hauntingly beautiful grounds studded with simple white tombstones marking the graves of countless Americans who had served their country in war and peace, as had President Kennedy. I stopped when we came to a spot just below the Custis-Lee Mansion. I could see across Memorial Bridge and to the Lincoln Memorial in the distance, even in the increasing fog and rain. "This is the place," I said quietly.

Later in the day I was introduced to a young Park Service ranger who had escorted Kennedy on a visit to Arlington a few weeks earlier. When I told him which spot I had chosen, the ranger nodded. "When President Kennedy was visiting a few weeks ago," he said, "he stopped in that same spot. He looked out, towards the monuments, and I heard him say that this was the most beautiful sight in Washington."

Final approval for the site came from a grieving Jackie, who visited it with me in the late afternoon. The weather was still miserable as we walked through the sea of graves. When we came to the spot I had chosen, Jackie approved it instantly and instinctively. She was buried at the same site in 1994.

———

John F. Kennedy was not a perfect man; no man is. He was a practical politician. Sometimes the political practices—particularly of his subordinates—took nasty forms. One incident, in particular serves as an illustration.

One day I received a call from an old associate, Rod Markley, Ford Motor Company's vice president in charge of government affairs, who said he had learned something he thought I would wish to know. He said that Red Duffy, Ford's vice president in charge of the company's East Coast plants selling to the Defense Department, had been told that unless his division made a financial contribution to the Democratic Party, the contracts would be canceled. I had worked with Duffy for years while at Ford. When I angrily asked Rod why Duffy had not reported what was clearly a grossly illegal act directly to me, Rod said Duffy feared that those in the Defense Department to whom I would refer the matter would retaliate against Ford.

I thanked Rod, hung up, and immediately phoned the air force inspector general, Lt. Gen. William H. "Butch" Blanchard. Blanchard had been a heroic B-17 bomber pilot in the Philippines; a B-29 group commander in India, China, and the Marianas; and a longtime friend from World War II. I said, "Butch, come down to my office and don't tell anyone—not the air force secretary or the chief of staff—that you're coming."

When Butch arrived, I told him the story and added: "I want

you to drop everything you're doing, fully investigate these charges, and report back directly to me."

After a month or so, I called Butch to ask what progress he had made. He replied that the situation was worse than had been reported. He had found other cases, involving other companies elsewhere in the country. At the end of six months, he placed a thick report on my desk documenting what had happened. When I asked who was responsible, he named a civilian who, he said, had been assigned to the air force procurement office by presidential assistant Kenny O'Donnell.

I telephoned the air force secretary and instructed him to fire the man that day, on my orders, without explanation. I then sent a copy of the report to O'Donnell with a one-sentence covering note that said the man no longer worked for the Defense Department. I never received a reply.

––––––––

John F. Kennedy had a very clear view of the role of a president. One day while in the Oval Office, I discussed the presidency with him. I drew this graph:

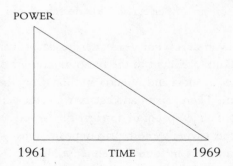

Power was plotted on the vertical axis and Time on the horizontal axis. "Mr. President," I said, "you came into office with a significant amount of power. I hope you go out with none, having expended it on what you and I believe is right for this nation." "Bob," he said, "that's exactly the way I feel." He thought that way, and I believe he would have acted that way.

President Kennedy also had the ability to stand back from an issue and see its broader implications. He acted with a sense of history and his place in it. During his presidency, a few of us gathered occasionally in the evening for discussions known as Hickory Hill Seminars. At one meeting, held in the family quarters of the White House, presidential aide Arthur Schlesinger brought his father, distinguished Harvard historian Arthur Schlesinger, Sr., as the featured guest. Pentagon demands unfortunately kept me away, so when I returned home later that night, I asked Marg, who had gone without me, "How did it go?"

"It was absolutely fascinating," she said. "No one could get a word in edgewise! The whole evening was devoted to Kennedy's questions: 'How do you judge a President?' 'What are the criteria?' 'Why do you view President X as greater than President Y?'" John F. Kennedy saw the world as history. He took the long view.

He was truly a great leader, with uncommon charisma and an ability to inspire. He moved the young and the old at home and abroad, touching the very best in them, a rare and priceless gift in political leaders. In an imperfect world, he raised our eyes to the stars.

And his legacy endures. For years after his death, I traveled with Marg as World Bank president to the remotest corners of the world, to isolated villages in India and Nigeria and Paraguay that had rarely seen an American. There, again and again, we came across his photograph, torn from a newspaper or a magazine, tacked on the wall of a hut, one of the owner's most prized possessions. People need heroes. They found one in John F. Kennedy. Had he lived, I firmly believe our nation and the world would have been the better.

———

It was not a secret that President Kennedy was deeply dissatisfied with Dean Rusk's administration of the State Department. But I was still surprised when, shortly after the president's death, I learned from Bobby and others that he had intended to ask me to replace Dean as secretary of state at the start of a second term. I would have declined the invitation for two reasons: I had deep respect and affection for Dean, and I did not consider myself qualified to serve as secretary of state. Later, after completing seven years as secretary of defense and another thirteen as World Bank president, I might have felt differently, but at the time, had Kennedy pressed me further, I would have urged him to appoint Mac Bundy, whose knowledge of history, international relations, and geopolitics was far greater than mine.

I have often spoken of Mac Bundy during this narrative. I should insert a special word here because his personality was so forceful and so influential during the years we worked together for Presidents Kennedy and Johnson. Throughout my life—whether at Ford, Defense, or the World Bank—I have tried to buttress my own abilities by associating with, and "borrowing" from, the ablest people I could find. If they were brighter than I, so much the better. Mac is one who falls in that category. A Harvard junior fellow at age twenty-two, biographer of Henry Stimson at twenty-nine, and dean of Harvard's Arts and Sciences Faculty at thirty-four, he possesses one of the keenest intellects I have ever encountered. And he was by far the ablest national security adviser I have observed over the last forty years.*

———

What would John F. Kennedy have done about Vietnam had he lived? I have been asked that question countless times over the last thirty years. Thus far, I have refused to answer for two reasons: Apart from what I have related, the president did not tell me what he planned to do in the future. Moreover, whatever his thoughts may have been before Diem's death, they might have changed as the

*My friend Henry Kissinger will take offense at this statement, but my reply to him will be "Although you bore the title 'national security adviser' and your office was in the White House, during those years you were in reality acting as secretary of state."

effect of that event on the political dynamics in South Vietnam became more apparent. Also, I saw no gain to our nation from speculation by me—or others—about how the dead president might have acted.

But today I feel differently. Having reviewed the record in detail, and with the advantage of hindsight, I think it highly probable that, had President Kennedy lived, he would have pulled us out of Vietnam. He would have concluded that the South Vietnamese were incapable of defending themselves, and that Saigon's grave political weaknesses made it unwise to try to offset the limitations of South Vietnamese forces by sending U.S. combat troops on a large scale. I think he would have come to that conclusion even if he reasoned, as I believe he would have, that South Vietnam and, ultimately, Southeast Asia would then be lost to Communism. He would have viewed that loss as more costly than we see it now. But he would have accepted that cost because he would have sensed that the conditions he had laid down—i.e., it was a South Vietnamese war, that it could only be won by them, and to win it they needed a sound political base—could not be met. Kennedy would have agreed that withdrawal would cause a fall of the "dominoes" but that staying in would ultimately lead to the same result, while exacting a terrible price in blood.

Early in his administration, President Kennedy asked his cabinet officials and members of the National Security Council to read Barbara Tuchman's book *The Guns of August*. He said it graphically portrayed how Europe's leaders had bungled into the debacle of World War I. And he emphasized: "I don't ever want to be in that position." Kennedy told us after we had done our reading, "We are not going to bungle into war."

Throughout his presidency, Kennedy seemed to keep that lesson in mind. During the Bay of Pigs crisis in April 1961, against intense pressure from the CIA and the military chiefs, he kept to his conviction—as he had made explicitly clear to the Cuban exiles beforehand—that under no conditions would the United States intervene with military force to support the invasion. He held to this position even when it became evident that without that support the invasion would fail, as it did.[1]

I saw the same wisdom during the tense days of the Cuban Missile Crisis. By Saturday, October 27, 1962—the height of the crisis—the majority of the president's military and civilian advisers were prepared to recommend that if Khrushchev did not remove the Soviet missiles from Cuba (which he agreed to the following day) the United States should attack the island.* But Kennedy repeatedly made the point that Saturday—both in Executive Committee sessions and later, in a small meeting with Bobby, Dean, Mac, and me—that the United States must make every effort to avoid the risk of an unpredictable war. He appeared willing, if necessary, to trade the obsolete American Jupiter missiles in Turkey for the Soviet missiles in Cuba in order to avert this risk. He knew such an action was strongly opposed by the Turks, by NATO, and by most senior U.S. State and Defense Department officials.[2] But he was prepared to take that stand to keep us out of war.

So I conclude that John Kennedy would have eventually gotten out of Vietnam rather than move more deeply in. I express this judgment now because, in light of it, I must explain how and why we—including Lyndon Johnson—who continued in policy-making roles after President Kennedy's death made the decisions leading to the eventual deployment to Vietnam of half a million U.S. combat troops. Why did we do what we did, and what lessons can be learned from our actions?

———

Despite the trauma of the assassination, the nation lived on without John F. Kennedy. On Sunday afternoon, November 24, while funeral preparations continued and workers readied the Oval Office for its new occupant, President Johnson met with Dean, Mac,

---

*Unbeknownst to us at the time, and quite contrary to CIA estimates, the Soviets then had approximately 160 nuclear warheads in Cuba, including scores of tactical nuclear weapons. A U.S. attack would almost surely have led to a nuclear exchange with devastating consequences. See the Appendix for further elaboration of this point.

George Ball, Henry Cabot Lodge (who was in Washington for pre-viously scheduled consultations), John McCone, and me in the office he had occupied as vice president in the Old Executive Office Building just west of the White House.

Lyndon Baines Johnson was one of the most complex, intel-ligent, and hardworking individuals I have ever known. He pos-sessed a kaleidoscopic personality: by turns open and devious, loving and mean, compassionate and tough, gentle and cruel. He was a towering, powerful, paradoxical figure, reminding me of a verse from Walt Whitman's "Song of Myself":

> *Do I contradict myself?*
> *Very well then I contradict myself;*
> *I am large, I contain multitudes.*

He was a masterful politician. He saw his role as one of identifying differences among the American people and then reconciling those differences so that the country could move forward toward a better life for all. In this sense, he assumed the presidency just at the time when he was most needed: a period of growing racial unrest and persistent economic inequalities.

Although Johnson had been part of the Kennedy administration for three years, none of us had worked closely with him. The distrust between the Kennedy and Johnson factions also must have made Johnson wonder whether he could expect complete loyalty from President Kennedy's cabinet members. Within a matter of days, if not hours, he came to understand that both Dean and I—devoted as we were to John Kennedy—had come to Washington to serve our nation, of which he was now the constitutional leader. Never once, in the years that followed, did he have reason to question our loyalty to him. But at the time he took office, I hardly knew him.

————

Between his ascendancy to the presidency and my departure from the Pentagon, President Johnson and I developed the strongest possible bonds of mutual respect and affection. However, our relationship was different from the one I had with President Kennedy, and more complicated. Johnson was a rough individual, rough on his friends as well as his enemies. He took every person's measure. He sought to find a person's weakness, and once he found it, he tried to play on it. He could be a bully, though he was never that way with me. He learned that I would deal straight with him, telling him what I believed rather than what I thought he wanted to hear, but also that once he, as the president, made a decision, I would do all in my power to carry it out. This kind of candid loyalty had always been my style, and I think that it reassured both President Kennedy and President Johnson. They knew that what they saw was what they got, that I would not tell them what they wanted to hear if I did not agree with them. Like all great leaders, what they wanted was results.

In a sense it was the same with Kennedy and Johnson as it had been with Henry Ford II. As long as I got the job done, they did not worry. They knew that my loyalty was unwavering, and that my goals were consistent with theirs.

Both presidents often asked for my advice and assistance on matters outside the secretary of defense's jurisdiction. This complicated my life.

An example of this occurred one fall. My son, Craig, had played on the St. Paul's School football team for three years and had been mentioned as an All–New England halfback, but Marg and I had never been able to see him play. His last game was scheduled for a weekend in November. I mentioned this to the president, suggesting I slip away on a Saturday afternoon and return to my office Sunday morning. Johnson grumbled about "taking all that time off," but I interpreted his comment as acquiescence.

As soon as Marg and I checked into our hotel in Concord, New Hampshire, on Saturday afternoon, I received a message to call the president immediately. When I did, he came on the line and shouted, "Where are you?" I patiently explained where I was and why. "I want you back here immediately to get that damn aluminum price down," he snapped. I said I knew nothing about the aluminum price, and, in any event, he had a commerce secretary to handle such matters. "Well, if you want to put your personal pleasure ahead of the welfare of your president and your country"— he paused—"then stay where you are." I said: "I'll make you a deal. Marg and I will see the game this afternoon and I'll be in my office early tomorrow morning." He slammed down the phone.

When I reached the Pentagon Sunday, I immediately called my former assistant Joe Califano at the White House and asked him to explain what had happened. The aluminum companies, anticipating higher costs, had raised their prices. Fearing this would trigger price inflation across the country, the president had demanded the increases be rolled back.

"What can we possibly do to accomplish that?" I asked Joe. We debated the issue for an hour or two, and finally hit on an idea: the government, with no real need, had continued to hold huge strategic reserves of raw materials, including aluminum, left over from the Korean War. Why not tell the aluminum companies we planned to release part of the reserves to the market? This would certainly force the price down.

I immediately put through a call to John Harper, president of Alcoa, and said, "John, you Republicans have been after us a long time to reduce the deficit. We've finally found a way to do so, and I hope you will support us. We plan to sell part of the government's aluminum stockpile and transfer the proceeds to the Treasury." "You SOB," he said. "You're trying to blackmail us. I'll be in your office tomorrow morning."

On Monday, John, along with Edgar Kaiser and his lawyer Lloyd Cutler, met with Joe and me. After a long discussion, we devised a plan that resulted in a price reduction, released part of the stockpile, and did so without disrupting the market.

The situation Johnson inherited in Vietnam could not have been more complex, difficult, or dangerous. The leader who had held South Vietnam's centrifugal forces together for nearly ten years had just been removed in a coup that Johnson had opposed. South

Vietnam lacked any tradition of national unity. It was besieged by religious animosities, political factionalism, corrupt police, and, not least, a growing guerrilla insurgency supported by its northern neighbor. Before Diem's death, even those who favored a coup against him had conceded the chances of putting in place stable political leadership to succeed him were fifty-fifty at best. Even this proved overly optimistic: two South Vietnamese governments came and went in the first ninety days of the Johnson administration, and four more within the next nine months.

Moreover, Johnson was left with a national security team that, although it remained intact, was deeply split over Vietnam. Its senior members had failed to face up to the basic questions that had confronted first Eisenhower and then Kennedy: Would the loss of South Vietnam pose a threat to U.S. security serious enough to warrant extreme action to prevent it? If so, what kind of action should we take? Should it include the introduction of U.S. air and ground forces? Launching attacks against North Vietnam? Risking war with China? What would be the ultimate cost of such a program in economic, military, political, and human terms? Could it succeed? If the chances of success were low and the costs high, were there other courses—such as neutralization or withdrawal— that deserved careful study and debate?

Lyndon Johnson inherited these questions (although they were not presented clearly to him), and he inherited them without answers. They remained unanswered throughout his presidency, and for many years thereafter. In short, Johnson inherited a god-awful mess eminently more dangerous than the one Kennedy had inherited from Eisenhower. One evening not long after he took office, Johnson confessed to his aide Bill Moyers that he felt like a catfish that had "just grabbed a big juicy worm with a right sharp hook in the middle of it."[3]

Contrary to popular myth, however, Lyndon Johnson was not oblivious to Vietnam when he became president. Although he had visited the country only once—in May 1961—and had attended few meetings on the subject during Kennedy's tenure, he was keenly aware of the problem and his responsibility to deal with it. Among his first acts as president was to schedule the November 24 meeting with his Vietnam advisers.

Some say he called this meeting for domestic political reasons. With an election coming within a year, the story goes, he feared that if he did not appear involved and firm he would face strident attacks from hard-line, right-wing Republicans.

I disagree. Of course, domestic politics was always in the forefront of his mind, and, yes, he feared the domestic political con-sequences of appearing weak. He also feared the effect on our allies if the United States appeared unable or unwilling to meet our security obligations. But most of all Johnson was convinced that the Soviet Union and China were bent on achieving hegemony. He saw the takeover of South Vietnam as a step toward that objective— a break in our containment policy—and he was determined to prevent it. Johnson felt more certain than President Kennedy that the loss of South Vietnam had a higher cost than would the direct application of U.S. military force, and it was this view that shaped him and his policy decisions for the next five years. He failed to perceive the fundamentally political nature of the war.

President Johnson made clear to Lodge on November 24 that he wanted to win the war, and that, at least in the short run, he wanted priority given to military operations over "so-called" social reforms. He felt the United States had spent too much time and energy trying to shape other countries in its own image. Win the war! That was his message.[4]

To do so required cleaning up the situation in the official American community in Saigon. Bickering, serious dissension, and downright hostility existed between embassy civilians and U.S. military officers. The president wanted a strong team, and he held the man in charge, Lodge, responsible.

Two days later National Security Action Memorandum (NSAM) 273 incorporated the president's directives into policy. It made clear that Johnson's policy remained the same as Kennedy's: "to assist the people and Government of South Vietnam to win their contest against the externally directed and supported Communist conspiracy" through training support and without the application of overt U.S. military force. But Johnson also approved planning for covert action against North Vietnam by CIA-supported South Vietnamese forces. First raised at the November 20, 1963, Honolulu conference, this proposal later became known as Operation Plan 34A.[5]

Two weeks later the president asked me to see him about Vietnam. He gave me quite a lecture. He was convinced the U.S. government was not doing all it should. He asked me to go to Saigon on my way home from a NATO meeting in Paris to see what more could be done, and he specifically asked whether planning for covert operations should be expanded.[6]

A small covert action program consisting of agent infiltration, propaganda distribution, intelligence collection, and general sabotage had been carried out against North Vietnam by South Vietnamese forces with U.S. backing and direction for several months. But Hanoi's rigid Communist control apparatus—including in nearly every North Vietnamese village and town "block committees" that detected even the smallest signs of change—guaranteed the program's ineffectiveness. Grasping for a way to hurt North Vietnam without direct U.S. military action, President Johnson wanted the covert program strengthened.

Bill Bundy accompanied me on the trip. Like his younger brother Mac, Bill had inherited the integrity and intelligence of their father, Harvey H. Bundy, longtime assistant to Henry Stimson. Together with John McNaughton, and later Paul Warnke (who succeeded John as assistant secretary of defense for international security affairs), Bill was one of my most trusted advisers on Vietnam.

At the end of our Paris talks, we boarded a military jet at Orly Airport, carrying a maximum fuel load, for a nonstop flight to South Vietnam. As we moved down the runway in heavy fog, jet engines gathering speed just before takeoff, a TWA passenger plane, having landed a moment before, suddenly loomed up in front of us. Our pilot, Captain Sutton, slammed on the brakes. We shuddered to a rough stop several seconds later (it seemed like an eternity). Tires, wheels, and brakes burst into flames, and we left the plane through the emergency exit. But Captain Sutton's superb piloting had saved us as well as the 150 or so passengers aboard the TWA plane.

―――――

Up to this time, the military intelligence reports I had gotten said we had made much progress in Vietnam. But on December 13, 1963, I received a memorandum from the Defense Intelligence Agency (DIA) stating that, while the Vietcong had not scored spectacular gains over the past year, they had sustained and even improved their combat capabilities. The report added that unless the South Vietnamese Army (ARVN) improved its operations, Vietcong activities would probably increase.[7]

My meetings in Saigon on December 19–20 reinforced this new and gloomy assessment. It became clear that the coup against Diem had left a political vacuum increasingly filled by ambitious ARVN officers more intent on political maneuvering in Saigon than military operations in the field. It also became clear that earlier reports of military progress had been inflated by the considerable falsification of data submitted by South Vietnamese officials to our military assistance command. John McCone reported to the president after our return: "It is abundantly clear that statistics received over the past year or more from the GVN officials and reported by the U.S. mission on which we gauged the trend of the war were grossly in error."[8]

At our Saigon meetings, Lodge and General Harkins agreed that the physical resources needed for South Vietnam to fight the war—including U.S. training assistance and logistical support—already existed. But they also agreed that the necessary South Vietnamese leadership did not. Still, they felt that while the situation was serious, it was by no means irreparable.

To strengthen the Vietnamese position, Harkins and Lodge tabled an expanded covert action program in response to my earlier request. It was later endorsed by the 303 Committee, the interagency group charged with reviewing such plans. Following recommendations from Dean, Mac, McCone, and me, the president approved a four-month trial program, beginning on February 1, 1964. Its goal was to convince the North Vietnamese that it was in their self-interest to desist from aggression in South Vietnam. Looking back, it was an absurdly ambitious objective for such a trifling effort—it accomplished virtually nothing.[9]

————

Upon my return to Washington on December 21, I was less than candid when I reported to the press. Perhaps a senior government official could hardly have been more straightforward in the midst of a war. I could not fail to recognize the effect discouraging remarks might have on those we strove to support (the South Vietnamese) as well as those we sought to overcome (the Vietcong and North Vietnamese). It is a profound, enduring, and universal ethical and moral dilemma: how, in times of war and crisis, can senior government officials be completely frank to their own people without giving aid and comfort to the enemy?

In any event, in two press interviews on December 21, I said, "We observed the results of a very substantial increase in Vietcong activity" (true); but I then added, "We reviewed the plans of the South Vietnamese and we have every reason to believe they will be successful" (an overstatement at best).[10]

I was far more forthright—and gloomy—in my report to the president. "The situation is very disturbing," I told him, predicting that "current trends, unless reversed in the next 2–3 months, will lead to neutralization at best or more likely to a Communist-controlled state."

The problem, I told him, lay with both Diem's successors and the U.S. mission. The South Vietnamese generals showed no talent for political administration, squabbled incessantly among themselves, and remained unable to check the Vietcong's progress on the battlefield. The worst fears of those who had opposed the coup seemed to be coming true.

The U.S. mission lacked leadership, was poorly informed, and was not working to a common plan. I strongly criticized Lodge for these problems. He maintained virtually no contact with Harkins and refused to share important cables from Washington. I stated that Lodge did not know how to administer a complex operation such as the U.S. mission in South Vietnam. I added that Dean and McCone agreed with me, that we all had tried to help him, but that Lodge—a loner all his life—simply could not take advice. For the time being, however, Lodge remained ambassador.[11]

———

Shortly after my return to Washington, the president received a memorandum from Senate Majority Leader Mike Mansfield (D-Mont.), recommending that the United States try for a neutral Southeast Asia—neither dependent on U.S. military support nor subject to Chinese domination through some sort of truce or settlement. The president asked Dean, Mac, and me for our reactions.[12]

All three of us felt Mansfield's path would lead to the loss of South Vietnam to Communist control with extremely serious consequences for the United States and the West. I stated the conventional wisdom among top U.S. civilian and military officials at the time:

In Southeast Asia, Laos would almost certainly come under North Vietnamese domination, Cambodia might exhibit a facade of neutrality but would in fact accept Communist Chinese domination, Thailand would become very shaky, and Malaysia, already beset by Indonesia, the same; even Burma would see the developments as a clear sign that the whole of the area now had to accommodate completely to Communism (with serious consequences for the security of India as well).

Basically, a truly "neutral" Southeast Asia is very unlikely to emerge from such a sequence of events, even if the U.S. itself tried to hold a firm position in Thailand, if Malaysia too tried to stand firm, and even if remote and uninvolved powers such as France backed the concept of "neutrality."

In the eyes of the rest of Asia and of key areas threatened by Communism in other areas as well, South Vietnam is both a test of U.S. firmness and specifically a test of U.S. capacity to deal with "wars of national liberation." Within Asia, there is evidence—for example, from Japan—that U.S. disengagement and the acceptance of Communist domination would have a serious effect on confidence. More broadly, there can be little doubt that any country threatened in the future by Communist subversion would have reason to doubt whether we would really see the thing through. This would apply even in such theoretically remote areas as Latin America.[13]

I have quoted extensively from my memo for two reasons: to show how limited and shallow our analysis and discussion of the alternatives to our existing policy in Vietnam—i.e., neutralization or withdrawal—had been; and to illustrate that the consequences of Southeast Asia's loss to U.S. and Western security were now being presented to President Johnson with greater force and in more detail than on previous occasions.

This memo hardened the president's preexisting attitude. As the likely failure of our training strategy became more apparent in the months ahead, we tilted gradually—almost imperceptibly—toward approving the direct application of U.S. military force. We did so because of our increasing fear—and hindsight makes it clear it was an exaggerated fear—of what would happen if we did not. But we never carefully debated what U.S. force would ultimately be required, what our chances of success would be, or what the political, military, financial, and human costs would be if we provided it. Indeed, these basic questions went unexamined.

We were at the beginning of a slide down a tragic and slippery slope.

———

The Joint Chiefs came forward with a proposal for more forceful moves in a memorandum to me on January 22, 1964. They asserted that the President in NSAM 273 had resolved "to ensure victory . . .

in South Vietnam." In fact he had done no such thing, certainly not regardless of the cost in human lives. The chiefs went on to say that "in order to achieve that victory, the Joint Chiefs of Staff are of the opinion that the United States must be prepared to put aside many of the self-imposed restrictions which now limit our efforts, and to undertake bolder actions which may embody greater risks."[14] But at what cost and with what chance of success? This memo, and subsequent ones given to me over the next four years, contained no answers to these crucial military questions.

I criticize the president, his advisers, and myself as much as the chiefs for this negligence. It was our job to demand the answers. We did not press hard enough for them. And the chiefs did not volunteer them. General Bruce Palmer, Jr., who in 1967 served in Vietnam as a corps commander and later deputy COMUSMACV, and in 1968 became army vice chief of staff, subsequently wrote: "Not once during the war did the JCS [Joint Chiefs of Staff] advise the Commander-in-Chief or the Secretary of Defense that the strategy being pursued most probably would fail and that the US would be unable to achieve its objectives."[15] I consider this a valid criticism, but we—their civilian superiors—erred equally by not forcing such an appraisal.

Why did we not ask these questions and demand answers? This is a subject I will return to in greater detail but it bears mentioning now that our failure was partially the result of having many more commitments than just Vietnam. Instability in Latin America, Africa, and the Middle East, and the continued Soviet threat in Europe all took up time and attention. We had no senior group working exclusively on Vietnam, so the crisis there became just one of many items on each person's plate. When combined with the inflexibility of our objectives, and the fact that we had not truly investigated what was essentially at stake and important to us, we were left harried, overburdened, and holding a map with only one road on it. Eager to get moving, we never stopped to explore fully whether there were other routes to our destination.

The Joint Chiefs also had stated in their memo that "we and the

South Vietnamese are fighting the war on the enemy's terms" and "have obliged ourselves to labor under self-imposed restrictions." These restrictions included "keeping the war within the boundaries of South Vietnam" and "avoiding the direct use of US combat forces." The chiefs recommended that we broaden the war to include U.S. air attacks on North Vietnam and shift from training the South Vietnamese to carrying out the war in both South and North Vietnam with U.S. combat forces. This recommendation for what, in effect, constituted a revolutionary change in U.S. policy rested on an exposition of two and a half pages, with little analysis or supporting rationale.[16]

The chiefs asked me to discuss their memo with the secretary of state, which I did; after that we briefed the president. He asked for specific proposals from the chiefs. They began to develop these over the next month, giving priority to plans for U.S. air attacks against the Ho Chi Minh Trail (a system of jungle supply routes through Laos and Cambodia into South Vietnam used by North Vietnam) and military and industrial targets in North Vietnam. The chiefs considered it "unlikely that the Chinese Communists would introduce organized ground units in significant numbers into the DRV [Democratic Republic of Vietnam (North Vietnam)]" and doubted Moscow would initiate "action which, in the Soviet judgment, would increase the likelihood of nuclear war."[17]

The thought of escalation to nuclear war arising from the chiefs' plan for U.S. operations in Vietnam had never entered my mind. But beginning then—and throughout the next four years—I was determined to minimize the risk that U.S. military action in Indochina would draw Chinese or Soviet ground or air forces into confrontation with the United States—whether with conventional or nuclear forces, either in Asia or elsewhere. President Johnson held the same view. It was a concern, among other reasons, that led us to oppose repeated recommendations over the next four years for a more rapid intensification of the air war and a more rapid expansion of the ground war.

———

At no time, as we shall see, did convincing evidence emerge that acceptance of the scale of operations recommended by the military in place of the lesser level approved by the president would have prevented the loss of South Vietnam. But the expanded operations most certainly would have resulted in greater loss of both U.S. and Vietnamese lives.

I addressed these issues on February 17, 1964, when I testified on our progress in Vietnam before the House Defense Appropriations Subcommittee. Representative Harry Sheppard (D-Calif.) said, "I compliment you for being forthright, Mr. Secretary, but sitting here analyzing your statement I find the following: 'I can conceive of no alternative other than to take all necessary measures within our capability to prevent a Communist victory.' " He pointed out that earlier I had described our policy as one of limited training and logistical support for the South Vietnamese, yet now I said we would provide "all" necessary support. What did I actually mean?

I paused for a moment before responding (with clear relevance to today): "Military capability alone cannot solve all of the problems in Vietnam or for that matter, in many other areas of the world." I went on to say, "The kind of war now going on in Vietnam can be won only by the Vietnamese people themselves. Among the conditions required to win such a war is *a strong, stable, and effective government which has the full loyalty and support of the people* [emphasis added]." I concluded my reply with these words: "I would be less than candid if I did not express to you our concern in those areas which lie beyond our own capabilities." I regularly repeated this point in statements to Congress and the press, as in my testimony before the Senate Appropriations Committee on July 22, 1964, when I said, "The primary problem in South Vietnam is not a military problem. The primary problem is a political and economic problem. Unless we can introduce political and economic stability in that country, there is not any possibility of a military solution."[18]

But under the pressure of events and without clearly recognizing where our actions might lead, we had begun to change course. The

The Early Years

1931: Eagle Scout. Scouting was a major influence in my life. It introduced me to the out-of-doors, which continues to be an abiding passion; exposed me to leadership training and opportunities; and, along with my church and my family, shaped my values.

(Photo courtesy the author)

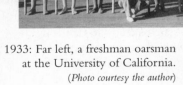

1933: Far left, a freshman oarsman at the University of California.

(Photo courtesy the author)

1937: Mt. Whitney (14,495 feet). A friend took this photo of me in an electrical storm, after we had backpacked to the top of the peak. The static electricity from a nearby lightning strike made my hair stand on end. I climbed Mt. Whitney again fifty years later, after a similar storm had killed several climbers.

(Photo courtesy the author)

World War II

In early 1943, while serving as a War Department consultant to the newly established Eighth Air Force in England, I was commissioned a captain in the U.S. Army Air Corps. (*Photo courtesy the author*)

The two I left behind. During the eighteen months I served overseas—in Britain, India, China, and the Marianas—Marg remained in Cambridge. Because of gas rationing, she was rarely able to use a car and traveled regularly on her bicycle, with our one-year-old daughter, Margy, sitting behind. (*Photo courtesy the author*)

Finishing my military service in early 1946 as a lieutenant colonel, I was awarded the Legion of Merit by the five-star chief of the Air Corps, General Hap Arnold. (*Photo courtesy the author*)

Building and Selling Cars

1946: The Whiz Kids. Several books have been written about the group of ten army officers who came to be known as the Whiz Kids. We went to work for Ford Motor Company in January 1946 to help Henry Ford II rebuild the company. Of the ten, one was fired, one quit, two committed suicide, and the remaining six—of whom two became president and one executive vice president—served as senior executives for a total of over 150 years. (*Photo courtesy the author*)

In the mid-fifties, as general manager of the Ford Division, I, along with my assistant general manager and sales manager, introduced our new models. These were exciting years as the automotive industry struggled to find the road to the future. Not everything we tried was a commercial success. In 1956, the *Automotive News* reported: "Chevrolet tried to sell speed this year. McNamara and Ford tried to sell safety. It looks like the public wants speed."
(*Photo courtesy the author*)

October 1960: After the board of directors of Ford Motor Company elected me president—the first president in the history of the company who had not been a member of the Ford family—Henry Ford II, chairman of the board, announced my election to the press. I left seven weeks later to become secretary of defense. (*Photo courtesy the author*)

January 19, 1961: The Transition begins. We received our introduction to
the problems of Southeast Asia from President Eisenhower, in a meeting
about which there are conflicting accounts to this day.
(*Photo courtesy the John F. Kennedy Library*)

January 20, 1961:
The swearing-in
of the Kennedy
cabinet. The most
exciting day of my
life. (*Photo courtesy
the John F. Kennedy
Library*)

October 1962: A meeting of the "Executive Committee." This was the group
that advised President Kennedy during the Cuban Missile Crisis. At the time,
we believed the danger was great; in recent years, we have learned it was far
more serious. We were, indeed, on the brink of nuclear disaster.
(*Photo courtesy the John F. Kennedy Library*)

March 1961: Shortly before the Bay of Pigs debacle, I met with the president and vice president. (*Photo courtesy AP/Wide World Photos*)

Bobby was ever present, by far the president's closest adviser.
(*Photo courtesy the author*)

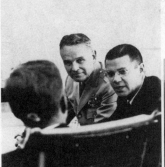

Dean Rusk, Max Taylor, and I were frequent visitors. (*Photos courtesy the John F. Kennedy Library*)

November 25, 1963: The Funeral March. If January 20, 1961, was the most exciting day of my life, November 25, 1963, was one of the saddest. (*Photo courtesy Robert Knudsen*)

The New President

November 24, 1963: The First Meeting. Among LBJ's first actions as president—while he was still in his vice-presidential quarters in the Old Executive Office Building and before he had moved into the Oval Office—was meeting with Dean Rusk, George Ball, Ambassador Lodge, and me to discuss Vietnam. His instructions were clear: Win!
(*Photo courtesy Cecil Stoughton / LBJ Library Collection*)

South Vietnam Begins to Unravel . . .

I did not persuade him. (*Photo courtesy the LBJ Library Collection*)

And he did not persuade me. (*Photo courtesy Yoichi R. Okamoto / LBJ Library Collection*)

Neither one of us was happy. (*Photo courtesy Yoichi R. Okamoto / LBJ Library Collection*)

We Could Find No Solution

May 1965: Cy Vance and I were both depressed as we began to contemplate the awesome decisions that lay ahead. (*Photo courtesy Yoichi R. Okamoto/LBJ Library Collection*)

July 27, 1965: The day the president made the fateful decision to embark on a major ground war in Southeast Asia. (*Photo courtesy Yoichi R. Okamoto/LBJ Library Collection*)

Interminable Meetings

February 1966: With Westy and Bus Wheeler in Honolulu.
(*Photo courtesy Yoichi R. Okamoto/LBJ Library Collection*)

With the chiefs at
the ranch in Texas.
(*Photos courtesy Yoichi R.
Okamoto/LBJ Library
Collection*)

March 1967: With Thieu and Ky in Guam. (*Photo courtesy the author*)

November 22, 1967: The Tuesday Lunch. The group was unaware that three weeks earlier, on November 1, I had presented a memo to the president which stated we could not win in Vietnam.

(*Photo courtesy Yoichi R. Okamoto/LBJ Library Collection*)

And Endless Briefings . . .

Of congressional leaders in the Cabinet Room. (*Photo courtesy Francis Miller/Life Magazine © Time Inc.*)

Of House and Senate members in the East Room of the White House. (*Photo courtesy Yoichi R. Okamoto/LBJ Library Collection*)

And of the press at the Pentagon. (*Photo courtesy the author*)

March 1964: Before Max and I left for Vietnam, President Johnson said he wanted to see a thousand photographs of me boosting Khanh, to demonstrate to the South Vietnamese people that the U.S. stood behind him every step of the way. To my everlasting embarrassment, LBJ got his wish. (*Photo courtesy Larry Burrows/Larry Burrows Collection*)

Max and I visit Vietnam again. (*Photo courtesy James Burke/*Life *Magazine © Time Inc.*)

1966: Another visit, this time with Ambassador Henry Cabot Lodge, Jr., who was serving a second term. (*Photo courtesy Ray Jewett/Army News Features*)

president informed Lodge on February 21 that "Secretaries Rusk and McNamara, with my approval, have already begun preparing specific plans for pressure against North Vietnam, both in the diplomatic and military fields." He added that I would be visiting Saigon early in March to obtain Lodge's views, after which "we should make definite decisions."[19]

On the same day, I asked the Joint Chiefs to examine a series of actions against North Vietnam designed "to induce that government to terminate its support and encouragement of the insurrection in South Vietnam and . . . Laos." I inquired how China might respond in Indochina, Thailand, South Korea, or Taiwan, and what U.S. air, sea, and land combat effort would be required to deal with their response. Given the importance and complexity of these issues—and the likelihood that they would confront us for some time to come— I suggested the chiefs set up a special planning unit for dealing with them.[20]

The chiefs replied in a long memorandum on March 2. In it, they reaffirmed their view of "the overriding importance to the security interests of the United States of preventing the loss of South Vietnam." To achieve this objective, they stated that we should be prepared to destroy military and industrial targets in North Vietnam, mine its harbors, and undertake a naval blockade. They recognized China might intervene militarily in response to such action, and acknowledged that a nonnuclear U.S. response might not force China to stop. They added that "nuclear attacks would have a far greater probability of" doing so, but even then they did not state their proposed program would prevent the loss of South Vietnam.[21]

It was clear: the chiefs recognized that their program involved a change in U.S. policy—including the possible use of nuclear weapons—but they nonetheless urged that it be adopted.

————

During these months, the situation in South Vietnam steadily worsened. The junta that had assumed power after the coup did little to arrest the decline. On January 29, 1964, a group of younger officers headed by Gen. Nguyen Khanh overthrew the divided, ineffectual government. Washington neither encouraged nor furthered this coup; in fact, the chronic chaos it symbolized reinforced President Johnson's growing anxiety and increased his concern that further political instability would disrupt the war effort. He felt we must therefore make Khanh "our boy."

A bantam figure with darting eyes and a goatee who often sported a red beret, Nguyen Khanh struck me as articulate, forceful, mercurial, shrewd, and intensely ambitious. He was only thirty-seven years old. A graduate of U.S. military training at Fort Leavenworth and, later, a division and corps commander, Khanh possessed extensive military experience, but he knew and understood little about politics and economic affairs. Despite these limitations, many Americans and others, including Britain's Robert Thompson, considered him the most able of South Vietnam's generals.

Before Max and I left for Saigon, the president called us to the White House. In his parting instructions, he said, "Bob, I want to see about a thousand pictures of you with General Khanh, smiling and waving your arms and showing the people out there that this country is behind Khanh the whole way."

The president got his wish. To my endless embarrassment, for several days in mid-March Americans picked up their newspapers and turned on their televisions to see images of me—looking very much like a politician on the hustings—barnstorming South Vietnam from the Mekong Delta to Hue, standing shoulder to shoulder with short, bouncy General Khanh before Vietnamese throngs in an attempt to promote him to his own people. And since we still did not recognize the North Vietnamese and Vietcong struggle as nationalist in nature, we never realized that encouraging public identification between Khanh and America may have only reinforced in the minds of many Vietnamese the view that his government drew its support not from the people but from the United States.

Within the constraints I referred to earlier, I tried to avoid misleading the public about our progress. While we refueled in Hawaii en route to Saigon, a reporter said, "You were quoted yesterday as saying the situation now in Vietnam was grave. Is that correct?" I replied, "Yes, I think so. As I reported . . . in October and again in December, the situation is serious. . . . We have had three governments in three months . . . the Viet Cong have sought to take advantage of the changes and have greatly increased the rate of their attacks, their acts of terror and harassment. The situation is serious."[22]

Back in Washington four days later, on March 16, I reported to the president that conditions in South Vietnam had unquestionably worsened since the coup. The weakening of the government's position in the past month had been particularly noticeable. North Vietnamese support for the insurgency continued to increase, but the most worrisome factor remained the Khanh government's uncertain viability. My tour of the country had convinced me Khanh did not have wide or deep political appeal; I sensed this, without speaking the language, simply by the blank expressions on most villagers' faces. Furthermore, his control of the army appeared uncertain.

I again discussed alternative courses of action. Withdrawal seemed unacceptable because of the domino effect. It was the same conclusion that had been put forward earlier on several occasions, and it remained poorly supported then as it had been before. I also discussed neutralization, concluding that de Gaulle's approach would lead to a Communist takeover in South Vietnam with results for Western security just as grave as U.S. withdrawal. No one thought to ask the question: If de Gaulle—who had as much to lose as we from such a "blow" to the West—could accept neutralization, why could not we?

The French president's public statements about neutralization may have lacked substance and therefore seriousness. A few weeks after my meeting with Johnson, French Foreign Minister Maurice Couve de Murville admitted to Dean Rusk that Paris lacked a specific neutralization plan and stated that France did not want

South Vietnam to fall into the Communist camp.[23] But, at a minimum, we should have pressed de Gaulle to go as far as he could to try to achieve his stated objective. We did not.

I also reported to the president that the chiefs' proposal for U.S. air attacks against North Vietnam had been debated at length. The risk of Chinese escalation and the possibility that air attacks would neither break the will nor decisively reduce the ability of the North to continue supporting the insurgency in the South were recognized. But, because no better alternative appeared to exist, the majority of the group meeting in Saigon favored such attacks! This was the sort of desperate energy that would drive much of our Vietnam policy in the years ahead. Data and analysis showed that air attacks would not work, but there was such determination to do something, anything, to stop the Communists that discouraging reports were often ignored.

Despite the views of the majority of those in the meetings in Saigon, I recommended against initiating air attacks. I pointed out that Khanh concurred with my view, claiming that his base in South Vietnam lacked sufficient strength to endure possible North Vietnamese retaliation. While I did not recommend increased American military involvement, I did agree to begin planning for U.S. air attacks in the North. But we did not even discuss the introduction of U.S. ground troops.[24]

I presented these recommendations to the president with the concurrence of all the senior military and civilian officials who had accompanied me, including Max Taylor, John McCone, and Bill Bundy. However, when the chiefs submitted their views, Marine Corps Commandant Gen. Wallace Greene and Air Force Chief of Staff Gen. Curtis LeMay disagreed with my report. Greene felt that if we were to stay and win in South Vietnam, that objective should be pursued with the full concentrated power of the United States (what that meant, precisely, he did not say). LeMay believed North Vietnam's and the Vietcong's logistical bases and reinforcement routes in Laos and Cambodia should be bombed. Dean concurred in my recommendations, and the president approved them.[25]

Others besides Greene and LeMay severely criticized my recommendations against immediate U.S. air attacks against the North. Such critics contended that the president's reluctance to bomb the North stemmed from his desire to avoid a domestic political crisis before the election.[26]

In 1964, as Lyndon Johnson was seeking election in his own right, many believed that he decided every issue on the basis of political expediency. But I did not. And I do not believe this explains why he then decided against air attacks on North Vietnam. Khanh himself opposed such action at that time. And I opposed it because I wished to avoid the risk of Chinese and/or Soviet retaliation if at all possible. Every president quite properly considers domestic politics, but I do not believe that the Kennedy and Johnson administrations' errors in Vietnam can be explained on that basis.

——————

On March 26, 1964, at the president's request, I delivered a major speech at an awards dinner in Washington outlining our position on Vietnam for the American public. By coincidence, the day before, Senate Foreign Relations Committee Chairman William Fulbright—later one of our most vocal critics—gave an important speech on the Senate floor entitled "Old Myths and New Realities," which presented views on Vietnam similar to those I outlined the following night. Regarding negotiations, Fulbright said, "It is difficult to see how a negotiation, under present military circumstances, could lead to termination of the war under conditions that would preserve the freedom of South Vietnam." Hence, he added:

> It seems clear that only two realistic options are open to us in the immediate future: the expansion of the conflict in one way or another, or a renewed effort to bolster the capacity of the South Vietnamese to prosecute the war successfully on its present scale. The matter calls for thorough examination by responsible officials in the executive branch; and until they have had an opportunity

to evaluate the contingencies and feasibilities of the options open to us, it seems to me that we have no choice but to support the South Vietnamese Government and Army by the most effective means available. Whatever specific policy decisions are made, it should be clear to all concerned that the United States will continue to meet its obligations and fulfill its commitments with respect to Vietnam.[27]

My own speech made several frank observations about Vietnam: I pointed out that "the situation in South Vietnam has unquestionably worsened"; that "the picture is admittedly not an easy one to evaluate and, given the kind of terrain and the kind of war, information is not always available or reliable"; that "the large indigenous support that the Viet Cong receives means that solutions must be as much political and economic as military"; and that "the road ahead in Vietnam is going to be long, difficult and frustrating." All true. But then I reviewed the same alternatives I had presented to the president, and a listener would have concluded I offered no answers to our problems. Moreover, I asserted:

> Communist China's interests are clear. It has publicly castigated Moscow for betraying the revolutionary cause whenever the Soviets have sounded a cautionary note. It has characterized the United States as a paper tiger and has insisted that the revolutionary struggle for "liberation and unification" of Vietnam could be conducted without risks by, in effect, crawling under the nuclear and the conventional defense of the Free World. Peiping thus appears to feel that it has a large stake in demonstrating the new strategy, using Vietnam as a test case. Success in Vietnam would be regarded by Peiping as vindication for China's views in the worldwide ideological struggle.[28]

We will not know whether my judgment of China's geopolitical objectives was right or wrong until Beijing opens its archives of the period. But at the time I expressed the common view of my senior associates—both military and civilian—with one exception: my personal assistant, Adam Yarmolinsky, though not an expert on

China, said our judgment was wrong. It demonstrates a point I made before: top government officials need specialists—experts—at their elbows when they make decisions on matters outside their own experience. If we had had more Asia experts around us, perhaps we would not have been so simpleminded about China and Vietnam. We had that expertise available during the Cuban Missile Crisis; in general, we had it available when we dealt with Soviet affairs; but we lacked it when dealing with Southeast Asia.

A few days later, NBC-TV correspondent Peter Hackes interviewed me in my Pentagon office. Toward the end of the interview, he asked, "Under what conditions would this country consider . . . backing forays into North Vietnam?" I replied that one of the options Max and I had reported to the president on our return from South Vietnam included just that: "the initiation of military action outside of South Vietnam, particularly against North Vietnam." I concluded that "whatever ultimate course of action is forced on us by the other side . . . must be thought of as a supplement to and not a substitute for progress within South Vietnam itself."[29]

I considered my statement a warning sign to all of what might lie ahead.

———

Around this time, in April 1964, General Khanh changed his mind and began thumping for an offensive against North Vietnam. Frustrated by the long and tedious war, irritated by a lack of progress in the South, and annoyed by Hanoi's continued intervention, Khanh increasingly looked North for a solution. In a meeting with Lodge on May 4, he suggested warning North Vietnam that any further interference in South Vietnam would lead to reprisals, and he specifically asked whether the United States would be prepared to bomb North Vietnam. The president suggested I stop off in Saigon on my return from a meeting with West German leaders in Bonn and join with Max to reexamine that question with Lodge, Harkins, and Khanh.

I met with Khanh in Saigon on May 13. He said he had indeed

changed his mind since my last visit in March. The covert Plan 34A operations against North Vietnam had not proven effective and would not likely become so (a judgment with which I agreed). Directly contradicting what he had said in March, Khanh argued that the fact that his base in the South lacked solidity and strength might be a reason to strike against the North at once, rather than wait for the weakness to be corrected.[30]

But before my departure from Saigon, Khanh suddenly changed his mind again. Now he told me that he did not want immediate air strikes against North Vietnam because he was not ready to use South Vietnamese forces for that purpose, and he did not wish to call on U.S. combat aircraft.

Lodge vehemently disagreed. He wanted to strike quickly against the North, both to cut off infiltration of men and supplies into the South and to destroy Hanoi's will to prosecute the war. Lodge also indicated that another coup might topple Khanh, in which case "the US should be prepared to run the country, possibly from Cam Ranh Bay." I could hardly believe my ears. But I could give the president no advice on how to prevent another coup or how to respond to one if and when it occurred.[31]

Amid this uncertainty and frustrating confusion, I made an impulsive and ill-considered public statement that has dogged me ever since. At a Pentagon news conference on April 24, the following exchange occurred:

REPORTER: Mr. Secretary, Senator [Wayne] Morse [D-Oreg.] has been calling this "McNamara's War." . . . What is your response to this?

MCNAMARA: . . . This is a war of the United States Government. I am following the President's policy and obviously acting in close cooperation with the Secretary of State. I must say [in that sense] I don't object to its being called McNamara's War. I think it is a very important war and I am pleased to be identified with it and do whatever I can to win it.[32]

What I was attempting to say was that I felt a responsibility to do everything I possibly could to protect the nation's interest in what had become a significant conflict. With reports on the war so subject to falsification by South Vietnamese and to such differing interpretations by U.S. military and political officials in both Saigon and Washington, the president and I considered it essential that one of his close associates visit Vietnam every thirty or sixty days and report to him, the National Security Council, and the American people through the press. The assignment had fallen to me. As a result, I had become more closely associated in the public mind with the war than any other senior Washington official. It was a fact, and I did not try to deny it. In another administration, it might have been another official. But in this administration, I was the one.

———

On May 15, 1964, the CIA submitted a special intelligence assessment on Vietnam to the president, Dean, Mac, and me. It reported bleak news:

> The over-all situation in South Vietnam remains extremely fragile. Although there has been some improvement in South Vietnam's military performance, sustained Viet Cong pressure continues to erode the government's authority throughout the country, undercut US and Vietnamese programs and depress South Vietnamese morale. We do not see any signs that these trends are yet "bottoming out." . . . If the tide of deterioration has not been arrested by the end of the year, the anti-Communist position in South Vietnam is likely to become untenable.[33]

With no other plan in sight likely to stem the "tide of deterioration," a few days later we authorized a four-month extension of the covert operations program beyond its scheduled termination on May 31. Although the chiefs conceded that Operation Plan 34A had accomplished little up to that point, they concluded that the program's potential "remains high." However, it proved no more effective subsequently than it had until then, and it may have provoked a later and very significant North Vietnamese response in the Tonkin Gulf.[34]

In the face of the CIA's gloomy assessment and the chiefs' strong recommendations, the president asked State and Defense to prepare an integrated political-military plan for graduated action against North Vietnam. In conjunction with this planning, the State Department drafted a resolution seeking congressional validation of expanded U.S. military action in Indochina.

This was the origin of what would become the Tonkin Gulf Resolution. It reflected President Johnson's oft-repeated warning that, if events ever forced us to expand the war, we must avoid the mistake President Truman had made in Korea, i.e., engaging in military operations without congressional approval. Congress will not accept any responsibility for a "crash landing" unless it has also been in on the "takeoff," said Johnson, and therefore he was determined to have congressional authorization of any major U.S. military action in Southeast Asia if he ever had to initiate it.

A small group under George Ball prepared and submitted a draft congressional resolution to the NSC on May 24. It authorized the president, upon the request of the South Vietnamese or the Laotian government, to "use all measures, including the commitment of armed forces" in their defense. We debated the draft at an NSC meeting the same day (without the president). I felt that should the president decide to use U.S. combat (as opposed to training) forces in Southeast Asia within the next two or three months, we should immediately go forward with the resolution. If not, we could wait.[35]

Although the situation was unraveling, we all recognized the risks of bombing the North or introducing U.S. combat forces into the South. Max believed the South Vietnamese government would neither lose nor win rapidly and said the U.S. military therefore preferred waiting until the fall before undertaking expanded action. We met with the president on May 26 but reached no conclusion. He asked us to discuss the matter further with Lodge and Harkins's successor as COMUSMACV, Gen. William C. Westmoreland, and Felt's successor as CINCPAC, Adm. U. S. Grant Sharp, Jr., in Honolulu.

Westy, who served as American field commander in Vietnam from 1964 to 1968, was a casting director's dream for the role of a general. He was handsome, craggy, decisive, ramrod straight. A West Point graduate, World War II and Korean War combat officer, and former U.S. Military Academy superintendent, Westy possessed neither Patton's boastful flamboyance nor LeMay's stubbornness but shared their determination and patriotism.

The Honolulu meeting convened on June 1 in CINCPAC's huge map room. In contrast to previous occasions, when at least some participants had been hopeful, almost everyone was apprehensive and gloomy. Lodge continued to believe things would get better, but he was a notable exception.

Discussion centered on a proposed action plan that had been drafted in Washington but not yet approved by the president, Dean, or me. Its opening moves would include a congressional resolution and communication with Hanoi,* followed by a series of graduated military pressures, culminating in limited air attacks against North Vietnam (which would be carried out by South Vietnamese forces to the greatest extent possible). A Special National Intelligence Estimate (SNIE) a few days earlier had concluded there was a reasonable chance such a plan would lead Hanoi to reduce the level of insurgency, although it stressed the possibility that Hanoi might hold on.[36]

In connection with the action plan, four points were discussed:

---

*During the summer of 1964, the Johnson administration initiated the first of several secret diplomatic contacts with North Vietnam through J. Blair Seaborn, Canada's representative on the International Control Commission (ICC), the body established to monitor compliance with the 1954 and 1962 Geneva Accords. Seaborn told Hanoi that if it agreed to cease its support for the Vietcong and end the conflict, the United States would provide it economic aid and diplomatic support. Otherwise, it could anticipate American air and naval attacks. North Vietnamese Foreign Minister Pham Van Dong replied that the United States must withdraw from South Vietnam and accept Vietcong participation in a "neutral" coalition government. The two sides were far apart.

Saigon remained unready either to mount air attacks against the North or to handle a military response against the South for several months; the possibility of Chinese intervention seemed to call for the preventive deployment of several U.S. divisions; the American public remained unconvinced of Southeast Asia's importance to U.S. security; and an appropriate congressional resolution made sense as a way of simultaneously demonstrating U.S. resolve and educating the country. However, the basic questions we had confronted for so long remained unposed and unanswered, and the conference ended inconclusively.[37] We came to no decision on the proposed action plan.

I have reported the Honolulu discussion in some detail for two reasons: (1) we came close to the brink of a major escalation—without adequately examining its consequences or alternatives—but at the last moment drew back; and (2) because no decision on an expanded military effort had been made, the administration decided to postpone presentation of the draft resolution to Congress until September, when it expected the Senate to have completed action on the Civil Rights Bill. Critics later charged that the president had carried the resolution around in his pocket for months waiting for an opportunity—or hoping to create one—to "slip" it through an unsuspecting Congress. That was not the case.

Just after my return from Honolulu, the chiefs (less the chairman) submitted a memo to me stating their belief that we had not defined a "militarily valid objective for Southeast Asia," nor had we approved a "military course of action to achieve that objective." They proposed two courses: a preferred one of breaking the North's will and capability and a "lesser" one of terminating its support of the southern insurgency. However, the chiefs failed to submit a plan for either course.[38]

When Max read the chiefs' memo, he declared that it was not "an accurate or complete expression of our choices." He further opposed their preferred course because it "raised considerably the risks of escalation."[39]

With the 1964 Republican presidential campaign heating up, Lodge felt he should resign to concentrate his energies on strengthening the moderate wing of his party. This afforded an occasion to try to strengthen the U.S. team in South Vietnam. That included, first of all, the strongest possible ambassador. Mac, Bobby, and I all volunteered for the assignment. The president chose Max Taylor and buttressed him with Alex Johnson. This, in addition to his replacing General Harkins with Westy, signaled the president's determination to do everything possible to increase the effectiveness of U.S. policy and operations in Indochina.

Shortly after the president had decided not to send me to South Vietnam as ambassador, and with the 1964 election ever present in his mind, he asked me to accept nomination as his vice presidential running mate. There had been press speculation about such an offer—Stewart Alsop, for example, had mentioned the possibility earlier in the year. However, knowing President Johnson as I did, I knew that if I answered yes, he might later reconsider and withdraw the invitation. In any event, I said no.

But the president still had plans for me. On August 1 he stated he wanted me to be his "number one executive vice president in charge of the Cabinet" during his next term.* Johnson never explained what he meant by that phrase, but he did call on me frequently for action in areas outside defense, and I did everything I could to fulfill his requests.

I refused Johnson's offer of the vice presidential nomination not because I thought little of the opportunity—quite the contrary. Looking back, if I could live my life over again, I would seize the chance to train for and seek elective office. There is no more

---

*This quotation (and certain others I will refer to in later chapters) is from tapes and transcripts of presidential recordings (hereafter cited as PR) in the Lyndon B. Johnson Library (hereafter cited as LBJL). The heretofore closed tapes and transcripts cover the following periods: November 1963–August 1964, November 1964, January 1965, June–July 1965, December 1965, and December 1966–February 1968. I thank LBJ Library Director Harry J. Middleton for arranging access to these materials and the NSC for expeditiously declassifying the notes I took on them for use in this book. It is important for readers to recognize that the Kennedy and Johnson libraries contain other tapes, which neither I nor other authors have yet had access to. As these become available, they may cast added light on the history of the war.

important task in a democracy than resolving the differences among people and finding a course of action that will be supported by a sufficient number to permit the nation to achieve a better life for all. That is both the challenge and the responsibility of the politician. But at the time, I lacked political skills and I knew it.

———

About this time, we received another statement from the CIA's Board of National Estimates. It addressed an inquiry the president had made a few days earlier concerning the likelihood of a "domino effect" in East Asia stemming from the fall of South Vietnam and Laos. The government's most senior, experienced group of intelligence analysts, who had no policy-making responsibilities and no prior policy decisions to defend, concluded:

> The loss of South Vietnam and Laos to the Communists would be profoundly damaging to the US position in the Far East, most especially because the US has committed itself persistently, emphatically, and publicly to preventing Communist takeover of the two countries. Failure here would be damaging to US prestige, and would seriously debase the credibility of US will and capability to contain the spread of Communism elsewhere in the area. Our enemies would be encouraged and there would be an increased tendency among other states to move toward a greater degree of accommodation with the Communists.

They went on to observe:

> Aside from the immediate joy in North Vietnam over achievement of its national goals, the chief effect would be upon Communist China, both in boosting its already remarkable self-confidence and in raising its prestige as a leader of World Communism. Peiping has already begun to advertise South Vietnam as proof of its thesis that the underdeveloped world is ripe for revolution, that the US is a paper tiger, and that local insurgency can be carried through to victory without undue risk of precipitating a major international war. The outcome in South Vietnam and

Laos would conspicuously support the aggressive tactical contentions of Peiping as contrasted with the more cautious position of the USSR. To some degree this will tend to encourage and strengthen the more activist revolutionary movements in various parts of the underdeveloped world.[40]

Their analysis seemed again to confirm my and others' fear—misplaced in retrospect, but no less real at the time—that the West's containment policy lay at serious risk in Vietnam. And thus we continued our slide down the slippery slope.

5

The Tonkin Gulf Resolution:

July 30–August 7, 1964

The closest the United States came to a declaration of war in Vietnam was the Tonkin Gulf Resolution of August 1964. The events surrounding the resolution generated intense controversy that continues to this day.

Before August 1964, the American people had followed developments in Vietnam sporadically and with limited concern. The war seemed far off. Tonkin Gulf changed that. In the short run, attacks on U.S. warships in the gulf and the congressional resolution that followed brought home the possibility of U.S. involvement in the war as never before. More important, in the long run, the Johnson administration invoked the resolution to justify the constitutionality of the military actions it took in Vietnam from 1965 on.

Congress recognized the vast power the resolution granted to President Johnson, but it did not conceive of it as a declaration of war and did not intend it to be used, as it was, as authorization for an enormous expansion of U.S. forces in Vietnam—from 16,000 military advisers to 550,000 combat troops. Securing a declaration of war and specific authorization for the introduction of combat forces in subsequent years might well have been impossible; not seeking it was certainly wrong.

———

Many people look upon the nine days from July 30 to August 7, 1964, as the most controversial period of the "Twenty-five-year War." No wonder. For three decades, intense debate has swirled around what happened in the gulf; how we reported what happened to the Congress and the public; the authority we sought from Congress in reaction to events; and how the executive branch under two presidents used that authority over the years that followed.

The key questions and my answers are these:

- Attacks by North Vietnamese patrol boats against U.S. destroyers reportedly occurred on two separate occasions—August 2 and August 4, 1964. Did the attacks actually occur?
  Answer: The evidence of the first attack is indisputable. In the first edition of this book, I stated "The second attack appears probable but not certain." On November 9, 1995, as the second edition was going to press, I learned in a meeting in Hanoi with General Vo Nguyen Giap, North Vietnam's Defense Minister during the war, that the presumed attack on August 4 did not occur.
- At the time—and still more so in later years—some elements of Congress and the public believed the Johnson administration deliberately provoked the attacks in order to justify an escalation of the war and to obtain, under a subterfuge, congressional authority for that escalation. Does this view have any merit?
  Answer: None at all.
- In response to the attacks, the president ordered a strike by U.S. naval aircraft against four North Vietnamese patrol boat bases and an oil depot. Was the strike justified?
  Answer: Probably.
- Would the congressional resolution have been submitted if the action in the Tonkin Gulf had not occurred and, without that action, would it have passed?
  Answer: Almost certainly a resolution would have been submitted to Congress within a matter of weeks, and very likely it would have passed. But the resolution would have faced far

more extensive debate, and there would have been attempts to limit the president's authority.

- Was the Johnson administration justified in basing its subsequent military actions in Vietnam—including an enormous expansion of force levels—on the Tonkin Gulf Resolution?

  Answer: Absolutely not. Although the resolution granted sufficiently broad authority to support the escalation that followed, as I have said, Congress never intended it to be used as a basis for such action, and still less did the country see it so.

The events in the Tonkin Gulf involved two separate U.S. operations: the Plan 34A activities and what were known as DESOTO patrols.

As I have said, in January 1964 the National Security Council had approved CIA support for South Vietnamese covert operations against North Vietnam, code-named Plan 34A. Plan 34A comprised two types of operations: in one, boats and aircraft dropped South Vietnamese agents equipped with radios into North Vietnam to conduct sabotage and to gather intelligence; in the other, high-speed patrol boats manned by South Vietnamese or foreign mercenary crews launched hit-and-run attacks against North Vietnamese shore and island installations. The CIA supported the South Vietnamese 34A operations, and MACV maintained close contact with them, as did General Krulak of the Joint Staff in Washington.

The 303 Committee—so named because it originally met in Room 303 of the Old Executive Office Building—reviewed the schedules of the clandestine operations. All of the CIA's covert operations worldwide required clearance by the 303 Committee. The president's national security adviser (Mac Bundy) chaired the group, whose other members at that time included the under-secretary of state (George Ball), the deputy secretary of defense (Cyrus R. Vance, who had succeeded Ros Gilpatric in early 1964), and the CIA's deputy director for plans (Richard Helms).

The CIA has often been called a "rogue elephant" by its critics, but I consider that a mischaracterization. During my seven years in the Defense Department (and I believe throughout the preceding and following administrations), all CIA "covert operations" (excluding spying operations) were subject to approval by the president and the secretaries of state and defense, or their representatives. The CIA had no authority to act without that approval. So far as I know, it never did.

DESOTO patrols differed substantially in purpose and procedure from 34A operations. They were part of a system of global electronic reconnaissance carried out by specially equipped U.S. naval vessels. Operating in international waters, these vessels collected radio and radar signals emanating from shore-based stations on the periphery of Communist countries such as the Soviet Union, China, North Korea, and, more to the point here, North Vietnam.[*1] These patrols resembled those of Soviet trawlers off our coasts. The information collected could be used in the event U.S. military operations ever became necessary against these countries. Fleet naval commanders— in this case, Pacific Fleet Commander Adm. Thomas Moorer— determined the frequency and course of DESOTO patrols and reviewed them with the Joint Staff in Washington.

Although some individuals knew of both 34A operations and DESOTO patrols, the approval process for each was compartmentalized, and few, if any, senior officials either planned or followed in detail the operational schedules of both. We should have.

Long before the August events in the Tonkin Gulf, many of us who knew about the 34A operations had concluded they were essentially worthless. Most of the South Vietnamese agents sent into North Vietnam were either captured or killed, and the seaborne attacks amounted to little more than pinpricks. One might well ask, "If so, then why were the operations continued?" The answer is that the South Vietnamese government saw them as a relatively low-cost means of harassing North Vietnam in retaliation for Hanoi's support of the Vietcong.

---

[*]The closest approach to North Vietnam was set at eight miles to the mainland and four miles to the offshore islands. Because the United States had no record of a North Vietnamese assertion regarding its territorial waters, Washington concluded that international waters extended to three miles offshore—the limit established by France when it controlled Indochina. Only *after* the Tonkin Gulf incidents did Hanoi claim a twelve-mile limit. At no time during August 1964 did U.S. ships approach closer than five miles to the offshore islands.

On the night of July 30, 1964, a 34A mission carried out by South Vietnamese patrol boats attacked two North Vietnamese islands in the Tonkin Gulf thought to support infiltration operations against the South. The next morning, the U.S. destroyer *Maddox* on a DESOTO patrol steamed into the gulf well away from the islands. Two and a half days later, at 3:40 P.M. (3:40 A.M. Washington time) on August 2, the *Maddox* reported it was being approached by high-speed boats. Within a few minutes it was attacked by torpedoes and automatic weapons fire. The *Maddox* reported no injuries or damage. No doubt existed that the vessel had been fired upon: crew members retrieved a North Vietnamese shell fragment from the deck, which I insisted be sent to my office to verify the attack; furthermore, North Vietnam, in its official history of the war, confirmed that it ordered the *Maddox* attacked. At the time of the incident, the *Maddox* lay in international waters, more than twenty-five miles off the North Vietnamese coast.[2]

At 11:30 A.M. on August 2, the president met with his senior advisers to study the latest reports and consider a U.S. response. Cy Vance represented my office. The group believed it was possible that a local North Vietnamese commander—rather than a senior official—had taken the initiative, and the president therefore decided not to retaliate. He agreed instead to send a stiff protest note to Hanoi and to continue the patrol, adding another destroyer, the *C. Turner Joy*.[3]

Max Taylor, by then ambassador in South Vietnam, opposed the decision not to retaliate. In a cable to the State Department late in the night of August 2, he said that our failure to respond to an unprovoked attack on a U.S. destroyer in international waters would be construed as an "indication that the U.S. flinches from direct confrontation with the North Vietnamese."[4]

At 3:00 P.M. the next day, Dean Rusk and I briefed members of the Senate Foreign Relations and Armed Services committees in closed session on the events of July 30 and August 2. We described the 34A operations, the attack on the DESOTO patrol, and why the president had decided not to retaliate. Although I have been unable to locate any record of the meeting, I believe we also stressed that we had no intention of provoking a North Vietnamese attack on the DESOTO patrol. We informed the senators that the DESOTO patrols, as well as the 34A operations, would continue, and in fact another 34A raid occurred about this time against the coast of North Vietnam (it was then early morning August 4 Saigon time).

———

At 7:40 A.M. Washington time (7:40 P.M. Saigon time) on August 4, the *Maddox* radioed that an attack from unidentified vessels appeared imminent. *Maddox*'s information came from highly classified reports from the National Security Agency, which had intercepted North Vietnamese instructions. An hour later the *Maddox* radioed that it had established radar contact with three unidentified vessels. A nearby U.S. aircraft carrier, the *Ticonderoga,* launched fighter aircraft to the *Maddox*'s and the *Turner Joy*'s assistance.

Low clouds and thunderstorms on this moonless night made visibility extremely difficult. During the next several hours, confusion reigned in the gulf. The *Maddox* and the *Turner Joy* reported more than twenty torpedo attacks, sighting of torpedo wakes, enemy cockpit lights, searchlight illumination, automatic weapons fire, and radar and sonar contacts.

As the situation intensified, Cy and I met with members of the Joint Staff to consider how to react. We agreed that, assuming the reports were correct, a response to this second unprovoked attack was absolutely necessary. While we had not accepted Max Taylor's view that the August 2 attack required retaliation, a second, and in our minds, unprovoked attack against U.S. vessels operating in international waters surely did. Therefore, we quickly developed a plan for carrier aircraft to strike four North Vietnamese patrol boat bases and two oil depots that supplied them.

At 11:40 A.M., I met with Dean, Mac, and the chiefs to review our options. We continued our discussion at an NSC meeting, and then at lunch with the president, Cy, and John McCone.

North Vietnamese attacks on U.S. destroyers on the high seas appeared to be so irrational (in that they were bound to escalate the conflict) that we speculated about Hanoi's motives. Some believed the 34A operations had played a role in triggering North Vietnam's actions against the DESOTO patrols, but others, pointing at 34A's ineffectiveness, found that explanation hard to accept. In any event, the president agreed that a second attack, if confirmed, required a swift and firm retaliatory strike.

The question then became: Did a second attack actually occur?

As I have said, visibility in the area at the time of the alleged attack was very limited. Because of that and because sonar soundings—which are often unreliable—accounted for most reports of the second attack, uncertainty remained about whether it had occurred. I therefore made strenuous efforts to determine what, indeed, had happened. At my request, Air Force Lt. Gen. David A. Burchinal, director of the Joint Staff, called Admiral Sharp in Honolulu several times to obtain details of the incident.

At 1:27 P.M. Washington time, Capt. John J. Herrick, DESOTO patrol commander aboard the *Maddox,* sent this "flash" message to Honolulu and Washington:

Review of action makes many reported contacts and torpedoes fired appear doubtful. Freak weather effects on radar and overeager sonar men may have accounted for many reports. No actual visual sightings by *Maddox*. Suggest complete evaluation before any further action taken.[5]

Forty-one minutes later, Sharp telephoned Burchinal and told him that, despite Herrick's message, there was "no doubt" in his mind a second attack had occurred. Captain Herrick sent another message at 2:48 P.M. Washington time, which read: "Certain that original ambush was bona-fide."[6]

I placed several calls myself to obtain as much information as possible. Because the facts remain in dispute even now, thirty years later, I wish to relate some of my conversations (recorded at the time) in detail. At 4:08 P.M., I called Admiral Sharp by secure phone and said, "What's the latest information on the action?"

"The latest dope we have, sir," replied Sharp, "indicates a little doubt on just exactly what went on. . . . Apparently the thing started by a sort of ambush attempt by the PTs." He added, "The initial ambush attempt was definite." However, he mentioned "freak radar echoes" and "young fellows" manning the sonars, who "are apt to say any noise is a torpedo, so that, undoubtedly, there were not as many torpedoes" as earlier reported. Sharp said the *Turner Joy* claimed three PT boats hit and one sunk, while the *Maddox* claimed one or two sunk.

"There isn't any possibility there was no attack, is there?" I asked Sharp. He replied, "Yes, I would say that there is a slight possibility."

I said, "We obviously don't want to do it [launch the retaliatory strike] until we are damn sure what happened."

Sharp agreed and said he thought he could have more information in a couple of hours.[7]

At 4:47 P.M., Cy and I met with the chiefs to review the evidence relating to the alleged second attack. Five factors in particular persuaded us it had occurred: the *Turner Joy* had been illuminated when fired on by automatic weapons; one of the destroyers had observed PT boat cockpit lights; antiaircraft batteries had fired on two U.S. aircraft overflying the area; we had intercepted and decoded a North Vietnamese message apparently indicating two of its boats had been sunk; and Admiral Sharp had determined there had probably been an attack. At 5:23 P.M., Sharp called Burchinal and said no doubt now existed that an attack on the destroyers had been carried out.[8]

At 6:15 P.M., the National Security Council met at the White House. I outlined the evidence supporting our conclusion and presented our proposed response. All NSC members concurred in the action, and the president authorized the launch of our naval aircraft.[9]

At 6:45 P.M., the president, Dean Rusk, the new Joint Chiefs chairman, Gen. Earle G. "Bus" Wheeler, and I met with congressional leaders to brief them on the day's events and our planned response. Explaining the basis for our retaliation, Dean told the leaders that North Vietnam had made a serious decision to attack our vessels on the high seas, that we should not interpret their action as accidental, that we must demonstrate U.S. resolve in Southeast Asia, and that our limited response would show we did not want a war with the North. The president informed the group that he planned to submit a resolution requesting Congress's support for U.S. combat operations in Southeast Asia should they prove necessary. Several of the senators and representatives said they would support this request.[10]

At 7:22 P.M., the *Ticonderoga* received the president's strike authorization message, as did a second carrier, the *Constellation* a few minutes later. The first planes took off from the carriers at 10:43 P.M. Washington time. In all, U.S. naval aircraft flew sixty-four sorties against the patrol boat bases and a supporting oil complex. It was considered a successful mission—a limited, but we thought appropriate, reply to at least one and very probably two attacks on U.S. vessels.

It did not take long for controversy to attach itself to the incident. On August 6, several senators disputed our report of what had occurred. The dispute was not resolved, and several years later (in February 1968), a Senate hearing was convened to reexamine the evidence. It also challenged the administration's reporting. In 1972, Louis Tordella, then deputy director of the National Security Agency, concluded that the intercepted North Vietnamese message, which had been interpreted as ordering the August 4 attack, had in fact referred to the August 2 action. Ray S. Cline, the CIA's deputy director for intelligence in 1964, echoed this judgment in a 1984 interview. And James B. Stockdale—a *Ticonderoga* pilot in 1964, who later spent eight years in a Hanoi prison and subsequently received the Congressional Medal of Honor—stated in his memoirs that he had seen no North Vietnamese boats while flying over the two destroyers on August 4, and he believed no attack had occurred.[11] The controversy has persisted until this day.

———

At 9:00 A.M. on August 6, 1964, Dean, Bus, and I entered the Senate Caucus Room and took our seats before a joint executive session of the Senate Foreign Relations and Armed Services committees to testify on the August 2 and 4 events in the Tonkin Gulf and in support of the joint congressional resolution then before both houses.

Dean began his prepared statement by stressing that "the immediate occasion for this resolution is of course the North Vietnamese attacks on our naval vessels, operating in international waters in the Gulf of Tonkin, on August 2nd and August 4th." He continued: "The present attacks . . . are no isolated event. They are part and parcel of a continuing Communist drive to conquer South Vietnam . . . and eventually dominate and conquer other free nations of Southeast Asia." I then described the two attacks in detail, and Bus stated the Joint Chiefs' unanimous endorsement of the U.S. retaliatory action, which they considered appropriate under the circumstances.

The committees' questioning centered on two separate issues: What had happened in the gulf? And was the resolution a proper delegation of power to the president to apply military force in the area?

Senator Wayne Morse vehemently challenged our description of events in the gulf, our military response, and the resolution itself:

> I am unalterably opposed to this course of action which, in my judgment, is an aggressive course of action on the part of the United States. I think we are kidding the world if you try to give the impression that when the South Vietnamese naval boats bombarded two islands a short distance off the coast of North Vietnam we were not implicated.
>
> I think our whole course of action of aid to South Vietnam

satisfies the world that those boats didn't act in a vacuum as far as the United States was concerned. We knew those boats were going up there, and that naval action was a clear act of aggression against the territory of North Vietnam, and our ships were in Tonkin Bay, in international waters, but nevertheless they were in Tonkin Bay to be interpreted as standing as a cover for naval operations of South Vietnam.

I think what happened is that Khanh got us to backstop him in open aggression against the territorial integrity of North Vietnam. I have listened to briefing after briefing and there isn't a scintilla of evidence in any briefing yet that North Vietnam engaged in any military aggression against South Vietnam either with its ground troops or its navy.

This last comment went contrary to voluminous, and ever-growing, evidence of North Vietnam's support for the Vietcong—by land and sea, with men and military equipment. The senator concluded his statement by asserting, "American naval vessels [were] conveniently standing by as a backstop" for South Vietnamese 34A operations.

In reply I said, "Our Navy played absolutely no part in, was not associated with, [and] was not aware of any South Vietnamese actions." As I have explained, the U.S. Navy did not administer 34A operations, and the DESOTO patrols had neither been a "cover" for nor stood by as a "backstop" for 34A vessels. Senator Morse knew these facts, for he had been present on August 3 when Dean, Bus, and I briefed senators on 34A and the DESOTO patrols. That portion of my reply was correct. However, I went on to say the *Maddox* "was not informed of, was not aware [of], had no evidence of, and so far as I know today had no knowledge of any possible South Vietnamese actions in connection with the two islands that Senator Morse referred to." That portion of my reply, I later learned, was totally incorrect; DESOTO patrol commander Captain Herrick had indeed known of 34A. My statement was honest but wrong.

The hearing then turned to a discussion of the resolution. Its key passages stated:

> Whereas naval units of [North Vietnam] . . . in violation of . . . international law, have deliberately and repeatedly attacked United States naval vessels lawfully present in international waters . . . and Whereas these attacks are part of a deliberate and systematic campaign of aggression . . . against its neighbors, . . . the United States is, therefore, prepared, as the President determines, to take all necessary steps, including the use of armed force, to assist any member or protocol state of the Southeast Asia Collective Defense Treaty requesting assistance in defense of its freedom.

Discussing the proposed language, Dean stressed it granted authority similar to that approved by Congress in the 1955 Formosa Resolution, the 1957 Middle East Resolution, and the 1962 Cuba Resolution. His prepared statement noted that "we cannot tell what steps may in the future be required," and he added: "As the Southeast Asia situation develops, and *if it develops in ways we cannot now anticipate, of course there will be close and continuous consultation between the President and the Congress* [emphasis added]."

Senate Foreign Relations Committee Chairman William Fulbright—who presided over the hearing, managed the resolution on the Senate floor, and later severely criticized the Johnson administration's handling of the Tonkin Gulf events—offered complimentary remarks that day: "The promptness and decision . . . which all of you exhibited on this occasion was commendable," he said.

Others present endorsed the resolution's extensive delegation of power to the president. Sen. Clifford P. Case (R-N.J.), for example, asked if the three resolutions previously referred to contained the broad language "as the President determines." "They have had language equivalent to that," responded Senator Fulbright. Senator Case declared his hearty support. The two committees favorably reported the resolution to the full Senate by a vote of 31–1, with Morse dissenting.[12]

During floor debate that afternoon, Sen. John Sherman Cooper (R-Ky.) had the following exchange with Senator Fulbright:

COOPER: Are we now giving the President advance authority to take whatever action he may deem necessary respecting South Vietnam and its defense, or with respect to the defense of any other country included in the [SEATO] treaty?

FULBRIGHT: I think that is correct.

COOPER: Then, looking ahead, if the President decided that it was necessary to use such force as could lead into war, we will give that authority by this resolution?

FULBRIGHT: That is the way I would interpret it.[13]

There is no doubt in my mind that Congress understood the resolution's vast grant of power to the president. But there is also no doubt in my mind that Congress understood the president would not use that vast grant without consulting it carefully and completely.

The Senate and House voted on the resolution the next day, August 7. The Senate passed it by a vote of 88–2, Morse and Ernest W. Gruening (D–Alaska) voting nay; the House approved it unanimously, 416–0.

———

Critics have long asserted that a cloak of deception surrounded the entire Tonkin Gulf affair. They charge that the administration coveted congressional support for war in Indochina, drafted a resolution authorizing it, provoked an incident to justify support for it, and presented false statements to enlist such support. The charges are unfounded.

The resolution grew out of the president's belief that should circumstances ever necessitate the introduction of U.S. combat forces into Indochina—as some of the Joint Chiefs had been suggesting since January 1964—such deployments should be preceded by congressional endorsement. For that purpose, the State Department had drafted a resolution in late May. However, because Max Taylor, as chairman of the Joint Chiefs, had recommended against initiating U.S. military operations at least until the fall—a recommendation that the president, Dean, Mac, and I concurred in—it had been decided to defer presenting the resolution to Congress until after the Civil Rights Bill cleared the Senate in September.

We had this schedule in mind until the North Vietnamese attacks on U.S. vessels led us to believe the war was heating up and to wonder what might happen next. This, in turn, led to our belief that a resolution might well be needed earlier than we had previously anticipated. The president may also have been influenced by what he saw as an opportunity to tie the resolution to a hostile action by Hanoi, and to do so in a way that made him appear firm but moderate, in contrast to Republican presidential candidate Barry Goldwater's hawkish rhetoric.

The charge of deliberate provocation has endured, in part, because some former government officials endorsed it. George Ball, in a 1977 BBC radio interview, stated: "Many of the people who were associated with the war . . . were looking for any excuse to initiate bombing. . . . The DESOTO patrol was primarily for provocation. . . . There was a feeling that if the destroyer got into some trouble, that would provide the provocation we needed."[14]

In contrast, Bill Bundy told the same radio audience that the United States did not intend to create a crisis and had not "engineered" the incidents as an excuse for military action. In fact, he said, "it didn't fit in with our plans at all, to be perfectly blunt about it. We didn't think the situation had deteriorated to the point where we had to consider stronger action on the way things lay in South Vietnam." Elsewhere he wrote, "The case on any Administration intent to provoke the incidents is not simply weak, it is nonexistent."[15]

He went on to make a different but no less crucial point:

> Miscalculation by both the U.S. and North Vietnam is, in the end, at the root of the best hindsight hypothesis of Hanoi's behavior. In simple terms, it was a mistake for an Administration sincerely

resolved to keep its risks low, to have the 34A operations and the destroyer patrol take place even in the same time period. Rational minds could not readily have foreseen that Hanoi might confuse them . . . but rational calculations should have taken account of the irrational. . . . Washington did not want an incident, and it seems doubtful that Hanoi did either. Yet each misread the other, and the incidents happened.[16]

I agree with both of these comments. And I believe Dean, Mac, and Max would agree as well.

Of course, if the Tonkin Gulf Resolution had not led to much more serious military involvement in Vietnam, it likely would not remain so controversial. But it did serve to open the floodgates. Nevertheless, the idea that the Johnson administration deliberately deceived Congress is false. The problem was not that Congress did not grasp the resolution's potential but that it did not grasp the war's potential and how the administration would respond in the face of it. As a 1967 Senate Foreign Relations Committee report concluded, in adopting a resolution with such sweeping language, "Congress committed the error of making a *personal* judgment as to how President Johnson would implement the resolution when it had a responsibility to make an *institutional* judgment, first, as to what *any* President would do with so great an acknowledgement of power, and, second, as to whether, under the Constitution, Congress had the right to grant or concede the authority in question [emphases in original]." I agree with both points.[17]

Senator Fulbright, in time, came to feel that he had been misled—and indeed he had. He had received definite assurances from Dean at the August 6, 1964, hearing (and I believe privately from LBJ as well) that the president would not use the vast power granted him without full congressional consultation. But at the February 20, 1968, hearing called to reexamine the affair, Senator Fulbright graciously absolved me of the charge of intentionally misleading Congress. "I never meant to leave the impression that I thought you were deliberating trying to deceive us," he said.

Senators Mike Mansfield, Claiborne Pell, and Stuart Symington made similar statements.[18]

The fundamental issue of Tonkin Gulf involved not deception but, rather, misuse of power bestowed by the resolution. The language of the resolution plainly granted the powers the president subsequently used, and Congress understood the breadth of those powers when it overwhelmingly approved the resolution on August 7, 1964. But no doubt exists that Congress did *not* intend to authorize without further, full consultation the expansion of U.S. forces in Vietnam from 16,000 to 550,000 men, initiating large-scale combat operations with the risk of an expanded war with China and the Soviet Union, and extending U.S. involvement in Vietnam for many years to come.

The question of congressional versus presidential authority over the conduct of U.S. military operations remains hotly contested to this day. The root of this struggle lies in the ambiguous language of the Constitution, which established the president as commander in chief but gave Congress the power to declare war.

In December 1990, just before the Persian Gulf War, I testified before the Senate Foreign Relations Committee on the possible use of U.S. forces there. A few days earlier, Secretary of Defense Richard B. Cheney had asserted that President Bush possessed the power to commit large-scale U.S. forces to combat in the gulf (ultimately we had 500,000 men and women there) under his authority as commander in chief. Senator Paul S. Sarbanes (D-Md.) asked my opinion of Cheney's assertion. I replied that I was not a constitutional lawyer and therefore declined to answer. Certain that I would repudiate Cheney's statement, Senator Sarbanes pressed me very hard for a reply.

Finally, I told the senator that he had asked the wrong question. The issue did not come down to legalities. It involved at its most basic level a question of politics: should a president take our nation to war (other than immediately to repel an attack on our shores) without popular consent as voiced by Congress? I said no president should, and I believed President Bush would not. He did not. Before President Bush began combat operations against Iraq, he sought—and obtained—Congress's support (as well as that of the U.N. Security Council).

President Bush was right. President Johnson, and those of us who served with him, were wrong.

6

The 1964 Election and Its Aftermath:

August 8, 1964–January 27, 1965

M any people today believe President Johnson put off making
decisions on Vietnam because he wanted to concentrate on
winning the 1964 presidential election. Some even allege that he
concealed an intention to expand vastly the war for political
reasons—that he wanted to paint the Republican candidate, Sen.
Barry M. Goldwater (R-Ariz.), as a warmonger and himself as a reasonable, peace-loving statesman.

If Lyndon Johnson had in mind a plan to escalate the war, he
never told me. And I believe he had no such plan. He never
indicated to me or to the Joint Chiefs that he wanted us to hold
back in Vietnam because of the election. In fact, there was still no
consensus among his advisers about what to do.

Throughout this period, military and political conditions in South
Vietnam rapidly worsened, heightening the dilemma we faced
between avoiding direct U.S. military involvement and preventing
the loss of South Vietnam. Deepening divisions over what to do in
the face of Saigon's accelerating decline added to our uncertainty

and muddled our policy. Running through our debates like a dark thread was the growing frustration and desperation we felt about a difficult and increasingly dangerous problem.

Barry Goldwater took a hard line on Vietnam throughout the 1964 campaign. In early March, he was quoted musing that ten years before, when France's Vietnam force was under siege at Dien Bien Phu, the United States might have done well to drop a low-yield atom bomb to defoliate the trees the attackers used for cover. The next day he amplified the point. Now that America was involved, he said, we should be "carrying the war to North Vietnam—ten years ago we should have bombed North Vietnam, with no risk to our lives." Needless to say, such bellicose talk alarmed many voters.[1]

President Johnson, meanwhile, seemed a model of moderation and restraint. One of his first—and, in many respects, most thoughtful—comments on Vietnam came in a speech to the American Bar Association in New York City on August 12. The phrases reflect the skill of his speechwriter (whom the record does not identify), but the beliefs were unquestionably the president's:

> Since the end of World War II, . . . we have patiently labored to construct a world order in which both peace and freedom could flourish.
>
> We have lived so long with crisis and danger that we accept, almost without division, the premise of American concern for threats to [that] order. . . .
>
> We have done this because we have, at painful cost, learned that we can no longer wait for the tides of conflict to touch our shores. Aggression and upheaval, in any part of the world, carry the seeds of destruction to our own freedom and perhaps to civilization itself.
>
> We have done this, lastly, for a reason that is often difficult for others to understand. We have done it because it is right that we should.
>
> Friendly cynics and fierce enemies alike often underestimate or ignore the strong thread of moral purpose which runs through the fabric of American history.

Of course, security and welfare shape our policies. But much of the energy of our efforts has come from moral purpose.

It is right that the strong should help the weak defend their freedom. . . .

It is right that nations should be free from the coercion of others.[2]

People have hotly debated whether President Johnson's foreign policy rested on moral grounds. I have no doubt that such considerations influenced him and many of his advisers, including me. Whether they should have—or should influence administrations today—remains highly controversial. Pragmatists and political realists argue they should not. I believe they should—as, for example, in avoiding indiscriminate bombing of North Vietnam or incurring the risk of the use of nuclear weapons. This issue again merits debate as America struggles to define its proper role in the post–Cold War world.

In any event, during these months and long after the election, President Johnson feared that the American right wing would push us ever more deeply into Indochina and expose us to ever greater risks of war with China and the Soviets. To counter this pressure, he said things that would return to haunt him. In August, for example, he declared, with obvious reference to Goldwater: "Some others are eager to enlarge the conflict. They call upon us to supply American boys to do the job that Asian boys should do. . . . Such action would offer no solution at all to the real problem of Vietnam." He added, "The South Vietnamese have the basic responsibility for the defense of their own freedom."[3] He repeated this formulation over and over during the campaign—in New Hampshire and Oklahoma, in Kentucky and Ohio.

Was he hiding something? To us behind the scenes, Johnson had made the goal in Vietnam crystal clear. "Win the war!" he told Dean Rusk, Mac Bundy, and me in his first meeting with us as president. He never deviated from that objective. But we could never show him *how* to win at an acceptable cost or an acceptable risk.

There was more he could have told the American people. While we had no agreed-upon plan to send in combat forces, a plan to use American airpower at a minimum had been under debate for months, and there was growing doubt that Saigon could continue for long to defend itself. The president disclosed none of this publicly. Had he done so, he probably would have had to add something like "We're in a helluva mess, and I don't know what may happen." But he did not.

Of course, total candor is not customary for politicians under such circumstances. Woodrow Wilson did not exhibit it during the 1916 presidential campaign, when he ran on the slogan "He Kept Us Out of War"—only to seek a declaration of war against the kaiser's Germany the following spring. Franklin Roosevelt did not exhibit it during the 1940 campaign, when he said he was not going to send American troops to fight in a European war—shortly before we entered World War II. President Johnson firmly believed that a Goldwater victory would endanger the United States and threaten world stability. He also believed that the end—Goldwater's defeat—justified the means. So what he said publicly during the campaign was accurate only in a narrow sense. It was the truth, but far from the whole truth.

Still, this failure to level with the public does not mean the president had plans up his sleeve to escalate the war. Although some of the Joint Chiefs had pressed for heavier military action in Vietnam since early 1964, William Westmoreland and Max Taylor, as well as South Vietnamese leader Nguyen Khanh, had urged postponing it. When Mac and I counseled Johnson to change course in late January 1965, we were uncertain what should be done—escalate or withdraw—while Dean resisted any change at all.

Judging from President Johnson's record during his long career, some may say that with an election hanging in the balance, he probably would have concealed a decision to go to war from the public. Perhaps so. But that is far different from saying that in 1964 he had made the decision. All the evidence indicates otherwise.

Goldwater attacked me as well as the president during the campaign. He liked to hammer at the issue of America's readiness to fight a war, nuclear or conventional, and he repeatedly alleged that I was trying to weaken America's defenses. On March 20, he made the "flat charge" that "Secretary of Defense McNamara and the State Department are engaged in unilateral disarmament." On August 11, he claimed, "Under our present defense leadership, with its utter disregard for new weapons, our deliverable nuclear capacity may be cut down by 90% in the next decade." On October 6, he toughened his allegation and accused me of "deliberately . . . phasing out 90% of our nuclear delivery capability." His campaign autobiography, *Where I Stand,* excerpted in *The Washington Post* that fall, asserted:

> The present Secretary of Defense has become the leading advo-cate—indeed the leading architect—of a so-called defense policy which, by the late 1960's and the early 1970's, will have turned the shield of the Republic into a Swiss-cheese wall, full of holes: a policy which will . . . encourage our enemies to become bolder, to risk the final, fatal step toward nuclear war. . . .
>
> I repeat: the architect of this policy is the present Secretary of Defense. In simplest terms, the defense policies of this Adminis-tration add up to *unilateral disarmament.*[4]

Now, the facts.

On February 3, 1964, I told Goldwater and other members of the Senate Armed Services Committee that the number of strategic nuclear weapons in our force structure would increase over the next five years and that the number of warheads—reflecting, in part, programs initiated by President Eisenhower and my prede-cessor, Tom Gates—would increase 74 percent, with the total megatonnage growing by 31 percent. On September 18, I declared publicly: "A full-scale nuclear exchange between the United States and the USSR would kill 100 million Americans during the first hour. It would kill an even greater number of Russians, but I doubt that any sane person would call this 'victory.'" It was my growing emphasis on—and public declaration of—our nuclear policy's severe limitations, and risks, that appeared particularly to infuriate Goldwater. His statement implied that he saw no real difference between conventional weapons and nuclear weapons. He went so far as to suggest the president should instruct commanders in Vietnam to use any weapons in our arsenal. I profoundly disagreed and said so.

But because Goldwater repeated his baseless and reckless allegations so loudly and often, President Johnson feared they were having their desired political effect. He therefore asked Dean and me to make statements before the Platform Committee at the Democratic Party's Atlantic City convention. Tradition dictates—wisely—that secretaries of state and defense stay out of partisan politics. But, to my regret, Dean and I gave in to the president and spoke at the convention.

At times it seemed like the senator from Arizona was running against me rather than Johnson. He blamed me for Ford Motor Company's decision to introduce the Edsel, whose costly failure in 1959 had marked one of the greatest financial losses in U.S. business history. He charged that I was similarly bankrupting our national security program. Goldwater knew I bore no responsibility for the Edsel's development. So insistent was he on this point that Ford Motor Company's former executive vice president Ernest R. Breech, who was a major financial contributor to Goldwater's campaign, finally wrote the senator's campaign headquarters and explained that "Mr. McNamara . . . had nothing to do with the plans for the Edsel car or any part of the program."[5] Yet the senator continued to make his charge, which found its way into newspaper morgues around the world. As a result, whenever I fell subject to criticism in later years, reporters would attach the epithet "father of the Edsel" to my name.*

---

*Years later, I finally asked my public affairs officer at the World Bank to distribute a copy of Breech's letter to the press each time the charge was made. The attacks eventually stopped.

Throughout the campaign, the administration struggled to balance two objectives in Vietnam: avoiding the introduction of U.S. combat forces while safeguarding South Vietnam from Communist control.

To do both became increasingly difficult. Meanwhile, conditions in South Vietnam, particularly in the political realm, worsened steadily, and in the face of what seemed like the Saigon government's imminent collapse, we remained deeply divided—in both Washington and Saigon—over what to do. We held meeting after meeting and exchanged memo after memo. We thrashed about, frustrated by Vietnam's complexity and our own differences and confusion. But we still failed to achieve consensus or solve the problem.

On August 13, Mac sent the president a memorandum about possible courses of action in Southeast Asia. It reflected his, Dean's, and my views as well as those of our colleagues in the State and Defense departments. This memo and its derivatives became the focus of our attention and acrimonious debate for the next five months.

The memo began with the admission "South Vietnam is not going well." It went on to state that Khanh's chances of staying in power were only fifty-fifty, that Saigon's leadership showed symptoms of defeatism, and that this, in turn, created pressure either to enlarge the war by introducing U.S. forces directly or seriously to consider a negotiated solution, which under current circumstances would be tantamount to surrender. The memo's only clear, unqualified recommendation was this: "We must continue to oppose any Vietnam [negotiating] conference" because "negotiation without continued military action will not achieve our objectives in the foreseeable future."

Mac listed possible military actions, from expanded covert operations to systematic U.S. air strikes against the North and its supply lines to the South. He endorsed a proposal by Max Taylor that we set January 1, 1965, as the target date for starting whatever expanded military action we might adopt.[6]

The Joint Chiefs agreed we should prepare plans for U.S. air strikes against North Vietnamese targets and the Ho Chi Minh Trail with the objective of destroying Hanoi's will to fight and its ability to continue to supply the Vietcong. That, in conjunction with our later ground effort, eventually became the military strategy we followed in subsequent years. Neither then nor later did the chiefs fully assess the probability of achieving these objectives, how long it might take, or what it would cost in lives lost, resources expended, and risks incurred.[7]

Fleshing out the air strategy, the chiefs formulated what came to be known as the "Ninety-four Targets List." It covered North Vietnam's airfields, lines of communication, military installations, industrial installations, and armed reconnaissance routes. They considered attacks on these targets necessary to prevent the collapse of America's position in Southeast Asia. The study did not mention that many of the strikes would have to be launched from airfields in South Vietnam, or that U.S. combat troops would be needed to keep the airfields safe.

When I read the recommendations, I asked the Joint Chiefs to evaluate the economic and military effects of striking the targets. Unbeknownst to me, my request touched off a sharp debate among the chiefs. In discussions on September 4, Army Chief of Staff Gen. Harold K. Johnson argued that the rationale for air strikes was gravely flawed. Although the chiefs had gone on record many times asserting that "the military course of action which offers the best chance of success remains the destruction [by air attack] of North Vietnam (DRV) will and capability as necessary to compel the DRV to cease providing support to the insurgencies in South Vietnam (RVN)," General Johnson disagreed. He pointed out that a growing body of evidence showed "the VC insurgency in the RVN could continue for a long time at its present or an increased intensity *even if* North Vietnam were *completely* destroyed [emphasis added]." For this reason, General Johnson told his colleagues that while bombing North Vietnam might dampen Vietcong operations in the South, "the war against the insurgency will be won in South Vietnam and along its frontiers." The general went on to propose that the "Ninety-four Targets List" be shelved unless the North Vietnamese or Chinese invaded South Vietnam or Laos. He thought this recommendation followed inescapably from the chiefs' own prediction that striking all ninety-four targets made a large-scale North Vietnamese or Chinese response "more than likely."[8]

But the "talking paper" that the chiefs discussed with Max and me on September 8 made no mention of this or General Johnson's other points.

This question of bombing's effectiveness that General Johnson had raised became a fundamental issue between the president and me, on the one hand, and the chiefs and military commanders in Vietnam on the other, for the next three and a half years. It was also the issue that triggered two highly contentious congressional hearings in 1966–67, in which most Armed Services Committee members and military witnesses testifying endorsed the view contested by General Johnson in 1964 (and supported by the president's and my subsequent decisions).

The division among the chiefs on this issue underscored more fundamental problems. Airpower advocates in the air force and navy accepted bombing's effectiveness as dogma and failed to examine precisely what it could accomplish in particular situations. The army (with the exception of the Special Forces) and the Marine Corps found it comparably difficult to conceptualize and implement effective antiguerrilla operations. And all the services (and I, as well) greatly underestimated Hanoi's determination, endurance, and ability to reinforce and expand Vietcong strength in the South.

The closest I came to getting a straight answer to my inquiry about the ninety-four targets appeared in a report of a war game, "Sigma II-64," conducted by the Joint Staff's Joint War Games Agency in mid-September 1964. It concluded that "industrial and military bombing" of North Vietnam "would not quickly cause cessation of the insurgency in South Vietnam" and, indeed, "might have but minimal effect on the (low) living standard" of the adversary.[9]

The government in Saigon was unraveling faster than we could even discuss our possible courses of action with the president. On September 6, Max cabled in exasperation that "only the emergence of an exceptional leader could improve the situation and no George Washington is in sight." Since the first days of the Kennedy administration, we had regarded political stability as a fundamental prerequisite for our Vietnam strategy. Now Max as much as said it appeared unattainable. A Special National Intelligence Estimate (SNIE) distributed shortly afterward echoed his judgment. It concluded, "The odds are against the emergence of a stable government capable of effectively prosecuting the war in South Vietnam."[10]

These two assessments should have led us to rethink our basic objective and the likelihood of ever achieving it. We did not do so, in large part because no one was willing to discuss getting out. We thought that would lead to a serious breach in the dike to contain the spread of Communism in Southeast Asia, and that we would not accept.

Because I relied heavily on SNIEs and will refer to them often in the pages ahead, let me explain what they were. In 1950 the CIA had created an independent unit called the Board of National Estimates (BNE). Its mission was to put together assessments of major political and military events, trends, and forecasts. These estimates drew on reports from the various intelligence agencies, including the State Department's Bureau of Intelligence and Research (INR) and those in the military services. Typically, the BNE would circulate draft versions of its estimates to the other agencies, and the BNE director would accept or reject their comments as he chose. The estimates then went to a top-level review committee, the U.S. Intelligence Board (USIB), and finally to the director of the CIA. He would send the finished estimates directly to the top: the president and his senior advisers.

Sherman Kent, a former Yale history professor, headed the BNE during most of my years as secretary of defense. Sherman, who looked like the original Mr. Chips, possessed one of the sharpest and toughest geopolitical minds I ever encountered. Even when I disagreed with him, which was not often, I held him in the highest regard. The reports prepared under his direction influenced me immensely.

When we finally met to discuss possible courses of action with the president on September 9, the substantial split among his military advisers became apparent. The air force chief of staff and the Marine Corps commandant believed it necessary to launch immediate air strikes against North Vietnam. The Joint Chiefs chairman (Bus Wheeler), the army chief of staff, the chief of naval operations, General Westmoreland, and Ambassador Taylor all believed we should not overstrain the currently weak Saigon regime by taking drastic action against the North.

South Vietnam's political instability deeply troubled President Johnson, and he wondered aloud whether it made all our efforts worthless. Max flatly stated we could not afford to let Hanoi win. Bus emphatically agreed, emphasizing the chiefs' unanimous belief that losing South Vietnam meant losing all Southeast Asia. Dean Rusk and John McCone forcefully concurred. But no one (including me) asked whether or how we could prevent it! The president ended the meeting by instructing Bus to tell those chiefs wishing to attack the North immediately that we would not enter our fighter in a ten-round bout when he was in no shape to last the first round. "We should get him ready to last three or four rounds at least," he grumbled. Conspicuously absent was any discussion by the president of the impact an escalation might have on the election, now just two months away.

Johnson was right to worry about South Vietnam's fragility. Just four days later came another near coup, this time by Catholics in the army who thought General Khanh was too cozy with the Buddhists. The Catholics marched troops into Saigon and seized several government installations before younger officers loyal to Khanh turned them back.

After talking to the president about this episode, Dean cabled Max that "the picture of bickering among [South] Vietnamese leaders has created an appalling impression abroad." He asked bitterly, "What can be the purpose of [our] commitment if South Vietnamese leaders themselves cannot declare a moratorium on personal rivalries?" Even Admiral Sharp began voicing doubts. He wired Bus Wheeler on September 25 that "the political situation in RVN is now so unstable as to raise some serious questions about our future courses of action. . . . Conceivably the decision could be one of disengagement." And the CIA concurred, saying, "The odds now favor a continuing decay of South Vietnamese will and effectiveness in coming weeks, sufficient to imperil the political base for present U.S. policy and objectives in South Vietnam."[11]

———

Amid this dismal state of affairs, on October 5, 1964, George Ball sent Dean, Mac, and me a sixty-two-page memorandum challenging the assumptions of our current Vietnam policy. Its depth, breadth, and iconoclasm were remarkable, as was the man who wrote it. A bearlike figure with a fine mind, sharp wit, and gifted pen, George was an Atlanticist who firmly believed in the primacy of America's relations with Europe. He had served as a member of the U.S. Strategic Bombing Survey in Germany at the end of World War II and as counsel to the French government during its Indochina ordeal in the 1950s. Because he was recognized as having a strong European bias, Dean, Mac, and I treated his views about Vietnam guardedly.

George began by stating the obvious: political conditions in Saigon had deteriorated markedly and there appeared little likelihood of establishing a government strong enough to vanquish the insurgency. He then posited four options for U.S. policy: (1) continue the present course of action; (2) take over the war; (3) mount an air offensive against the North; and (4) work for a political settlement. He analyzed each. He saw the present course leading to a downward spiral of political and military weakness. Taking over the war would lead to heavy loss of American lives in the jungles and rice paddies. Bombing the North would neither break its will nor significantly hurt its ability to support the Vietcong. (He also said an air offensive would do nothing to strengthen our negotiating position, but he revised this judgment early the next year).

In particular, George questioned the premise "that we can take offensive action while controlling the risks." In pungent—and prophetic—words, he wrote: "Once on the tiger's back we cannot be sure of picking the place to dismount."*

That left only Option 4. Noting that we had given "almost no attention to the possible political means of finding a way out," George concluded, "we should undertake a searching study of this question without further delay."

He was absolutely correct on both counts. But his memo did not take us very far toward that political solution. He argued that a negotiated settlement should include

(a) The effective commitment of North Vietnam to stop the insurgency in the South;

(b) The establishment of an independent government in Saigon capable of cleaning up the remaining elements of insurgency once Hanoi has ceased its direct support;

(c) Recognition that the Saigon Government remains free to call on the United States or any other friendly power for help if it should again need assistance; and

(d) Enforceable guarantees of the continued independence of the Saigon Government by other signatory powers.[12]

Dean, Mac, and I strongly endorsed these objectives. But we agreed that advocating a political solution with no effective means to achieve it was tantamount to advocating unconditional withdrawal. We weighed that possibility in terms of its potential effect on America's global security. We saw a world where the Hanoi-supported Pathet

*But he failed to note we were already in that position!

Lao continued to push forward in Laos, where Sukarno appeared to be moving Indonesia ever closer to the Communist orbit, where Malaysia faced immense pressure from Chinese-supported insurgents, where China had just detonated its first atomic device and continued to trumpet violent revolution, where Khrushchev and his successors in the Kremlin continued to make bellicose statements against the West. In light of all those threats, we viewed unconditional withdrawal as clearly unacceptable.

George shared that conclusion. It was this internal contradiction that flawed his memo. He was correct in identifying the problem we faced. He was correct in examining the risks inherent in the actions we contemplated. He was correct in urging that more attention be given to negotiations. And he was correct in spelling out the objectives of negotiation. But it was *not* clear that this proposed action would achieve those objectives.

Dean, Mac, and I discussed the memo with George on Saturday, November 7. I have been unable to locate a set of notes of the meeting, but I believe we made our views clear. George acknowledged there were "conspicuous *lacunae*" in his "very preliminary paper." He said he offered it "to suggest areas of exploration that could lead to other options."[13]

We seriously erred by not carrying out that exploration. I fault all four of us. George's memo represented the effort of an honest man pushing a series of propositions that deserved thorough debate at the highest levels. He had our respect—but he deserved more than that. We should have immediately discussed the memo with the president; instead, Johnson did not focus on it until February 24 the next year, when George passed it to him through presidential aide Bill Moyers. And we should have returned the memo to George and insisted he quickly submit it to experts from the State Department, the CIA, the Defense Department, and the NSC for evaluation and analysis. That we did not reflected our belief that he had not found a way to achieve the objective we all sought. During the winter and spring of 1965, George's thinking evolved toward my position, negotiations following military pressure against the North.

Watching Dean and me struggle with Vietnam, Mac Bundy made an observation I will never forget. He pointed out that the secretary of state was looking to a solution through military means and that I, the secretary of defense, was looking to negotiations. This irony said much about the deeply vexing problem we faced.

––––––

The situation in South Vietnam slipped further throughout October as Khanh's authority diminished and calls for the return of civilian government increased. Toward the end of the month, the Joint Chiefs sent me a memorandum expressing their deep concern. They proposed a new and intensified program of military action, which included U.S. air operations over both North and South Vietnam. They premised their recommendations on the unacceptability of U.S. withdrawal from South Vietnam or Southeast Asia. The chiefs felt so alarmed—and so insistent about action—that they asked me to forward their memo to the president at the earliest feasible time.[14]

I met with Bus Wheeler on November 1, 1964 to discuss their concerns. He said the chiefs felt so strongly that, if the president decided against additional military action, most of them believed the United States should withdraw from South Vietnam. Max Taylor had an entirely different view. Asked by me to comment on the chiefs' proposals, he said they amounted to a departure from the long-standing principle of the Kennedy and Johnson administrations "that the Vietnamese fight their own war in South Vietnam." Several weeks before, Westy had cabled that "unless there are reasonable prospects of a fairly effective government in South Vietnam in the immediate offing, then no amount of offensive action by the U.S. either in or outside South Vietnam has any chance by itself of reversing the deterioration now underway."[15]

Faced with such sharply conflicting advice, the president on November 2 set up a working group under Bill Bundy to review the policy alternatives yet again. The next day, LBJ won the election in what was then the greatest landslide in American history.

The Working Group started from scratch.* It conducted an exhaustive review of assumptions, premises, and options, beginning with a reassessment of our position in South Vietnam and our objectives in Southeast Asia. The process took four weeks and yielded some alarming observations. Preparing for a meeting with the president on December 1, the team wrote a draft that said in part:

> We cannot guarantee to maintain a non-Communist South Vietnam short of committing ourselves to whatever degree of military action would be required to defeat North Vietnam and probably Communist China militarily. Such a commitment would involve high risks of a major conflict in Asia, which could not be confined to air and naval action but would almost inevitably involve a Korean-scale ground action and possibly even the use of nuclear weapons at some point.

The chiefs downplayed these risks, arguing that they were "more acceptable than the alternatives of continuing the present course or withdrawal from Southeast Asia." But it was precisely such risks that President Johnson and I were determined to avoid. Our efforts to do so greatly influenced the controversial way we managed the air campaign against North Vietnam in subsequent years.[16]

Above all else, we wanted to avoid the risk of nuclear war.

The president and I were shocked by the almost cavalier way in which the chiefs and their associates, on this and other occasions,† referred to, and accepted the risk of, the possible use of nuclear weapons. Apart from the moral issues raised by nuclear strikes, initiating such action against a nuclear-equipped opponent is almost

---

*In addition to Assistant Secretary of State William Bundy, the Working Group included Vice Adm. Lloyd M. Mustin, senior operations officer of the Joint Chiefs; Harold Ford, senior China-Asia officer at CIA; and John T. McNaughton, assistant secretary of defense for international security affairs.

†See, for example, Chapter 4, p. 111; Chapter 9, p. 234; and Chapter 10, p. 275.

surely an act of suicide. I do not want to exaggerate the risks associated with the chiefs' views, but I believe that even a low risk of a
catastrophic event must be avoided. That lesson had not been
learned in 1964. I fear neither our nation nor the world has fully
learned it to this day. (Because this issue is so vitally important to our
security, I elaborate on it in the Appendix.)

The president received a progress report on November 19.
Dean told him the study group had begun to focus on three options:
(1) a negotiated settlement on any basis obtainable;* (2) a sharp
increase of military pressure on North Vietnam; and (3) an "in
between" course of increased pressure on North Vietnam with
simultaneous efforts to keep open channels of communication in
case Hanoi desired a settlement. He assured the president that we
would not allow irresistible momentum to develop for any one
option and, therefore, he would be free to make whatever decision
he believed to be in the country's best interests.

———

December 1 was sunny and cold, and the first snow of the season
had covered everything with a thin layer of white. President
Johnson had returned from Thanksgiving at the LBJ Ranch to make
decisions with his senior Vietnam advisers on the Working Group's
recommendations. The presence of Max Taylor—who had flown in
from Saigon—and Vice President Hubert Humphrey signaled the
meeting's importance. The president once again listened to laments
about South Vietnam's volatile political situation and warnings that
the country's loss would seriously undermine our containment
policy.

The Working Group presented three options (the option of a
negotiated settlement "on any basis obtainable" was not even
referred to):

*When the Joint Chiefs' representative working on the report had been asked how badly the
loss of South Vietnam would shake the faith and resolve of other non-Communist nations, he
replied succinctly: "Disastrously or worse," and added, "South Vietnam is a military keystone."

A. Continuing the present course indefinitely with little hope of avoiding defeat.

B. Undertaking a sharp, intensive bombing campaign against North Vietnam's communication lines to the South and the ninety-four targets proposed by the chiefs, with the object of forcing Hanoi to stop supporting the Vietcong and/or enter negotiations.

C. Undertaking the same bombing campaign in a graduated manner, with the same objectives but at lesser risk of a larger war.

Deep differences existed even among the military men: the chiefs favored Option B; Max preferred Option A with gradual movement to Option C; Westy wanted to keep pursuing Option A for six more months.

To complicate matters still further, the CIA had submitted its judgment on the effectiveness of bombing shortly before the meeting. It echoed the chiefs' view that North Vietnam's transportation system and industrial base lay vulnerable to aerial attack. But the CIA went on to stress that because North Vietnam's economy was overwhelmingly agricultural and largely decentralized in a myriad of villages that were essentially self-sustaining, bombing would neither create insurmountable economic problems nor inhibit Hanoi's ability to supply enough men and materiel to continue the guerrilla war in the South. The CIA also observed that North Vietnam's leaders saw the collapse of the Saigon government—and victory—as quite near. Therefore, they would likely endure substantial bombing without changing course.[17]

In retrospect, it is clear that our presentation to the president was full of holes. We failed to confront several basic questions:

• If, at the time of President Kennedy's death, we believed only the South Vietnamese themselves could win the war (and this required political stability), what made things different now?

• What was the basis for believing that a bombing program— either "intensive" or "graduated"—would force Hanoi to stop supporting the Vietcong and/or negotiate?

- Assuming North Vietnam could be forced to negotiate, what U.S. objectives might be achieved in such negotiations?
- What U.S. ground forces might Options B and C require, both to protect air bases in the South and to prevent the collapse of the South Vietnamese army while the bombing was underway?
- What U.S. casualties might each option entail?
- How would Congress and the American public react to the course we chose?

No wonder President Johnson became totally frustrated. He confronted an intractable situation. His anxiety and desperation poured out in a stream of questions and comments: "What can we do?" "Why not say, 'This is it!'?" "What resources do we have?" "If they need dollars, give 'em." "The day of reckoning is coming." "I am hesitant to sock my neighbor if my fever is 104 degrees. I want to get well first . . . so when we tell Wheeler to slap, we can take a slap back."

To this last comment, Max replied, "I doubt that Hanoi will slap back."

"Didn't MacArthur say the same just before the Chinese poured into Korea?" Johnson snapped.

The president finally decided: "I want to give Max one last chance to achieve political stability. If that doesn't work, then I'll be talking to you, General Wheeler [about bombing the North]." He conditionally approved a two-phase plan. Phase One would consist of armed reconnaissance flights against infiltration routes in Laos, along with reprisal strikes against the North Vietnamese in response to any attacks on U.S. targets. In the meantime, Max would use the prospect of Phase Two—an air campaign against North Vietnam—as an incentive for South Vietnam's leaders to put their house in order.[18]

———

So Max went back to Saigon bearing a message for the South Vietnamese generals: continued U.S. support would require political stability, and this meant the generals must stop scheming against one another and against their government. The injunction proved futile. The Saigon generals remained as fractious as ever. Shortly after Max's return, they dissolved a major arm of the government, effectively enacting another coup. Its aim appeared to be to replace civilian with military rule.

The action infuriated Max. He took it as a personal affront and demanded that the South Vietnamese leaders meet with him, then chewed them out as a drill instructor might a squad of raw recruits. Perhaps something was wrong with his French, he said sarcastically (he spoke the language fluently), for the officers had obviously not understood his injunction for stability. "You people have broken a lot of dishes, and now we have to see how we can straighten out this mess." The reprimand produced some shamefaced grins and considerable resentment toward Max, but no concrete results.

Partly in frustration, partly in desperation, Max sent Washington a year-end appraisal that said, among other things, "If worse comes to worst . . . we might seek to disengage from the present . . . relationship with the GVN [government of South Vietnam], withdrawing the bulk of our advisers. . . . By this means we might . . . disengage ourselves from an unreliable ally and give the GVN the chance to walk on its own legs and be responsible for its own stumbles."[19]

Those of us who read Max's cable failed to focus on this passage. We (and, I believe, Max too) wished to do nothing that might lead to a break in the "containment dike" as long as there appeared to be some alternative. With hindsight, it seems painfully clear the very course Max referred to—pursuing our program to the point where the South Vietnamese asked us to leave or a chaotic situation developed that forced us to withdraw our advisers—would have cost the United States far less in lives lost, resources expended, and erosion of our containment policy. It is clear that disengagement was the course we should have chosen.

We did not.

Instead, we continued to be preoccupied by the question of what military course to follow. In a personal cable to Max on

December 30, the president expressed irritation with the Joint Chiefs' repeated pleas for permission to bomb the North. "Every time I get a military recommendation," he pointedly reminded Max, "it calls for large-scale bombing. I have never felt that this war will be won from the air. . . . What is much more needed and would be more effective is . . . appropriate military strength on the ground. . . . I am ready to look with great favor on that kind of increased American effort." This suggestion for large-scale deployment of U.S. ground troops came from out of the blue.[20]

Max responded with one of the most comprehensive and thoughtful analyses we received from Saigon during the seven years I wrestled with Vietnam:

> We are faced here with a seriously deteriorating situation characterized by continued political turmoil, irresponsibility and division within the armed forces, lethargy in the pacification program, some anti-U.S. feeling which could grow, signs of mounting terrorism by VC [Vietcong] directly at U.S. personnel and deepening discouragement and loss of morale throughout SVN [South Vietnam]. Unless these conditions are somehow changed, . . . we are likely soon to face . . . installation of a hostile government which will ask us to leave while it seeks accommodation with the National Liberation Front [the Vietcong's political wing] and Hanoi. . . . There is a comparatively short time fuse on this situation.

He then turned to the question of ground combat, cautioning the president that, by a standard military rule of thumb, defeating the Vietcong would require a massive deployment of troops:

> The lack of security for the population is the result of the continued success of the VC subversive insurgency for which the foundation was laid in 1954–55 and which has since grown to present proportions [of approximately 100,000 well-trained guerrillas]. . . . It enjoys the priceless asset of a protected logistic sanctuary in the DRV and in Laos. I do not recall in history a successful anti-guerrilla campaign with less than a 10 to 1 numerical

superiority over the guerrillas and without the elimination of assistance from outside the country.

Max stressed the ratio in South Vietnam had never exceeded five to one in the past two years, and there appeared no likelihood of achieving a satisfactory ratio at any foreseeable time in the future.

He then asked rhetorically, What should we do? We could not, he observed, "change national characteristics, create leadership where it does not exist, raise large additional GVN forces or seal porous frontiers to infiltration." To get results, he believed, we would have to add a new element, and the "only one which offers any chance of the needed success in the available time . . . is the program of graduated air attacks directed against the will of the DRV" and aimed at creating "a situation favorable to talking with Hanoi." He shared the president's conviction that guerrilla war could not be won from the air. But that was not his goal. Rather, it was "to bring pressure on the will of the chiefs of the DRV." Max ended his long telegram by warning that "we are presently on a losing track and must risk a change" because "to take no positive action now is to accept defeat in the fairly near future."[21]

———

But we took no action. In early January, the Vietcong mauled two elite South Vietnamese units in major battles. Combined with intelligence reports that North Vietnamese Army regulars had begun entering the South, the defeats sharpened our fear that Hanoi and the Vietcong were preparing an all-out offensive that Saigon and its army would not be able to withstand. South Vietnam seemed on the brink of total collapse.

These events made me conclude, painfully and reluctantly, that the time had come to change course. On January 27, 1965—just one week after the inauguration—Mac and I gave President Johnson a short but explosive memorandum. We discussed it at length with him and Dean that morning in the Executive Mansion's Treaty

Room, where Abraham Lincoln had consulted his cabinet during the Civil War. Mac and I believed events were at a critical juncture, and we wanted the president to know how that affected our thinking. We told LBJ that

> both of us are now pretty well convinced that our current policy can lead only to disastrous defeat. What we are doing now, essentially, is to wait and hope for a stable government. Our December directives make it very plain that wider action against the Communists will not take place unless we can get such a government. In the last six weeks that effort has been unsuccessful, and Bob and I are persuaded that there is no real hope of success in this area unless and until our own policy and priorities change.
>
> The underlying difficulties in Saigon arise from the spreading conviction there that the future is without hope for anti-Communists. More and more the good men are covering their flanks and avoiding executive responsibility for firm anti-Communist policy. Our best friends have been somewhat discouraged by our own inactivity in the face of major attacks on our own installations. The Vietnamese know just as well as we do that the Viet Cong are gaining in the countryside. Meanwhile, they see the enormous power of the United States withheld, and they get little sense of firm and active U.S. policy. They feel that we are unwilling to take serious risks. In one sense, all of this is outrageous, in the light of all that we have done and all that we are ready to do if they will only pull up their socks. But it is a fact—or at least so McNamara and I now think.
>
> The uncertainty and lack of direction which pervade the Vietnamese authorities are also increasingly visible among our own people, even the most loyal and determined. Overtones of this sentiment appear in our cables from Saigon, and one can feel them also among our most loyal staff officers here in Washington. The basic directive says that we will not go further until there is a stable government, and no one has much hope that there is going to be a stable government while we sit still. The result is that we are pinned into a policy of first aid for squabbling politicos and passive reaction to events we do not try to control. Or so it seems.
>
> Bob and I believe that the worst course of action is to

continue in this essentially passive role which can only lead to eventual defeat and an invitation to get out in humiliating circumstances.

We see two alternatives. The *first* is to use our military power in the Far East and to force a change in Communist policy. The *second* is to deploy all our resources along a track of negotiation, aimed at salvaging what little can be preserved with no major addition to our present military risks. Bob and I tend to favor the first course, but we believe that both should be carefully studied and that alternative programs should be argued out before you.

Both of us understand the very grave questions presented by any decision of this sort. We both recognize that the ultimate responsibility is not ours. Both of us have fully supported your unwillingness, in earlier months, to move out of the middle course. We both agree that every effort should still be made to improve our operations on the ground and to prop up the authorities in South Vietnam as best we can. But we are both convinced that none of this is enough, and that the time has come for harder choices.

You should know that Dean Rusk does not agree with us. He does not quarrel with our assertion that things are going very badly and that the situation is unraveling. He does not assert that this deterioration can be stopped. What he does say is that the consequences of both escalation and withdrawal are so bad that we simply must find a way of making our present policy work. This would be good if it was possible. Bob and I do not think it is.[22]

After months of uncertainty and indecision, we had reached the fork in the road.

7

The Decision to Escalate:

January 28–July 28, 1965

The six months that followed our "fork-in-the-road" memo marked the most crucial phase of America's thirty-year involvement in Indochina. Between January 28 and July 28, 1965, President Johnson confronted the issues spelled out in our memorandum and made the fateful choices that locked the United States onto a path of massive military intervention in Vietnam, an intervention that ultimately destroyed his presidency and polarized America like nothing since the Civil War.

During this fateful period, Johnson initiated bombing of North Vietnam and committed U.S. ground forces to South Vietnam, raising the total U.S. troop strength from 23,000 to 175,000—with the likelihood of another 100,000 in 1966 and perhaps even more later. All of this occurred without adequate public disclosure or debate, planting the seeds of an eventually debilitating credibility gap.

How did it happen? Why did President Johnson fail to take the American people into his confidence? Why was General Westmoreland's military strategy not exhaustively debated? Why did we escalate rather than withdraw amid a rapidly worsening situation? Why did we fail to foresee the implications of our actions? How did domestic political forces—particularly the president's aspirations for the Great Society and pressures from ultraconservative forces in both parties—influence Vietnam policy, if at all? What hopes, fears, perceptions, and judgments—accurate and inaccurate—combined to shape our thinking and decisions?

———

The same day President Johnson received our memo, he sent Mac Bundy to Saigon to appraise the prospects for stable government there and to advise whether to initiate U.S. military action against North Vietnam. Those who leaned toward support of such action—including Mac, Max Taylor, and me—believed it would increase South Vietnam's confidence in America's willingness to fight on its behalf, thereby strengthening its morale and political structure.

The situation in Saigon confirmed Mac's worst fears: the South Vietnamese generals continued to fight among themselves and against the Buddhists; the politicians remained totally ineffectual; the religious sects persisted in their street demonstrations and protests. Mac cabled the president: "The current situation among non-Communist forces gives all the appearances of a civil war within a civil war."[1]

On the third day of Mac's visit, the Vietcong, using dynamite charges and mortar shells, attacked a South Vietnamese Army headquarters and a U.S. air base near Pleiku, about 240 miles north of Saigon. Eight American servicemen died and over 100 suffered injuries. With the support of Max and General Westmoreland, Mac promptly recommended a retaliatory air strike against North Vietnam of the kind that had been under consideration in Washington for months. The Pleiku attack and our reaction to it contributed significantly to the escalation that ensued.

As soon as the president received Mac's recommendation, he convened a National Security Council meeting attended by congressional leaders in the Cabinet Room. Although a strike against the North carried added risk because Soviet Premier Alexei Kosygin was then visiting Hanoi, almost everyone present—including Soviet specialist Tommy Thompson and George Ball—urged a response to the Vietcong attack. Only Sen. Mike Mansfield spoke forcefully against it. Looking straight at the president across the cabinet table, he cautioned that, even if Hanoi directed the attack, it should have "opened many eyes." "The local populace in South Vietnam is not behind us," Mansfield stated, or "else the Viet Cong could not have carried out their surprise attack." He urged Johnson to weigh this fact carefully, because a reprisal strike meant that America would no longer be "in a penny ante game." The president heard Mansfield out, then ordered the strike, basing his action on the authority granted by the Tonkin Gulf Resolution.[2]

Mac returned to Washington the next evening with a report that stated:

> The situation in Vietnam is deteriorating and without new U.S. action defeat appears inevitable. . . . The stakes in Vietnam are extremely high. . . . The international prestige of the United States, and a substantial part of our influence, are directly at risk in Vietnam. There is no way of unloading the burden on the Vietnamese themselves, and there is no way of negotiating ourselves out of Vietnam which offers any serious promise at present. . . . Any negotiated withdrawal today would mean surrender on the installment plan.

Mac therefore recommended a policy of graduated and sustained bombing of North Vietnam. He cited two objectives: in the long run, he hoped it would affect the North's will—moving them to reduce their support of the Vietcong and/or to negotiate; in the short run, he believed it would produce a "sharp immediate increase in optimism in the South."

Would the proposed course of action change the long-term prognosis? Mac did not promise that it would. He stressed that "the prospect in Vietnam is grim" and that "there are a host of things the Vietnamese need to do better." But "there is one grave weakness in our posture in Vietnam which is within our power to fix," he continued, "and that is a widespread belief that we do not have the will and force and patience and determination to take the necessary action and stay the course."

His final paragraph stressed a major point: "At its very best the struggle in Vietnam will be long. It seems to us important that this fundamental fact be made clear and our understanding of it be made clear to our own people."[3] As I will relate, it was not.

Mac presented his report at an NSC meeting on February 8, 1965, attended by congressional leaders. The president favored the proposed bombing program but characterized it as a step to defeat aggression "without escalating the war." At best, this was an understatement that thoroughly ignored the magnitude of the change in U.S. military operations the program entailed. Johnson knew this, but, fearing the public implications, he chose to stilt his comments and, hopefully, the comments of others: in response to a question from Sen. Everett Dirksen about what he could say to the press, Johnson urged him not to imply that the United States was seeking to "broaden the war."[4]

Although the president withheld this change in policy from the public, he sought the advice of many experienced people outside government, especially ex-President Eisenhower. He asked Lt. Gen. Andrew Goodpaster, Ike's former military assistant and, at the time, a member of the Joint Staff, to brief the former president. He also invited Eisenhower to meet with him and his senior advisers at the White House.

I attended the meeting on February 17. The president, Mac, Bus Wheeler, Andy Goodpaster, and I—all junior officers in World War II—gathered around the cabinet table for two and a half hours that afternoon to hear the general's views on the bombing decision and Vietnam generally. Ike began by saying LBJ's first duty was to contain Communism in Southeast Asia. He then stated that bombing could help achieve that objective. It would not end the infiltration, but it would help by weakening Hanoi's will to continue the war. He believed the time, therefore, had come for the president to shift from retaliatory strikes to a "campaign of pressure." When someone present—I do not remember who—said it might take a very large force—eight U.S. divisions—to prevent a Communist takeover of South Vietnam, Eisenhower stated he hoped they would not be needed; but if they were, "so be it." If the Chinese or Soviets threatened to intervene, he said, "We should pass the word back to them to take care lest dire results [i.e., nuclear strikes] occur to them."[5]

Ike's strong words were echoed in a rare and powerful personal memo from Dean Rusk to the president, in which he said, "I am convinced it would be disastrous for the United States and the Free World to permit Southeast Asia to be overrun by the Communist North." He added, "I am also convinced that everything possible should be done to throw back the Hanoi–Viet Cong aggression"— even at "the risk of major escalation." As for withdrawal, Dean wrote: "Negotiation as a cover for the abandonment of Southeast Asia to the Communist North cannot be accepted."[6]

President Johnson finally decided on February 19 that regular strikes against the North would begin, but he again refused Mac's advice to announce the decision publicly. This judgment would eventually cost him dearly. In February 1965, polls showed the American people strongly backed his Vietnam policies. When asked, "Should the U.S. continue its present efforts in South Viet-Nam, or should we pull our forces out?" 64 percent said "continue" and only 18 percent said "pull out." But these numbers changed dramatically over the next three years, as Johnson's continued lack of candor steadily diminished popular faith in his credibility and leadership.[7]

Why did President Johnson refuse to take the American people into his confidence? Some point to his innate secretiveness, but the answer is far more complex. Two factors in particular influenced him. One was his obsession with securing Congress's approval and financing of his Great Society agenda; he wanted nothing to divert attention and resources from his cherished domestic reforms. The other was his equally strong fear of hard-line pressure (from conservatives in both parties) for greater—and far riskier—military action that might trigger responses, especially nuclear, by China and/or the

Soviet Union. The president coped with his dilemma by obscuring it—an unwise and ultimately self-defeating course.

President Johnson's fears about failure in Vietnam made him accept bombing, overriding whatever hesitation he still harbored about South Vietnam's instability.*[8] As a result, sustained U.S. bombing of North Vietnam, kept secret from the American public, finally began on March 2. On that day over 100 aircraft launched from carriers in the South China Sea and air bases in South Vietnam struck an ammunition depot in North Vietnam. Operation Rolling Thunder, as the air program came to be known, had begun. It would continue for three years and drop more bombs on Vietnam than had been dropped on all of Europe in World War II.

————

Wars generate their own momentum and follow the law of unanticipated consequences. Vietnam proved no exception. President Johnson's authorization of Operation Rolling Thunder not only started the air war but unexpectedly triggered the introduction of U.S. troops into ground combat as well.

As preparation for U.S. air strikes accelerated in February, Westy sought ground forces to protect the bases from which the strikes were launched. He began by requesting two marine battalions for Da Nang. This request startled and alarmed Max. While he had urged an air campaign, he had strenuously opposed ground deployments, and he immediately cabled Washington, urging a rejection of Westy's request. As Max later put it: "Once you put that first soldier ashore, you never know how many others are going to follow him."[9] But the need appeared pressing and the commitment small, and besides, how could the president decline a field

*Nothing could banish those fears, including George Ball's October 5, 1964, memorandum, which, as I have said, George passed to the president through Bill Moyers on February 24, and Johnson asked to be discussed on February 26. It had been overtaken by a second memo George submitted on February 13 (which Mac, Tommy Thompson, and I endorsed), advocating bombing as a means to "increase United States bargaining power . . . to the point where a satisfactory political solution" became possible. In view of Ike's comments, Dean's memo, and the change in George's position, the result was preordained before the February 26 meeting.

commander's petition for ground troops to protect the lives of U.S. airmen? Johnson approved Westy's request.

Some have argued that Westy and the Joint Chiefs had much larger deployments in mind—what one scholar has called a "foot-in-the-door" strategy—when they first requested U.S. Marines to guard South Vietnamese airfields launching Rolling Thunder strikes. By implication, they suggest Westy and the chiefs concealed from the president and me a clear intention to start with small troop deployments, knowing this would inevitably lead to more.[10]

I am not persuaded. All of us should have anticipated the need for U.S. ground forces when the first combat aircraft went to South Vietnam—but we did not. The problem lay not in any attempt to deceive but rather in a signal and costly failure to foresee the implications of our actions. Had we done so, we might have acted differently.

It should also be noted that at that time the Joint Chiefs remained deeply split among themselves over the proper strategy to follow in Vietnam. Although they unanimously endorsed the air campaign in a February 11 memo to me, Gen. Bruce Palmer, Jr.— then army vice chief of staff—later observed that

> the Army did not agree that bombing North Vietnam would produce the desired results, and the Navy wasn't too sure about it. It was the Air Force and the Marine Corps that were the tough proponents of air power. It was General Wheeler who talked the other Chiefs into submitting an agreed paper on the theory that if we submitted a split paper this would hand over a basic military judgment to the Secretary of Defense and put him in a difficult spot of having to make the decision, him and the President.

"Where I fault ourselves," Palmer added, referring to army policy makers, "was to agree in a JCS decision to go ahead and try these things anyway . . . to 'see' if they could work."[11]

Westy later said he, too, had been opposed to sustained bombing before the introduction of U.S. ground forces. "I frankly did not support the bombing campaign, in principle, until actually '66 when

I had . . . enough troops to protect ourselves." He agreed to Rolling Thunder not because he believed it would significantly affect the North's will or its ability to resupply the South but rather because of its expected boost to South Vietnamese morale.[12]

Senior army officers and field commanders proved far more realistic about the potential of airpower in Vietnam than did senior air commanders. For their part, senior air force generals and navy admirals were probably equally realistic about the limitations of ground operations. Each could see clearly the weaknesses of the other but was unable to realize their own limitations. I shared each group's skepticism, but I did not sense—nor was I made aware of— the important and revealing divisions among them. These divisions were therefore never fully debated at the highest level. They should have been.

The president had always been skeptical of what bombing could accomplish. He wanted to see more ground progress in South Vietnam. On March 2, he ordered Army Chief of Staff Gen. Harold K. Johnson to Saigon to appraise the situation and tell him what more needed to be done.

He sent the best. "HK" Johnson had survived the Bataan Death March and endured three years of deprivation and suffering as a Japanese prisoner of war in World War II. From those experiences he had developed an iron will, extraordinary toughness of mind and spirit, and a fierce integrity.*

*Such qualities made him typical of what I saw and admired in so many other senior U.S. military leaders with whom I served: Max Taylor, Bus Wheeler, Westy Westmoreland, George Brown, Larry Norstad, Dave Shoup, Arleigh Burke, Dave McDonald, Andy Goodpaster, and many, many more. These men were not—and their successors today are not—what they are so often portrayed to be by those who simply do not know the military: trigger-happy war-mongers. Oliver Stone's fanciful movie *JFK,* for example, includes a scene in which President Johnson, during the 1964 campaign, is made to say, in effect: "Gentlemen, you give me my election and I will give you your war."

Such a scene is disgraceful. These men put their lives—and the lives of the men they felt responsible for and led into battle—at risk for all of us. To suggest that military leaders want war is to misunderstand what motivates them. As I make clear throughout this book, I never hesitated to disagree with the Joint Chiefs when I thought them parochial in vision or wrong in judgment; but I never forgot that they—and the soldiers, sailors, and airmen of all ranks they commanded—were motivated by a deep and noble desire to serve their country, and a willingness to sacrifice their lives if necessary to achieve that end.

General Johnson heard a grim assessment when he reached Saigon. Max told him the "basic unresolved problem" remained inadequate security for the South Vietnamese people; this problem derived, in large part, from our inability to achieve numerical superiority of even five-to-one over the Vietcong, whereas recent successful counterinsurgency operations—as in the Philippines and Malaya—suggested the need for numerical superiority of ten- or even twenty-to-one. Westy recommended the United States take "whatever measures . . . necessary to postpone indefinitely the day of collapse."

So, not surprisingly, when General Johnson prepared his report, it included a recommendation for more ground troops. Among other things, he proposed expanding the air campaign against North Vietnam; creating a multinational anti-infiltration force along the Demilitarized Zone (DMZ); and deploying a U.S. Army division, approximately 16,000 soldiers, near Saigon or in the central highlands to the north of the city.

The president and I met with General Johnson and the other chiefs at the White House on March 15 to review his report. At the meeting, General Johnson estimated it could take 500,000 U.S. troops five years to win the war.[13] His estimate shocked not just the president and me but the other chiefs as well. None of us had been thinking in anything approaching such terms.

———

About this time another incident occurred which, though unrelated to the war, underscores the vital point that all of us struggling with Vietnam—but most of all the president—faced a hundred other problems every day. On March 17, the Reverend Martin Luther King, Jr., and his followers won a federal court order allowing them to march, unobstructed and unmolested, from Selma to Montgomery, Alabama, to protest black disfranchisement in the South. We had received intelligence reports that they would be confronted by violent mobs of white racists. Alabama Gov. George Wallace, who had received the same reports, refused state protection for the marchers.

I told President Johnson he must exercise his powers as commander in chief to federalize the Alabama National Guard, thereby removing it from Governor Wallace's "do-nothing" control. The president flatly refused.

When I strenuously objected, he said, "That's what's wrong with you, Bob. You just don't understand politics. Most Alabamians will be so incensed by any violence resulting from Wallace's failure to act that they will dump him come the next election. That's what I want."

"I want to dump Wallace just as much as you do," I told him, "but I don't want to see scores—if not hundreds—of people injured or killed in the process."

Reluctantly Johnson gave in.

The historic march from Selma to Montgomery took place March 21–24, 1965. Federalized troops and U.S. marshals along the route greatly reduced incidents of violence, although one march participant, Viola Liuzzo, died from gunshots fired at her car.

The night after the march, I arrived home from the Pentagon about 9:00 P.M., tired and hungry, to find our oldest child, Margy, awaiting me. She had come home from college to spend a holiday with her mother and me. Delighted to see her, I asked if she had had a pleasant trip home.

"Oh, Daddy, it was horrible!" she said. "I spent thirty-three hours on a bus."

"Why in God's name did you do that?" I asked.

"I joined Martin Luther King to march from Selma to Montgomery." I immediately dialed LBJ and said, "Mr. President, I know how you agonized over the decision to federalize the Alabama Guard. But knowing how much you love Margy, I am sure you will realize now you were right. She was one of the marchers!"

————

The divisions over Vietnam remained deep. They fell into several categories. Some continued to advocate bombing the North. Others believed resolution of the conflict required winning in the South.

Still others came to believe the war could not be won, and the United States must therefore pursue negotiations. It would be misleading to oversimplify the story by categorizing individuals whose positions shifted back and forth over time, but it would not be incorrect simply to say that we, as a government, failed to address the fundamental issues or to solve the problem.

Our actions during the spring and summer of 1965 demonstrated that point as we dealt with repeated requests for additional troops. On March 17, Westy sought another marine battalion for base security at Da Nang. Oley Sharp requested still another battalion on March 19. The following day the Joint Chiefs submitted their own plan. Fearing the war was being lost, they pressed for the deployment of a marine division to the northern provinces and an army division to the central highlands for offensive operations. A decision loomed on major new deployments.[14]

We met at the White House on April 1. Dean, Mac, and I questioned the wisdom of the chiefs' proposal. Anti-American sentiment lay just beneath the surface in South Vietnam, and committing large numbers of U.S. troops risked igniting it. The president accepted our judgment. He deferred the chiefs' proposal but agreed to Westy's and Oley's two-battalion request and, much more important, agreed to change the marines' mission from base security to active combat. While we scaled down troop deployments, we broadened their mission significantly. American ground forces would now directly enter the war.[15]

The president's agreement to commit more U.S. troops to the South and to change their mission—without at the same time intensifying U.S. air strikes against the North—troubled John McCone. At an NSC meeting (and in a memo to Dean, Mac, Max, and me) the next day, McCone urged significantly expanding the bombing program, arguing that the present program would not force Hanoi to change its policy.

I agreed that we could not force the Vietcong and North Vietnamese to change their policy through the present bombing program alone. The Joint Chiefs—with one or two exceptions—

also believed that bombing, by itself, would not force a change. Bombing would only work, they agreed, if accompanied by actions in the South that convinced the Vietcong and North Vietnamese they could not win. Doing that would require increasing numbers of U.S. ground troops to supplement the South Vietnamese Army's flagging efforts.

McCone did not accept this view. He thought we could effect a change through bombing. I believed we could not—short of genocide, which neither he nor anyone else recommended.[16] When Mac prepared a directive reporting the president's April 1 decisions to the concerned government departments, Johnson instructed him to write that "premature publicity [should] be avoided by all possible precautions. The actions themselves should be taken in ways that should minimize any appearance of sudden changes in policy. . . . The President's desire is that these movements and changes should be understood as being gradual and wholly con- sistent with existing policy."[17]

Dean, George, Max, and I all testified before congressional com- mittees in the days that followed. Each of us assured our listeners that President Johnson, in George's words, had "every intention of keeping in the closest consultation with the Congress on all moves of this kind." But statements like these only enlarged the adminis- tration's growing credibility gap.

As U.S. military action increased, a political resolution of the Viet- namese war remained much on our minds. On March 6, Mac had reported to the president on a discussion with Dean and me the night before:

> Two of the three of us [referring to himself and me] think that the chances of a turnaround in South Vietnam remain less than even. . . . There remains a real question in our minds as to how much we should open the door to a readiness for "talks." This is a point on which both Dean, and Bob especially, are quite concerned. They

both feel, for somewhat different reasons, that it is important to show that we are ready to talk about Vietnam—always on our own terms—in all appropriate international channels. . . . But Bob goes a lot further. He believes that we should find a way to have real talks in an international meeting. (I think his motivation is that we will need a conference table if things go worse, as he expects.)[18]

Mac accurately conveyed my concern. At this point in 1965, I believed we should make every possible effort to spark negotiations leading to an end to the conflict. This remained my position until I left the Pentagon three years later.

Two negotiating proposals existed by early April. United Nations Secretary-General U Thant proposed a three-month ceasefire across the border between North and South Vietnam, and seventeen non-aligned nations called for negotiations "without preconditions." President Johnson dismissed the former but responded to the latter in a major speech at Johns Hopkins University on April 7.

In this speech, he broadcast his readiness for unconditional discussions. At the same time, he emphasized, "We will not be defeated. We will not grow tired. We will not withdraw, either openly or under the cloak of a meaningless agreement. . . . And we must be prepared for a long continued conflict." Seeking to coax the Vietcong and North Vietnamese into a settlement, he then outlined a billion-dollar development plan for Southeast Asia, which he said was "within the reach of a cooperative and determined effort."[19]

Hanoi quickly denounced the speech and advanced their own, "Four Points" peace formula, which remained their basis for settlement throughout the conflict. They proposed that we recognize the Vietnamese people's basic national rights, including the right to live without foreign troops; that Vietnam's two "zones" abstain from any foreign military alliances pending reunification; and that reunification be settled by the Vietnamese people in both zones. All of this we could accept. But the final point—that "the internal affairs of South Vietnam must be settled by the South Vietnamese people themselves *in accordance with* the program of the South Vietnam National Front for Liberation [emphasis added]"—proved the crux of dispute. Accepting it meant accepting Communist control of South Vietnam.

———

Meanwhile, the Joint Chiefs, CINCPAC, Westy, and I all continued to react on a day-to-day basis to the gathering force of events when we—and especially I, as secretary—should have been far more forceful in developing a military strategy and a long-term plan for the force structure required to carry it out.

On April 6, the CIA informed President Johnson that Hanoi had infiltrated a North Vietnamese Army battalion into the central highlands and other regular units near Da Nang. The chiefs responded to these moves by requesting deployment of two more brigades (approximately 8,000 men) to South Vietnam. Westy seconded their proposal, but Max did not. Learning of the request only after it had been made, he fired off an angry cable to the White House, saying, "It shows a far greater willingness to get into the ground war than I had discerned in Washington during my recent trip."[20]

With the situation deteriorating and feeling something more must be done, the president leaned toward approving the chiefs' proposal. Because of Max's concern, however, he asked me to meet in Honolulu with Max and other senior officials to review the proposed deployments.

We did so on April 20, 1965. Sitting around a large conference table beneath a bank of clocks at Pacific Command Headquarters, we began by discussing the bombing program against North Vietnam. A few days earlier, Max had expressed his view when he cabled Dean: "No amount of bombardment . . . is going to convince Hanoi to call off its action . . . without real progress in South Vietnam against the VC. Hanoi must be convinced that the VC cannot win here."

Quite simply, he said bombing could not do the job alone. I

shared this conclusion then, I continued to share it during my remaining time as secretary and—as I will comment later—I have seen, read, and heard nothing in subsequent years that leads me to change my view. Although one or two of the Joint Chiefs disagreed with me (and my position later generated intense controversy) everyone at the meeting—Max, Westy, Bus, Oley, Bill Bundy, and John McNaughton—agreed that bombing alone was not the answer.

We turned our attention, therefore, to what could be done in the South. General agreement existed on the need for more U.S. forces to prevent Saigon's collapse. But how many? Pursuing what strategy? With what effect? Here, significant disagreement emerged. Bus, Oley, and Westy renewed the request for two divisions, plus the two brigades Max had resisted, and they added the requirement for logistical support forces. The total troops involved came to approximately 60,000 men. With Max's support, I opposed the two divisions—there had been no clear explanation of how they would be used—but I agreed to support the other requests. This meant a marked increase in U.S. strength in Vietnam, from 33,000 to 82,000.[21]

I presented my recommendations to the president at a Cabinet Room meeting on April 21. I urged him to approve the deployments promptly, in order to bolster South Vietnam against an expected Communist offensive while preventing "a spectacular defeat of GVN [South Vietnamese] or U.S. forces." I knew these larger deployments, coupled with the troops' new combat mission, meant inevitably higher casualties and closer public attention to the war. I therefore urged President Johnson to inform congressional leaders about both the "contemplated deployments" and the recent "change in mission of U.S. forces in Vietnam."[22] But the president did not want to do so, and when he cabled to Max his approval of the Honolulu recommendations, he stated: "It is not our intention to announce the whole program now but rather to announce individual deployments at appropriate times." Shortly after, in early May, he presented a supplemental appropriation request to

Congress, saying: "This is not a routine appropriation. . . . Each member of Congress who supports this request is also voting to persist in our effort to halt communist aggression in South Viet Nam." The bill passed 408–7 in the House and 88–3 in the Senate.[23]

———

George Ball, who also attended the April 21 meeting, responded to the Honolulu recommendations with a plea that we "should not take such a hazardous leap into space without exploring the possibilities of a settlement." The president replied, "All right, George, I'll give you until tomorrow to get me a settlement plan. If you can pull a rabbit out of the hat, I'm all for it."[24]

Ball submitted a settlement plan to the president that night. He began it by saying, "We must be prepared for a settlement that falls somewhere short of the goals we have publicly stated, but that still meets our basic objectives [i.e., an independent South Vietnam, not under Communist control]." None of us—the president, Dean, Mac, or I—disagreed with that position. But, again, George's paper failed to show how to achieve the objectives we all sought.

George said we should not accept a coalition government of the Laotian type but that we should permit Vietcong members to campaign in free elections. He added, "We could not, of course, agree to any arrangement worked out on these terms without insisting that the Viet Cong units in the South be broken up and that the Viet Cong be absorbed into the national life of the country." The president, Dean, Mac, and I agreed with all of this as well. But George did not spell out how to achieve "free elections," given North Vietnam's insistence that a settlement must be "in accordance with the program of the South Vietnam National Front for Liberation." Nor did he show how to achieve the other objectives he recommended.[25]

What George *did* recommend—and we perhaps failed to implement properly—was to ask intermediaries (e.g., Sweden, the Soviets, the seventeen nonaligned nations) to make clear to Hanoi that we would accept the position he had outlined. We made one contact with a North Vietnamese representative in Paris within a matter of weeks. We attempted many other contacts over the next three years. But we failed to utilize all possible channels and to convey our position clearly.

A few days later, I asked John McNaughton to draft a one-week bombing pause proposal. I hoped it might trigger a sequence of actions leading Hanoi either to negotiate or to reduce its support of the insurgency, while bolstering domestic and international support for the administration's policy. Like all of my subsequent pause proposals, it provoked considerable controversy. Many senior military leaders opposed it because they feared North Vietnam would exploit it to boost infiltration. Some of the president's advisers feared Hanoi would entrap us by offering to negotiate provided the pause continued, thus allowing North Vietnam to maintain, or even increase, its support of the Vietcong under the cover of a bombing suspension. Still others feared U.S. right-wingers would brand it an act of weakness and demand heavier bombing if it failed to produce quick results.

But criticism of President Johnson's Vietnam policy among liberal intellectuals and members of Congress had grown markedly in recent weeks, and, irked, Johnson sought to answer and still it if possible. It was this—rather than any personal faith that a pause at this stage would spark negotiations—that led him to accept my proposal.

In any event, an unpublicized pause began on May 13. That same day our ambassador to Moscow, Foy Kohler, was instructed to deliver a message to his North Vietnamese counterpart. It read: "The United States Government has taken account of the repeated suggestions . . . by Hanoi representatives that there can be no progress toward peace while there are air attacks on North Viet-Nam. . . . The United States will be very watchful to see whether in this period of pause there are significant reductions in . . . armed actions by [Vietcong and North Vietnamese] forces."[26] Hanoi's ambassador refused to see Kohler. A lower-ranking American diplomat hand-delivered the message to the North Vietnamese embassy that evening. It was returned, without comment, the next morning in a plain white envelope marked "Embassy of US of A."

Feeling rebuffed and still fearing right-wing criticism, the president indicated his intention to resume bombing at a White House meeting on May 16. I urged a delay, believing we should follow the original plan for a seven-day pause to give Hanoi more time to consider how to respond. But the president felt that Hanoi, if interested, should have responded by now. We finally compromised on six days. Bombing resumed on May 18.

———

The next three weeks marked a period of increasing frustration and anxiety for the president and those of us advising him. Political instability in South Vietnam intensified—if that was possible. Catholics and Buddhists in and out of the military plotted against the civilian government of Phan Huy Quat. One coup barely had failed before another hatched by young South Vietnamese officers succeeded. They installed Army Gen. Nguyen Van Thieu—forty-two years old—as chief of state and Air Force Gen. Nguyen Cao Ky—thirty-five years old—as prime minister. Deputy Ambassador Alex Johnson described Ky as an "unguided missile." He was. He drank, gambled, and womanized heavily. He dressed ostentatiously; often when I saw him he sported a zippered black flying suit belted with twin pearl-handled revolvers. He also made extreme statements: when asked by a journalist whom he most admired, he replied, "I admired Hitler. . . . We need four or five Hitlers in Vietnam." Bill Bundy characterized Ky and Thieu in hindsight as "the bottom of the barrel, absolutely the bottom of the barrel!"[27]

Meanwhile, a growing realization of bombing's ineffectiveness intensified the pressure to expand the ground war. On June 3, Max cabled Washington: "We should . . . make very clear that we do not believe that any feasible amount of bombing is of itself likely to cause the DRV [North Vietnam] to cease and desist its actions in the south. Such a change in DRV attitudes can probably be brought about only when . . . there is also a conviction on their part that the tide has turned or soon will turn against them in the south."[28]

Two days later, he sent another cable describing a South Vietnamese Army plagued by poor leadership and desertions and racing toward collapse. Having opposed a U.S. combat role in the South for months, Max now wrote with grim resignation, "It will probably be necessary to commit U.S. ground forces to action."[29]

Dean, Mac, Bill, George, Tommy Thompson, and I gathered in Dean's office on Saturday afternoon, June 5, to discuss Max's message. Suddenly and unexpectedly the president walked in. He clearly was lonely. Lady Bird was away, he said, and he had come over for some company. What he got instead was a cold shower.

He read Max's telegram with growing anxiety. Dean tried to be hopeful, but I said, "We're looking for no more than a stalemate in the South. Can we achieve it? I don't know. The communists still think they're winning."

The president listened. He seemed troubled and pensive. "The great danger," he concluded darkly, "is we'll pick up a very big problem any day."[30]

How right he was.

The bombshell exploded on June 7. On that day, Westy sent a cable to the Pentagon that stated:

> The conflict in Southeast Asia is in the process of moving to a higher level. Some PAVN [North Vietnamese] forces have entered SVN [South Vietnam] and more may well be on the way. . . . So far the VC have not employed their full capabilities in this campaign. . . . ARVN [South Vietnamese Army] forces on the other hand are already experiencing difficulty in coping with this increased VC capability. Desertion rates are inordinately high. Battle losses have been higher than expected. . . . As a result, ARVN troops are beginning to show signs of reluctance to assume the offensive and in some cases their steadfastness under fire is coming into doubt. . . . The force ratios continue to change in favor of the VC. . . . The GVN cannot stand up successfully to

this kind of pressure without reinforcement. . . . I see no course of action open to us except to reinforce our efforts in SVN with additional U.S. or third country forces as rapidly as is practical during the critical weeks ahead. . . . The basic purpose of the additional deployments recommended . . . is to give us a substantial and hard hitting offensive capability on the ground to convince the VC that they cannot win.

Westy said he needed 41,000 more combat troops now and another 52,000 later. This would increase total U.S. strength from 82,000 to 175,000. The last paragraph of his cable read: "Studies must continue and plans developed to deploy even greater forces, if and when required." His request meant a dramatic and open-ended expansion of American military involvement.[31]

Of the thousands of cables I received during my seven years in the Defense Department, this one disturbed me most. We were forced to make a decision. We could no longer postpone a choice about which path to take. The issue would hang over all of us like a menacing cloud for the next seven weeks.

———

We began our deliberations in the Oval Office the next morning. South Vietnam seemed to be crumbling rapidly, with the only apparent antidote a massive injection of U.S. troops. "We're in a hell of a mess," I told the others. But, like them, I did not know how to solve it.[32]

Our discussion continued on June 10. Someone—I do not recall who—began by saying, "The American people feel we are withholding information." I shared this thought. We had long gotten "behind the curve" of public opinion.

The president peppered us with various questions, among them:

Q. Would U.S. forces beyond 175,000 be needed?
A. That seemed the most that could be used effectively to backstop ARVN.

Q. How do we extricate ourselves?
A. Hope for a settlement lay in stalemating the Vietcong and keeping the North under pressure.

Q. What should be our objective?
A. Some said stalemate. Others saw our goal as self-determination for South Vietnam.

Q. Had we left any stone unturned on the negotiating front?
A. Opening contact with the Vietcong. But this risked a heavy blow to Saigon morale and promised little hope of success. Dean believed dealing with the Vietcong really meant a cover for defeat.

Q. Did the May bombing pause produce any adverse effects?
A. Little in Saigon. It killed off one point used by critics. But the outcry both at home and abroad remained: Where are we heading? Mac and I recommended more explanation, urging the president to make clear what he intended to do through a major speech.

During the meeting, the president directed that Westy be asked what military strategy and tactics should be followed; how the Vietcong and North Vietnamese would respond; how many casualties the United States would suffer; what responses could be expected to U.S. actions, and when they would occur. The lack of answers to such questions handicapped our decision making in the months ahead.[33]

The force of events, quickening by the day, deepened my concern about the potential extent of our involvement. In a telephone conversation with President Johnson that evening, I told him, "In the back of my mind, I have a very definite limitation on commitment in mind, and I don't think the chiefs do. In fact, I know they don't."

"Do you think that [Westy's request] is just the next step with them up the ladder?" he asked.

"Yes," I said. "They hope they don't have to go any further. But Westmoreland outlines in his cable the step beyond it. And he doesn't say that's the last."[34]

In the midst of this uncertainty and chaos, I met the press on June 16. When asked, "Do you foresee a build-up beyond the 70,000 to 75,000 man level?" I replied, "The Secretary of State and I and the President have repeatedly said that we will do whatever is necessary to achieve our objective in South Vietnam. . . . I can only give that answer to your question." When asked, "What is the overall American strategy?" I said, "Our objective, our strategy is to convince the North Vietnamese that their Communist-inspired, directed, and supported guerrilla action to overthrow the established government in the South cannot be achieved, and then to negotiate for the future peace and security of that country."[35]

On the same day, Andy Goodpaster went to Eisenhower's Gettysburg farmhouse at LBJ's direction to brief the former president on Westy's troop request. Ike's advice was simple and direct: the United States had now "appealed to force" in Vietnam and therefore "we have got to win." Westy's request should be approved.

President Johnson read polls the next afternoon that showed a public prepared for further action. Sixty-five percent approved his handling of the war; 47 percent favored sending more troops. This was double those "not sure" (23 percent); two and a half times those wishing to "keep the present number" (19 percent); and more than quadruple those wanting to "take troops out" (11 percent).[36]

But the president knew how quickly the public could change. He told me on June 21:

I think that in time . . . it's going to be difficult for us to very long prosecute effectively a war that far away from home with the divisions that we have here and particularly the potential divisions. And it's really had me concerned for a month and I'm very depressed about it because I see no program from either Defense or State that gives me much hope of doing anything except just praying and grasping to hold on during [the] monsoon [season] and hope they'll quit. And I don't believe they're ever goin' to quit. And I don't see . . . that we have any . . . plan for victory militarily or diplomatically. . . . Russell* thinks we ought to take one of these [regime] changes to get out of there. I do not think we can get out of there with our treaty like it is and with what all we've said and I think it would just lose us face in the world and I just shudder to think what all of 'em would say.[37]

The president felt tortured. I sensed it, and others did as well. Henry Graff, a Columbia University historian who interviewed Johnson during these days, later wrote that the president told him he spent many sleepless nights thinking about how he would feel "if my President told me that my children had to go to South Vietnam in a Marine company . . . and possibly die."[38]

Lyndon Johnson often resorted to theatrics, and cynics will say his words reflected such behavior. But they did not. No president I have known who exercises his authority to send Americans into harm's way feels otherwise. I shared the president's feelings.

Decisions were deferred as we groped for the least bad road to follow. While the debate raged, reporters pressed Johnson about recent Senate requests for further congressional action—going beyond the Tonkin Gulf Resolution—before he deployed more U.S. troops. He deflected the questioners by saying, "Anybody [who] has read the resolution" could see it authorized the president "to take all—all—all necessary measures" he thought necessary in the situation.[39]

The president's comments followed advice he had received from Senator Mansfield (who opposed more troops) and Senator Dirksen (who supported reinforcements). Both had urged him not to resurrect the issue with Congress because both feared it would tear the nation apart; whichever way the vote went, it would hurt the war effort. That was the answer Johnson wanted to hear, but it was the wrong answer. There is no "right" moment to obtain popular

*Richard B. Russell (D-Ga.), Johnson's old Senate mentor and powerful chairman of the Senate Armed Services Committee.

consent for military action through a vote of Congress. Debate will always arise over how and when to do so. The fact is it *must* be done—even if a divisive vote risks giving aid and comfort to our adversary. We did not do it, and we would learn the hard way that a government must accept that risk in order to lead a united country into war and maintain support. Instead of working toward unity, we chose to sweep the debate under the Oval Office carpet. Are we wiser today?

————

We remained in constant turmoil over Vietnam between mid-June and mid-July. Every few days we received a message from Max or Westy reporting further deterioration in Saigon's situation or presenting further arguments for more troops. We attended one meeting after another. I spent countless hours with the Joint Chiefs in "The Tank" debating Westy's shifting plans and requirements. Bill Bundy and his associates continually reviewed diplomatic alternatives. And the president examined every facet of this complex and difficult problem with varying combinations of his senior advisers almost daily.

On June 18, George Ball sent the president another eloquently argued memorandum. As had been the case with his October 1964 memo, it too, had not been analyzed and debated by senior officials in either the State or the Defense Department. Initially, it was sent only to the president and Dean; except for the secretary, no one in the State Department received a copy, not even Bill Bundy. George urged the president to limit additional deployments to "no more" than 100,000—a level very similar to the total of 95,000 I had proposed on June 10. However, the South Vietnamese Army's mounting losses and Westy's recommendations soon pushed Dean and us beyond the 100,000 level. Therefore, when George at a meeting on June 23 suggested holding at the 100,000 level and, if this forced us out of South Vietnam, retreating to Thailand and trying to hold there, Dean and I strongly objected. We doubted Thailand could stand if South Vietnam fell. I urged approval of

Westy's troop request but also more extensive negotiating efforts than had yet been made.

Faced with such disagreement, the President asked George and me to develop our separate proposals in detail. He gave us a week.[40]

We immediately set about our task. As George did so, he made a significant shift: up to this time, he had advocated limiting, not refusing, further deployments; exploring, not urging, disengagement. But no more. Rather than try to hold in South Vietnam, George now concluded we must "cut our losses" as soon as possible by making whatever deal we could with North Vietnam. Bill Bundy could not accept this and began preparing a third paper laying out a "middle way"—i.e., holding the line with the present level of about 85,000 U.S. troops.

While working on my paper, I received another disquieting cable from Westy. It pointed to a long and costly war requiring increasing numbers of American troops, including substantially more forces in 1966 than he had previously implied. After discussing it with the Joint Chiefs, I prepared a draft on June 26 incorporating Westy's views that I circulated to Dean, Mac, George, and Bill, soliciting their comments.

My memo centered on the idea that U.S. and South Vietnamese military strength should be increased "enough to prove to the VC that they cannot win and thus to turn the tide of the war." Westy estimated this would require a total of 175,000 U.S. troops in 1965 (and an undetermined number more in 1966). I therefore recommended that figure. I accompanied this recommendation with proposals for expanded military action against North Vietnam and expanded diplomatic initiatives designed to open a dialogue with Hanoi, Beijing, and the Vietcong. I concluded with an "estimate of success," which said:

> The success of this program from a military point of view turns on whether the increased effort stems the tide in the South; that in turn depends on two things—on whether the South Vietnamese

hold their own in terms of numbers and fighting spirit, and on whether the U.S. forces can be effective in a quick reaction reserve role, a role in which they have not been tested. The number of U.S. troops is too small to make a significant difference in the traditional 10:1 government-guerrilla formula, but it is not too small to make a significant difference in the kind of war which seems to be evolving in Vietnam—a . . . conventional war in which it is easier to identify, locate and attack the enemy.[41]

My draft shocked Mac, who replied with a memo "designed to raise questions and not to answer them." And raise questions he did. "My first reaction," he wrote, "is that this program [a doubling of presently planned U.S. strength in South Vietnam, a tripling of air effort against North Vietnam, and a new and very important program of naval quarantine] is rash to the point of folly." He presciently raised a question that later proved fundamental: "Is there any real prospect that U.S. regular forces can conduct the anti-guerrilla operations which would probably remain the central problem in South Vietnam?" He referred to former President Eisenhower's statement that it was the prospect of nuclear attack that had brought an armistice in Korea and suggested we "at least consider what realistic threat of larger action is available to us for communication to Hanoi." He ended with the question "Do we want to invest 200 thousand men to cover an eventual retreat? Can we not do that just as well where we are?"[42]

Except for Mac's reference to nuclear weapons, and the implication that we should consider threatening their use, I shared all his views and concerns. But the challenge was to lay out the answers—not just the questions. The three papers (George's, Bill's, and mine) went to the White House the night of July 1. But to them was added—unbeknownst to me and I believe unbeknownst to George and Bill—one more.

As I have indicated, Dean rarely wrote the president, and I had never known him to do so on a matter relating to military matters without informing me. In this case he did, in order to express his deepest convictions and his greatest fears, which he clearly did not believe George's paper addressed. I want to quote Dean's exact words, because his view—that if we lost South Vietnam, we increased the risk of World War III—influenced others of us to varying degrees as well. He wrote:

> The integrity of the U.S. commitment is the principal pillar of peace throughout the world. If that commitment becomes unreliable, the communist world would draw conclusions that would lead to our ruin and *almost certainly to a catastrophic war*. So long as the South Vietnamese are prepared to fight for themselves, we cannot abandon them without disaster to peace and to our interests throughout the world [emphasis added].[43]

The reader may find it incomprehensible that Dean foresaw such dire consequences from the fall of South Vietnam, but I cannot overstate the impact our generation's experiences had on him (and, more or less, on all of us). We had lived through appeasement at Munich; years of military service during World War II fighting aggression in Europe and Asia; the Soviet takeover of Eastern Europe; repeated threats to Berlin, including that of August 1961; the Cuban Missile Crisis of 1962; and, most recently, Communist Chinese statements that the South Vietnam conflict typified "wars of liberation," which they saw spreading across the globe. George's memo failed to address these underlying concerns, and President Johnson turned away from it.

Mac forwarded the four papers to the president with a covering memo of his own. In it, he shifted his position from the thoughts expressed to me the day before. "My hunch," he wrote, "is that you will want to listen hard to George Ball and then reject his proposal. Discussion could then move to the narrower choice between my brother's course and McNamara's."[44]

We met with the president the following day. He seemed deeply torn over what to do. After much discussion, he ended the meeting by asking me to visit Saigon once again to analyze further military requirements with Max and Westy. He sent Averell Harriman to Moscow to explore reconvening the Geneva Conference (a mission

I strongly supported). And he directed George to examine opening direct contact with Hanoi's representative in Paris (another move toward negotiation that I also applauded).[45]

The latter contact, code-named XYZ, opened in August and involved secret talks in Paris between former U.S. Foreign Service officer Edmund Gullion and Mai Van Bo of North Vietnam. Gullion probed the meaning of Hanoi's public and private statements to determine if there was a chance for substantive negotiations. After potentially encouraging early talks, North Vietnam abruptly closed the channel during September.

In the midst of the July debates, the president brought to Washington a bipartisan group of elder statesmen who became known as the Wise Men. He called on this group, whose composition differed somewhat from one gathering to another, several times. On this occasion, he asked it to review the war's progress and advise him on how to proceed.

The Wise Men comprised an impressive group with knowledge, experience, and prestige. On this occasion, they included Dean Acheson, a major architect of U.S. foreign policy during the early Cold War as secretary of state to President Truman; retired five-star Gen. Omar Bradley, another panel member, radiated the quiet, cool professionalism of America's military establishment; John Cowles, liberal Republican publisher of the *Minneapolis Star and Tribune* and *Look* magazine, exemplified the internationalism of leading U.S. newspapers and journals; attorney and diplomat Arthur Dean, who had served as Eisenhower's negotiator during the Korean armistice talks, shared Cowles's liberal Republicanism and dedication to bipartisan internationalism; Ros Gilpatric symbolized the continuities between JFK's and LBJ's stewardship of national security affairs; millionaire industrialist Paul Hoffman, who had headed the Marshall Plan, typified American business know-how harnessed in the service of American foreign policy; distinguished Harvard chemist George Kistiakowsky personified the interrelationship of science and politics in the nuclear era; Duke University law professor Arthur Larson, who had served several presidents since 1933, signified the alliance between academia and government forged during World War II; Robert Lovett had served with distinction as undersecretary of state and secretary of defense in the Truman administration; Lovett's World War II colleague and former American proconsul in occupied Germany, John McCloy, completed the impressive roster. All these men projected the determination, confidence, and assurance of a generation steeped in the successes of World War II and the early Cold War.

A subpanel of the larger group—Bradley, Gilpatric, Kistiakowsky, Larson, and McCloy—met with Dean, Tommy, Bill, and me on the morning of July 8. We briefed them thoroughly, answered their questions, and urged them to report their frank opinions to the full panel. All but Larson advised committing "whatever" forces were needed to prevent South Vietnam from falling under Communist control. Several members, in fact, criticized our previous actions as "too restrained."

They expressed their views later that day to the full panel, which—except for Hoffman—fully agreed. Acheson and Arthur Dean, in particular, strongly resisted Hoffman's call for negotiations; this was no time to "turn over our Far East policy to the UN" or anyone else, said Arthur Dean. McCloy, speaking for the group, told Dean Rusk and me: "We are about to get our noses bloodied but you've got to do it. You've got to go in."

That evening, Acheson, Bradley, Cowles, Arthur Dean, Lovett, and McCloy met with the president in the Cabinet Room. Acheson reported to former President Truman a few days later that, after listening to Johnson complain about his problems, "I blew my top & told him . . . that he had no choice except to press on. . . . With this lead my colleagues came thundering in like the charge of the Scots Greys at Waterloo. . . . Bob Lovett, usually cautious, was all out, &, of course, Bradley left no doubt that he was with me all the way. I think . . . we scored." But they failed to "score" on their belief, strongly expressed to Dean Rusk and me, that the administration must fully explain the military situation and the need for more troops to the American public. Cowles and Lovett both faulted the president for "painting too rosy a picture" of the war.[46]

About this time, congressional conservatives began pressing for large increases in defense spending to support the added programs under way and the further efforts then in prospect. Representatives Gerald Ford and Melvin Laird urged a supplemental defense appropriation of $1 to $2 billion and the call-up of at least 200,000 reserves. Senator Dirksen also urged the president to seek "additional authority and more money—a good deal of money."[47] Meanwhile, the Great Society had reached a critical juncture: the Senate had finally approved Medicare, and it would soon enter conference; other major Great Society legislation—including immigration reform, the antipoverty program, aid to Appalachia, and the Clean Air Act—had yet to be acted on. President Johnson believed higher defense appropriations would kill his proposals for the greatest social advance since the New Deal. Today we see his actions as subterfuge—what is commonly called deceit—but in the process we often overlook his deep desire to address our society's ills.

On July 14, 1965, as I prepared to leave for Saigon, Johnson met with a *Newsweek* editor, James Cannon. Cannon queried him about his overriding goal as president. "To make life better and more enjoyable and more significant" for all our people, he replied. When Cannon asked him how he squared this with his more conservative Senate record, he said, "I'm more aware of the problems of more people than before. I am more sensitive to the injustices we have put on the Negro, for instance, because I see and talk to him more now. I'm a little less selfish, a little more selfless. . . . In this place, you can't go any higher and the only thing you want to do is what's right."[48]

Many who read these words may view them as self-serving propaganda, the effort of a consummate actor to lead people to see him as different than he really was. I do not believe that was the case. It is sad that LBJ's frequent efforts to dissemble robbed his reputation of the deep responsibility he felt to right the wrongs that afflicted so many of our people.

President Johnson devoted nearly every waking minute to advancing his programs, whether they related to civil rights, the Great Society, or the Vietnam War. One evening that summer, during congressional debate over the Voting Rights Act, Marg and I dined alone with the president and Lady Bird in the family quarters of the White House. The four of us sat around a small table eating and talking when the president suddenly leaned down, picked up the phone hanging beneath his place setting on the table, and said to the White House operator: "Get me Ev Dirksen."

The Senate minority leader was soon on the line. I could hear only half the conversation, but it went like this: "Ev," the president said, pausing for emphasis, "you lost the God-damned vote today." He was referring to an important procedural vote that might determine the bill's ultimate success or failure. I could hear Dirksen sputtering, "What the hell do you mean I lost it? Your God-damned southern Democrats deserted you!"

The president listened patiently, then said smoothly, "Ev, I knew the southern Democrats were going to desert me. I depended on you to produce enough Republicans to offset that." They bantered back and forth for several more minutes. Finally, Johnson said, "Look, Ev, there's something you want. What is it? I want to tell you there's something I want; it's the Voting Rights Act." They then made a deal over the phone. That was President Johnson, working constantly in pursuit of his legislative objectives—in this case, working to achieve one of the greatest contributions to racial peace in this century.

On another occasion, he had asked me to join him in a Cabinet Room meeting with business and labor leaders. The meeting had nothing to do with defense—he wished to obtain their support for the Civil Rights Bill—but, as I have said, he often involved me in matters unrelated to my primary responsibilities. For an hour he pleaded with his guests to pressure their congressmen to vote for the bill. He appeared to be making little progress. Finally, in total frustration, he said, "Gentlemen, you all know Zephyr"—I doubt anyone in the room, besides me, knew she was the Johnsons' longtime black cook. "Last summer, as she, Bird, and I drove through Mississippi on our way back to Washington from the ranch, Bird said, 'Lyndon, would you please stop at the next gas station? I want to relieve myself.' I said, 'Surely.' We did, returned to the car, and drove on a while when Zephyr said, 'Mr. President, would you mind stopping by the side of the road?' 'Why do you want to stop?' I asked. 'I want to relieve myself.' 'Why the hell didn't you do it at that gas station when Bird and I did?' 'Cause they wouldn't let me,' she replied." With that, LBJ pounded the table and in a bitter voice said, "Gentlemen, is *that* the kind of a country you want? It's not the kind *I* want." Some will say it was theater. I know it was not.

Thus far, Johnson's presidency has been judged largely on Vietnam. But I believe future historians, less influenced by the divisiveness of the war, will offer a more balanced assessment, crediting him with two legislative landmarks: the Civil Rights Act of 1964 and the Voting Rights Act of 1965. Without these two pieces of legislation, our country would surely be in flames today, literally and figuratively. I think history will record them among the greatest political achievements in this century. And Lyndon Johnson's expansive vision of our future—the Great Society—remains a goal to strive for, tragically unfulfilled thirty years after he put it forward.

———

Before leaving Washington on the night of July 14, I phoned President Johnson to discuss my mission to Saigon and Vietnam generally. We talked about how we had arrived at this point, and what we should do in the critical days ahead:

PRESIDENT: We know, ourselves, in our own conscience, that when we asked for this Tonkin Gulf Resolution, we had no intention of committing this many . . . ground troops.

MCNAMARA: Right.

PRESIDENT: And we're doin' so now and we know it's goin' to be bad, and the question [is]: do we just want to do it out on a limb by ourselves?

MCNAMARA: . . . If we do go as far as my paper suggested—sending numbers of men out there—we ought to call up reserves. . . . Almost surely, if we called up reserves, you would want to go to the Congress to get additional authority. This would be a vehicle for drawing together support. Now you'd say, "Well, yes, but it also might lead to extended debate and divisive statements." I think we could avoid that. I really think if we were to go . . . and say to them, "Now, this is our situation, we cannot win with our existing commitment, we must increase it if we are going to win in this limited way we define 'win.' It requires additional troops. Along with that approach, we are . . . continuing this political initiative to probe for a willingness to negotiate a reasonable settlement here. And we ask your support under these circumstances." I think you'd get it from them under those circumstances. And that's a vehicle by which you both get the authority to call up the reserves and also tie them into the whole program.

PRESIDENT: Well, that makes sense.

MCNAMARA: I don't know that you want to go that far and I'm not pressing you to. It's my judgment you should. But my judgment may be in error here.

PRESIDENT: . . . Does Rusk generally agree with you?

MCNAMARA: Yes. . . . He very definitely does. He's a hardliner on this in the sense that he doesn't want to give up South Vietnam under any circumstances—even if it means going to general war. Now, he doesn't think we ought to go to general war; he thinks we ought to try to avoid it. But if that's what's required to hold South Vietnam, he would go to general war.[49]

I met with Westy in Saigon on July 16–17, 1965. The meetings reinforced many of my worst fears and doubts. Westy said he needed 175,000 troops by year's end and another 100,000 in 1966. Skeptical that aerial attacks could reduce the flow of men and materiel from North to South below the levels required to overwhelm South Vietnamese and U.S. forces, I probed Westy and his staff about the bombing's effectiveness. What I heard did nothing to lessen my skepticism. After a long discussion, I finally said:

These are my conclusions, but I would like you to prove me wrong:

1. The VC [and North Vietnam] can recruit a lot more people than they currently have. We should be prepared to increase our strength accordingly.
2. It has not taken many supplies to support the VC in the past. It doesn't take many supplies now. And, I don't think it's going to take many in the future.
3. Because it takes so few supplies, aerial attacks are not going to cut into the VC logistics to a damaging degree. I am not saying that we should stop our aerial attacks. However, I do say that we are going to need a lot more men in the South to effectively counter this on the ground.[50]

I then probed about the role U.S. forces would play in South Vietnam. Two weeks earlier, I had directed the Joint Staff to study the problem of military strategy and tactics and to assess "the assurance the U.S. can have of winning in South Vietnam if we do everything we can." I insisted the study make clear what our strategy would be. Bus Wheeler asked Andy Goodpaster to undertake the study. Using an ad hoc group, he produced a 128-page report, which I received the day I left for Saigon.

In answer to the question "Can we win if we do everything we can?" it stated, "Within the bounds of reasonable assumptions, . . . there appears to be no reason we cannot win if such is our will—and if that will is manifested in strategy and tactical operations." But the report also candidly cautioned that any "assessment of the assurance the U.S. can have of winning in SVN if we do 'everything we can' must remain to a degree tentative for many reasons, including in particular the limited experience in SVN to date with offensive operations approximating the kind envisaged herein."[51]

That was the key unknown. Westy and the Joint Chiefs believed the Vietcong and North Vietnamese would move to what Hanoi's defense minister, Vo Nguyen Giap, had termed the "Third Stage," large-unit operations, which we could meet and eliminate through conventional military tactics ("search and destroy" operations). A further implicit assumption existed: that if the Vietcong and North Vietnamese did not move to the Third Stage, U.S. and South Vietnamese troops could wage effective antiguerrilla operations.

Although I questioned these fundamental assumptions during my meetings with Westy and his staff, the discussions proved superficial. Looking back, I clearly erred by not forcing—then or later, in either Saigon or Washington—a knock-down, drag-out debate over the loose assumptions, unasked questions, and thin analyses underlying our military strategy in Vietnam. I had spent twenty years as a manager identifying problems and forcing organizations—often against their will—to think deeply and realistically about alternative courses of action and their consequences. I doubt I will ever fully understand why I did not do so here.

On July 21 I returned to Washington and presented the report I had prepared along the way to the president. It began with a frank but disturbing assessment:

> The situation in South Vietnam is worse than a year ago (when it was worse than a year before that). After a few months of stalemate, the tempo of the war has quickened. A hard VC push is now on to dismember the nation and to maul the army. . . . Without further outside help, the ARVN is faced with successive tactical reverses, loss of key communication and population centers particularly in the highlands, piecemeal destruction of ARVN units . . . and loss of civilian confidence.

I continued:

> There are no signs that we have throttled the inflow of supplies for the VC or can throttle the flow while their material needs are as low as they are. . . . Nor have our air attacks in North Vietnam

produced tangible evidence of the willingness on the part of Hanoi to come to the conference table in a reasonable mood. The DRV/VC [Democratic Republic of North Vietnam/Vietcong] seem to believe that South Vietnam is on the run and near collapse; they show no signs of settling for less than a complete take-over.

I then reviewed the three alternatives we had examined so many times before: (1) withdraw under the best conditions obtainable— almost certainly meaning something close to unconditional surrender; (2) continue at the present level—almost certainly forcing us into Option 1 later; or (3) expand our forces to meet Westy's request, while launching a vigorous effort to open negotiations— almost certainly staving off near-term defeat but also increasing the difficulty and cost of withdrawal later.

I was driven to Option 3, which I considered "prerequisite to the achievement of any acceptable settlement." I ended by expressing my judgment that "the course of action recommended in this memorandum—if the military and political moves are properly integrated and executed with continuing vigor and visible determination—stands a good chance of achieving an acceptable outcome within a reasonable time." Subsequent events proved my judgment wrong.[52]

───────

While I was in Saigon, Cy Vance had cabled me that it was the president's "current intention" to approve the troop levels he anticipated I would recommend. During the week after I returned, we met at least once a day for deliberations until the president decided. The deliberations at various times included all senior national security officials—in particular, the Joint Chiefs and the service secretaries (Paul Nitze, Eugene Zuckert, and Stanley Resor). All supported the recommendations, except George Ball.

The president approved the expanded program on July 27 and announced his decision to the American public in a midday speech on July 28. But he did not approve the proper way to finance it. I estimated that it would entail roughly $10 billion in additional expenditures through fiscal 1966. The president, with support from some key members of Congress, decided to hold his initial appropriation request far below that estimate, promising a further request in January, "when the figures would be firmer." He also flatly refused my advice to increase taxes to pay for the war and thus avert inflation. I submitted my spending estimate and proposed tax increase in a highly classified draft memorandum known to only a handful of people. Not even the treasury secretary or the chairman of the Council of Economic Advisers knew about it.

When the president read the draft memo and its financing provisions, he said, "What's your vote count?" (I knew what he meant: he believed a tax bill would not pass Congress.)

"I don't have a vote count," I replied. "I know it will be difficult, but that's what you have legislative liaison people for."

"You get your ass up to the Hill and don't come back till you have the vote count."

I did. And of course the votes were not there. I told the president this and said, "I would rather fight for what's right and fail than not try."

He looked at me, exasperated. "Goddammit, Bob, that's what's wrong with you—you aren't a politician. How many times do I have to remind you that after FDR tried to pack the Supreme Court and failed, he couldn't get Congress to pass the time of day."

He exaggerated, but I understood his point: he was protecting his Great Society programs. Had he not at the same time vastly enlarged the credibility gap—which eroded his very ability to build the Great Society—I could have agreed with him.

Meanwhile, Bill Bundy had prepared a list of actions covering every aspect of a presidential announcement, from notifying Congress to informing the American people. It was a superb program. And as presidential aides Douglass Cater and John

Gardner—both strong liberals—emphasized, time still existed for Johnson to educate the public about the problems he faced and the actions he proposed, and to gain their support. Cater reported that "present criticism represents [nothing] more than a marginal group of malcontents. Gardner is confident that a poll devoted solely to intellectuals would show as high popularity as among any other group."[53]

But the advice of Bundy, Cater, and Gardner was not followed. Instead, the fact that the nation had embarked on a course carrying it into a major war was hidden.

Why?

The president understood the magnitude of the decision he had made—and the price he would likely pay for the way he announced it. But he felt trapped between two bitter choices: subterfuge versus the twin dangers of escalatory pressure and the loss of his social programs.

We were sinking into quicksand.

A Host of Other Crises Impinged on Vietnam

May 1967: A long-scheduled meeting with British Prime Minister Harold Wilson, planned to permit the prime minister and LBJ to review the state of the world, focused instead on the likelihood of a major war in the Middle East. (*Photo courtesy the author*)

June 6, 1967: We met in the Situation Room to consider how to respond to Premier Kosygin's message over the hot line. It said, in effect: If you want war, you will get war. (*Photo courtesy Yoichi R. Okamoto/LBJ Library Collection*)

June 23, 1967: Meeting with Kosygin at Glassboro. The president asked me
to tell the Soviet leader why we believed deployment of a Soviet anti-ballistic
missile system would destabilize the nuclear balance between NATO and the
Warsaw Pact. My statement infuriated Kosygin but led, ultimately, to the
Anti-Ballistic Missile and SALT treaties, which were signed a few years later.
(*Photo courtesy the LBJ Library Collection*)

But There Were Moments of Play

During my seven years in the Pentagon, the secretary of agriculture, Orville Freeman, and I played about 2,500 games of squash. We played evenly—poorly, but very competitively. (*Photo courtesy Art Rickerby/Life Magazine © Time Inc.*)

SUMMIT

FRICTION PITCH
FISSURE JERN

WIND TUNNEL

GOLDEN STAIRCASE

WALL STREET

LOWER SADDLE

Over several summer holidays, I climbed Wyoming's Grand Teton (13,766 feet) with each member of my family, including Marg. We followed the route shown in the photo. It was named after the man who pioneered it in 1937, my friend and guide Glen Exum. (*Photo courtesy Al Read*)

Occasionally, Marg and I backpacked
in the wilderness areas of Colorado.
(*Photos courtesy the author*)

1981: With my children, Kathy and Craig, I took Marg's ashes to her favorite
campsite in the Snowmass Maroon Bells Wilderness, near our home in Aspen.
With my broken wrist in a cast, Craig and I are on Buckskin Pass at 12,500
feet on the way to her resting place, which lies below Snowmass Peak
(14,092 feet). (*Photo courtesy the author*)

The Secretary's Wife

Parade

MRS. ROBERT McNAMARA: WIFE OF A MAN UNDER FIRE
by LLOYD SHEARER

February 27, 1966

February 1966: Marg spoke at the University of California, Los Angeles, in place of Lady Bird Johnson.

Marg's Program: Reading Is Fundamental

In 1966, aghast at fifth and sixth grade public school students' inability to read, Marg started, by herself, Reading Is Fundamental, a program to stimulate interest in reading. It sought to motivate poor and underprivileged children to want books and to acquire reading skills. Fifteen years later, when she died, 70,000 volunteers were distributing 11 million books annually to 3 million children. RIF continues to be an active, vigorous organization under the direction of Ann Richardson, the wife of the former attorney general, Elliot Richardson. (*Top: photo courtesy The Smithsonian Institution; bottom: photo courtesy the author*)

Marg was a tireless promoter who enlisted the help of many of her friends to publicize R.I.F. Vice-President Rockefeller, John Chancellor, and Ted Kennedy were among those she called on. (*Photos courtesy the author*)

January 16, 1981: President Carter awarded Marg the Medal of Freedom, our nation's highest civilian award, seventeen days before she died. (*Photo courtesy the Jimmy Carter Library*)

THE SECRETARY OF DEFENSE
WASHINGTON

February 23, 1968

Dear Mr. President

I cannot find words to express to you the feelings that lie in my heart.

Fifty-one months ago you asked me to serve in your cabinet. No other period in my life has brought so much struggle -- or so much satisfaction. The struggle would have been infinitely greater and the satisfaction immeasurably less if I had not received your full support every step of the way.

No man could fail to be proud of service in an Administration which has recorded the progress yours has in the fields of civil rights, health and education. One hundred years of

My handwritten note of farewell expressed my deep respect and affection for a man and a president whose burdens were soon to prove unbearable. (*Courtesy the LBJ Library Collection*)

neglect can not be overcome overnight.
That you have pushed, dragged, and
cajoled the nation into basic reforms
from which my children and my
childrens' children will benefit for
decades to come. I know the price
you have paid, both personally and
politically. Every citizen of our land
is in your debt.

I will not say goodbye — you
know you have but to call and
I will respond.

Sincerely
Bob

February 29, 1968: The president's experiences on my last day as secretary were a portent of the troubles that lay ahead of him. Rain marred the honors ceremony and forced cancellation of the flyover, and the elevator stuck between floors as he was on his way to my office. A near-hysterical Secret Service used emergency measures to evacuate him. (*Top: photo courtesy Mike Geissinger/LBJ Library Collection; bottom: photo courtesy Yoichi R. Okamoto/LBJ Library Collection*)

A Lovely Surprise

The award of the Medal
of Freedom.

A beautiful gift from Lady
Bird. (*Photos courtesy Yoichi R.
Okamoto/LBJ Library Collection*)

On the day I left the Pentagon, Marg and I went to Aspen for a month of
skiing. We interrupted our holiday to attend a brief meeting in the Caribbean.
On our way back, while passing through the Miami airport, we ran into
Jackie Kennedy. It was a lovely surprise for all of us. (*Photo courtesy the author*)

The World Bank

September 1973: Each year, in September, the president of the World Bank
and the managing director of the International Monetary Fund co-chair a
meeting of their governors and the finance ministers and governors of central
banks from across the globe. In September 1968, six months after I left the
Defense Department, I put forward a five-year program to double the bank's
technical and financial assistance to the developing countries. Although
quite controversial, it was accepted. At the 1973 meeting in Nairobi, it was
followed by an equally ambitious program to raise the productivity—and
hence the incomes—of the "absolute poor," the several hundred million
human beings living, literally, on the margin of life.

A Labor of Love

Pope John Paul II had expressed great interest in the bank's program to accelerate economic and social advance in the developing world. He invited me to visit him. I did. We found much to agree on, but we agreed to disagree on "family planning."
(*Photo courtesy the author*)

April 1980: I negotiated with Deng Xiaoping the reentry into the World Bank of the People's Republic of China, beginning a relationship which has been immensely satisfying to both parties. Deng had just announced the goal of quadrupling China's GNP from 1980 to 2000, with the intention of distributing the benefits broadly across Chinese society. Few thought he could achieve his objectives. He will, in fact, surpass them.
(*Photo courtesy the author*)

Recent Years

1982: The Einstein Peace Prize. Awarded to me for my efforts to reduce the risk of nuclear war. (*Photo courtesy the author*)

1987: An Honorary Oxford Degree. The citation read: "He beats swords into plowshares." (*Top: photo courtesy Martin Argles*/The Guardian*; bottom: photo courtesy the author*)

1991: Addressing a Conference on Global Development. Having served as president of the World Bank for thirteen years, I resigned in 1981. Since then, I have pursued the interests closest to my heart: reducing the risk of nuclear war; accelerating economic and social advance in the developing countries; exploring alternative means of reducing conflict between and within nations in the post-Cold War world; and addressing the polarization of our society and the marginalization—the "unemployability"—of increasing numbers of our people. (*Photo courtesy the author*)

1987: Former secretaries of defense debate defense policy. (*Photo courtesy the author*)

Today—and Tomorrow?

While writing this manuscript, I took time off for a winter climb of
Homestake Peak (13,200 feet) on the Continental Divide in Colorado.
The peak is approached from a system of huts, the first two of which I
built, in memory of Marg, for public use on national forest land. My
companion on the climb was Dr. Ben Eiseman, the former vice-chairman
of the American College of Surgeons. At the time, we were both in our late
seventies. We hope to continue skiing and climbing until the day we die!
(*Photo courtesy the author*)

8

The Christmas Bombing Pause, An Unsuccessful Attempt to Move to Negotiations

July 29, 1965–January 30, 1966

I have heard it said about the difference between results and consequences that results are what we expect, consequences are what we get. This certainly applies to our assumptions about Vietnam in the summer and fall of 1965. Reality collided with expectations. We had no sooner begun to carry out the plan to increase dramatically U.S. forces in Vietnam than it became clear there was reason to question the strategy on which the plan was based. Slowly, the sobering, frustrating, tormenting limitations of military operations in Vietnam became painfully apparent. I had always been confident that every problem could be solved, but now I found myself confronting one—involving national pride and human life—that could not.

My sense of the war gradually shifted from concern to skepticism to frustration to anguish. It shifted not because of growing fatigue, as was sometimes alleged, but because of my increasing anxiety that more and more people were being killed and we simply were not accomplishing our goals.

In the days following President Johnson's July 28, 1965, announcement, most Americans—intellectuals, members of Congress, the press, the people in the street—expressed support for his decision. When, in late August, a Gallup poll asked: "Do you approve or disapprove of the way the Johnson Administration is handling the situation in Vietnam?" 57 percent approved versus 25 percent who disapproved. This compared with 48 percent versus 28 percent two months earlier. A Harris survey in September reported that "the American people are nearly 70–30 behind the proposition that Vietnam should be the ground on which the United States should take its stand against communism in Asia," and it pointed out that "a majority of the public believe that the Vietnam fighting will go on for several years."[1]

At this very moment when public support for the war appeared more solid than ever, more signs of trouble appeared. At a National Security Council meeting on August 5, Max Taylor—who had become a presidential adviser after Henry Cabot Lodge, Jr., returned for a second stint as ambassador in Saigon—confidently predicted that the Communist offensive would be defeated by year's end, and that 1966 could be "a decisive year" for the United States.[2] But that same day, the Joint Staff completed another war game, Sigma II-65, that cast serious doubt on Max's predictions and the assumptions underlying our military strategy. Contrary to the belief that we could force and win large-scale ground operations, the Sigma II-65 report noted "considerable feeling among participants that Viet Cong adoption of the strategy of avoiding major engagements with U.S. forces would make it extremely difficult to find and fix enemy units. . . . Viet Cong experience in the jungles [and] guerrilla warfare . . . would pose serious problems, even for well-equipped and highly mobile U.S. regulars." As for bombing, the report noted, "There was considerable feeling . . . that [the] punishment being imposed could and would be absorbed by the Hanoi leadership . . . based on the fact that the country is basically a subsistence economy centering on the self-sustaining village. . . . Industrial activities constitute such a limited portion of the total economy that even [its] disruption seemed an acceptable price" to pay.[3]

The report's conclusions disturbed me greatly but seemed to have little impact on others in the Pentagon and elsewhere in the government. This may have reflected the fact that the news from Vietnam in August had been encouraging. United States forces had won a significant victory in their first major engagement with Vietcong forces, a battle that was fought between August 18 and August 21 on the Batangan Peninsula, south of the marine base at Chu Lai. This operation, together with a series of statements in *Newsweek* in the fall of 1965 by Bernard Fall, a renowned Indochina scholar and perceptive observer who stressed the determinative weight of America's growing presence in Vietnam, persuaded many the U.S. effort could not fail.*[4]

As U.S. troops poured into Vietnam, General Westmoreland issued a classified paper spelling out America's objective in the South and the military strategy to achieve it. Entitled "Concept of Operations in the Republic of Vietnam" and dated September 1, 1965, the paper defined our objective as "ending the war in the Republic of Vietnam by convincing the Viet Cong and the DRV [Democratic Republic of (North) Vietnam] that military victory is impossible, thereby forcing an agreement favorable to the RVN [Republic of (South) Vietnam] and the United States." The ground war would unfold in three phases, each with a specific timetable. Phase 1 would be to halt the Communists' advances—"to stop losing the war"—and would extend through December 31, 1965. Phase 2 would involve taking the offense against Communist forces and expanding the pacification program aimed at "winning the hearts and minds" of South Vietnam's peasantry. It would run from January 1 through June 30, 1966. Unless the Communists gave up, Phase 3 would kick in "to destroy or render militarily ineffective the

---

*Growing concern about the effectiveness of U.S. military operations led Fall gradually to abandon his belief that American technology and power could not but prevail. By the time of his death in 1967, he had reversed the stand he took in *Newsweek* in 1965.

remaining organized VC units and their base areas." It would begin July 1, 1966, and run through December 31, 1967. The paper stressed that "for political and psychological reasons, the conflict must retain primarily a Vietnamese character at all times." This condition, clearly, was not to be met.[5]

Westy also sketched how he planned to carry out his responsibilities under the two-pronged military strategy that the president, the Joint Chiefs, and senior officials including me had accepted as a basis for ending the war. The main prong—the ground war—was intended to show Hanoi and the Vietcong that they could not take the South by force. The ancillary prong—bombing the North—was intended both to reduce Hanoi's will and ability to support the Vietcong and to increase the cost of trying to do so. We believed the two prongs would force a settlement.

Some critics have asserted that the United States lacked a military strategy in Vietnam. In fact, we had one—but its assumptions were deeply flawed. Beneath Westy's strategy lay the implicit assumption that pacification and bombing would prevent the Communists from offsetting losses inflicted by U.S. and South Vietnamese Army forces through recruitment in the South and reinforcement from the North. That key assumption grossly underestimated the Communists' capacity to recruit in the South amid war and to reinforce from the North in the face of our air attacks. Moreover, American military and civilian leaders assumed the U.S. and South Vietnamese military could force the Vietcong and North Vietnamese regulars to slug it out on the battlefield in a more or less conventional war. Then U.S. mobility and firepower, together with bombing to choke off supplies and reinforcements from the North, would force them into a settlement. If the Vietcong and North Vietnamese Army refused to fight on our terms and reverted to hit-and-run tactics, as some believed they would, we had assumed the U.S. and South Vietnamese forces, backed by a strong pacification program, could wage an effective antiguerrilla war. And, finally, we believed that the pacification program in the South would serve as our insurance policy, keeping the insurgents from being able to find supplies and recruit fighters there. Westy had outlined such a strategy at our July 17 meeting in Saigon, and I had alluded to it in my July 20 memo to the president.

All these assumptions proved incorrect. We did not force the Vietcong and North Vietnamese Army to fight on our terms. We did not wage an effective antiguerrilla war against them. And bombing did not reduce the infiltration of men and supplies into the South below required levels or weaken the North's will to continue the conflict.

With Washington's tacit agreement, Westy fought a war of attrition, whose major objective was to locate and eliminate the Vietcong and North Vietnamese regular units. No alternative to this "search-and-destroy" strategy seemed viable, given the decision not to invade North Vietnam with its attendant risk of triggering war with China and/or the Soviet Union (a risk we were determined to minimize) and our unwillingness to expand massively our ground operations into Laos and Cambodia. Westy reasoned that destroying the Vietcong and North Vietnamese regular units would enable Saigon to stabilize itself politically and win the allegiance of the South Vietnamese people, thereby forcing the adversary either to withdraw or to negotiate a settlement favorable to South Vietnam.

Military historian and former career army Maj. Andrew F. Krepinevich has accused Westmoreland of self-delusion. He argues that Westy "simply developed a strategy to suit the Army's preferred *modus operandi,* force structure, and doctrine." He goes on to explain: "Denied the opportunity to win a decisive battle of annihilation by invading North Vietnam, [the army] found the attrition strategy best fit the kind of war it had prepared to fight. . . . It was nothing more than the natural outgrowth of its organizational recipe for success—playing to America's strong suits, material abundance and technological superiority, and the nation's profound abhorrence of U.S. casualties." Krepinevich continues:

In developing its Vietnam strategy to use operational methods successful in previous wars, the Army compromised its ability to successfully combat . . . insurgency operations at anything approaching an acceptable cost. In focusing on the attrition of enemy forces rather than on defeating the enemy through denial of his access to the population, MACV [Military Assistance Command, Vietnam] missed whatever opportunity it had to deal the insurgents a crippling blow. . . . Furthermore, in attempting to maximize Communist combat losses, the Army often alienated the most important element in any counterinsurgency strategy—the people.[6]

Gen. William E. DePuy, Westmoreland's operations officer and principal planner in 1965–1968, made a somewhat different but equally telling point in a 1988 interview, when he said: "[We] eventually learned that we could not bring [the Vietcong and North Vietnamese] to battle frequently enough to win a war of attrition. . . . We were arrogant because we were Americans and we were soldiers or Marines and we could do it, but it turned out that it was a faulty concept, given the sanctuaries, given the fact that the Ho Chi Minh Trail was never closed. It was a losing concept of operation."[7]

Why this failure? Gen. Bruce Palmer, Jr., whose views on the air war I quoted earlier, offered a compelling explanation. The chiefs, Palmer writes, "were imbued with the 'can do' spirit and could not bring themselves to make . . . a negative statement or to appear to be disloyal."[8]

That certainly explains part of the failure. But the president, I, and others among his civilian advisers must share the burden of responsibility for consenting to fight a guerrilla war with conventional military tactics against a foe willing to absorb enormous casualties in a country without the fundamental political stability necessary to conduct effective military and pacification operations. It could not be done, and it was not done.

———

That fall the Communists matched our military escalation, recruiting more troops in the South, strengthening air defenses in the North, and boosting infiltration of men and supplies down the Ho Chi Minh Trail. Quite simply, they were adapting to the larger U.S. presence. Westy responded in early September by requesting 35,000 more troops, taking us from 175,000 to 210,000 by the end of the year. Pressure to raise it further still increased with each passing day. In mid-October, Westy sent us revised estimates of his 1966 requirements. Instead of the 275,000 he had previously said he would need by July 1966, he now wanted 325,000, with the possibility of even more later, and with no guarantee that the United States would achieve its objectives.[9]

Westy's troop requests troubled us all. We worried that this was the beginning of an open-ended commitment. The momentum of war and the unpredictability of events were overwhelming the Joint Chiefs' calculations of late July and Westy's predictions of early September. I sensed things were slipping out of our control.

That fear was reinforced when the chiefs urged expanding U.S. air attacks against North Vietnam to include targets in the Hanoi-Haiphong area and others closer to China. The president and I rejected their request, in part because we doubted such attacks would significantly impair the Vietcong's ability to persevere in the South or persuade Hanoi to desist, but also because such moves would increase the risk of a confrontation with China, as had happened in Korea only fifteen years before.[10]

Given the growing division within the government over the air campaign, I asked the president to authorize a special group to study bombing's impact on Hanoi's will and ability to continue the war. President Johnson agreed and appointed Tommy Thompson, Max Taylor, John McNaughton, and Bill Bundy. The Thompson Group, as it came to be known, submitted its report on October 11. Its conclusions closely paralleled the judgments the president and I had reached, and the reasoning behind them. Escalating the air war could trigger a strong military reaction by the Chinese and/or Soviets. Mining Haiphong and other harbors could lead to the sinking of Soviet ships and increase North Vietnam's dependence on overland transport from China, thereby increasing Beijing's more radical influence on Hanoi. North Vietnam seemed less willing to negotiate while under attack. The Thompson Group recommended a long bombing pause to test Hanoi's interest in talks.[11]

———

Elsewhere in Asia, events took place in the fall of 1965 that, in hindsight, significantly altered the regional balance of power and substantially reduced America's real stake in Vietnam. At the time, however, we failed to recognize their implications.

China suffered several serious setbacks. In early August, conflict erupted between India, which was a Soviet ally, and Pakistan, a Chinese ally, over the territory of Kashmir in the foothills of the Himalayas. China exploited New Delhi's preoccupation with the crisis to advance military forces on its border with India and demand territorial concessions. But India won its conflict with Pakistan, leaving the Chinese forces in a vulnerable position, from which they quickly retreated. The net effect, geopolitically, was a gain for the Soviets and a loss for the Chinese.

China also lost ground in Indonesia, which was shaken by a major political realignment in October. Up to that time, Jakarta had appeared to be moving into China's orbit. On August 17, for example, Indonesian leader Sukarno lashed out strongly against Washington and spoke of a "Peking-Jakarta-Hanoi–Phnom Penh" axis. But soon after the Chinese-supported Indonesian Communist Party (PKI) launched a coup that ultimately failed miserably. Anti-Communist feeling and primitive xenophobia swept the country; in the resulting violence, Sukarno was driven from power and 300,000 or more PKI members were killed. The largest and most populous nation in Southeast Asia had reversed course and now lay in the hands of independent nationalists led by Suharto (who remains in power to this day). China, which had expected a tremendous victory, instead suffered a permanent setback.

George F. Kennan, whose containment strategy was a significant factor in our commitment to South Vietnam's defense, argued at Senate hearings on February 10, 1966, that the Chinese had

"suffered an enormous reverse in Indonesia, . . . one of great significance, and one that does rather confine any realistic hopes they may
have for the expansion of their authority." This event had greatly
reduced America's stakes in Vietnam. He asserted that fewer
dominoes now existed, and they seemed much less likely to fall.*[12]

Kennan's point failed to catch our attention and thus influence
our actions. But words uttered by Chinese Defense Minister
Marshal Lin Biao on September 2, 1965, did. Expounding the
concept of "people's war," Lin called on the "rural areas of the
world" (developing countries) to take over "the cities" (industrialized nations) through militant local revolutions. He ridiculed
American forces in Vietnam and said the "classic struggle" of the
Vietnamese people must bring ignominious defeat to an overex-
tended United States. The Johnson administration—including me—
interpreted the speech as bellicose and aggressive, signaling an
expansionist China's readiness to nourish "local" forces across the
world and to give a helping push when the time came. Lin's remarks
seemed to us a clear expression of the basis for the domino theory.

In retrospect, one can see the events of autumn 1965 as clear
setbacks for China, which contributed to its turn inward and the
Cultural Revolution the following year. This destructive chain of
events led to China's withdrawal from active involvement in international affairs for more than a decade. But, blinded by our
assumptions and preoccupied with a rapidly growing war, we—like
most other Western leaders—continued to view China as a serious
threat in Southeast Asia and the rest of the world.

———

As China turned inward, the United States increased its presence in
Vietnam. The war took on more and more the appearance and
flavor of an American enterprise. This led to some outbreaks of
criticism in the United States, but polls continued to show broad

---

*George would, I am sure, be pained to think that any senior U.S. government official viewed
our intervention in Vietnam as a logical extension of "containment." It is unlikely he ever visu-
alized extending the strategy globally to this extent.

public support for President Johnson's policy. In Congress, approximately ten senators and seventy representatives could be counted severe critics—including such influential figures as William Fulbright, Mike Mansfield, and Wayne Morse—but, on the whole, the legislative branch remained supportive. The press, except for a few well-known columnists, also continued to back the president.

Antiwar protest had been sporadic and limited up to this time and had not compelled attention. Then came the afternoon of November 2, 1965. At twilight that day, a young Quaker named Norman R. Morrison, father of three and an officer of the Stoney Run Friends Meeting in Baltimore, burned himself to death within forty feet of my Pentagon window. He doused himself with fuel from a gallon jug. When he set himself on fire, he was holding his one-year-old daughter in his arms. Bystanders screamed, "Save the child!" and he flung her out of his arms. She survived without injury.

After Morrison's death, his wife issued a statement:

Norman Morrison [gave] his life to express his concern over the great loss of life and human suffering caused by the war in Vietnam. He was protesting our Government's deep military involvement in this war. He felt that all citizens must speak their convictions about our country's action.[13]

Morrison's death was a tragedy not only for his family but also for me and the country. It was an outcry against the killing that was destroying the lives of so many Vietnamese and American youth.

I reacted to the horror of his action by bottling up my emotions and avoided talking about them with anyone—even my family. I knew Marg and our three children shared many of Morrison's feelings about the war, as did the wives and children of several of my cabinet colleagues. And I believed I understood and shared some of his thoughts. There was much Marg and I and the children should have talked about, yet at moments like this I often turn inward instead—it is a grave weakness. The episode created tension at home that only deepened as dissent and criticism of the war continued to grow.

Three weeks later, on November 27, an estimated 20,000 to 35,000 antiwar protesters marched on the White House. Sponsored by SANE (the Committee for a Sane Nuclear Policy) and led by Sanford Gottlieb, one of the most active and responsible antiwar organizers, the march remained peaceful and orderly. A few days later, Dr. Benjamin Spock, the nationally known pediatrician, and Professor H. Stuart Hughes of Harvard, the co-chairmen of SANE, sent Ho Chi Minh a cable saying SANE had sponsored the march and urged him to accept U.S. offers for negotiation. They added, "Demonstrations will continue but will not lead to a U.S. pullout."[14]

Many more demonstrations were to follow.

Surprising as it may seem to some, I felt great sympathy for the protesters' concerns. Mary McGrory, a *Washington Star* syndicated columnist, correctly portrayed my attitude when she wrote on December 3, 1965:

> Secretary of Defense Robert S. McNamara regards recent peace demonstrations with neither alarm nor dismay.
>
> His undoubtedly is a minority view in the Pentagon, but the civilian manager of the military establishment is an advocate of free speech.
>
> "This nation has a tradition of protecting free speech and the right of dissent," he says. "Our policies become stronger as the result of debate."
>
> The secretary is an admirer of Norman Thomas, the venerable Socialist leader who was the most effective orator at last Saturday's demonstration here. But he takes issue with Thomas' contention that he "would rather see America save her soul than her face in Southeast Asia."
>
> "How do you save your soul?" McNamara asks. "Do you save your soul by pulling out of a situation, or do you save it by fulfilling your commitments?"[15]

While protests mounted across America, the expansion of North Vietnamese and Vietcong military operations led Westy again to reconsider, and substantially increase, his estimate of U.S. troop requirements. At the same time, several of us in Washington renewed our efforts to find ways to move toward negotiations. These two issues dominated debate within the administration during November, December, and January.

On November 7, 1965, I sent the president a memo that, along with two others, dated November 30 and December 7, formed the basis for much of the discussion in the next several weeks. The memo opened with this statement:

> The February decision to bomb North Vietnam and the July approval of Phase I deployments make sense only if they are in support of a long-run United States policy to contain Communist China. China—like Germany in 1917, like Germany in the West and Japan in the East in the late 30's, and like the USSR in 1947—looms as a major power threatening to undercut our importance and effectiveness in the world and, more remotely but more menacingly, to organize all of Asia against us.
>
> . . . There are three fronts to a long-run effort to contain China (realizing that the USSR "contains" China on the north and northwest): (a) the Japan-Korea front; (b) the India-Pakistan front; and (c) the Southeast Asia front. Decisions to make great investments today in men, money and national honor in South Vietnam make sense only in conjunction with continuing efforts of equivalent effectiveness in the rest of Southeast Asia and on the other two principal fronts. The trends in Asia are running in both directions—for as well as against our interests; there is no reason to be unduly pessimistic about our ability over the next decade or two to . . . keep China from achieving her objectives until her zeal wanes. The job, however—even if we can shift some responsibilities to some Asian countries—will continue to require American attention, money, and, from time to time unfortunately, lives.
>
> Any decision to continue the program of bombing North Vietnam and any decision to deploy Phase II forces—involving as they do substantial loss of American lives, risks of further esca-

lation, and greater investment of U.S. prestige—must be predicated on these premises as to our long-run interests in Asia.

I have quoted these passages at length because, with hindsight, they provide an example of the kind of totally incorrect appraisal of the "Chinese Threat" to our security that pervaded our thinking. Among other shortcomings, they took no account of the centuries-old hostility between China and Vietnam (which flared up again once the United States withdrew from the region) or of the setbacks to China's political power caused by the recent events in India, Pakistan, and Indonesia, which I have just described. And yet, as far as I can recall and the record indicates, they reflect the views of all, or almost all, senior U.S. policy makers. Here again, the lack of expertise and historical knowledge seriously undermined U.S. policy.

My memorandum continued with a somber appraisal of the situation in South Vietnam. It noted that guerrilla war continued at high intensity; Vietcong attacks, sabotage, and terrorism showed no signs of abating; the Thieu-Ky government had survived but accomplished little; and, worst of all, Saigon's political control over the countryside—where most South Vietnamese lived—had weakened.

After citing our current political objective in South Vietnam—an independent, non-Communist state—I wrote, "The question whether we should be prepared ultimately to settle for a 'compromise solution' . . . may have to be faced soon." After analyzing alternative courses open to us, I recommended: (1) increasing U.S. troop commitments to 350,000 by the end of 1966, compared with the 275,000 Westy had estimated in July; (2) implementing a month-long bombing pause similar to what I had proposed in July and the Thompson Group had recommended in October; and (3) making an all-out effort to start negotiations. I recognized negotiations at that time appeared unlikely to succeed, but I argued a bombing pause "would set the stage for another pause, perhaps in late 1966, which might produce a settlement." If a pause proved fruitless, I recommended intensifying Rolling Thunder strikes against North Vietnam—not to win the war (which I considered impossible, short of genocidal destruction) but as one prong of our two-prong strategy to prove to the Vietcong and North Vietnamese that they could not win in the South while penalizing Hanoi's continued support of the war.

I was hardly encouraging. Indeed, I told the president "that none of these actions assures success. There is a small but meaningful risk that the course I have recommended . . . will lead the Chinese or Russians to escalate the war. U.S. killed-in-action can be expected to increase to 500–800 a month. And the odds are even that the DRV/VC will hang on doggedly, effectively matching us man-for-man . . . and that, despite our efforts, we will be faced in early 1967 with stagnation at a higher level."

But I saw no other way. I could only conclude that "the best chance of achieving our objectives, and of avoiding a costly national political defeat, lies in the combination of political, economic and military steps described in this memorandum. If carried out vigorously, they stand the best chance of achieving an acceptable resolution of the problem within a reasonable time."[16]

The president initially expressed deep skepticism toward my recommendations. In his memoirs, he stated, "The May pause had failed, and I thought that Hanoi would probably view a new cessation in the bombing as a sign of weakness." There were other good men and good arguments against it: Dean Rusk doubted Hanoi would respond positively; Bus Wheeler and the Joint Chiefs anticipated North Vietnam would exploit it militarily and confuse our action with weakness; Henry Cabot Lodge believed it would demoralize South Vietnam and drive a wedge between Saigon and Washington; Clark Clifford an outside adviser to the President, feared it would signal a lack of U.S. resolve and increase the pressure to hit North Vietnam even harder. I knew I faced an uphill battle.[17]

——

There things stood for several weeks while the president went to his Texas ranch to convalesce from gallbladder surgery and Dean left on a trip to Latin America. During that time, the weight of opinion within the government toward a pause started to shift, as we received sobering news on the military front, severe criticism of our negotiating position, and an indication from the Soviets that they would try to help start talks if we paused.

The first major battle between U.S. and North Vietnamese forces occurred November 14–19, 1965, in the Ia Drang Valley in west-central South Vietnam, near the Cambodian border. Two North Vietnamese regiments engaged the First Cavalry Division and the First Battalion of the Seventh Cavalry in fierce fighting amid elephant grass and anthills as high as a man's head. When the battle ended, the North Vietnamese left behind over 1,300 dead. The United States had 300 men killed. At first glance, Ia Drang seemed a sound U.S. military victory. American soldiers, as expected, fought bravely and well. But the North Vietnamese had chosen where, when, and how long to fight. This proved to be the case all too often as the war went on.

The Ia Drang battle confirmed intelligence reports from MACV that enemy infiltration into the South had been much greater than anticipated. As a result, there now appeared to be nine North Vietnamese regiments in South Vietnam, as opposed to the three reported earlier. Vietcong regiments, likewise, had more than doubled, from five to twelve. The infiltration rate had tripled from three regiments a month in late 1964 to at least nine a month. And all this had occurred amid an intense U.S. interdiction bombing campaign.[18]

Westy looked at these trends and rightly concluded that enemy force levels in the future would be much higher than he had estimated. He therefore cabled Washington on November 23 requesting 200,000 more troops in 1966—twice his July 1965 estimate. This would bring total U.S. forces in Vietnam by the end of 1966 to 410,000, in contrast to his original estimate of 275,000.[19]

The message came as a shattering blow. It meant a drastic—and arguably open-ended—increase in U.S. forces and carried with it the likelihood of many more U.S. casualties. The request and its implications were so great that I decided to fly with Bus Wheeler to Saigon to assess the situation personally.

My meetings with Lodge, Westy, Bus, and Oley Sharp on November 28 and November 29 confirmed my worst fears. The valor and courage of U.S. troops impressed me immensely, but I saw and heard many problems. The U.S. presence rested on a bowl of jelly: political instability had increased; pacification had stalled; South Vietnamese Army desertions had skyrocketed. Westy's talk of 400,000 U.S. troops by the end of 1966, with the possibility of at least 200,000 more in 1967, combined with evidence that North Vietnam could move 200 tons of supplies a day down the Ho Chi Minh Trail *despite* heavy interdiction bombing—more than enough to support the likely level of Communist operations, taking account of supplies the Vietcong obtained in the South—shook me and altered my attitude perceptibly. This came through in my remarks to the press when I left Saigon:

> We have stopped losing the war. . . . But despite the fact that we've had that success, . . . [the Vietcong and North Vietnamese] have more than offset the very heavy losses which they have suffered. The level of infiltration has increased, and I think this represents a clear decision on the part of Hanoi to . . . raise the level of conflict. . . . The decision by the Vietcong [and North Vietnamese Army] to stand and fight [at the recent battle of Ia Drang], recognizing the level of force we can bring to bear against them, expresses their determination to carry on the conflict that can lead to only one conclusion. It will be a long war.[20]

I returned to Washington to offer the president a bleak choice between but two options: go for a compromise solution (entailing less than our objective of an independent, non-Communist South Vietnam) or meet Westy's requests and intensify bombing of North Vietnam. I cautioned that these latter actions would by no means guarantee success, that U.S. killed-in-action could rise to 1,000 a month, and that we might be faced in early 1967 with a "no decision" at an even higher level of violence, destruction, and death.

I did not state a preference between these two unhappy options. But I did say that if U.S. troop levels and air attacks were increased, we should preface those steps with a three- to four-week bombing pause. My thinking was simple; as I told the president: "I am seriously concerned about embarking on a markedly higher level of war in Vietnam without having tried, through a pause, to end the war or at least having made it clear to our people that we did our best to end it."[21]

The first option I presented—standing pat militarily and accepting a compromise political solution—received no serious attention. Others did not address it, and I did not force the issue. I should have, even though conditions in South Vietnam made it unlikely that the Saigon government could have survived a showdown with the Communists.

The second option—a bombing pause—had initially been greeted coolly within the government but received more attention because of two developments in November. A series of discussions between the recently deceased U.S. Ambassador to the United Nations Adlai Stevenson and U.N. Secretary-General U Thant came to public attention through a *Look* magazine article by Eric Sevareid. It implied that Washington was unwilling to negotiate.[22] And at a quiet luncheon with Mac Bundy on November 24, Soviet Ambassador to Washington Anatoly Dobrynin, no doubt acting under instructions, said that if the United States stopped bombing for two to three weeks, Moscow would use its influence to get Hanoi to negotiate.[23] This set the stage for the debate that followed.

It began in earnest on the afternoon of December 2, when I telephoned President Johnson at his ranch. I told him that, since returning from Saigon, I had grown "more and more convinced that we ought definitely to think of some action other than military action as the only program. . . . I personally believe we should go ahead and raise our budgets, raise our strengths, [and] increase our deployments out there to gradually meet Westmoreland's require- ments. But I think if we do that by itself, it's suicide and we ought definitely to accompany it—or even, perhaps, precede it—by some other action." My concern was this: "I think pushing 300,000, 400,000 Americans out there without being able to guarantee what it will lead to is a terrible risk and a terrible problem." I urged Johnson to accompany additional ground deployments "with some kind of political program—a pause or what have you." He listened noncommittally.[24] I told the president that Dean, Mac Bundy, and I would explore the alternatives before coming down to visit him.

For the next five days we held intensive discussions in Washington. By the end of that time, most of the president's advisers favored trying a pause. I prepared another memorandum, this time recommending that Westy's troop request be approved and laying out a step-by-step approach to a long bombing pause that I hoped might start a chain reaction toward an eventual settlement. Dean, Mac, and I traveled to Texas on December 7 to argue our case.

The president listened carefully but remained skeptical. He saw the same dangers that worried the Joint Chiefs—increased infiltration, misinterpretation as a sign of weakness, a potential barrier to the resumption of bombing. A string of comments illustrated his frustration and confusion: "What is the best course?" "We're getting deeper and deeper in. I bogged my car down. I don't want a bulldozer to come and get me." "Where we were when I came in—I'd trade back to where we were."[25]

The president weighed the issue and then called us to the Cabinet Room on December 17, 1965, for two final days of debate. Leaning forward until his chest pressed against the large oval table, he opened the first session by saying he was willing to "take any gamble" that might produce results. I pressed my case hard that day and the next, at one point laying out my deepest concerns and fragile hopes:

MCNAMARA: A military solution to the problem is not certain—one out of three or one in two. Ultimately we must find . . . a diplomatic solution.

PRESIDENT: Then, no matter what we do in the military field, there is no sure victory?

MCNAMARA: That's right. We have been too optimistic. . . .

RUSK: I'm more optimistic, but I can't prove it.

MCNAMARA: I'm saying: we may not find a military solution. We need to explore other means. . . . Our military action approach is an unacceptable way to a successful conclusion. . . . This seems a contradiction. I come to you for a huge increase in Vietnam—400,000 men. But at the same time it may lead to escalation and undesirable results. I suggest we now look at other alternatives.[26]

Johnson left the meetings inclined to try at least a short bombing pause, I thought, but still undecided. On December 22, the White House and Saigon announced a thirty-hour ceasefire, including a bombing halt over North Vietnam, beginning Christmas Eve. When the president returned to Texas shortly before Christmas, I continued to hope he would authorize the long pause, tied to efforts to move to negotiations. Matters stood there when I took my family to Aspen, Colorado, for the holidays.

———

On Christmas morning, the president decided to extend the "ceremonial" pause for another day or two. When I received the news, I did something I had never done before: I used my personal access to the president to make an end run around my colleagues.

From the Mountain Chalet, a modest but popular lodge in downtown Aspen—I recall we paid four dollars per night for each of our children in the bunk room—I called the ranch on the evening of December 26. There was little privacy for a call from the secretary of defense, through the lodge operator, to the president of the United States. However, the always dependable White House switchboard quickly connected me with the president at a friend's home in Round Mountain, Texas.

He quickly agreed when I asked if I might come to the ranch alone to discuss Vietnam. I then called the Pentagon and arranged for an air force jet to pick me up the next day. On

December 27, a friend drove me down to Grand Junction, where the plane was waiting. I arrived at the LBJ Ranch outside Austin at 6:30 P.M.

The president and Lady Bird greeted me at their airstrip. We returned to the ranch house and dined with their younger daughter, Luci. After dinner, the president and I retired alone to the living room. For the next three hours, we discussed the pause before a crackling fire. I stressed my judgment that the possibility of sparking talks that might ultimately lead to peace outweighed the military disadvantages of deferring resumption of the bombing.

The president listened intently, weighing the pros and cons. He finally agreed to extend the pause for an indefinite period and to mount a massive diplomatic effort to move Hanoi toward negotiations. We agreed I should call Dean Rusk and others in Washington to explain what he wanted done. Although Dean was against extending the pause, he went along because he understood I had already convinced the president.

After breakfast the next morning, we made more calls from the president's small office at the ranch. I phoned Averell Harriman, who eagerly agreed when the president asked him to press for negotiating help in Eastern Europe. We called George Ball, whom the president made responsible for coordinating the diplomatic offensive; and Arthur Goldberg—Adlai Stevenson's successor as U.N. ambassador—whom he instructed to see U Thant and the Pope.

I left the ranch shortly after noon and returned to Aspen, very pleased with the course events had taken. Yet I felt a strong sense of guilt for having gone around my colleagues to win my case. It was the only time I did so in my seven years as secretary.*

---

*Because my trip to the LBJ Ranch has not been reported in the literature describing the origin of the pause, I began to question my memory. As I wrote these paragraphs, therefore, I asked the Johnson Library to search the president's "Daily Diary" logs for evidence of what I have related. They found a detailed record of the events, including a notation that we dined on "quail, rice, peas, and coconut pudding for dessert."

The bombing pause over North Vietnam continued on a day-to-day basis for more than a month—until the end of January 1966. But controversy over both political moves and military actions raged throughout this period.

The administration launched an open and intense diplomatic offensive. In addition to the Harriman and Goldberg missions, it sent Vice President Humphrey to the Philippines and India, and Assistant Secretaries of State G. Mennen "Soapy" Williams and Thomas Mann to Africa and Latin America. Each man publicized Washington's desire to start peace negotiations. Dean also promulgated a fourteen-point program inviting North Vietnam to enter into "negotiations without preconditions."

Throughout the pause, the Joint Chiefs urged resuming operations against the North immediately, asserting that cessation of bombing placed U.S. forces "under serious and progressively increasing military disadvantage." I told them I would advise the president to do so if they could show me how the pause was hurting us in the South.[27]

They did not reply.

Meanwhile, the United States intensified its air strikes along the Ho Chi Minh Trail in Laos, and American field commanders in South Vietnam stepped up ground operations. Early in January, they launched the biggest attack to date against the Vietcong near Saigon and later that month staged the largest amphibious operation since the Inchon landing in Korea, in Quangngai Province above the thirty-fourth parallel. More U.S. troops arrived in country.

The debate resumed at the White House on January 10. Johnson, believing the pause had produced nothing, was inclined to start bombing again in a few days. I urged him to give the pause—and the possibility of starting talks—more time, sensing no military disadvantage in waiting until the end of the month. Bus disagreed. "Every day makes a difference," he said on behalf of the chiefs.[28]

On January 12, Oley Sharp urged resuming—and intensifying—the bombing to include interdicting lines of communication from

China. He argued that such a campaign would "bring the enemy to the conference table or cause the insurgency to wither from lack of support." The chiefs concurred in a separate memo six days later.[29]

However, that same day—January 18, 1966—I received an analysis showing that the North Vietnamese could infiltrate 4,500 men a month, along with supplies sufficient to support a substantial combat effort in South Vietnam, despite our interdiction campaign. This assumed a heavy level of bombing, whose magnitude was reflected in the fact that in December 1965 we had dropped 50 percent more tonnage than had been expended in the peak month of the Korean War.[30] The CIA independently confirmed this analysis. Its Board of National Estimates concluded that mining harbors and bombing the extra targets proposed by Oley Sharp and the chiefs—airfields, petroleum stocks, power plants—would not have a "critical impact on the combat activity of the Communist forces in South Vietnam." Deputy Director for Plans for the CIA Dick Helms put the point bluntly to President Johnson at a meeting on January 22: "Increased bombing in the North could not stop movement of supplies to the South."[31]

This controversy over what bombing could or could not do was the latest round of a debate about airpower that had followed both World War II and the Korean War. The debate intensified during the next two years, and the issue remains in dispute to this day.

Still, the president faced a hard decision. Newspaper columnist Walter Lippmann captured his predicament in a piece published in mid-January. "At bottom," Lippmann wrote, "the President has to choose between a bigger war and an unattractive peace." Richard Russell echoed that thought on the Senate floor: "I believe we must decide whether or not we are willing to take the action necessary to win the war in Vietnam and bring a conclusion to our commitment. The only other alternative I can see is to pull out—and this the overwhelming majority of Americans are not prepared to do."[32]

I offered my thoughts to President Johnson on the morning of January 17. "My own feeling," I told him, "is . . . that we are well-advised to continue the pause through Tet [i.e., late January] in order to allow an ample period of time to elapse for North Vietnam to respond to any one of these several lines of contact and establish firmly in the minds of our own public and of the international public that we gave a reasonable time for them to respond."

"I think you know where my leanings are and how I feel about it," he responded. "Except for you, I doubt we'd have gone on as long as we have gone, and I am not sorry for it at all. I want to be patient and understanding and reasonable; on the other hand, I think you know my natural inclination."[33]

The implication was clear: Johnson clearly believed that the pause had been a mistake and that the bombing had to be resumed. Although I remained convinced the Joint Chiefs had overestimated interdiction's effectiveness, I now recognized resumption was necessary. We had to start bombing again to blunt criticism that the pause was leading to even higher levels of infiltration, and to avoid sending the wrong signal to Hanoi, Beijing, and our own people. Yet Dean and I were fearful of right-wing pressure to attack targets near the China border, as had been done shortly before Beijing intervened in the Korean War. We urged that the bombing program be kept under tight control—and more limited than the chiefs wished—to minimize the risk of Chinese intervention.

The president now sought a broad consensus for the decision he planned to make. He called in four of the "Wise Men" (Clark Clifford, Arthur Dean, Allen Dulles, and John McCloy) on January 28. They endorsed resuming air operations against the North and increasing U.S. troop levels in the South. At a National Security Council meeting two days later, the president decided to end the pause. A Harris poll released the same day reported that "the vast majority of Americans would support an immediate escalation of the war—including all-out bombings of North Vietnam and increasing U.S. troop commitments to 500,000 men."[34]

———

What effects did the Christmas Bombing Pause produce? Some critics have argued that the increased U.S. air operations against the Ho Chi Minh Trail in Laos and ground operations in South Vietnam during the pause undercut whatever message we sought to convey. In any case, its failure to produce diplomatic results almost certainly soured President Johnson on the use of extended bombing pauses.

Many observers criticized our pattern of public diplomacy as naive or worse. Chester Cooper subsequently offered this comment:

> Where finely tooled instruments were required, we used a sledge-hammer. Where confidential and careful advance work was necessary, we proceeded with the subtlety of a Fourth of July parade. Where a dramatic, surprise proposal may have stirred Hanoi's interest, we made a public spectacle of every melodramatic move. Instead of maximizing the effect of our fourteen-point peace package, we buried it in the razzmatazz of sudden, noisy, and florid VIP trips. In short, the President was acting like a ringmaster of a three-ring circus, rather than the focal point of a carefully worked out exercise in diplomacy.[35]

If Cooper was right, then all of us who advised the president on this issue must share the blame.

The administration had made one attempt at quiet diplomacy. On December 29, it instructed the U.S. ambassador to Burma, Henry A. Byroade, to inform his North Vietnamese counterpart, Consul General Vu Huu Binh, that the bombing pause might be extended if Hanoi reciprocated "by making a serious contribution toward peace." A Hanoi radio broadcast several days later denounced the pause as a "trick" and repeated its "third point," that "the internal affairs of South Vietnam must be settled . . . in accordance with the program of the . . . National Front for Liberation" (the Vietcong's political arm). And shortly after the pause ended, Vu approached Byroade merely to restate Hanoi's hard line in response to the message Byroade had given him.[36]

Was the pause successful? It clearly did not lead immediately to negotiations. But, then, few who favored it thought that it would.

We viewed it as a step in a process that might ultimately bring about a negotiated settlement, and thus an end to the war.

Was it such a step? If not, did it fail because of our clumsiness or Hanoi's intransigence—or some combination of both? We will not know the answers until Hanoi opens its archives.

9

Troubles Deepen:

January 31, 1966–May 19, 1967

A s I was starting this chapter, a book appeared by George C. Herring, a historian who has devoted himself to study of the Vietnam War for over a decade. He writes:

> McNamara's influence began to wane after the December 1965 bombing pause. The secretary of defense had pushed the pause and accompanying peace initiative and LBJ, grudgingly and against his better judgment, had endorsed it. When it failed, as Johnson predicted it would, McNamara's infallibility was challenged and the president held him responsible for a major policy failure. After December 1965, moreover, the once indomitable secretary of defense was increasingly skeptical that the war could be won militarily, and as his skepticism grew and more and more manifested itself in his policy recommendations, his influence declined still further. At some point late in his tenure, he was cut off from some information because of his growing opposition to the war and his suspected ties to dovish Senator Robert Kennedy.[1]

I wish Herring were right. My influence—and therefore my responsibility as a key participant in Vietnam decision making—continued until I left the Pentagon in late February 1968. I had been skeptical, and grew increasingly skeptical, of our ability to achieve our political objectives in Vietnam through military means, but this did not diminish my involvement in the shaping of Vietnam policy.

During the fifteen months that followed the Christmas Bombing Pause, the war and its casualties grew substantially; debates over ground strategy, pacification, and especially bombing intensified dramatically; and war-related pressures on the Johnson administration, my family, and me increased almost daily. Dissent began to grow, although public support remained strong overall. Three more fitful and amateurish attempts to start negotiations failed, and the period ended with still another request from General Westmoreland to escalate. This time, he asked for 200,000 more troops along with a geographic expansion of the war. Both Westy and the Joint Chiefs stated their belief that this program would require mobilizing the reserves and utilizing the nation's full military capability, including the possible use of nuclear weapons. They recognized these actions could lead to confrontation with China and/or the Soviet Union in Southeast Asia or elsewhere, but they considered such steps necessary to shorten what they predicted would otherwise be five more years of war.

All of this demonstrated that our policy was failing: bombing and ground operations were not working, and our diplomatic initiatives, such as they were, were proving clumsy and ineffective. These harsh facts led me to conclude, in a highly controversial memo to President Johnson on May 19, 1967, that it was time to change our objectives in Vietnam and the means by which we sought to achieve them. The memo foreshadowed the break between us over Vietnam that ultimately led to my departure.

————

The year 1966 began with an event that deeply depressed me: McGeorge Bundy left the administration. In November 1965, John McCloy and Henry Ford II, heading a search committee for a new

Ford Foundation president, approached Mac and offered him the post. The job was clearly a plum: the Ford Foundation was the largest foundation in the country and was spending approximately $200 million a year to advance human welfare around the world.*

About the same time McCloy interviewed Mac for the job, he interviewed me, though I doubt he considered me as qualified as Mac. In any event, I knew I was not, and I told him so. Moreover, I felt a responsibility not to leave the government at that time, although the work the Ford Foundation was doing fascinated me.

Mac Bundy's departure was a grievous loss. He and I had not always agreed, but Mac brought to government service a highly disciplined mind of extraordinary quality and an insistence that we focus on the fundamental foreign policy issues confronting our nation, however difficult they might be. He could have left the administration because of the attractiveness of the Ford Foundation job alone, but I doubt that was the case. I speculate the true reason was his deep frustration with the war. I believe he was frustrated not only with the president's behavior but also with the decision-making process throughout the top echelons in both Washington and Saigon. He certainly had good cause to feel that way.

Walt Rostow succeeded Mac as national security adviser. He was an extraordinarily bright man with a warm personality and an open approach with his colleagues. But Walt viewed our Vietnam involvement, the conduct of our operations, and the prospects for achieving our political and military objectives there very uncritically. Optimistic by nature, he tended to be skeptical of any report that failed to indicate we were making progress. Years later, at an LBJ Library conference in March 1991, he continued to assert that

---

*One can think of that as mobilizing 2,000 of the world's most capable scholars and policy analysts (at $100,000 each in compensation, expenses, and overhead) to focus on the most critical economic, political, social, and security problems facing humankind. As I later observed after serving as a Ford Foundation trustee for seventeen years, the foundation did just that under Mac's leadership. When I became World Bank president, I borrowed or "stole" many of their ideas concerning population planning, poverty reduction, agricultural research, and environmental preservation—ideas enormously helpful, to the World Bank and me, in dealing with problems in developing nations.

America's decision to intervene in Vietnam, and the way we prosecuted the war, had proved beneficial to our nation and the region.[2]

———

As the Christmas Bombing Pause ended in late January 1966, President Johnson requested my views on the military outlook in Vietnam. In a memorandum of January 24, 1966, I expressed to him my belief that the Communists had decided to continue vigorously prosecuting the war in the South. They appeared to believe that the war would be a long one, that time was on their side, and that their staying power was superior to ours. They recognized that the large U.S. intervention in 1965 signaled our determination to avoid defeat, and that more U.S. deployments could be expected. I reasoned that the Communists would therefore enlarge their forces by heavier recruitment in the South and expanded infiltration from the North. The Joint Chiefs and I estimated they could increase their combat battalions by 50 percent in 1966 and sustain this larger force on infiltrated supplies of only 140 tons per day, utilizing no more than 70 percent of the Ho Chi Minh Trail's capacity.

To blunt this expected buildup, I recommended increasing U.S. troop levels by 200,000 (as Westy had previously requested), raising the total from 179,000 to 368,000 by year's end, and expanding air operations as planned. But I warned this increased effort probably would not put a "tight ceiling" on enemy operations in South Vietnam because bombing could reduce, but not stop, the supply flow from North Vietnam.

This led me to offer a somber assessment:

Even though the Communists will continue to suffer heavily from our ground and air action, we expect them, upon learning of any U.S. intentions to augment its forces, to boost their own commitment and to test U.S. capabilities and will to persevere at a higher level of conflict and casualties (U.S. killed-in-action with the recommended deployments can be expected to reach 1000 a month.) . . . It follows, therefore, that the odds are about even that, even with the recommended deployments, we will be faced in early 1967 with a military standoff at a much higher level, with pacification hardly underway and with the requirement for the deployment of still more U.S. forces.

This prospect intensified my conviction that the United States needed negotiations leading to a diplomatic resolution of the conflict. I hoped our increased effort would "condition [Hanoi] toward [such] negotiations and an acceptable end to the war."[3]

———

Between 1965 and 1967, Westy intensified his pursuit of an attrition strategy aimed at inflicting more casualties on the Vietcong and North Vietnamese than they could replace. But the facts proved otherwise. However much Westy, I, and many others wished differently, the evidence showed that our adversaries—through a combination of recruitment in the South and infiltration from the North—expanded their combat numbers substantially. Vietcong and North Vietnamese forces increased in size throughout 1966 and into 1967.

From the beginning of our involvement in Vietnam, the South Vietnamese forces had been giving us poor intelligence and inaccurate reports. Sometimes these inaccuracies were conscious attempts to mislead; at other times they were the product of too much optimism. And sometimes the inaccuracies merely reflected the difficulty of gauging progress accurately.

But I insisted we try to measure progress. As I have emphasized, since my years at Harvard, I had gone by the rule that it is not enough to conceive of an objective and a plan to carry it out; you must monitor the plan to determine whether you are achieving the objective. If you discover you are not, you either revise the plan or change the objective. I was convinced that, while we might not be able to track something as unambiguous as a front line, we could find variables that would indicate our success or failure. So we measured the targets destroyed in the North, the traffic down the Ho Chi Minh Trail, the number of captives, the weapons seized, the enemy body count, and so on.

The body count was a measurement of the adversary's manpower losses; we undertook it because one of Westy's objectives was to reach a so-called crossover point, at which Vietcong and North Vietnamese casualties would be greater than they could sustain. To reach such a point, we needed to have some idea what they could sustain and what their losses were.

Critics point to use of the body count as an example of my obsession with numbers. "This guy McNamara," they said, "he tries to quantify everything." Obviously, there are things you cannot quantify: honor and beauty, for example. But things you can count, you ought to count. Loss of life is one when you are fighting a war of attrition. We tried to use body counts as a measurement to help us figure out what we should be doing in Vietnam to win the war while putting our troops at the least risk. Every attempt to monitor progress in Vietnam during my tenure as secretary of defense was directed toward those goals, but often the reports were misleading.

In the spring of 1967, Westy concluded that the crossover point had at last been reached; the enemy's numbers had stabilized and, perhaps, diminished. The CIA, by contrast, never perceived a diminution in enemy strength. In a May 23, 1967, report, its analysts concluded, "Despite increasingly effective 'search and destroy' operations . . . the Vietnamese Communists have continued to *expand* their Main Forces, both by infiltration and by local recruitment. . . . It appears that the Communists can continue to sustain their overall strength during the coming year [emphasis added]."[4]

Whichever judgment was correct—Westy's or the CIA's—I took little comfort, because the Vietcong and North Vietnamese still largely controlled their casualties in a guerrilla war in jungle terrain by choosing where, when, and how long to fight. What is more, by the spring of 1967 they possessed sufficient forces to prevent any substantial extension of the pacification program—particularly in the rural areas where most South Vietnamese lived.

The disagreement between Westmoreland and the CIA was frustrating but unsurprising. Although we had been trying to measure the war's progress realistically, getting accurate data remained difficult. With the numbers we had, there was room for great disparities in analysis, of which this dispute is a good example. The CIA felt that the North Vietnamese had much greater staying power than the administration (and Westy) believed. It turned out the CIA was correct.

How were we to decide which interpretation to accept? This task was hellishly complex when we were not even sure of the accuracy of the reports the interpretations were based on. Without question, we sometimes received erroneous reports. Years later this led to a painful sequence of events when the CBS network mistakenly portrayed Westy as having lied to the president and me. At issue was his reporting of the enemy's so-called Order of Battle—the strength of the Vietcong and North Vietnamese forces in the field.

A 1982 *CBS Reports* documentary, "The Uncounted Enemy: A Vietnam Deception," alleged that Westy ordered his senior intelligence officers knowingly to understate enemy strength in order to bolster his claims of military progress. In effect, CBS argued that by deliberately underreporting Vietcong/North Vietnamese strength in South Vietnam, Westy could demonstrate greater progress through his attrition strategy than had in fact been achieved. I address this issue now to make crystal clear that, while deep differences existed between Westy and me over the course of the war in the South (and between the Joint Chiefs and me over the air war in the North), these differences in no way reflected personal antagonism or lack of trust.

My involvement with the CBS film began on June 6, 1981, shortly before I retired as World Bank president, when *CBS Reports* producer George Crile III telephoned me at my office. Crile, whom I knew socially—he was the former son-in-law of friends Joe and Susan Mary Alsop—said CBS was preparing a program on Vietnam in which he knew I would wish to participate. He said that CBS had clear evidence, along with supporting testimony from Military

Assistance Command, Vietnam, and CIA personnel, that General Westmoreland had consciously deceived the president and me on the Order of Battle.

I told Crile I did not believe it. He replied that the evidence was incontrovertible. I continued to deny such a possibility. Crile finally asked if he could outline and substantiate the charges in a meeting with me. I said I would almost certainly not change my mind, but, because of our past relationship, I agreed to see him.

We met at the end of the day on June 16. During a thirty-minute conversation in my World Bank office and a car ride to my house, Crile presented his evidence. It boiled down to this: Westy reported enemy strength as x, whereas some of his military intelligence officers, supported by some CIA analysts, estimated it as x plus y. The CBS network alleged Westy had ordered his subordinates to insert the lower figure in MACV reports to Washington.

A highly technical, ambiguous, and even elusive issue, the controversy swirled around competing definitions of "the enemy." The United States faced an extraordinarily diverse enemy force in Vietnam—regular North Vietnamese Army units, individual North Vietnamese soldiers infiltrated into the South as fillers, Vietcong guerrillas recruited in the South and organized into military units, and a wide assortment of paramilitary personnel. The paramilitaries ranged from peasants equipped with rifles and organized into informal military groups to black-pajama-clad villagers functioning as saboteurs and informers. The issue became where to draw the line when reporting "enemy strength." Westy excluded more of the nonregular forces than did some of his intelligence officers and some CIA analysts.

The dispute—within both MACV and the Washington intelligence community—grew bitter. It extended over a long period and became well known to CIA Director Dick Helms, the president, me, and other senior government officials. It aroused deep emotions, which outlived the war. Several individuals opposed to Westy's judgment consented to interviews with CBS in which they stated—either explicitly or implicitly—that he deliberately and grossly misled President Johnson and me. This included the program's main witness and paid "informant," former CIA analyst Sam Adams.

When I met with Crile, I explained to him why I believed such a charge lacked merit. He refused to believe me. The documentary was aired on the night of January 23, 1982. Westy demanded an apology from the network, and, when it was not forthcoming, he filed a $120 million libel suit against them that fall.

Although I knew the libel trial would be a nasty, "dirty" confrontation, because of my immense respect for the dedication with which Westy had served our country over several decades, I volunteered in the summer of 1983 to testify on his behalf.

Westy's attorney, Dan Burt of the Capital Legal Foundation, learned that Crile had secretly—and without my permission—taped some of his telephone conversations with me. Believing the tapes would substantiate Westy's claim that Crile knew before the program aired that reason existed to believe the charges unfounded, Burt sought to obtain the tapes. According to him, CBS's counsel initially denied that any such tapes existed. A CBS News editor who had worked on the program told Burt that Crile's secretary said the tapes were in his bottom left-hand desk drawer. They were not. They later turned up in a trunk at Crile's home—but the portions containing my denial of the allegation against Westy had been erased.[5]

In due time, CBS asked to depose me. I agreed. At my deposition on March 26–27, 1984, network attorney David Boies began by saying he presumed I would have no objection to the deposition being videotaped. When I inquired how the videotape might be used, he replied, "In whatever way we choose." When I inquired whether this included transmission over commercial television networks, he said yes. My lawyer had advised me that if I could not remember details about events that had occurred sixteen years previously, I should simply reply, "I do not recall." I could well imagine the effect of twenty to thirty such repetitions broadcast on *The CBS Evening News*. I therefore said I would not consent to videotaping. Boies said in a threatening voice that CBS had the legal right to demand that I be videotaped. I said I would go to jail instead. Boies finally decided to proceed without the taping but reserved the right to return to the issue later. He never did. I later learned that Dick Helms, called to depose for the same trial, also refused to be videotaped. The network took his case to court. But after many months and substantial legal expenses, Dick prevailed.

In my deposition and in court testimony on December 6, 1984, I stated that the president and I knew about the differing opinions of enemy strength within MACV and the CIA during 1966–67; that I leaned toward the more inclusive (and larger) estimate; that Westy had not tried to deceive us; and that even had he tried—which was inconceivable—he could not have succeeded because of the alternative information channels available to us. Boies sought to discredit my testimony by alleging I had consistently misrepresented military progress in Vietnam. The trial ended in February 1985 in an out-of-court settlement, with both sides claiming victory. But the combination of the program and the widespread press coverage of the libel trial sadly caused further erosion in the American people's faith in the integrity of their government and its leaders, both military and civilian.

Despite our differences in judgment, Westy and I did our utmost to keep U.S. troops in the field as well supplied and well protected as possible. As the war heated up and passions increased, some critics of the Johnson administration alleged that material shortages had compromised our soldiers' safety. This was not the case. As Bus Wheeler wrote me on April 23, 1966, "There have been no shortages in supplies for the troops in Vietnam which have adversely affected combat operations or the health or welfare of the troops. No required air sorties [a sortie is one attack mission by one aircraft] have been canceled. As a matter of fact the air support given our forces is without parallel in our history."[6]

American soldiers in Vietnam faced many obstacles and miserable conditions: an elusive and deadly enemy, booby traps and ambushes, fire ants and leeches, dense jungles, deep swamps, and sweltering heat. Where large-unit engagements occurred, U.S. troops usually prevailed. They fought bravely. They answered their nation's call and endured many hardships—both "in country" and, sadly, after coming home as well.

It was not the valor of American soldiers in Vietnam that was ever in dispute but how they should operate in the field. This issue became the focus of considerable disagreement between Westy and the marines (along with some army elements) during this period. Convinced that the "search and destroy" strategy played to Vietcong and North Vietnamese strengths, its critics—in particular, the marines—favored an alternative counterinsurgency strategy that combined population protection with gradual liberation of Vietcong-controlled villages. Although deeply divided, the military never fully debated their differences in strategic approach, or discussed them with me in any detail. As secretary of defense, I should have forced them to do both.

Westy's attrition strategy relied heavily on firepower. Shells and napalm rained down on Vietcong and North Vietnamese base areas in South Vietnam. It often proved difficult to distinguish combatants from noncombatants. Between 1965 and 1967, U.S. and South Vietnamese air forces dropped over a million tons of bombs on the South, more than twice the tonnage dropped on the North.[7] Fighting produced more and more civilian casualties and squalid refugee camps. The increasing destruction and misery brought on the country we were supposed to be helping troubled me greatly. This also undermined, in an unintended but profound way, the pacification program designed to extend security to the countryside and win the "hearts and minds" of the South Vietnamese people. And it hurt any effort at building popular support for the Saigon government, which was crucial to defeating the Vietcong.

A corrupt Saigon bureaucracy and poor coordination between South Vietnamese and Americans (and among Americans as well) also dogged our efforts. Funds promised for many projects never reached their destination, and many local officials regarded pacification as a threat to their perquisites and power. Villagers traumatized by war often greeted the effort with apathy or caution. We never adequately addressed how such a program should be administered or by whom, especially in the absence of an effective and responsible South Vietnamese government. When we tried to accelerate pacification's progress, we merely failed more quickly.

In the fall of 1966, I advised the president to reorganize the pacification program—then under the ambassador's control. I urged that we place both military operations and pacification programs under MACV's direct command. The idea stirred considerable bureaucratic opposition in both Saigon and Washington, so I changed tack. I recommended centralizing lines of command and clarifying responsibilities, leaving military operations under Westy and the pacification program under Deputy Ambassador William Porter. If, after a fair trial, the plan did not work, I advised putting both operations under Westy. This was never done, a serious mistake.[8]

Meanwhile, the air war intensified. Sorties against North Vietnam grew from 25,000 in 1965 to 79,000 in 1966 to 108,000 in 1967, and the tonnage of bombs dropped rose from 63,000 to 136,000 to 226,000.[9] Bombing inflicted damage on the North; it diverted manpower and resources that otherwise might have gone to military uses; it hampered the movement of men and supplies to the South. But there was a heavy price: American pilots were lost; captured U.S. airmen provided Hanoi with hostages; the number of civilian casualties multiplied. Moreover, the continued pounding of a small nation by a superpower gave the North Vietnamese a powerful propaganda tool. And, in the end, bombing did not achieve its basic goals: as Rolling Thunder intensified, U.S. intelligence estimated that infiltration *increased* from about 35,000 men in 1965 to as many as 90,000 in 1967, while Hanoi's will to carry on the fight stayed firm.[10]

I did not believe that strategic bombing would work unless it targeted production sources, denied access to basic products, and prevented the use of substitute products and means. But production sources for North Vietnam and the Vietcong lay in the Soviet Union and China. The United States could not reasonably target those sources except by political (not military) means. Similarly, I believed that bombing to interdict the flow of men and supplies would work only in specific instances. It was unlikely to be effective in North Vietnam and Laos because of the nature of the terrain, the low volumes of supplies required, and the ability to substitute alternative routes and means of distribution, especially in North Vietnam's manpower-intensive environment. All this led me to conclude that no amount of bombing of the North—short of genocidal destruction, which no one contemplated—could end the war.

The Joint Chiefs felt differently and pressed for a more ambitious bombing program in the spring of 1966. They favored attacking petroleum storage facilities near Hanoi and Haiphong, claiming this would deal North Vietnam a mortal blow. The president and I hesitated to attack these facilities for several reasons, including the danger that a nearby Soviet ship might accidentally be hit, risking a confrontation between nuclear superpowers.*

Finally, in late June 1966, we authorized the attacks. Petroleum storage facilities were struck, but the loss hindered the North Vietnamese for only a short time. They quickly adapted, dispersing fuel in underground tanks and concealed fifty-five-gallon drums scattered throughout the country, and offset the raids by extracting increased oil shipments by rail from China and by off-loading from

---

*Our concern over the risk of confrontation with the Soviets was borne out the following summer, when I was summoned to the Pentagon one Sunday morning. Moscow was protesting that U.S. warplanes had struck one of their merchant ships docked at Campha harbor, northeast of Haiphong. Assured following an investigation by Adm. Oley Sharp that the story lacked merit, I instructed my public affairs office to issue a scathing denial. Some weeks later, the commander of the U.S. Air Force in the Pacific, Gen. John D. Ryan, on a trip to Thailand discovered that a flight of four U.S. aircraft had indeed struck the Soviet ship while attacking nearby antiaircraft batteries. When the planes had returned to their base in Thailand after the mission, two of the four pilots reported the story to their wing commander, a colonel, who then ordered the gun camera film destroyed and the after-action reports altered. The colonel was later court-martialed and fined. To my knowledge, this was the only occasion during my seven years at the Defense Department that an outright lie by a military officer affected my understanding and explanation of an event.

Soviet tankers anchored offshore onto barges, which ferried the oil to transfer points dotted along the many estuaries in the Red River delta.

The failure of the June raids significantly to impede North Vietnam's will and ability to continue supporting the war in the South led me to consider other options. In the summer of 1966, I requested a group of distinguished scientists working on contract with the JASON division of the Pentagon's Institute for Defense Analyses—among them President Eisenhower's former science adviser, George Kistiakowsky, and Jerome Wiesner, president of MIT—to study the problem. They concluded the bombing had indeed been ineffective and recommended building a "barrier" as an alternative means of checking infiltration. This concept, which had first come to my attention in the spring of 1966, would involve laying down a complex belt of mines and sensors across the Demilitarized Zone and the Laotian panhandle to the west. (The sensors would guide our attack aircraft to enemy forces on the move.) The barrier would be costly, but because our bombing was ineffective, I authorized it and assigned Lt. Gen. Alfred D. Starbird to oversee its development. The Joint Chiefs reacted coolly to this idea but did not actively oppose it. Once it was put in place, the barrier was intended to increase infiltration losses. And it did.*

Meanwhile, the chiefs continued to press for heavier air attacks against the North throughout the fall of 1966 and into 1967. Our differences came to light in open Senate hearings. As Bus Wheeler and I testified before the Senate Armed Services Committee in January, this exchange took place:

SECRETARY MCNAMARA: I don't believe that the bombing up to the present has significantly reduced, nor any bombing that I could contemplate in the future would significantly reduce, the actual flow of men and material to the South.

---

*My account of the anti-infiltration barrier (or McNamara Line, as it came to be called by some) is based on recollection rather than the contemporary record—largely because the August 1966 JASON study has yet to be declassified.

SENATOR CANNON: Do the military advisers agree with you on that question?

SECRETARY MCNAMARA: I think General Wheeler should answer that question.

GENERAL WHEELER: As I have said, I believe our bombing in the North has reduced the flow. I do not discount the effect to the extent that some other people do.[11]

The statements hinted at the deepening disagreement between the chiefs and me, and the inevitable—and growing—friction it produced.

———

Throughout the long months of debate over ground strategy, pacification, and bombing, efforts to stimulate movement toward a negotiated settlement continued, but they were sporadic, amateurish, and ineffectual.

Critics argue the Johnson administration never mastered the delicate task of waging peace in the midst of waging limited war. Three diplomatic ventures initiated during this period demonstrate the merit of this charge: the Ronning Missions in the spring of 1966 and two code-named undertakings—Marigold in the second half of that year and Sunflower in early 1967. These three contacts illustrate our general approach to achieving a political settlement in Vietnam during 1966 and early 1967—and why we failed.

After the abortive Christmas Bombing Pause, which, its critics charged, had led to increased U.S. casualties and increased pressure to expand air attacks, the president indeed grew hesitant about any more initiatives. However, much to his annoyance, he confronted another such attempt just two months later. This time it originated not with me but with Canadian Prime Minister Lester Pearson. In March, retired Canadian diplomat and old Far Eastern hand Chester A. Ronning traveled to Hanoi and brought back a message from North Vietnamese Premier Pham Van Dong that, if the Americans stopped the bombing "for good and unconditionally, we will talk."[12]

The Canadians considered Pham's message a bona fide peace move; to them, it seemed an advance beyond Hanoi's earlier insistence on U.S. acceptance of the Four Points before negotiations. Many in Washington did not agree. They distrusted Pearson's and Ronning's prior open criticism of Washington's Vietnam policy and felt Pham's words contained deliberate and clever ambiguities—for example, the use of the word *talks* rather than *negotiations* seemed to imply only preliminary contacts, not substantive discussions. The president, moreover, hesitated to stop the bombing again without some reciprocal concession from Hanoi. Thus the Johnson administration refused to authorize another pause. In retrospect, we were mistaken in not having Ronning at least probe the meaning of Pham's words more deeply.

A few months later, in June 1966, Poland's representative to the ICC,* Januscz Lewandowski, returned to Saigon from a trip to Hanoi with what he termed "a very specific peace offer." He reported the North Vietnamese open to a "political compromise" to end the war and willing to go "quite a long way" to achieve it. Lewandowski passed his information to the dean of Saigon's diplomatic corps, Italian Ambassador Giovanni D'Orlandi; D'Orlandi transmitted it to Ambassador Henry Cabot Lodge; and Lodge reported it to Washington. The channel became known as Marigold.[13] Secret talks took place throughout the summer between Lodge and Lewandowski, the lanky Lodge frequently crouching in the back of a private car en route to D'Orlandi's office or apartment to avoid detection.

In September, the president authorized Arthur Goldberg to deliver a major speech to the U.N. General Assembly in which Goldberg announced the United States would stop "all bombing of North Vietnam the moment we are assured, privately or otherwise,

---

*Established in 1954 to monitor compliance with the Geneva Agreements, the ICC comprised representatives from Canada, India, and Poland.

that this step will be answered promptly by a corresponding and appropriate de-escalation of the other side."[14]

Since the Christmas Bombing Pause of 1965, we had insisted Hanoi reduce its ground activity at the same time we stopped bombing. The North Vietnamese appeared to have viewed this as an effort to force them to deescalate under the threat of continued bombing. They refused to move under such pressure. Seeking to bridge the gap, we now said, in effect: "Give us private assurances of more than 'talk,' and we will immediately cease bombing, after which you will be expected to reciprocate by reducing infiltration and military operations in the South." This was designed to provide Hanoi with a face-saving way of decreasing the level of its military activity and became known as the Phase A–Phase B Formula.

Based on this new formula, Lewandowski in November claimed to have secured North Vietnam's agreement to meet with the United States in Warsaw beginning on December 5, 1966. On December 2 and 4, American aircraft struck new targets around Hanoi in raids originally planned for November 10 but postponed because of bad weather. The Poles reacted angrily at this unfortunate timing but agreed to proceed as planned. United States Ambassador John Gronouski met Polish Foreign Minister Adam Rapacki on December 6. The North Vietnamese did not show. The Poles continued, however, to try to bring the two sides together. Gronouski and Rapacki met again on December 13. That very day (and the following day as well) the United States again bombed targets around Hanoi—this time with twice the intensity of the early December raids.

How could such a thing happen? Senior U.S. officials suspected Hanoi might misread this second round of attacks on the eve of talks. Lodge, Gronouski, Undersecretary of State Nicholas Katzenbach, Tommy Thompson, and I had all desperately urged the president to postpone them. But Johnson, still influenced by the aftereffects of the Christmas Bombing Pause, felt postponement would be interpreted as weakness. He rejected our suggestion.

The reaction came quickly. On December 15, Rapacki

informed Gronouski that the U.S. bombing raids had scotched the talks. A Russian embassy official in Washington subsequently told John McNaughton that Moscow believed there had been a favorable atmosphere for negotiations, but the attacks had "ruined it." He added that there were forces in Hanoi interested in compromise, but they could not "become active in an environment in which bombs . . . are falling in Hanoi."[15]

Did the December bombing raids destroy a serious effort toward peace? One U.S. official who followed these developments, Chet Cooper, believed the North Vietnamese "at most . . . had given Lewandowski a hunting license, rather than any definitive commitment." Nick Katzenbach later characterized Marigold as a "phoney." Either—or neither—may have been right.

A few weeks later, a third peace initiative (Sunflower) led to an even greater fiasco—one that for a time severely strained U.S.-British relations. The initiative involved three separate contacts: a direct approach to the North Vietnamese embassy in Moscow; a personal letter from President Johnson to Ho Chi Minh; and an effort by British Prime Minister Harold Wilson, working through Soviet Premier Alexei Kosygin.

The initiative began in early January 1967, when the Russians informed our Moscow embassy that if we asked to see the North Vietnamese chargé d'affaires, preliminary contacts might result, perhaps leading to serious talks. The senior U.S. official then in Moscow, John Guthrie, met with his Hanoi counterpart, Le Chang, on January 10. Guthrie reported that Chang appeared nervous, listened silently, and said nothing. He did, however, invite Guthrie back for a second meeting. On that occasion, Guthrie sketched a scenario for how the war might end: a ceasefire, followed by troop withdrawals, elections, political participation by the National Liberation Front, and eventually reunification of North and South Vietnam. Chang again listened silently. A week later, on January 27, he invited Guthrie to come again. This time, Chang greeted him with a long and insulting polemic.

On February 6, Prime Minister Wilson welcomed Alexei

Kosygin on an official visit to London. A short bombing pause associated with the Vietnamese Tet holiday had just begun. Wilson and Kosygin discussed North Vietnamese Foreign Minister Nguyen Duy Trinh's recent statement that talks "could begin" if the bombing stopped unconditionally. When Kosygin could not, or would not, guarantee that talks would start after a bombing cessation, Wilson put forward the Phase A–Phase B Formula. But evidence of increased North Vietnamese infiltration led the president to harden his position on mutual deescalation in a personal letter to Ho Chi Minh on February 8. The United States asked Wilson to withdraw Phase A–Phase B and replace it with a new and demanding formula: Washington would stop bombing if Hanoi stopped infiltration. Wilson reacted angrily but passed the proposal to Kosygin.

The United States then reluctantly approved Wilson's last-minute proposal to extend the Tet bombing pause by several hours so that Kosygin could present the new formula to Hanoi. David K. E. Bruce, our able ambassador to London and an old friend of mine (I later served as a pallbearer at his funeral) asked for forty-eight hours. The president agreed to only six. Kosygin promised to do what he could, but he was furious. Bruce telephoned Dean Rusk to say the deadline was ridiculous; Kosygin could not possibly contact Hanoi and report back in so short a time. He urged Dean to see the president and ask for several more days.

Dean refused, and well he might have. I had been in the Cabinet Room and had supported the president when, in exasperation, he said we had already extended the pause twice and ruled out another extension. His decision rested on evidence that North Vietnam had boosted infiltration during each pause, and the Joint Chiefs' charge that this increased American casualties in the South. In addition, in this case we had learned of a very large North Vietnamese troop movement. Before Wilson even had a chance to get the Russian's reply, the bombing resumed.

Two years later, Wilson told a television audience: "I believe we got very near . . . then the whole thing was dashed away." A forty-eight-hour extension, he said, might have done it. At about the same time, Tommy Thompson, again serving as ambassador to Moscow, reported that Soviet Ambassador to Washington Anatoly Dobrynin said, "Kosygin's statements in London . . . were not made out of thin air"—in other words, the Russians had reason to believe the North Vietnamese had been ready to move toward negotiations.[16]

Were Wilson and Kosygin right? Again, we may never know. But of one thing I am certain: we failed miserably to integrate and coordinate our diplomatic and military actions as we searched for an end to the war.

———

From early 1966 through mid-1967, public support for the administration's Vietnam policy remained surprisingly strong, despite rising U.S. casualties and increasing media scrutiny of the war. After the Christmas Bombing Pause, polls showed about two-thirds of Americans took a middle-of-the-road position on the war. For example, on February 28, 1966, Louis Harris reported, "There is 'consensus' in the country today on one point about the Vietnam war: the American people long for an honorable end to hostilities, but by 2 to 1 they believe we have to stay and see it through." Harris also reported, however, that "more and more the American people are becoming split between those who favor an all-out military effort to shorten the war and those who prefer negotiations to the risk of escalation." His conclusion: "If there is a movement of opinion in the country it is toward seeking a military solution to what is generally regarded as a frustrating stalemate."[17] Advocates of Sen. Richard Russell's "get it over with or get out" approach appeared to be gaining in popularity.

Pressure from the left—those urging us to do less or to withdraw—would culminate in early 1968 in substantial opposition that contributed to President Johnson's decision not to seek reelection. But that was not our major concern in 1966 and most of 1967. The president, Dean, and I worried far more about pressure from the right. Hawks charged we were forcing our military to fight with one hand tied behind its back and demanded we unleash the full weight of America's military might.

We believed, however, that in a nuclear world an unlimited war over Vietnam posed totally unacceptable risks to the nation and, indeed, to the world. In Dean's words, we therefore "tried to do in cold blood what perhaps could only be done in hot blood." Lady Bird captured our dilemma when she wrote in her diary, "A miasma of trouble hangs over everything. The temperament of our people seems to be 'you must either get excited, get passionate, fight and get it over with, or we must pull out.' It is unbelievably hard to fight a limited war."[18]

Nevertheless, dissent on the left—vocal and often violent—began to grow, particularly in the universities. These dissenters frequently targeted me as a symbol of America's "war machine." During one week in June 1966, faculty and students at both Amherst College and New York University walked out as I received honorary degrees. A short time earlier, picketers had hooted at me when I addressed my younger daughter Kathy's graduating class at Chatham College.

I respected these students' right to dissent and the spirit in which most of them did so. "There is a serious dimension to the protest among some students today," I said at Chatham, adding: "But whatever comfort some of the extremist protest may be giving our enemy . . . let us be perfectly clear about our principles and our priorities. This is a nation in which freedom of dissent is absolutely fundamental." On another occasion I said, "I don't think we can have a democracy without freedom to dissent." I believed so then, and I believe so today.[19]

What disturbed me most during my campus visits was the realization that opposition to the administration's Vietnam policy increased with the institution's prestige and the educational attainment of its students. At Amherst, those protesting my presence wore armbands. I counted the number and calculated the percentage of protesters in each of four groups: graduates, cum laude graduates, magna cum laude graduates, and summa cum laude graduates. To my consternation, the percentages rose with the level of academic distinction. Some of the largest and most intense campus demonstrations occurred at premier institutions such as Berkeley and Stanford.

An early and ugly demonstration took place at Harvard University in the fall of 1966. Professor Richard Neustadt, of Harvard's Kennedy School, invited me to address a group of undergraduates. At about the same time, Henry Kissinger, who was then teaching a Harvard graduate seminar in international relations, asked me to meet with his class. I accepted both invitations and extended my trip to include a visit to my alma mater, the Harvard Business School.

I traveled to Cambridge on November 7 unaccompanied by security personnel, as was my custom wherever I went in the United States during my seven years as secretary.*

My chauffeur—who had driven Franklin Roosevelt when he served as assistant secretary of the navy under President Wilson—did occasionally carry a pistol. And there was also a fountain pen–like tear gas dispenser in the limousine's rear compartment. One day, after attending a meeting of the Kennedy family to review plans for the slain president's grave site, I asked Eunice Shriver (President Kennedy's sister) if she needed a ride. She asked to be driven to the Wardman Park Hotel. As Eunice and I rode up Connecticut Avenue together, I decided to show her how the tear gas dispenser worked. I rolled the window down a bit, held the dispenser up to it, and pressed. Because we were moving so fast, there was a vacuum, which drew the fumes into the car. Eunice—who planned to make a speech at the Wardman Park—began choking and screaming. I had incapacitated her by the time we arrived.

My visit at the Harvard Business School proceeded in an orderly fashion, and the discussion across the Charles River, with the undergraduates at Quincy House—while far more lively and bordering on the contentious—proved highly stimulating for me. However,

---

*The world has changed greatly in the past thirty years: today, while playing tennis in Washington, I often see on adjacent courts cabinet officers or their spouses who must be protected by security people even while engaging in recreation.

trouble began as I left Quincy House for Henry's class in Langdell Hall, several blocks away. Quincy House exits onto Mill Street, a brick lane barely wide enough for a car. The university had provided a station wagon and campus policeman to drive me to Langdell. As I entered the car, a mob of students quickly surrounded it.

Then all hell broke loose. Students pressed in around the car and began rocking it. The driver, fearing harm to both himself and me, slammed the car into gear and began driving into the students gathered in front.

"Stop!" I shouted. "You'll kill someone!"

He jammed the car into reverse and started backing up. By then, students had gathered in the rear. "I'm getting out," I said.

"You can't do that," he warned. "They'll mob you."

By then the crowd had grown to several hundred angry young people. Anyone who has experienced an uncontrolled mob knows it is a fearful thing. I wrenched open the door, stepped out of the car, and in a loud voice said, "OK, fellas, I'll answer one or two of your questions. But remember two things: We're in a mob and someone might get hurt and I don't want that. I also have an appointment in five minutes."

I asked who was in charge, and a young man named Michael Ansara, president of Harvard's Students for a Democratic Society chapter (a radical protest group), produced a microphone. I suggested we get on the car's hood, where we could see and be seen.

"Before you start your questions," I began, "I want you to know I spent four of the happiest years of my life on the University of California, Berkeley, campus doing some of the things you are doing today."

This was greeted by catcalls and massive pushing and shoving. Thinking I could avert further violence by making clear that their threat would not intimidate me, I added, "I was tougher than you then and I'm tougher today. I was more courteous then and I hope I am more courteous today."

After a few questions, it became clear the danger was only increasing, so I concluded my remarks, jumped off the car, rushed through a Quincy House door the campus policeman had opened for me, and found myself in an underground tunnel extending several blocks and linking a number of Harvard buildings. My escort through the maze was Barney Frank, a Harvard undergraduate who later became U.S. representative for Massachusetts's Fourth Congressional District. Frank and I ran through the maze, lost the students, and emerged in Harvard Yard. I kept my commitment to meet with Kissinger's class, somewhat unnerved. Then I spent a half hour calming myself by browsing through one of Harvard Square's delightful bookstores.

Later I joined Dick Neustadt and other Harvard faculty friends for dinner. The conversation proved frank but friendly. For the first time, I believe, I voiced my feeling that, because the war was not going as hoped, future scholars would surely wish to study why. I thought we should seek to facilitate such study in order to help prevent similar errors in the future. This thought ultimately led to the "Pentagon Papers."

Shortly after I returned to Washington, I received a note from Harvard College Dean John U. Munro about the incident. He wrote:

> I hope you will accept our deeply felt apology for the discourteous and unruly confrontation forced upon you yesterday by members of the Harvard College community. We appreciated very much your willingness to take time during your visit to talk with undergraduates, and we are much disturbed by the unpleasant finale in the streets. Such rudeness and physical confrontation have no place in the university world, and we are appalled that it should happen here at Harvard.

I thanked Dean Munro for his note in a letter the next day, adding:

> No apology was necessary, however. Having spent four active years at Berkeley, I believe I understand both the intense interest

of the students in the vital issues of our time and their desire to express that interest in a manner which commands public attention. Occasionally, all of us allow our zeal to exceed our judgment, but such behavioral aberrations should not be a basis for curbing dissent—dissent is both the prerogative and the preservative of free men everywhere.[20]

Antiwar sentiment continued to be directed at me from many sources. Sometimes it came from those I cared about most. Marg and I had remained very close to both Jackie and Bobby Kennedy, talking to them on the phone frequently and visiting whenever I had time. Bobby had grown to be one of my best friends. When I first met him, he had seemed a rough, tough character who believed that in politics the end justifies the means. But during the eight years I knew him, he grew thirty years in terms of his values and his understanding of the world.

Some people inside and outside the administration were surprised that I remained so close to the Kennedys, given President Johnson's mistrust of them. The tension between LBJ and Bobby was well-known and reciprocal. But just as Henry Ford II had not cared whether I lived in Ann Arbor or refused to donate to the Republicans as long as I produced profits, Lyndon Johnson accepted my closeness to the Kennedys because he understood my loyalty to the presidency and to him. This was true even when he and I split irreconcilably over Vietnam.

Jackie, of course, did not represent the same political threat to the president as Bobby, but she thought no less deeply than her brother-in-law about the issues of the day. At one point during my long process of growing doubt about the wisdom of our course, Jackie—this dear friend whom I admired enormously—erupted in fury and tears and directed her wrath at me. I was so overwhelmed by her feelings that I still remember every detail of the incident.

Marg was traveling, so I had gone to New York to dine with Jackie. After dinner, we sat on a couch in the small library of her Manhattan apartment discussing the work of Chilean poet and

Nobel Prize winner Gabriela Mistral. Both us were especially fond of her poem "Prayer." It is a plea to God to grant forgiveness to the man Mistral loved, who had committed suicide. She writes, "You say he was cruel? You forget I loved him ever . . . To love (as YOU well understand) is a bitter task."

Jackie was indeed a glamorous woman. But she was also extremely sensitive. Whether her emotions were triggered by the poem or by something I said, I do not know. She had grown very depressed by, and very critical of, the war. In any event, she became so tense that she could hardly speak. She suddenly exploded. She turned and began, literally, to beat on my chest, demanding that I "do something to stop the slaughter!"

My encounters with other protesters became louder and uglier. One of the more disturbing was in August 1966. My family and I were waiting to board a plane at Seattle airport after having climbed Mount Rainier with Jim and Lou Whittaker (Jim was the first American to conquer Mount Everest). A man approached, shouted "Murderer!" and spat on me. Then, during the Christmas holidays, while I was lunching with Marg at a restaurant on top of Aspen Mountain, a woman came to the table and in a voice loud enough to be heard across the room, screamed, "Baby burner! You have blood on your hands!"

These incidents naturally upset me. Even more distressing, the tensions hurt my family. Marg developed a dangerous ulcer that required surgery the following summer. My son, Craig, who was only a teenager, sometime later also developed an ulcer.

Occasionally the stress and strain would be eased by a lighter moment. In November 1966, Yevgeny Yevtushenko, one of the Soviet Union's most popular poets, visited the United States. In a gesture typical of the "outreach" practiced by the Kennedy clan, Bobby invited him to a large dinner party at his home, Hickory Hill. About 2:30 A.M., after Yevtushenko and I had spent hours talking of poetry, the Cold War, Vietnam, and a hundred other topics—he had been drinking heavily—I asked where he was staying and whether we could take him home. He eagerly accepted the offer, and my chauffeur drove him, Marg, and me to the Statler Hotel. As he staggered out of the car, he turned and said, "They say you are a beast. But I think you are a man."

About the same time, an amusing incident followed an evening with Sam Brown. A friend of one of my children, Sam had organized and led massive public protests against the administration's policies in Vietnam. After one such march in front of the White House, Sam came to our home for dinner. He and I talked for hours in the library after leaving the table. As Sam got up to leave, his parting words were "Well, I guess no one who loves the mountains as much as you do can be all bad."*

———

Congressional and public concern deepened during the fall of 1966. Liberals and moderates stepped up demands for negotiations, while conservatives clamored for more forceful military action. At the same time, the media began to present increasingly skeptical reports about the war's progress. Neil Sheehan wrote an article for the October 9, 1966 *New York Times Magazine* entitled "Not a Dove, but No Longer a Hawk," in which he said that during his first tour in Vietnam, as a United Press International reporter in 1962–1964, he had believed in basic U.S. aims. But after his second tour, as a *Times* reporter in 1965–1966, he realized he had been "naive in believing the non-communist Vietnamese could defeat the Communist insurgency and build a decent and progressive social structure."

The administration's relations with Congress cooled further as a result of an unfortunate incident involving Bobby Kennedy, by this time a senator from New York and a dove on Vietnam. Bobby returned from Paris in early February 1967 with what appeared to him to be a legitimate North Vietnamese peace feeler. Word of this

---

*Nearly thirty years later, when President Clinton nominated Sam Brown as U.S. ambassador to the Conference on Security and Cooperation in Europe (CSCE), strong opposition emerged among conservatives in the Senate because of his antiwar activities. Sam asked me to write a letter on his behalf to the Senate Foreign Relations Committee, which I gladly did. But his nomination was never confirmed, and he assumed the CSCE post with nonambassadorial rank.

leaked to *Newsweek,* which printed the story in its February 5 issue. President Johnson hit the roof, believing Bobby had leaked it to his own advantage. He had not. The president met with Bobby on February 6 and reportedly said: "The war will be over this year, and when it is, I'll destroy you and every one of your dove friends. You'll be dead politically in six months."[21]

President Johnson never directed at me the anger and mistrust he felt toward Bobby. But their enmity put me in a difficult position. Johnson knew that Bobby and I spoke frequently and that the subject was often Vietnam. I was scrupulously careful not to betray the president's confidences or mention anything Bobby could use politically against the president. I never hesitated to tell the president what I thought, and I was quite as open with Bobby about my feelings regarding Vietnam.

The accumulating stresses and tensions took their toll on those of us who had to make the decisions, and I was not exempt. Some nights in 1967 I had to take a pill in order to sleep. My friend David Lilienthal, a former chairman of the Atomic Energy Commission, confided to his diary around this time that he had observed a "harassed and puzzled look in the no longer sprightly" secretary of defense. And *The Washington Post* on May 21, 1967, reported that both Dean and I had begun to show the war's strain. Dean wrote in his memoirs that by the following year he was "bone-tired" and survived on a daily diet of "aspirin, scotch, and four packs of Larks." He was well on the way to that condition in 1967.[22]

In part because of the newspaper reports, and because I believed the president might benefit politically by replacing Dean and me, I told him in the spring of 1967: "We should not . . . rule out . . . changing key subordinates in the U.S. government to meet the charge that 'Washington is tired and Washington is stale.' "[23]

———

As one diplomatic initiative after another fizzled, my frustration, dis-enchantment, and anguish deepened. I could see no good way to win—or end—an increasingly costly and destructive war.

More Buddhist uprisings in South Vietnam in the spring of 1966 intensified my anxiety. This internecine strife underscored the Saigon government's fragility and lack of popular appeal. It bothered me that South Vietnamese battled one another while the enemy pressed at the gates. At the height of the crisis, in early April, John McNaughton and I prepared what we called a "Possible 'Fall-back' Plan" based on the belief that "while the military situation is not going badly, the political situation is in 'terminal sickness' and even the military prognosis is of an escalating stalemate." We concluded that we should consider seizing on the troubles as the vehicle for U.S. disengagement.[24]

In a meeting on April 2, 1966, the president made an elliptical remark about "being ready to make a terrible choice—perhaps take a stand in Thailand," which indicated he was similarly inclined.[25] But he, I, and others remained fearful of the costs—international and domestic—that would flow from getting out. And the immediate crisis passed a short time later when the South Vietnamese government used force to quell the disturbances.

Looking back, I deeply regret that I did not force a probing debate about whether it would ever be possible to forge a winning military effort on a foundation of political quicksand. It became clear then, and I believe it is clear today, that military force—especially when wielded by an outside power—just cannot bring order in a country that cannot govern itself.

Most of my colleagues viewed the situation quite differently. They saw (or wished to see) steady political and military progress. In the summer of 1966, Dean commented that "the situation has reached the point where North Vietnam cannot succeed." Walt wrote, "Mr. President, you can smell it all over: Hanoi's operation, backed by the Chicoms, is no longer being regarded as the wave of the future. . . . We're not in, but we're moving." Lodge cabled that "the military side of this war is going well. . . . This means that the real danger—and the only real danger—would be if the American people were to lose heart and choose 'to bring the boys home.' This would indeed be the first domino to fall." And White House

Vietnam assistant Robert W. Komer reported after a trip to South Vietnam that he was "both an optimist and a realist." Little support existed among the president's senior advisers for the view I expressed to Averell Harriman on June 23, 1966, that an acceptable military solution was not possible and therefore we should "get in direct touch" with the North Vietnamese and Vietcong to work out the best settlement obtainable.[26]

My disagreement with the president's other senior advisers deepened as the year progressed. The divergence grew increasingly sharp and obvious. In a meeting that fall, Lodge reported that the United States had been successful in the "military war," and that by next spring, he expected "a very different military situation indeed." Westy agreed.[27] After visiting South Vietnam again in mid-October, I did not.

I told the president in a lengthy report that I saw "no reasonable way to bring the war to an end soon." Many factors influenced my thinking, and I laid them out for him in unvarnished detail:

Enemy morale has not broken—he apparently has adjusted to our stopping his drive for military victory and has adopted a strategy of keeping us busy and waiting us out (a strategy of attriting our national will). He knows that we have not been, and he believes we probably will not be, able to translate our military successes into the "end products" [that count]—broken enemy morale and political achievements by the GVN [Government of (South) Vietnam].

The one thing demonstrably going for us in Vietnam over the past year has been the large number of enemy killed-in-action resulting from the big military operations. Allowing for possible exaggeration in reports, the enemy must be taking losses . . . at the rate of more than 60,000 a year. The infiltration routes would seem to be one-way trails to death for the North Vietnamese. Yet there is no sign of an impending break in enemy morale and it appears that he can more than replace his losses by infiltration from North Vietnam and recruitment in South Vietnam.

. . . Pacification has if anything gone backward. As compared with two, or four, years ago, enemy full-time regional forces and part-time guerrilla forces are larger; attacks, terrorism and sabotage have increased in scope and intensity; . . . we control little, if any, more of the population; the VC [Vietcong] political infrastructure thrives in most of the country, continuing to give the enemy his enormous intelligence advantage; full security exists nowhere (not even behind the U.S. Marines' lines and in Saigon); in the countryside, the enemy almost completely controls the night.

Nor has the Rolling Thunder program of bombing the North either significantly affected infiltration or cracked the morale of Hanoi. There is agreement in the intelligence community on these facts.

In essence, we find ourselves—from the point of view of the important war (for the [hearts and minds] of the people)—no better, and if anything worse off. This important war must be fought and won by the Vietnamese themselves. We have known this from the beginning. But the discouraging truth is that, as was the case in 1961 and 1963 and 1965, we have not found the formula, the catalyst, for training and inspiring them into effective action.

What should we do about this unhappy situation? I perceived no "good" answer, and therefore offered none. I could only advise the president to level off U.S. military involvement for the long haul while pressing for talks, hoping these combined efforts would prevent the other side from waiting us out, avoid endless escalation of U.S. deployments, avert the risk of a larger war, and increase the prospects for a negotiated settlement through continued pressure.

Whatever my hopes, I conceded "the prognosis is bad that the war can be brought to a satisfactory conclusion within the next two years. The large-unit operations probably will not do it; negotiations probably will not do it. *While we should continue to pursue both of these routes in trying for a solution in the short run, we should recognize that success from them is a mere possibility, not a probability* [emphasis in original]."*[28]

---

*To achieve these goals, I recommended a multipronged course of action: leveling off U.S. ground forces in the South at 470,000; installing an anti-infiltration barrier along the Ho Chi Minh Trail; leveling off Rolling Thunder strikes against the North; and vigorously pursuing pacification.

It was a sobering—indeed anguishing—scenario. But I could see no better way at the time.

Under secretary of State Nick Katzenbach generally shared my views. Nick had been attorney general but had been moved to State because of the president's dissatisfaction with Dean's administration of the department. The CIA described my evaluation of the situation as "sound, perceptive and very much in line with our own." Not so the Joint Chiefs. The *Pentagon Papers* characterized their reaction as "predictably rapid—and violent," a fair summary of the chiefs' feelings. They sharply challenged my assessment of the military situation, my recommendation to level off U.S. deployments, and my advice that we press ever harder for negotiations while giving primary emphasis to pacification and political self-sufficiency in South Vietnam. They felt so strongly that they asked me to forward their views to the president, which I did.[29]

The differences between me and the chiefs were not hidden, yet they also were not addressed. Why? Most people wish to avoid confrontation. They prefer to finesse disagreement rather than to address it head-on. Also, I speculate that LBJ—like all presidents—wanted to avoid an open split among his key subordinates, especially during wartime. So he swept our divergence of opinion under the rug. It was a very human reaction. But I regret that he, Dean, and I failed to confront these differences among us and with the chiefs directly and debate them candidly and thoroughly.

The differences and contradictions continued, even within individuals. In December, Lodge told the president he expected "brilliant military results in 1967" and similar political improvements, but he added: "It might take five years to complete the job." After visiting Saigon in early February 1967, Bus reported "the VC/NVA [Vietcong/North Vietnamese Army] can no longer hope to win militarily in South Vietnam." And yet—less than six weeks later, on March 18, 1967—Westy requested 200,000 more troops (which would raise the total from 470,000 to 670,000); urged expanding ground operations into Laos and Cambodia; advocated heavier bombing and mining of North Vietnam; and contemplated an amphibious invasion north of the Demilitarized Zone. This meant mobilizing the reserves, boosting active duty forces by 500,000 men, and spending another $10 billion annually on the war—in addition to the roughly $25 billion already directed toward Southeast Asia out of a total Pentagon budget of approximately $71 billion.[30]

We discussed these recommendations at the White House on April 27. In his memoirs, Westy states I "wrung" from him an estimate of how long it would take "to wind down our involvement" if U.S. forces were increased by 200,000; increased by 100,000; or kept at 470,000. He finally said two years, three years, and five years, respectively. At one point in the meeting, President Johnson asked him: "When we add divisions, can't the enemy add divisions? If so, where does it all end?"[31]

At this meeting, Bus noted, "The bombing campaign is reaching the point where we will have struck all worthwhile fixed targets except the ports." Consistent with that fact, I advised the president at our Tuesday Luncheon on May 2, 1967, not only to reject the chiefs' proposal to expand the bombing (except for destroying remaining electric power facilities) but to limit it to the area below the twentieth parallel (the "panhandle" south of Hanoi and Haiphong through which most troops and supplies flowed south).

I understood and empathized with the potential concern of military men about withholding punishment from the adversary. But I based my recommendation on several factors: Bus's April 27 comment; my belief that closing the ports through bombing and mining posed an unacceptable risk of confrontation with the USSR; the conclusions of U.S. Consul General Edmund Rice in Hong Kong and Sir Robert Thompson in Malaysia that Rolling Thunder had strengthened rather than diminished Hanoi's will; the fact that U.S. pilot losses per sortie north of the twentieth parallel ran six times higher than losses south of that line; and my judgment that the damage inflicted by air attacks north of that line did not justify the higher loss of American life. Cy Vance, Nick Katzenbach, Dick Helms, Walt Rostow, and Bill Bundy endorsed my recommendation, as did Mac Bundy—out of government but still in touch with the president—in a separate memorandum to him on May 3. Evaluations by the CIA supported this position.[32]

My concern and skepticism came to a head later that month in the long and controversial memorandum I submitted to the president on May 19, 1967. Advancing positions the *Pentagon Papers* later described as "radical," the memo crystallized my growing doubts about the trend of events and set the stage for the increasingly sharp debate that followed. Because of its importance, I wish to quote from it extensively.

I began:

> This memorandum is written at a time when there appears to be no attractive course of action. The probabilities are that Hanoi has decided not to negotiate until the American electorate has been heard in November 1968. Continuation of our present moderate policy, while avoiding a larger war, will not change Hanoi's mind, so is not enough to satisfy the American people; increased force levels and actions against the North are likewise unlikely to change Hanoi's mind, and are likely to get us in even deeper in Southeast Asia and into a serious confrontation, if not war, with China and Russia; and we are not willing to yield. So we must choose among imperfect alternatives.

I proceeded to discuss the situation in the United States:

> The Vietnam war is unpopular in this country. It is becoming increasingly unpopular as it escalates—causing more American casualties, more fear of its growing into a wider war, more privation of the domestic sector, and more distress at the amount of suffering being visited on the noncombatants in Vietnam, South and North. Most Americans do not know how we got where we are, and most, without knowing why, but taking advantage of hindsight, are convinced that somehow we should not have gotten this deeply in. All want the war ended and expect their President to end it. Successfully. Or else.
>
> This state of mind in the U.S. generates impatience in the

political structure of the United States. It unfortunately also generates patience in Hanoi. (It is commonly supposed that Hanoi will not give anything away pending the trial of the U.S. elections in November 1968.)

In South Vietnam:

[In Vietnam] the "big war" in the South between the U.S. and the North Vietnamese military units (NVA) is going well. We staved off military defeat in 1965; we gained the military initiative in 1966; and since then we have been hurting the enemy badly, spoiling some of his ability to strike. . . . [But] throughout South Vietnam, supplies continue to flow in ample quantities. . . . The enemy retains the ability to initiate both large- and small-scale attacks. . . .

Regrettably, the "other war" against the VC is still not going well. Corruption is widespread. Real government control is confined to enclaves. There is rot in the fabric. . . . The population remains apathetic. . . . The National Liberation Front (NLF) continues to control large parts of South Vietnam, and there is little evidence that the [pacification] program is gaining any momentum. The Army of South Vietnam (ARVN) is tired, passive and accommodation-prone, and is moving too slowly if at all into pacification work.

In North Vietnam:

Hanoi's attitude toward negotiations has never been soft nor open-minded. . . . They seem uninterested in a political settlement and determined to match U.S. military expansion of the conflict. . . . There continues to be no sign that the bombing has reduced Hanoi's will to resist or her ability to ship the necessary supplies south. Hanoi shows no signs of ending the large war and advising the VC to melt into the jungles. The North Vietnamese believe they are right; they consider the Ky regime to be puppets; they believe the world is with them and that the American public will not have staying power against them. Thus, although they may have factions in the regime favoring different approaches, they believe that, in the long run, they are stronger than we are for the purpose.

And in the Communist bloc:

> The dominant Soviet objectives seem to continue to be to avoid direct involvement in the military conflict and to prevent Vietnam from interfering with other aspects of Soviet-American relations, while supporting Hanoi to an extent sufficient to maintain Soviet prestige in International Communism.
>
> China remains largely preoccupied with its own Cultural Revolution. The Peking Government continues to advise Hanoi not to negotiate and continues to resist Soviet efforts to forge a united front in defense of North Vietnam. There is no reason to doubt that China would honor its commitment to intervene at Hanoi's request, and it remains likely that Peking would intervene on her own initiative if she believed that the existence of the Hanoi regime was at stake.

I then addressed, carefully, and at length, the rationale behind Westy's proposed course of action:

> Proponents of the added deployments in the South believe that such deployments will hasten the end of the war. None of them believes that the added forces are needed to avoid defeat; few of them believe that the added forces are required to do the job in due course; all of the proponents believe that they are needed if that job is to be done faster. The argument is that we avoided military defeat in 1965; that we gained the military initiative in 1966, since then hurting the enemy badly, spoiling much of his ability to strike, and thus diminishing the power he could project over the population; and that even more vigorous military initiative against his main forces and base areas will hurt him more, spoil his efforts more, and diminish his projected power more than would be the case under presently approved force-deployment levels. This, the argument goes, will more readily create an environment in South Vietnam in which our pacification efforts can take root and thrive; at the same time—because of our progress in the South and because of the large enemy losses—it will more rapidly produce a state of mind in Hanoi conducive to ending the war on reasonable terms.

But this course entailed grave risks and repercussions, which also had to be addressed:

> The addition of the 200,000 men, involving as it does a call-up of Reserves and an addition of 500,000 to the military strength, would . . . almost certainly set off bitter Congressional debate and irresistible domestic pressures for stronger action outside South Vietnam. Cries would go up—much louder than they already have—to "take the wraps off the men in the field." The actions would include more intense bombing—not only around-the-clock bombing of targets already authorized, but also bombing of strategic [civilian] targets such as locks and dikes, and mining of the harbors against Soviet and other ships. Associated actions impelled by the situation would be major ground actions in Laos, in Cambodia, and probably in North Vietnam. The use of tactical nuclear and area-denial-radiological-bacteriological-chemical weapons would probably be suggested at some point if the Chinese entered the war in Vietnam or Korea or if U.S. losses were running high while conventional efforts were not producing desired results.

Quite simply, escalation threatened to spin the war utterly out of control. I felt this danger had to be prevented. I told the president,

> There may be a limit beyond which many Americans and much of the world will not permit the United States to go. The picture of the world's greatest superpower killing or seriously injuring 1000 noncombatants a week, while trying to pound a tiny backward nation into submission on an issue whose merits are hotly disputed, is not a pretty one. It could conceivably produce a costly distortion in the American national consciousness and in the world image of the United States—especially if the damage to North Vietnam is complete enough to be "successful."

All of this led me to come down hard against Westy's request. I stressed that Vietnam must be considered in its larger Asian context. Expressing a view far different from the one I had held in earlier years, I pointed to the Communists' defeat in Indonesia and the Cultural Revolution then roiling China, arguing that these events showed the trend in Asia now ran in our favor, thus reducing South Vietnam's importance. I urged we "eliminate the ambiguities from our minimum objectives" and base our policy on two principles:

(1) Our commitment is only to see that the people of South Vietnam are permitted to determine their own future.
(2) This commitment ceases if the country ceases to help itself.

I therefore proposed a politico-military strategy that raised the possibility of compromise: restricting the bombing to interdiction of the infiltration "funnel" below the twentieth parallel; limiting additional deployments to 30,000, after which a firm ceiling should be imposed; and adopting a more flexible bargaining position while actively seeking a political settlement.

I frankly acknowledged the difficulties of this approach:

Some will insist that pressure, enough pressure, on the North can pay off or that we will have yielded a blue chip without exacting a price in exchange for our concentrating on interdiction; many will argue that denial of the larger number of troops will prolong the war, risk losing it and increase the casualties of the American boys who are there; some will insist . . . Hanoi will react [with] increased demands and truculence; . . . and there will be those who point out the possibility that the changed U.S. tone may cause a "rush for the exits" in Thailand, in Laos and especially inside South Vietnam, perhaps threatening cohesion of the government, morale of the army, and loss of support among the people. Not least will be the alleged impact on the reputation of the United States and of its President.

But I considered the difficulties, and risks, of this approach fewer and smaller than those of any other approach. After much thinking, struggling, and searching, I had concluded—and I bluntly told President Johnson—that "the war in Vietnam is acquiring a momentum of its own that must be stopped" and that Westy's approach "could lead to a major national disaster."

I believed my recommended course, on the other hand, offered the "combined advantages of being a lever toward negotiations and towards ending the war on satisfactory terms, of helping our general position with the Soviets, of improving our image in the eyes of international opinion, of reducing the danger of confrontation with China and with the Soviet Union, and of reducing U.S. losses."[33]

Walt Rostow, describing the reactions to my memorandum, said with some understatement that it aroused "dangerously strong feelings" within the government.[34] Could I have handled the issues confronting us with less pain to the president and, most of all, with greater effect in shortening the war? I now believe I could have and should have. I did not see how to do so at the time. Today, it is clear to me that my memorandum pointed directly to the conclusion that, through either negotiation or direct action, we should have begun our withdrawal from South Vietnam. There was a high probability we could have done so on terms no less advantageous than those accepted nearly six years later—without any greater damage to U.S. national security and at much less human, political, and social cost to America and Vietnam.

10

Estrangement and Departure:

May 20, 1967–February 29, 1968

My May 19, 1967, memorandum to the president unleashed a storm of controversy. It intensified already sharp debate within the administration. It led to tense and acrimonious Senate hearings that pitted me against the Joint Chiefs of Staff and generated rumors they intended to resign en masse. It accelerated the process that ultimately drove President Johnson and me apart. And it hastened my departure from the Pentagon.

The crush of events that summer and fall made it increasingly hard for the president and the senior officials in State, Defense, and the National Security Council to focus sharply on Vietnam. We were confronted with a deluge of other crises and problems: a Middle East war that led to the first use of the hot line between Moscow and Washington; a Soviet Anti-Ballistic Missile program that threatened to upset the nuclear balance between East and West; a looming conflict between Greece and Turkey over Cyprus that endangered NATO's eastern flank; race riots in our major cities; and, of course, rising protests against the war, which included a massive attempt to shut down the Pentagon. The press started reporting symptoms of stress affecting senior personnel, including me. President Johnson began hinting that he would not seek reelection in 1968.

———

For two weeks after my memo, the Joint Chiefs responded with no fewer than seven memoranda to the president and me. As the *Pentagon Papers* later observed, the "Washington papermill must have broken all previous production records."[1]

The chiefs took particular exception to my recommendation that we "eliminate the ambiguities from our minimum objectives" in Vietnam. As I have said, I had urged that we base our policy on two principles: "(1) Our commitment is only to see that the people of South Vietnam are permitted to determine their own future"; and "(2) This commitment ceases if the country ceases to help itself." This formulation, asserted the chiefs, "does not support correct U.S. national policy and objectives in Vietnam and should not be considered further." They charged that my statement contradicted existing U.S. policy and goals as outlined in NSAM 288, which, they pointed out, still served as the governing policy document on the war.

In fact, NSAM 288 was a brief note dated March 17, 1964, from Mac Bundy to Dean Rusk, me, the chairman of the Joint Chiefs, and others. It said that the president had decided to adopt advice I had given in a report submitted the day before. That document stated: "I recommend you make clear to the agencies of the government that we are prepared to furnish assistance and support to South Vietnam for as long as it takes to bring the insurgency under control." But the report included this key qualification: "There were and are sound reasons for the limits imposed by our present policy—*the South Vietnamese must win their own fight* [emphasis added]."[2] The chiefs were mistaken: our policy had not changed. But they were also right: in recent years the policy had not been adhered to.

The cardinal question had never gone away: If the South Vietnamese government, such as it was, could not gain and keep its people's support and defeat the insurgents, could we do it for them?

The chiefs also urged heavier U.S. attacks against the North by land, sea, and air. They felt so strongly about this that they asked me to bring their recommendations to the president's attention, which of course I did. On May 20, they sent me another memo repeating their view that invasions of North Vietnam, Laos, and Cambodia might become necessary, involving the deployment of U.S. forces to Thailand and, quite possibly, the use of nuclear weapons in southern China. All of this, they emphasized, highlighted the need to mobilize U.S. reserves.[3] Their continued willingness to risk a nuclear confrontation appalled me.

To help resolve my disagreement with the chiefs over bombing, I had asked CIA Director Dick Helms to have agency analysts assess the alternatives. The resulting report stated categorically, "We do not believe that any of the programs . . . is capable of reducing the flow of military and other essential goods sufficiently to affect the war in the South or to decrease Hanoi's determination to persist in the war." This conclusion, the CIA explained, was based on stubborn facts: "The excess capacity on the road networks . . . provides such a deep cushion that it is almost certain that no interdiction program can neutralize the logistics target system to the extent necessary to reduce the flow of men and supplies to South Vietnam below their present levels."[4]

The chiefs rejected this analysis out of hand and continued to press for a stepped-up bombing campaign.

Sharp differences existed not only between senior civilian and military officials, but also within the military itself. For example, about this time Navy Secretary Paul Nitze and I received a short briefing from a unit called the Navy Vietnam Appraisal Group. I recalled the episode recently when Eugene Carroll, a retired rear admiral, forwarded to me a reminiscence from the man who had served as its director, Rear Admiral Gene R. La Rocque. It read in part:

Sometime in 1967, Paul Nitze, the Secretary of the Navy, called me to his office and said that after a conversation with Secretary McNamara that he, Paul Nitze, wanted me to form a group of about 10 Admirals and a Marine General to assess the situation in Vietnam and recommend possible military options for the U.S.

Nitze made it clear that he and Mr. McNamara were not interested in events which had already transpired as they were well aware of those events. Rather, he directed the group to focus on an appraisal of the situation as it existed in 1967 and the options open to the U.S.

Pursuant to the Navy Secretary's instructions, I formed a group of 10 Admirals and one Marine Brigadier General and set to work. During our visit to Vietnam, we held discussions with Generals Westmoreland, Momyer, Cushman and with Admirals and their staffs at sea. We questioned officers at all levels, troops in the field, as well as officers and men aboard the ships at sea off Vietnam and the Riverene portals.

For about six months the group evaluated a series of options including building a wall on the northern and western boundaries of South Vietnam, mining the harbors, massive air attacks, and destroying the flow of traffic on the Red River. These and other options examined were evaluated as insufficient to achieve a military victory.

One additional option which called for the dispatching of U.S. troops to North Vietnam would, by Marine Corps estimates, have required an addition of at least 500,000 more U.S. troops in the area. Our group determined that this might well provoke an intervention by China into North Vietnam. . . .

The appraisal my group provided demonstrated that a military victory in Vietnam was highly unlikely and it was our intent to report this formally to the Secretary of the Navy, the Secretary of Defense and senior officials in the Pentagon. The informal nature of our group, the absence of an official directive to establish the group and the existing political situation involving the White House prevented dissemination of the results of the group's appraisal. The Vice Chief of Naval Operations, Admiral Horacio Rivero, personally and forcefully made it clear to me that distribution of the report would be detrimental to the U.S. prosecution of the war and my future in the Navy. His adamant opposition blocked subsequent distribution of the report.

In his cover letter, Admiral Carroll told me, "It was Gene La Rocque's independent spirit and determination to report the facts, not politically correct positions, concerning the situation in Vietnam that led to his early retirement [from the navy] after a career on the fast track." Carroll and La Rocque went on to become cogent civilian critics of U.S. military thinking.[5]

The onslaught of memos from the chiefs did not persuade me. On June 12, Cy Vance and I again counseled the president to reject their plan. We cited the CIA analysis and said we were convinced that a large-scale escalation could lead to disaster: "Nothing short of toppling the Hanoi regime will pressure North Vietnam to settle so long as they believe they have a chance to win the 'war of attrition' in the South. . . . actions sufficient to topple the Hanoi regime will put us into war with the Soviet Union and China." We also argued that the chiefs' plan would be costly in American lives: many of their recommended targets were heavily defended, and hitting them would involve losses per sortie several times higher than the program we proposed. The president accepted our recommendations on June 13.[6]

Readers must wonder by now—if they have not been mystified long before—how presumably intelligent, hardworking, and experienced officials—both civilian and military—failed to address systematically and thoroughly questions whose answers so deeply affected the lives of our citizens and the welfare of our nation. Simply put, such an orderly, rational approach was precluded by the "crowding out" which resulted from the fact that Vietnam was but one of a multitude of problems we confronted.

Any one of the issues facing Washington during the 1960s justified the full attention of the president and his associates. Thus, in late May 1967, we received CIA reports of an imminent Egyptian invasion of Israel. Very likely, Egypt would be supported by other Arab states, such as Jordan and Syria. And, we feared, if it were necessary to achieve its objective—destruction of the Jewish state— Egypt would receive support from the Soviet Union as well. Israel, of course, had similar information.

A meeting between President Johnson and British Prime Minister Harold Wilson had long been planned for June 2 to review our common interests around the world. When the day arrived, the imminent Arab-Israeli war had crowded all other issues off the agenda. We compared our intelligence estimates and our conclusions about the conflict's outcome. We agreed on all points, including who would win: Israel—beyond a shadow of a doubt. One side, I recall, anticipated an Israeli victory within ten days; the other expected it within seven. But we also agreed the consequences of such a war would be difficult to predict and to control, and therefore we should do everything possible to prevent it.

The CIA's intelligence was superb but disquieting. It reported that Israel planned to preempt Egypt's attack. From one point of view, this seemed reasonable; a preemptive strike would undoubtedly cause fewer Israeli casualties. However, from our point of view, if Israel attacked first, it risked losing U.S. popular support should American intervention become necessary to stop the Soviets from moving against it.

In late May, Israeli Foreign Minister Abba Eban had visited Washington, and President Johnson had invited him to the White House family quarters, where he asked Dean and me to join him in urging Eban to persuade the Israeli cabinet to cancel the preemptive strike. We thought we had succeeded. Instead, Israel moved against Egypt on June 5. The war lasted six days, and during that period Israel inflicted a devastating defeat on Egypt, Jordan, and Syria, seizing control of the Sinai Peninsula, the Gaza Strip, the West Bank of the Jordan River, and the Golan Heights.

On June 5, as usual, I arrived at the Pentagon at 7:00 A.M. Within an hour, my phone rang and a voice said, "This is General 'Smith' in the War Room." (We maintained an admiral or a general on duty in the War Room twenty-four hours a day, seven days a week.) The general said, "Premier Kosygin is on the 'hot line' and asks to speak to the president. What should I tell him?"

"Why are you calling me?" I said.

"Because the 'hot line' ends in the Pentagon," he replied.

A legacy of the Cuban Missile Crisis, the "hot line" had been installed in August 1963 but had never been used except to test its effectiveness. I did not even know its Teletype circuits ended below my office. I told the general, "Patch the circuit over to the White House Situation Room, and I'll call the president."

I knew President Johnson would be asleep, but I put through the call. As I expected, a sergeant posted outside the president's bedroom answered the phone. I told him I wanted to speak to the president.

"The president is asleep and doesn't like to be awakened," he remarked.

"I know that, but wake him up."

The president, I later learned, had been taking calls from Dean and Walt Rostow about the crisis since 4:30 A.M. He came on the line. "What in the hell are you calling me for at this hour of the morning?" he growled sleepily.

"Mr. President, the 'hot line' is up and Kosygin wants to speak to you. What should we say?"

"My God, what *should* we say?" he replied.

"I suggest I tell him you will be in the Situation Room in fifteen minutes. In the meantime, I'll call Dean and we'll meet you there."

Over the next several days, we exchanged messages over the hot line with Kosygin. The situation became particularly tense on June 10, as the Israelis scored military gains against Syria. At one point, Kosygin said, in effect, "If you want war, you will get war." That, of course, was furthest from our thoughts.

How could the Soviet premier have reached this conclusion? He did so because, after Israel had so clearly defeated Egypt and Jordan, it appeared to be moving in ways that threatened Damascus. Johnson responded by informing Kosygin that the Israelis would accept a ceasefire once the Golan Heights had been secured. At the same time, he agreed we should move the Sixth Fleet closer to the Syrian coast to make clear to the Soviets that we would respond to any action by them in the region. Within hours, Israel and Syria had accepted a ceasefire and the Sixth Fleet stopped its eastward movement. The exchange of messages had clarified the situation. But the episode illustrates how delicate U.S.-Soviet relations around the world remained in the midst of the Cold War. It partially explains the chiefs' feelings about the necessity of "prevailing" in Indochina. And it illustrates the numerous other pressing issues that prevented us from devoting our full attention to Vietnam.

———

By now it was clear to me that our policies and programs in Indochina had evolved in ways we had neither anticipated nor intended, and that the costs—human, political, social, and economic—had grown far greater than anyone had imagined. We had failed. Why this failure? Could it have been prevented? What lessons could be drawn from our experiences that would enable others to avoid similar failures? The thought that scholars would surely wish to explore these questions once the war had ended was increasingly on my mind.

In June 1967, I decided to ask John McNaughton, my assistant secretary for international security affairs (ISA), to start collecting documents for future scholars to use. I told him to cast his net wide, including relevant papers not just from our department but also from the State Department, the CIA, and the White House. Because I wanted the work done as objectively as possible, I said to John that I would not be personally involved. "Tell your researchers not to hold back," I instructed. "Let the chips fall where they may." Perhaps out of the same impulse that prompted me to say this, I never thought to mention the project to the president or the secretary of state. It was hardly a secret, however, nor could it have been with thirty-six researchers and analysts ultimately involved.

The document collecting started on June 17, 1967—one month before McNaughton's tragic death in an air accident—under the direction of Leslie H. Gelb, who was then a member of the ISA staff and is now president of the Council on Foreign Relations. He and his task force assembled memos, position papers, cables, and field reports stretching back more than twenty years. Les told a researcher several years later: "All I had to do was call up and say: 'McNamara asked. . . . I would go see people, explain the study, and say I wanted the following kinds of material. . . . They all said, 'Yeah, sure.' . . . No one refused a thing."[7]

By early 1969, going far beyond the collection of raw materials for scholars, they had completed a 7,000-page study of America's Vietnam policy since World War II. It had shortcomings, in part reflecting the natural limitations of history written close to the event and in part because Les and his team in fact lacked access to White House files and some top-level State Department materials. But overall the work was superb, and it accomplished my objective: almost every scholarly work on Vietnam since then has drawn, to varying degrees, on it.

But as with so much involving Vietnam, this effort to assist scholars was also a lesson in unintended consequences. In 1971, Daniel Ellsberg, who had worked for Gelb, leaked the document to *The New York Times.* The editors christened it the Pentagon Papers and began running excerpts, to the intense embarrassment of officials from both the Johnson and Nixon administrations. When the first excerpt appeared on Sunday, June 13, President Nixon's Justice Department reacted immediately, using every legal means at its command to block further publication.

Though I was long since out of the Defense Department, I found myself tangentially involved behind the scenes. On Monday evening, June 14, *The Times*'s Washington bureau chief, James B. "Scotty" Reston, and his wife, Sally, dined with Marg and me at our home. The phone rang, a call for Scotty, which he took in the library. After a few minutes, he came back to the table holding a piece of paper. He reported that *The Times*'s editors and lawyers had drafted a statement "respectfully declining" Attorney General John Mitchell's request to desist from further publication of the papers. Then he read us the draft and asked what I thought. I said *The Times* should continue printing them but should hedge its position by making clear it would obey any order issued by the Supreme Court. Ultimately, of course, the Court allowed *The Times* to go ahead.

Because of the papers, those of us involved in Vietnam decision making came under scrutiny and criticism that was sharper than ever. Wild rumors circulated about why I had started the project. One report even alleged I had done so at Robert Kennedy's behest, to undermine LBJ and help Bobby's 1968 presidential campaign. That was nonsense. But when Dean later asked me why I had not told him or the president about the project, I felt chagrined. I should have.

Dean Rusk was one of the most dedicated servants of this nation I ever met. His devotion to the president—and to the presidency— shone through in many ways, not least in an episode that occurred during the summer of 1967.

Dean phoned me one hot afternoon to ask if he could come to my office. I told him the secretary of state does not come to the secretary of defense's office; it is the other way around. "No, no," he said. "It's a personal matter." I said I did not care whether it was personal or official business—I would be in his office in fifteen minutes.

When I arrived, he pulled a bottle of whiskey out of his desk drawer, poured a drink for himself, and said, "I must resign."

"You're insane," I said. "What are you talking about?"

He said his daughter planned to marry a black classmate at Stanford University, and he could not impose such a political burden on the president. It may be hard for readers today to understand what went through his mind. But it was very clear to me at the time: he believed that because he was a southerner, working for a southern president, such a marriage—if he did not resign or stop it—would bring down immense criticism on both him and the president.

When I asked him if he had talked to the president, he said no, he did not wish to burden him.

"Burden him hell!" I said. "You'll really burden him if you resign. And I know he won't permit it. If you won't talk to the president, I will."

Dean did, and the president reacted as I expected—with congratulations for the impending marriage. So far as I was aware, the marriage had absolutely no effect—political or personal—on Dean or the president.

————

In early July 1967, the president asked me to visit Vietnam to assess the situation once more. I took along Nick Katzenbach and Bus Wheeler. In Saigon, we listened to optimistic briefings from General Westmoreland and Ellsworth Bunker, the distinguished diplomat who had succeeded Lodge as U.S. ambassador in April. "The situation is not a stalemate," said Westy. "We are winning slowly but steadily, and the pace can accelerate if we reinforce our successes." Bunker generally echoed this appraisal. He also believed the war was being won but added a crucial qualification (which had been at the heart of President Kennedy's position): "In the end, they [the South Vietnamese] must win it themselves." Westy apparently did not share that view; he again requested 200,000 additional U.S. troops. I remained opposed, for the reason Bunker had noted.[8]

The slow pace of the war, the mounting casualties, and the increasing polarization it was generating at home frustrated and troubled the president. When Nick, Bus, and I reported our findings on July 12, following our return, he at one point asked, "Are we going to be able to win this goddamned war?"

The optimistic briefings I had received in Saigon had momentarily eased my long-standing doubts about the war's progress in the South. I told the president, "There is not a military stalemate," and said that if we stuck to our program we would win—contingent, of course, on the performance of the South Vietnamese government. But I remained skeptical about the effectiveness of bombing and told him I still opposed military requests to expand it.[9] Subsequent events reawakened, and reconfirmed, my skepticism about the ground war as well.

By now my position on the bombing campaign had become public and intensely controversial. While liberals and moderates criticized President Johnson for failing to deescalate the war, hawks in both parties—fully supported by the Joint Chiefs—pressed for a widening of the war. The latter group worried Johnson, Dean, and me most. Polls showed public sentiment moving in their direction. A Harris survey in mid-May, for example, reported slightly stronger support for increased military pressure than for withdrawal (45 versus 41 percent).[10]

This rising hawkishness manifested itself in the Senate Armed Services Committee's Preparedness Investigating Subcommittee, chaired by John Stennis (D-Miss.). Stennis and his colleagues— Stuart Symington (D-Mo.), Henry Jackson (D-Wash.), Howard Cannon (D-Nev.), Robert Byrd (D-W.Va.), Margaret Chase Smith (R-Me.), Strom Thurmond (R-S.C.), and Jack Miller (R-Iowa)— took a hard line on airpower and had harshly criticized the administration's bombing program for months. When they learned through the chiefs in June that the president had accepted my recommendation to keep the bombing limited, they went on the warpath. They announced their intention to call top military leaders—and me—for testimony.

The hearings, which took place in August, were intended to pressure the White House to lift the bombing restrictions. While they failed to do that, President Johnson considered them a political disaster. He later told Bus: "Your generals almost destroyed us with their testimony before the Stennis Committee. We were murdered in the hearings."[11]

The day before they began, the president warned me about the heat I would face. "I am not worried about the heat, as long as I know what we are doing is right," I told him. He looked at me without saying another word. Not surprisingly, the president's political antennae were more sensitive than mine.[12]

The hearings, which went on in executive session for seven long days between August 9 and August 29, proved to be one of the most stressful episodes of my life. Senator Stennis made his views plain in his opening remarks. "The question is growing in the Congress as to whether it is wise to send more men if we are going to just leave them at the mercy of the guerrilla war without trying to cut off the enemy's supplies more effectively. . . . My own personal opinion is that it would be a tragic and perhaps fatal mistake for us to suspend or restrict the bombing."

A parade of top navy, air force, and army officers then testified, including all five Chiefs of Staff and the five senior commanders involved in the bombing campaign. Each fully supported Stennis's views. In essence, they told the senators:

- The air war in the North was an important and indispensable part of the U.S. strategy for fighting the war in the South.
- The bombing had inflicted extensive damage and disruption on North Vietnam, holding down the infiltration of men and supplies, restricting the number of forces that could be sustained in the South, and reducing the ability of those forces to mount major sustained combat operations, resulting in fewer U.S. casualties.
- Without the bombing, North Vietnam could have doubled its forces in the South, which would have made it necessary for us to send as many as 800,000 additional troops at a cost of $75 billion more just to hold our own.
- Repairing bomb damage tied up 500,000 North Vietnamese who would otherwise be free to support more directly the insurgency in the South.
- A cessation of the bombing now would be a "disaster," resulting in increased U.S. losses and an indefinite extension of the war.
- The bombing had been much less effective than it might have been—and could still be—if civilian leaders would heed military advice and lift the overly restrictive controls they had imposed on the campaign. . . . The slow tempo of the bombing, its concentration well south of vital targets near Hanoi and Haiphong, the toleration of a sanctuary in Cambodia, the failure to close or neutralize Haiphong harbor—these and other rules kept the bombing from achieving decisive results.
- The "doctrine of gradualism" and the long delays in approving targets of real significance, moreover, gave North Vietnam time to build up formidable air defenses, contributing to U.S. aircraft and pilot losses, and enabled North Vietnam to prepare for the anticipated destruction of its facilities (such as POL [petroleum,

oil, lubricants]) by building up reserve stocks and dispersing them.[13]

The generals and admirals hammered at what they considered the central problem in the way we were fighting the war—meddling by the civilians in Washington. In their minds, it stood in the way of victory and got men killed. I strongly believed we were saving American lives without penalizing progress in the war.

Finally, on August 25, the subcommittee invited me to respond. I was left with quite a case to rebut. I began my testimony by reminding the senators that our bombing campaign had three objectives:

1. To reduce the flow and/or increase the cost of the continued infiltration of men and supplies from North to South.
2. To raise the morale of the South Vietnamese people, who, at the time the bombing started, were under severe military pressure.
3. To make clear to North Vietnam's leaders that as long as they continued their aggression against the South, they would pay a price in the North.

These had been our objectives when we started bombing in February 1965, and they remained our objectives in August 1967. I spent all day patiently and systematically elaborating them for the senators and explaining the inherent limitations of bombing. I said we had learned that no amount of it—short of annihilating the North and its people, which no responsible person would propose—could reduce the flow of men and supplies to the South below what was required to support the current level of enemy operations. Nor could any amount of bombing short of annihilation break the North's will to continue the conflict. I stressed that the air war in the North was no substitute for the ground war in the South, that bombing would not allow us to win on the cheap.

The reason bombing supply lines had not proved decisive, I told the senators, was that North Vietnam had a highly diversified and resilient transportation system consisting of rails, roads, waterways, and trails. On these the North Vietnamese moved trains, trucks, barges, sampans, human porters, and bicycles (each of which, I noted, was capable of carrying a load of up to 500 pounds). This transport system was low-tech, easy to maintain, and possessed a capacity many times larger than necessary to carry the limited tonnage needed for military operations in the South. That was the point. Intelligence studies estimated that enemy forces in the South needed only 15 tons a day of externally supplied material other than food. The logistics pipeline from North to South, even under intense air attack, possessed an output capacity of over 200 tons daily. I pointed out that, to date, we had flown 173,000 bombing sorties against North Vietnam—a huge total even when compared with Allied attacks on Germany during World War II. Fully 90 percent of those had been directed against supply lines.

Next I turned to the issue of fixed targets in the North—factories, power plants, storage depots, and the like. These accounted for only 10 percent of our strikes. I explained that we made decisions about these targets on a target-by-target analysis, balancing the target's military importance against its cost in U.S. and Vietnamese lives and the risks of expanding the war. The chiefs had recommended 359 targets to the president and me, of which 302, or 85 percent, had been approved. Of the 57 not approved, the chiefs themselves acknowledged 7 to be of limited value; 9 were small petroleum facilities accounting for less than 6 percent of North Vietnam's remaining storage capacity; 25 were nonpetroleum targets of lesser importance in heavily defended areas, which were not, in my judgment, worth the loss of American lives that would result from the attacks. Five lay too close to China; and the final 11 were still on the table.

I tried to make clear that the importance attached to fixed targets reflected a fundamental misconception of North Vietnam's simple economic needs and the outside sources of its war-making capacity. Although we had rendered inoperative 85 percent of North

Vietnam's central electrical generating capacity, the total capacity was less than one-fifth the output of the Potomac Electric Power Company's plant in Alexandria, Virginia. Moreover, the USSR and China—not indigenous factories or refineries—produced most of its war supplies.

I pointed out that the regular monthly report "An Appraisal of the Bombing of North Vietnam," which was prepared jointly by the CIA and the Defense Intelligence Agency and distributed to all senior civilian and military officials right up to the president, invariably concluded with these words: "The stepped-up air campaign has caused major changes in the air defense system and widespread disruption of economic activities in North Vietnam. However, the North Vietnamese still retain the capability to support activities in South Vietnam and Laos at present or increased combat levels and force structures."[14]

If we still wanted to expand the air war, I told the senators, there was one new objective that some would propose adding: "bombing the ports and mining the harbors, particularly at Haiphong in an attempt to prevent entry into Vietnam of the supplies needed to support combat in the South." But I explained in detail why that was unlikely to work. I said there could be no question that such bombing would interfere seriously with North Vietnam's imports of war-supporting materials.

But far less than the present volume of imports would provide the essentials for continued North Vietnamese military operations against South Vietnam. As I have mentioned, estimates of the total tonnage required start at 15 tons per day of non-food supplies. This can be quintupled and still be dwarfed by North Vietnam's actual imports of about 5,800 tons per day. And its import capacity is much greater. The ports together with the roads and railroad from China have an estimated capacity of about 14,000 tons a day.

The great bulk of North Vietnamese imports now enters through Haiphong . . . This includes most of the war-supporting material, such as trucks, generators, and construction equipment but this category of supply represents only a small percentage of total sea imports. And little if any of the imported military equipment (which is estimated by intelligence sources to total 550 tons per day) comes by sea. Moreover, this present heavy reliance on Haiphong reflects convenience rather than necessity. Haiphong represents the easiest and cheapest means of import. If it and the other ports were to be closed, and on the unrealistic assumption that closing the ports would eliminate all seaborne imports, North Vietnam would still be able to import over 8,400 tons a day by rail, road, and waterway. And even if, through air strikes, its road, rail, and Red River waterway capacity could all be reduced by 50 percent, North Vietnam could maintain roughly 70 percent of its current imports. Since the daily importation of military and war-supporting material totals far less than this, it seems obvious that cutting off seaborne imports would not prevent North Vietnam from continuing its present level of military operations in the South. . . .

The North Vietnam seacoast runs for 400 miles. Many locations are suitable for over-the-beach operations. The mining of Haiphong or the total destruction of Haiphong port facilities would not prevent offshore unloading of foreign shipping. Effective interdiction of this lighterage, even if the inevitable damage to foreign shipping were to be accepted, would only lead to total reliance on land importation through communist China. The common border between the two countries is about 500 air miles long.[15]

The case against expanding the air war was clear. All you had to do was look at the numbers. But my testimony generated considerable controversy.

Senator Cannon was not interested in discussing our objectives. Instead, he zeroed in on my unwillingness always to follow the military's advice on the use of force in Vietnam. "As long ago as October 1965," he said, "these targets . . . were unanimously recommended by the Joint Chiefs of Staff. I am wondering whether or not you have confidence in the members of the Joint Chiefs . . . , and just what the reason is that their recommendations on military matters and military targets are not followed."

I replied that "the Constitution gives the responsibility of Commander in Chief to a civilian, the President, and I am sure it didn't intend that he would exercise that by following blindly the recommendations of his military advisers. So you must assume that under the Constitution it was recognized that the President would act contrary to his advisers at times.

"The Constitution," I went on, "recognizes that other factors than the narrow military factors must be taken account of by the Commander in Chief in making decisions in this area, and that, of course, is exactly what has happened. It isn't at all a question of confidence in the Chiefs. If we didn't have confidence in the Chiefs, they wouldn't be Chiefs."[16]

The discussion went downhill from there. An exchange between Senator Thurmond and me illustrates the rising tension in the hearing room:

"Mr. Secretary, I am terribly disappointed with your statement. I think it is a statement of placating the Communists. It is a statement of appeasing the Communists. It is a statement of no-win."

I took strong exception: "There has been no witness before this committee . . . [who] has said the approval of the 57 targets . . . would act to shorten the war in any significant way."[17]

At the end of a long and bitterly trying day, I made a concluding statement. It was a plea to reason:

> The tragic and long drawn-out character of [the] conflict in the South makes very tempting the prospect of replacing it with some new kind of air campaign against the North. But however tempting, such an alternative seems to me completely illusory. To pursue this objective would not only be futile, but would involve risks to our personnel and to our Nation that I am unable to recommend."[18]

The subcommittee issued a unanimous report severely criticizing me for micromanaging the war. Asserting that "careful controls and restrictive ground rules had resulted in the application of our air power in a manner which was of limited effectiveness," the senators concluded: "We cannot, in good conscience, ask our ground forces to continue their fight in South Vietnam unless we are prepared to press the air war in the North in the most effective way possible. . . . Logic and prudence requires that the decision be with the unanimous weight of professional military judgment."[19]

Soon after the hearings, reports circulated that my testimony had provoked a near revolt among the chiefs. Some years later, a journalist, Mark Perry, wrote that following my appearance, Bus called a meeting of the chiefs, at which they decided to resign en masse. Marine Corps Commandmant Gen. Wallace Greene and Chief of Naval Operations Adm. Thomas Moorer subsequently denied the account. I doubt it as well.[20]

But strong differences of judgment did divide us. And the frictions they caused created stress, which took its toll. Bus suffered a serious heart attack during early September, the first of many that would eventually kill him. But before the end of the year, Bus returned to serve the administration by offering his advice in private meetings and public testimony in a direct but noninflammatory and nonconfrontational way, just as he had during the Stennis hearings. And all the other senior military commanders with whom I worked over seven years remained dedicated, loyal servants of their commander in chief and their nation.

––––––

The deepening differences among the president's advisers on Vietnam came through clearly in two communications from CIA Director Richard Helms to President Johnson during this period. On August 29, Dick sent him a personal evaluation of the effects of the bombing on the North. It pointed out that, since March 1967, we had flown over 10,000 bombing sorties per month against North Vietnam—a 55 percent increase over the same period in 1966. Despite this escalation and "despite the increasing hardships, economic losses and mounting problems in management and logistics caused by the air war," he concluded, "Hanoi continues to meet its own needs and to support its aggression in South Vietnam. *Essential military and economic traffic continues to move* [emphasis added]."[21]

Two weeks later, on September 12, he sent the president an extraordinary second memo attached to a thirty-three-page report. The documents have only recently been declassified. The memo warned the president: "The attached paper is sensitive, particularly if its existence were to leak. It comes to you in a sealed envelope." It continued:

> Since part of my job is to examine contingencies and since our involvement in Vietnam has many facets, I recently asked one of my most experienced intelligence analysts in the Office of National Estimates to attempt to set forth what the United States stake is in that struggle. The device which he chose for the purpose was a paper on the "Implications of an Unfavorable Outcome in Vietnam." I believe that you will find it interesting. *It has not been given and will not be given to any other official of the Government* [emphasis in original].
>
> Without indicating his reasons, the writer consulted some thirty or more people in this Agency. There was a considerable diversity of view as to details and degrees of emphasis. Yet the paper represents much fuller agreement among those consulted than might have been expected on so difficult a subject.
>
> I would emphasize that the paper was not intended as an argument for ending or for not ending the war now. We are not defeatist out here. It deals narrowly with the hypothetical question which the author put to himself, i.e., what would be the consequences of an unfavorable outcome for American policy and American interests as a whole.[22]

Helms was right to say the report was political dynamite. After two dozen pages of sophisticated reporting and analysis, it concluded:

> The foregoing discussion has roamed widely over many areas and possibilities. Any very precise or confident conclusions would misrepresent what has been said and exceed what sober judgment

would allow. The following are the broad and essential impressions which this paper has intended to convey:

a. An unfavorable outcome in Vietnam would be a major setback to the reputation of U.S. power which would limit U.S. influence and prejudice our other interests in some degree which cannot be reliably foreseen.

b. Probably the net effects would not be permanently damaging to this country's capacity to play its part as a world power working for order and security in many areas.

c. The worst potential damage would be of the self-inflicted kind: internal dissension which would limit our future ability to use our power and resources wisely and to full effect, and lead to a loss of confidence by others in the American capacity for leadership.

d. The destabilizing effects would be greatest in the immediate area of Southeast Asia where some states would probably face internal turmoil and heightened external pressures, and where some realignments might occur; similar effects would be unlikely elsewhere or could be more easily contained.

The report ended with these words:

Any honest and dispassionate analysis must conclude that, if the U.S. accepts failure in Vietnam, it will pay *some* price in the form of new risks which success there would preclude. The frustration of a world power, once it has committed vast resources and much prestige to a military enterprise, must be in some degree damaging to the general security system it upholds. In the case of Vietnam, there does not seem to be a common denominator which permits such eventual risks to be measured reliably against the obvious and immediate costs of continuing war. Presumably those who have to make the agonizing choices were aware of that already. If the analysis here advances the discussion at all, it is in the direction of suggesting that *the risks are probably more limited and controllable than most previous argument has indicated* [emphasis added].[23]

I never saw the memo until I wrote this book. To my knowledge, President Johnson never showed it to anyone else.

Some people would say this fact in itself reveals an idiosyncratic secretiveness in the president that inevitably led to flawed decisions on Vietnam. One of his closest advisers, commenting on an early draft of this text, wrote that I had failed to emphasize properly the weakness of LBJ's decision-making approach: "He did not like working toward a decision in company—he wanted to go one-on-one. He never let anyone see his hole card in any context. His unwillingness, for example, to explore acceptable 'peace terms' doomed the bombing pauses to failure. In sum, his way of doing business was a major factor contributing to the deficiencies—repeatedly apparent in this narrative—of the Administration's management of the war."

Lyndon Johnson, like all of us, made his own trouble sometimes. Having a senior adviser submit a memo questioning the fundamental premise underlying our involvement in a war, and not allowing him to discuss it with his colleagues, is certainly no way to run a government. One could point to other examples of Johnson's so-called autocratic style. But I think it is simplistic to attribute a president's failure to such factors. Subordinates ought to find ways to compensate for idiosyncrasies in their leader's style. It remained our responsibility to identify the contradictions in policy, force them to the surface, and debate them. Had we done so, we might have changed the policy.

Dick Helms's secret memo shows that, in the fall of 1967, the CIA's most senior analysts believed we could have withdrawn from Vietnam without any permanent damage to U.S. or Western security. At the same time they were expressing that view, I was stating to the Stennis subcommittee the judgment—supported by CIA/DIA analyses—that we could not win the war by bombing the North. And my May 19 memo had reported that we would continue suffering heavy casualties in South Vietnam with no assurance of winning there either.

How, in the face of such factors, does one explain the administration's failure to push harder for negotiations and contemplate withdrawal? The answer is that the Joint Chiefs and many others in the government took an entirely different view of the war's progress, that influential members of Congress and the public shared that view, and that the president was heavily swayed by their opinion.

The ferocity of this opposing view came through on September 7, in a syndicated newspaper column attacking me. It said:

> There are signs that the administration is getting fed up with the deceit, wrong decisions and dictatorial arrogance of Robert Strange McNamara, the man who never yet has been right about Vietnam or any other military matter. The major visible sign of McNamara's slippage in the court of LBJ is the fact that, for the first time, military men seem free to voice the opposition to McNamara which always has been present. . . . The fact that the chiefs are now fighting him openly can only mean, it seems to me, that there is certain knowledge now that the White House is withdrawing some of that support.[24]

The author was none other than Barry Goldwater.

———

In reality, during and after the Stennis hearings, the Johnson administration was in the midst of the most intense diplomatic initiatives with Hanoi it had ever undertaken. The secret initiative, known by the code name Pennsylvania, started in July, lasted three months, and helped pave the way for the meeting of U.S. and North Vietnamese representatives in Paris on May 10, 1968.

When I returned to my Pentagon office one Monday morning in mid-June, after an absence of several days, I found on my desk a stack of cables that had accumulated from all over the world. They included one addressed to Dean Rusk, with a copy to me, from Henry Kissinger in Paris. Henry, who was attending a Pugwash meeting—an international conference of scientists and intellectuals—reported he had just made a contact that might interest us. He had met a Frenchman, Herbert Marcovich, who stood ready to establish a direct contact between the United States and North Vietnam in order to explore the conditions for peace. A second

Frenchman, Raymond Aubrac, had come into the picture when Henry expressed willingness to take up the matter with Washington. Now he was asking what to tell them.

I called John McNaughton and asked what action had been taken on the cable. None, he said.

I asked what he thought should be done.

"What do you think?" he replied warily.

"I asked first," I said.

"We've made a lot of abortive attempts to open negotiations with no results, and this may prove to be another of those dead ends," he said. "But why don't we explore it in ways that won't involve costs or risks?" I totally agreed and said I would take the cable to the Tuesday Lunch with Dean and the president.

When I broached the subject at lunch the next day, Dean and the president said, "Oh Bob, this is just another of those blind alleys that lead nowhere. We've been down them before. Forget it." They had good reason to feel as they did. But although this matter clearly fell within the secretary of state's responsibility, I finally persuaded them to let me handle it. I promised I would do so in a way that brought no embarrassment to the United States.

I then began a series of exchanges with Henry. My first step was to probe Aubrac's and Marcovich's backgrounds. Aubrac, it turned out, was a left-wing Socialist, and Marcovich a scientist. As the weeks went by, Aubrac appeared the shrewder of the two politically. He was an old friend of Ho Chi Minh, who had stayed at Aubrac's house in Paris while negotiating with the French government in 1946 and was the godfather of Aubrac's daughter.

I also sought Henry's advice about how we should proceed. He performed superbly, offering invaluable advice on approaching the North Vietnamese and responding to their proposals. He also proved an extraordinarily accurate reporter of messages between the two sides.

By early July, we had reached a point where I felt confident we should ask Aubrac and Marcovich to travel to Hanoi. We asked them to present again the Phase A–Phase B Formula, whereby the

United States would suspend or end the bombing based on a commitment by North Vietnam to take reciprocal action.

Aubrac and Marcovich arrived in Hanoi on July 21. Ho was ill but agreed to see his old friend Aubrac. Aubrac and Marcovich then met with Premier Pham Van Dong for lengthy discussions. Following their presentation, the premier said, "We want an unconditional end of bombing and if that happens, there will be no further obstacles to negotiations." He appeared willing to maintain the channel, and suggested Aubrac and Marcovich send future messages to him through North Vietnam's consul general in Paris, Mai Van Bo.[25]

While Aubrac and Marcovich were in Hanoi, I took time off to attend to Marg. Her ulcer had grown increasingly painful, and it finally became clear she needed surgery. The operation took place at Johns Hopkins University Hospital in early July. The surgery left her very weak and in great pain. So we decided to take a vacation in Wyoming. Marg, Craig, and I flew to Jackson Hole, at the foot of the Teton Range of the Rockies, one of the most majestic in the world. There, while Marg relaxed at an inn, Craig and I climbed the Grand Teton. We were joined by two other father-and-son teams, one headed by my army secretary, Stan Resor, the other by Glen Exum, who had pioneered our route thirty years before. It was a wonderful break that combined exhausting physical activity, the powerful beauty of the peaks, the satisfaction that comes from accomplishing a difficult and sometimes dangerous ascent, and the strong sense of companionship that binds people in such circumstances.

After the climb, Craig and I rented a car, fashioned a bed in the backseat for Marg, and drove down to Aspen, Colorado. We looked forward to seeing the vacation house we had under construction in nearby Snowmass Village—and we wanted to check the damage caused by antiwar protesters, who had twice tried to burn it down. The damage proved minor, but we were far from reassured: the would-be arsonists had made a serious effort to destroy it. The FBI reported other such attempts in later years. For example, after Patty Hearst had been arrested for "Symbionese Liberation Army" activities in the 1970s, agents found floor plans of our Snowmass house in the group's Berkeley garage. Each of our bedrooms had been clearly labeled with the name of its occupant. Returning from a hike one afternoon in the mountains around Aspen to the house we had rented for our stay, Craig and I found it surrounded by a mob of chanting demonstrators. We ducked out of sight. Soon after that incident, we gave up on our vacation and flew home to Washington.

Aubrac and Marcovich left Hanoi on July 26, 1967, and returned to Paris. Henry met them an hour after they arrived and sent us their comments. I discussed his cable with the president and Dean at the Tuesday Lunch on August 8, saying it was "the most interesting message on the matter of negotiations which we have ever had."[26] I obtained their approval to draft new instructions for Henry, which I dictated the next day:

MEMORANDUM FOR DR. KISSINGER

You may give your contacts the following message and ask that they deliver it to Pham Van Dong:

> The United States is willing to stop the aerial and naval bombardment of North Vietnam if this will lead promptly to productive discussions between representatives of the U.S. and the DRV [Democratic Republic of (North) Vietnam] looking toward a resolution of the issues between them. We would assume that, while discussions proceed either with public knowledge or secretly, the DRV would not take advantage of the bombing cessation or limitation. Any such move on their part would obviously be inconsistent with the movement toward resolution of the issues between the U.S. and DRV which the negotiations are intended to achieve. . . .

The U.S. is ready to have immediate private contact with the DRV to explore the above approach or any suggestions the DRV might wish to propose in the same direction.

The president approved the memorandum on August 11, and Henry returned to Paris, where he and Chester Cooper held a series of meetings with Aubrac and Marcovich beginning on August 17. According to Chet, the Frenchmen "repeatedly pressed us as to how they could convince the North Vietnamese that the U.S. was seriously interested in negotiations when our bombing had reached record levels of intensity." They asked whether, during their next trip to North Vietnam, the United States would reduce its bombing "as a signal to Hanoi that their mission was seriously regarded by the United States." Henry and Chet promised to raise the issue with Washington. They did, and on August 19 the president agreed to suspend bombing within a ten-mile radius of Hanoi from August 24 to September 4 to ensure Aubrac's and Marcovich's safety and demonstrate the validity of Henry's role as intermediary.[27]

What we did not anticipate or have the sense to prevent was a series of major attacks on North Vietnam just before the planned pause. Because the weather had been poor over North Vietnam, the air force and the navy had built up a backlog of targets to be hit. On August 20, when the skies cleared, the United States flew over 200 weather-postponed sorties, more than any previous day in the war. Heavy bombing near Hanoi, Haiphong, and the Chinese border continued for the next two days.

Aubrac and Marcovich never made it to Hanoi. On August 21, North Vietnam rejected their visa application, explaining that the bombing made it too dangerous to visit the capital. The North Vietnamese added pointedly that allowing them to come at that time, as Aubrac told it, "would have discredited us and ultimately you." Once again, we had failed miserably to coordinate our diplomatic and military actions.[28]

Both sides kept the channel open, however. On September 8, Marcovich told Bo that Henry would be coming to Paris on September 9 for about ten days. Bo commented that if there was no bombing of Hanoi during that period, "something could well happen." We made sure there was no bombing of Hanoi, but attacks against other areas continued, including a heavy raid on Haiphong on September 11. That day North Vietnam rejected our August 9 proposal in a blast of angry rhetoric. Its statement said, in

part: "The American message has been communicated after an escalation of the attacks against [Haiphong] and under the threat of continuation of the attacks against Hanoi. It is clear that this constitutes
an ultimatum to the Vietnamese people. . . . It is only after the
unconditional stopping by the United States of the bombing and all
other acts of war against the Democratic Republic of Vietnam, that
it would be possible to engage in conversations."[29]

Commenting on these developments in a cable to Washington
that day, Henry said the United States had two options: "(a) to take
the message at face value and end the A–M channel; or (b) to treat
the message as a first step in a complicated bargaining process. On
balance," he wrote, I would favor going along a little further." We
all agreed, but we stood poorly prepared to present proposals that
would bring Hanoi to the table.[30]

The inadequacy of our thinking on this issue had come through
clearly in a conversation I had two weeks before with Averell
Harriman, who was now the State Department official assigned to
look after any possible Vietnam negotiations. Averell had advised
that if we were seriously interested in negotiations, we would have
to redefine our objective. He pointed out that the North Vietnamese would never give us an unconditional surrender. I agreed
and said we must therefore "make up our minds that the only way
to settle this is by having a coalition government. We cannot avoid
that." Averell concurred. But, sadly, neither of us forced a debate
within the administration on that fundamental issue, and no such
proposal was presented to Hanoi.[31]

The president, Dean, and I met on September 12 to talk about
Henry's cable. The president wondered why we could not stop the
bombing if it led to prompt and productive discussions. I agreed.
But Dean asked: "Are we prepared to go through with a series of
talks that may not be productive?" We compromised and sent
Henry a message to deliver to Bo through Marcovich. On September 13, U.S. planes again hit around Hanoi and Haiphong.
Henry reported that when he met Marcovich that day, "M. replied
that every time I brought a message we bombed the center of a

North Vietnamese city. If this happened one more time he was no longer prepared to serve as a channel."[32]

We debated the issue again on September 26 at a Tuesday Lunch. Nick Katzenbach pushed hard to keep the channel open, saying there was now dialogue for the first time since February and "the tone of the communications was less strident than before." He added, "It is important to try to get them to talk, even at the price of not hitting within the Hanoi circle."

Walt Rostow protested, "I do not see any connection between bombing and negotiations."

"I do not think we are going to get negotiations by bombing," Nick replied acidly. Though he, Dean, and I all agreed that piecemeal bombing of fixed targets in the North had little effect on the war, we were unable to settle on a formula that would bring Hanoi to the bargaining table. And so the debate continued.[33]

Later that same day, Nick sent the president a memo urging we keep open the Pennsylvania channel. He wrote that this was his own view and he did not know whether Dean agreed. The memo began: "The significance of the Paris-Kissinger exercise lies in the fact that it is the closest thing we have yet had to establishing a dialogue with North Vietnam." Because North Vietnam had repeatedly cited bombing escalations as prejudicial to discussions, Nick urged the president to "eliminate all possible doubt" about the sincerity of our negotiating efforts. He explained:

> I do not believe that Hanoi is presently likely to enter into serious discussions. But I think that it is important in terms of both circumstances and public relations that we test that possibility to the hilt. I do not think we pay a heavy price in delaying hitting again a very small percentage of the targets in North Vietnam. We know that destruction of those targets this week or next week can have absolutely no significance in terms of the conduct of the war. There is an outside chance that it could have some impact on the search for peace. And I would play along with that chance— which I acknowledge to be very small indeed—because the consequences are so great.[34]

The president reluctantly accepted Nick's advice. He gave a major speech in San Antonio, Texas, on September 29 based on the Pennsylvania initiative, which came to be known as the San Antonio Formula. It went further than any previous U.S. public statement by saying we would stop the bombing if there would be private assurances this would lead promptly to productive discussions, and on the assumption North Vietnam would not take military advantage of the halt, meaning it would not increase the flow of men and supplies to the South.

The president's speech did not move Hanoi. When Marcovich met with Bo on October 2, North Vietnam's consul general called it "insulting."[35]

Hanoi continued to criticize our offer as conditional—dependent on "prompt productive discussions." We refused to change the wording, even though I, for one, argued that it was not that important. If we stopped the bombing, we could resume it anytime, no matter what we said, if North Vietnam did not bargain in good faith. The debate continued within the administration with no more unity than before.

On October 18, we met to discuss whether the Pennsylvania channel should be abandoned. To varying degrees, Dean, Nick, Walt, Max Taylor, and Henry recommended keeping it open. Presidential counselors Abe Fortas and Clark Clifford urged closing it. I strongly disagreed. I believed that if we stopped bombing, talks would quickly follow; that some possibility existed this would lead to a settlement; and that we must move toward a settlement in the next twelve months if only because public support for the war could not be maintained for long. The president instructed Henry to inform North Vietnam of our continued willingness to talk but also to express our dissatisfaction with the results to date.[36]

On October 20, Bo refused to see Aubrac and Marcovich, remarking, "There is nothing new to say. The situation is worsening. There is no reason to talk again." That marked the end of Pennsylvania, except for the foundations it laid for negotiations in 1968.[37]

The next day, Saturday, October 21, 1967, 20,000 angry antiwar demonstrators marched on the Pentagon, determined to shut it down.

We had learned of the march well in advance. On September 20, the president met with me and others to discuss how to deal with it. I told him we faced a difficult problem—difficult because the Pentagon has no natural defenses. A huge building—the world's largest when it was constructed during World War II—it is ringed by an asphalt road and acres of grass. You can walk up to it on all five sides.

We decided to surround the building with troops armed with rifles, standing shoulder-to-shoulder in the middle of the asphalt ring, and to station U.S. marshals between them and the protesters. We knew a single line of soldiers could not possibly prevent a mob of thousands from rushing the building—unless they fired their weapons, which we did not intend to permit. Therefore, Bus and I, with his troop commanders, agreed to station reinforcements in the Pentagon's center courtyard, a grassy area where employees like to sit in the sun during lunch. If pressure from the crowd forced a breach in the troop line, soldiers from inside the building would pour out to close it. So as not to aggravate tensions, we decided to drop those reinforcements into the courtyard using helicopters at night.

I told the president no rifle would be loaded without my permission, and I did not intend to give it. I added that Bus, Deputy Attorney General Warren Christopher, and I would personally monitor the operation from my office and the Pentagon roof.

The day before the march, Undersecretary of the Army David E. McGiffert circulated a memo to all participating troops, marshals, and military police through the army chief of staff. It spelled out the guidelines of their mission:

> In support of civil authority, we have the very delicate and difficult job of both upholding constitutional rights of free assembly

and expression and protecting government operations and property. We cannot tolerate lawlessness; neither can we tolerate interference with the legitimate exercise of constitutional rights. . . .

We must avoid either overreacting or under-reacting. We
must behave with dignity and firmness. We must act in a way
which holds to the absolute minimum the possibility of bloodshed
and injury; which minimizes the need for arrest; which distin-
guishes to the extent feasible between those who are and are not
breaking the law, and which uses minimum force consistent with
the mission of protecting the employees (military and civilian), the
operations, and the property of the Government.[38]

As I reread Dave's words nearly three decades later, I still feel
immense pride in the professional, responsible way the U.S. Army
and the U.S. Marshal Service planned and executed an almost
impossible task.

"There were two separate parts of the rally," *The Washington
Post* reported.

The first was the gathering at the Reflecting Pool between the
Washington Monument and the Lincoln Memorial. This one had
the structure of taste and human respect. The crowd there had to
be over 50,000. It was orderly and it was made up primarily of
college students. The second gathering was the one in front of the
Pentagon. This was smaller; 20,000 the Pentagon said. The front
ranks of it, 3000 probably, was made up of troublemakers who put
a deep gash in the antiwar movement."[39]

The front ranks indeed included many troublemakers, who used
every device to provoke the troops to violence. Young women
rubbed their breasts against soldiers standing at attention with rifles
at their sides and even unzipped their flies; the soldiers did not
move. Protesters threw mud balls, picket signs, leaflets, sticks, and
rocks at the troops; they stayed in place. A wave of demonstrators
tried to break the line, but the troops fell back against the Pentagon's
doors and the reinforcements from the courtyard flowed out to
help hold the crowd. A few protesters managed to get into the

building but were quickly ejected. Eventually, the crowd began to disperse. But thousands stayed into the night, building fires on the grounds. The last demonstrators did not leave until the following afternoon.

The Post's report on the demonstration included this statement: "Although the potential for violence was high throughout the afternoon and into the night, not a shot was fired and no serious injuries were reported."[40]

I watched the whole thing from the roof of the building and other vantage points. Years later a reporter asked if I had been scared. Of course I was scared: an uncontrolled mob is a frightening thing—luckily, in this case, frightening but ineffective. At the same time, I could not help but think that had the protesters been more disciplined—Gandhi-like—they could have achieved their objective of shutting us down. All they had to do was lie on the pavement around the building. We would have found it impossible to remove enough of them fast enough to keep the Pentagon open.

———

President Johnson continued to reach out for advice. For help in deciding what changes, if any, he should make in the conduct of the war, he solicited Mac Bundy's judgment, and he asked the Wise Men to meet again on November 2.*

Mac replied with a memo on October 17. His position—summed up in the statement "I think your policy is as right as ever and that the weight of the evidence from the field is encouraging"—reflected the later consensus of the Wise Men. Ironically, Mac advised the president in the same memo: "I would not listen too closely to anyone who comes from a distance and spends only one day looking at the evidence."[41] He might have added: "In particular, don't listen too closely to a group, however distinguished, which hears only part of the evidence."

The group that gathered around the big table in the Cabinet

*See Chapter 7, for the first gathering of the Wise Men in July 1965.

Room on the morning of November 2 was somewhat different from the group in 1965, when the Wise Men had urged the president to commit whatever forces were needed to keep Vietnam from falling under Communist control. Paul Hoffman, George Kistiakowsky, and Arthur Larson were gone—uninvited because they were known to be against Johnson's Vietnam policy. Bob Lovett and Jack McCloy were absent too, invited but unable to attend. The eleven now at the table were Dean Acheson, George Ball, Omar Bradley, Mac Bundy, Clark Clifford, Art Dean, Doug Dillon, Abe Fortas, Cabot Lodge, former State Department official Bob Murphy, and Max Taylor.

When the president opened the meeting, he laid out five questions:

1. What could we do that we are not doing in South Vietnam?
2. Concerning the North, should we continue what we are doing, should we mine the ports and take out the dikes, or should we eliminate our bombing of the North altogether?
3. Should we adopt a passive policy of willingness to negotiate, should we aggressively seek negotiations, or should we bow out?
4. Should we get out of Vietnam?
5. What positive steps should the administration take to unite and better communicate with the nation?

Johnson was asking the right questions. But in his poker-playing fashion, he had held back crucial knowledge the Wise Men needed to give fully informed answers. They had been briefed the night before by Bus Wheeler and George Carver, CIA Vietnam specialist and continuing optimist about the war. But they had received no written materials. In particular, they did not receive Rear Admiral La Rocque's devastating report that a military victory in Vietnam was highly unlikely. Nor did they see Dick Helms's analysis that the risks of U.S. disengagement were limited and controllable.

And, to my disappointment, the president did not disclose to them a memorandum I had given him the day before. It represented my appraisal of the dilemma into which we had steered the country and my best judgment of how we should deal with it. My cover note pointed out the grim reality we had to face: "Continuation of our present course of action in Southeast Asia would be dangerous, costly in lives, and unsatisfactory to the American people." Without saying it in so many words, I indicated I understood just how hard it would be for the president to consider abandoning the conventional wisdom on Vietnam and changing course. But that was what I was recommending: "The attached memorandum outlines an alternative program [to the program we are presently following]."

I assured the president "the memo represents my personal views," and I went on, "Because these may be incompatible with your own, I have not shown the paper to Dean Rusk, Walt Rostow or Bus Wheeler. After you have read it, if you wish me to discuss my proposals with them and report back to you our joint recommendations, I will do so." I hoped the president, after studying my memo, would let me distribute it to my senior civilian and military associates for intensive debate and deliberation. I recognized my recommendations were highly controversial, and quite possibly unwise, but they addressed fundamental questions that demanded answers.

As we will see, it did not happen.

I began the memorandum itself by looking to the coming year. I stressed my overwhelming conviction that "continuing on our present course will not bring us by the end of 1968 enough closer to success, in the eyes of the American public, to prevent the continued erosion of popular support for our involvement in Vietnam." Yet, during this period, we would "be faced with requests for additional ground forces requiring an increased draft and/or a call-up of reserves." This, in turn, would lead to a doubling of U.S. casualties in 1968. I cited the best estimates we had: "10,900 to 15,000 additional American dead and 30,000 to 45,000 additional wounded requiring hospitalization."

I repeated what I had said many times before about the bombing: it would neither reduce the conflict in the South below existing levels nor break the North's will to fight. "Nothing," I stressed,

> can be expected to break this will other than the conviction that they cannot succeed. This conviction will not be created unless and until they come to the conclusion that the U.S. is prepared to remain in Vietnam for whatever period of time is necessary to assure the independent choice of the South Vietnamese people. The enemy cannot be expected to arrive at that conclusion in advance of the American public. And the American public, frustrated by the slow rate of progress, fearing continued escalation, and doubting that all approaches to peace have been sincerely probed, does not give the appearance of having the will to persist. As the months go by, there will be both increasing pressure for widening the war and continued loss of support for American participation in the struggle. There will be increasing calls for American withdrawal.
>
> There is, in my opinion, a very real question whether under these circumstances it will be possible to maintain our efforts in South Vietnam for the time necessary to accomplish our objectives there.

I emphasized that the Joint Chiefs' recommendations for bringing the conflict to a speedy conclusion—geographic expansion of the ground war and intensification of the bombing—gave no reasonable hope of doing so while carrying major risks of widening the war. I therefore concluded the only sensible course involved "the stabilization of our military operations in the South . . . along with a demonstration that our air attacks on the North are not blocking negotiations leading to a peaceful settlement." I recommended these specific steps:

- Announce a policy of stabilization
- Halt the bombing of North Vietnam before year's end in order to bring about negotiations
- Review ground operations in the South in order to reduce U.S. casualties, transfer greater responsibility to the South Viet-

namese for their own security and lessen the war's destructiveness to South Vietnam.[42]

The Wise Men had no clue that all this was going on. Unsurprisingly, in the absence of new information, their preconceived notions about the military and political situation in South Vietnam determined their answers. With respect to the ground war in the South, they saw great improvement and progress, and urged the president to press ahead with the current program. With respect to bombing of the North, all except George Ball agreed it should continue. With respect to negotiations, eight of the eleven predicted the Communists would never negotiate: once the enemy understood it could never win, it would simply reduce hostilities and eventually give up. With respect to whether we should get out, they unanimously said no. Finally, with respect to how to unite the American people, they advised emphasizing "light at the end of the tunnel" instead of battles, death, and danger.[43]

This represented the accumulated wisdom of America's foreign policy establishment, the most experienced leaders in their fields, men who had spent the past two decades dealing—successfully—with the challenges and perils of the Cold War. If they felt as they did, and Ellsworth Bunker and Westy continued to report progress from the field, how could President Johnson be expected to break out of his mind-set and confront the uncomfortable truths and unpalatable choices that I had laid before him the previous day?

I never received a reply from the president to my memorandum.* Much later, I learned he had sent a copy of it to Dean Rusk for his reaction, with instructions to show it to no one. And he asked Walt Rostow to disclose the memo's substance, but not its author, to Nick Katzenbach, Max Taylor, William Westmoreland, Ellsworth Bunker, Clark Clifford, and Abe Fortas for comment. Not until I undertook research on this book did I discover this

---

*The Johnson Library holds a memo from Walt Rostow to the president on December 4, 1967, that says: "Herewith a draft letter from you to Sec. McNamara which represents a consensus of all the advice presented to you." But President Johnson never sent me the letter.

or learn their reactions. At one extreme was Nick, who expressed almost total agreement. At the other was Abe Fortas, who thought the author of the memo had probably seen too many protest marches. "The analysis and recommendations," he wrote,

> are based, *almost entirely,* upon an assessment of U.S. public opinion and an *unspoken assumption* as to the effect that should be given to it. I am in *total disagreement.* . . . I can think of nothing *worse* than the suggested program. . . . It *will, indeed, produce demands* in this *country* to *withdraw*—and, in fact, it must be appraised for what it is: *a step in the process of withdrawal.* And in my opinion, it means *not* domestic appeasement, but domestic repudiation (which it would deserve); a powerful tonic to Chinese Communist effectiveness in the world; and a profound retreat to the Asia dominoes [emphases in original].[44]

Clark Clifford disliked the memo too. He wrote: "I disagree with the recommendations presented in the memorandum. . . . I believe that the course of action suggested therein will retard the possibility of concluding the conflict rather than accelerating it." As for my proposal to halt the bombing, he said: "I am at a loss to understand the logic." He contended that stabilization "would be interpreted to be exactly what it is: a resigned and discouraged effort to find a way out of a conflict for which we had lost our will and determination." He ended by saying that "the President and every man around him wants to end the war. But the future of our children and grandchildren require that it be ended by accomplishing our purpose, i.e., the thwarting of the aggression by North Vietnam, aided by China and Russia."[45]

Mac Bundy, whom Johnson did not consult on my memo, sent the president a summary commentary on the Wise Men's meeting. He urged him to start a high-level review that "could establish a pattern of gradually decreasing cost that would be endurable for the five to ten years that I think are predicted by most of the wisest officials in Vietnam." "If one thing is more clear than another," he wrote, "it is that we simply are not going to go on at the present rate for that length of time."[46]

Why did President Johnson not force a full and open debate on issues that so sharply and clearly divided his most senior advisers? Perhaps his failure was rooted in his realization that the problem of Vietnam was intractable, that there was no satisfactory solution—no way to bring his advisers to consensus. Perhaps he saw clearly that the decision about changing the war's direction rested with him—and it was a decision he could not bring himself to make.

My November 1 memorandum did do one thing: it raised the tension between two men who loved and respected each other—Lyndon Johnson and me—to the breaking point. Four weeks later, President Johnson announced my election as president of the World Bank and my departure from the Defense Department at an unspecified date.

———

I do not know to this day whether I quit or was fired. Maybe it was both.

I had long been interested in the developing countries. In a highly controversial speech before the American Society of Newspaper Editors in Montreal on May 18, 1966, I spoke on that subject. I said, "There is among us . . . a tendency to think of our security problem as being exclusively a military problem." I disagreed. "A nation can reach the point at which it does not buy more security for itself simply by buying more military hardware, and we are at that point." I believe the relationship between defense expenditures and security takes the shape of a curve in which, up to a point, security increases as defense expenditures increase, then the curve flattens out and may even decline. I judged the United States to be on the flat of that curve in 1966. I believe we are on it today.

Rather than increase military spending, I told the editors, we should assist "those developing countries which genuinely need and request our help and which as an essential precondition are willing and able to help themselves." I noted that the already dangerous gap between rich and poor nations was widening, and that poverty within nations produced social and political tensions that often spilled over into conflict between nations. In sum, I believed that we would achieve greater security by transferring marginal dollar expenditures from defense to foreign aid.

One did not expect to hear such a speech from a defense secretary in time of war. It led to harsh criticism from hawks in Congress and caused the president (with whom it had not been cleared) considerable pain. But it reflected my beliefs. It was those beliefs that shaped my reply to George Woods in the spring of 1967, when over lunch he told me his five-year term as president of the World Bank ended on December 31 and he wished me to succeed him. I expressed considerable interest. I added, however, that I had told all who had made similar job offers—including, among others, a Wall Street partnership that proposed to pay me $2.5 million annually in 1967 dollars—that I would not consider such matters so long as the president wanted me to stay in my present post.

I had reported the conversation to the president at the time, and it had not come up again until September or October, when out of the blue he asked if anything further had developed. I told him I was still interested in George's proposal but would stay at the Defense Department as long as the president desired.

"You deserve whatever you want from this government," he said. "My obligation is to help you, and you can have whatever is within my power to bestow."

"People have obligations to the president, not the reverse," I replied. We left it at that.

On November 8, George visited my office, and we rode together to the White House, where I had a lunch to attend. He said the bank's new president would be selected soon, and he planned to tell Joe Fowler—the secretary of the treasury and the U.S. governor of the bank, whose duty it was to come up with nominees—that I was his candidate. But it was not until years later that George told me what Joe and the president had done. Before submitting my name to the board of directors of the bank, Joe went to clear the nomination with the president. George said that Joe, who was hoping to become the bank president himself, told LBJ that it was customary to submit three names. In typical fashion, the president replied, "OK, it's McNamara, McNamara, McNamara."

On November 27, the London *Financial Times* printed a rumor of my nomination. Two days later George and five World Bank directors came to my office and offered me the post. I accepted. The next day President Johnson announced I would be leaving the Pentagon to go to the World Bank.

One of the great ironies is that I do not know whether the president himself knew exactly how and why my departure came about. He knew I was loyal to the presidency and to him. And, as I have said, I sensed his equally strong feelings toward me, despite our deep differences over Vietnam. He must have assumed I had thought of resigning, and I believe he felt relieved that I had not.

Why, then, did I leave? It was not because I was ill, although newspapers reported such stories, and the president told his aides he was worried I might commit suicide, as had Truman's first defense secretary, James V. Forrestal. It has since become a common assumption that I was near emotional and physical collapse. I was not. I was indeed feeling stress. I was at loggerheads with the president of the United States; I was not getting answers to my questions; and I was tense as hell. But I was not under medical care, not taking drugs except for an occasional sleeping pill, and never contemplated suicide.

The fact is I had come to the conclusion, and had told him point-blank, that we could not achieve our objective in Vietnam through any reasonable military means, and we therefore should seek a lesser political objective through negotiations. President Johnson was not ready to accept that. It was becoming clear to both of us that I would not change my judgment, nor would he change his. Something had to give.

Many friends, then and since, have told me I was wrong not to have resigned in protest over the president's policy. Let me explain why I did not. The president (with the exception of the vice president) is the only elected official of the executive branch. He appoints each cabinet officer, who should have no constituency other than him. That is how cabinet officers are kept accountable to the people. A cabinet officer's authority and legitimacy derives from the president. It is also true, however, that, because of their frequent public exposure, some cabinet officers develop power independent of the president.

To a degree, I held such power, and some said I should have used it by resigning, challenging the president's Vietnam policy, and leading those who sought to force a change.

I believe that would have been a violation of my responsibility to the president and my oath to uphold the Constitution.

I will never forget what Dean Acheson told me. Dean said that when he had served as undersecretary of the treasury in the early 1930s, under Franklin Roosevelt, he had found himself unable to accept the president's monetary policy. So he had resigned—silently. Roosevelt had told him he was the only official he had ever known to resign as the Constitution intended. I never forgot the lesson.*

Simply put, despite my deep differences with Lyndon Johnson over Vietnam, I was loyal to the presidency and loyal to him, and I sensed his equally strong feelings toward me. Moreover, until the day I left, I believed I could influence his decisions. I therefore felt I had a responsibility to stay at my post.

———

Between November 29 and when I left the Pentagon three months later, crisis piled on top of crisis: North Vietnamese troops laid siege to the marine base at Khe Sanh in the far northwestern corner of South Vietnam; North Korea seized the U.S. intelligence ship *Pueblo* in international waters off the Korean peninsula on January

---

*Cy Vance did much the same as secretary of state in the spring of 1980. Disagreeing with President Carter's attempt to rescue U.S. embassy hostages in Iran and feeling he could no longer influence the president's decision, he told Carter he planned to resign—after the attempted rescue, and whether it succeeded or failed.

23, 1968; a week later, the Vietcong blasted their way into the American embassy compound in Saigon, launching the bloody Tet Offensive.

In my last official act on Vietnam, on February 27, 1968, I opposed Westy's renewed appeal for 200,000 additional troops on economic, political, and moral grounds. My successor, Clark Clifford, later adopted the same position.

As the day of my departure neared, I wrote this letter to LBJ:

February 23, 1968

Dear Mr. President:

I cannot find words to express to you the feelings that lie in my heart.

Fifty-one months ago you asked me to serve in your Cabinet. No other period in my life has brought so much struggle—or so much satisfaction. The struggle would have been infinitely greater and the satisfaction immeasurably less if I had not received your full support every step of the way.

No man could fail to be proud of service in an Administration which has recorded the progress yours has in the fields of civil rights, health, and education. One hundred years of neglect cannot be overcome overnight. But you have pushed, dragged, and cajoled the nation into basic reforms from which my children and my children's children will benefit for decades to come. I know the price you have paid, both personally and politically. Every citizen of our land is in your debt.

I will not say goodbye—you know you have but to call and I will respond.

Sincerely
Bob[47]

Marg had already written the president and Lady Bird and received a moving reply from LBJ that said in part:

We both felt so bleak through this business of separation. You know that if I were to wait for a "convenient time" to part with

Bob, it would be about 24 hours before I leave office myself. I have never admired or enjoyed anyone more than your husband. As for the days ahead, they are bright with the promise of a line from your own letter. Though our lives will change, you wrote, we will not. Lady Bird and I will never change our feelings for both of you. They are lasting in admiration and gratitude.

With love, L.B.J.[48]

When the president arrived for my farewell ceremony at the Pentagon on February 29, we boarded the elevator to my office. As we rode up it got stuck between floors. The sergeant operating the elevator called maintenance on the emergency phone. The maintenance man asked, "Do you have a full load?" "We sure do," the sergeant replied. We stayed stuck for ten or fifteen minutes; the Secret Service, needless to say, was frantic. Finally, an agent climbed through the car roof and secured our release.

We then moved to the parade ground in front of the Pentagon's River Entrance. Though nobody felt like celebrating because we were at war, protocol had to be observed, so the military had organized a full-fledged farewell ceremony in my honor, complete with speeches, a band, an honor guard, an artillery salute, and a flyover by navy and air force jets. It seemed almost fitting that the ceremony took place in a driving storm of sleet and rain, which forced cancellation of the flyover and short-circuited the public address system. Everyone left chilled and soaked.

The day before, President Johnson had awarded me the Medal of Freedom in the White House East Room, before a gathering of family, friends, and Washington officialdom. Seven years earlier I had stood in that very room and proudly taken my oath of office. For a person whose image is one of cool efficiency, I become very emotional at times, and so it was this day. When my turn came to speak, I looked at the president and began, "I cannot find words to express what lies in my heart today," then could say nothing more as I choked back conflicting feelings of pride, gratitude, frustration, sadness, and failure. Had I been able to speak, this is what I might have said:

> Today, I end 1,558 days of the most intimate association with the most complex individual I have ever known. Many in this room believe Lyndon Johnson is crude, mean, vindictive, scheming, untruthful. Perhaps at times he has shown each of these characteristics. But he is much, much more. I believe that in the decades ahead, history will judge him to have done more—for example, through such legislation as the Civil Rights Act, the Voting Rights Act, and the Great Society legislation—to alert us all to our responsibility toward the poor, the disadvantaged, and the victims of racial prejudice than any other political leader of our time. But for Vietnam, a war which he inherited—and which admittedly neither he nor we managed wisely—we would have been much further along in solving those problems.

Thirteen years later, on January 16, 1981, I returned to the East Room with Marg. This time it was she who was honored and I who watched. President Carter awarded *her* the Medal of Freedom for her work in founding Reading Is Fundamental, a program to encourage disadvantaged youth to read. Marg was at the end of a long battle with cancer. When she died, seventeen days after the ceremony, 70,000 volunteers were working in her organization across the country.

11

The Lessons of Vietnam

M y involvement with Vietnam ended the day after I left the East Room. The war, of course, went on for another seven years. By the time the United States finally left South Vietnam in 1973, we had lost over 58,000 men and women; our economy had been damaged by years of heavy and improperly financed war spending; and the political unity of our society had been shattered, not to be restored for decades.

Were such high costs justified?

Dean Rusk, Walt Rostow, Lee Kwan Yew, and many other geopoliticians across the globe to this day answer yes. They conclude that without U.S. intervention in Vietnam, Communist hegemony—both Soviet and Chinese—would have spread farther through South and East Asia to include control of Indonesia, Thailand, and possibly India. Some would go further and say that the USSR would have been led to take greater risks to extend its influence elsewhere in the world, particularly in the Middle East, where it might well have sought control of the oil-producing nations. They might be correct, but I seriously question such judgments.

When the archives of the former Soviet Union, China, and Vietnam are opened to scholars, we will know more about those countries' intentions, but even without such knowledge we know that the danger of Communist aggression during the four decades of the Cold War was real and substantial. Although during the 1950s, 1960s, 1970s, and 1980s the West often misperceived, and therefore exaggerated, the power of the East and its ability to project that power, to have failed to defend ourselves against the threat would have been foolhardy and irresponsible.

That said, today I question whether either Soviet or Chinese behavior and influence in the 1970s and 1980s would have been materially different had the United States not entered the war in Indochina or had we withdrawn from Vietnam in the early or mid-1960s. By then it should have become apparent that the two conditions underlying President Kennedy's decision to send military advisers to South Vietnam were not being met and, indeed, could not be met: political stability did not exist and was unlikely ever to be achieved; and the South Vietnamese, even with our training assistance and logistical support, were incapable of defending themselves.

Given these facts—and they are facts—I believe we could and should have withdrawn from South Vietnam either in late 1963 amid the turmoil following Diem's assassination or in late 1964 or early 1965 in the face of increasing political and military weakness in South Vietnam. And, as the table opposite suggests, there were at least three other occasions when withdrawal could have been justified.

I do not believe that U.S. withdrawal at any of these junctures, if properly explained to the American people and to the world, would have led West Europeans to question our support for NATO and, through it, our guarantee of their security. Nor do I believe that Japan would have viewed our security treaties as any less credible. On the contrary, it is possible we would have improved our credibility by withdrawing from Vietnam and saving our strength for more defensible stands elsewhere.

DATE OF WITHDRAWAL	U.S. FORCE LEVELS IN SOUTH VIETNAM	US KILLED IN ACTION	BASIS FOR WITHDRAWAL
November 1963	16,300 advisers[a]	78	Collapse of Diem regime and lack of political stability
Late 1964 or early 1965	23,300 advisers	225	Clear indication of South Vietnam's inability to defend itself, even with U.S. training and logistical support
July 1965	81,400 troops	509	Further evidence of the above
December 1965	184,300 troops	1,594	Evidence that U.S. military tactics and training were inappropriate for the guerrilla war being waged
December 1967	485,600 troops	15,979	CIA reports indicating bombing in the North would not force North Vietnam to desist in the face of our inability to turn back enemy forces in South Vietnam
January 1973	543,400 troops (April 1969)	58,191[b]	Signing of Paris Accords, marking an end of U.S. military involvement

[a]This and all subsequent figures in the table have been supplied by the U.S. Army Center of Military History, Washington, D.C.
[b]As of December 31, 1968, the number of U.S. killed-in-action in Vietnam totaled 30,568.

———

It is sometimes said that the post–Cold War world will be so different from the world of the past that the lessons of Vietnam will be inapplicable or of no relevance to the twenty-first century. I disagree. That said, if we are to learn from our experience in Vietnam, we must first pinpoint our failures. There were eleven major causes for our disaster in Vietnam:

1. We misjudged then—as we have since—the geopolitical intentions of our adversaries (in this case, North Vietnam and the Vietcong, supported by China and the Soviet Union), and we exaggerated the dangers to the United States of their actions.

2. We viewed the people and leaders of South Vietnam in terms of our own experience. We saw in them a thirst for—and a determination to fight for—freedom and democracy. We totally misjudged the political forces within the country.

3. We underestimated the power of nationalism to motivate a people (in this case, the North Vietnamese and Vietcong) to fight and die for their beliefs and values—and we continue to do so today in many parts of the world.

4. Our misjudgments of friend and foe alike reflected our profound ignorance of the history, culture, and politics of the people in the area, and the personalities and habits of their leaders. We might have made similar misjudgments regarding the Soviets during our frequent confrontations—over Berlin, Cuba, the Middle East, for example—had we not had the advice of Tommy Thompson, Chip Bohlen, and George Kennan. These senior diplomats had spent decades studying the Soviet Union, its people and its leaders, why they behaved as they did, and how they would react to our actions. Their advice proved invaluable in shaping our judgments and decision. No Southeast Asian counterparts existed for senior officials to consult when making decisions on Vietnam.

5. We failed then—as we have since—to recognize the limitations of modern, high-technology military equipment, forces, and doctrine in confronting unconventional, highly motivated people's movements. We failed as well to adapt our military tactics to the task of winning the hearts and minds of people from a totally different culture.

6. We failed to draw Congress and the American people into a full and frank discussion and debate of the pros and cons of a large-scale U.S. military involvement in Southeast Asia before we initiated the action.

7. After the action got under way and unanticipated events forced us off our planned course, we failed to retain popular support in part because we did not explain fully what was happening and why we were doing what we did. We had not prepared the public to understand the complex events we faced and how to react constructively to the need for changes in course as the nation confronted uncharted seas and an alien environment. A nation's deepest strength lies not in its

military prowess but, rather, in the unity of its people. We failed to maintain it.

8. We did not recognize that neither our people nor our leaders are omniscient. Where our own security is not directly at stake, our judgment of what is in another people's or country's best interest should be put to the test of open discussion in international forums. We do not have the God-given right to shape every nation in our own image or as we choose.

9. We did not hold to the principle that U.S. military action—other than in response to direct threats to our own security—should be carried out only in conjunction with multinational forces supported fully (and not merely cosmetically) by the international community.

10. We failed to recognize that in international affairs, as in other aspects of life, there may be problems for which there are no immediate solutions. For one whose life has been dedicated to the belief and practice of problem solving, this is particularly hard to admit. But, at times, we may have to live with an imperfect, untidy world.

11. Underlying many of these errors lay our failure to organize the top echelons of the executive branch to deal effectively with the extraordinarily complex range of political and military issues, involving the great risks and costs—including, above all else, loss of life—associated with the application of military force under substantial constraints over a long period of time. Such organizational weakness would have been costly had this been the only task confronting the president and his advisers. It, of course, was not. It coexisted with the wide array of other domestic and international problems confronting us. We thus failed to analyze and debate our actions in Southeast Asia—our objectives, the risks and costs of alternative ways of dealing with them, and the necessity of changing course when failure was clear—with the intensity and thoroughness that characterized the debates of the Executive Committee during the Cuban Missile Crisis.

These were our major failures, in their essence. Though set forth separately, they are all in some way linked: failure in one area contributed to or compounded failure in another. Each became a turn in a terrible knot.

Pointing out these mistakes allows us to map the lessons of Vietnam, and places us in a position to apply them to the post–Cold War world.

Although clear evidence has existed since the mid-1980s that the Cold War was ending, nations throughout the world have been slow to revise their foreign and defense policies in part because they do not see clearly what lies ahead.

As the Iraqi invasion of Kuwait, the civil war in the former Yugoslavia, and the turmoil in Chechnya, Somalia, Haiti, Sudan, Burundi, Armenia, and Tajikistan make clear, the world of the future will not be without conflict, between disparate groups within nations and extending across national borders. Racial, religious, and ethnic tensions will remain. Nationalism will be a powerful force across the globe. Political revolutions will erupt as societies advance. Historic disputes over political boundaries will endure. And economic disparities among nations will increase as technology and education spread unevenly around the world. The underlying causes of Third World conflict that existed long before the Cold War began remain now that it has ended. They will be compounded by potential strife among states of the former Soviet Union and by continuing tensions in the Middle East. It is such tensions that in the past forty-five years have contributed to 125 wars causing 40 million deaths in the Third World.[1]

In these respects, the world of the future will not be different from the world of the past—conflicts within and among nations will not disappear. But relations between nations will change dramatically. In the postwar years, the United States had the power—and to a considerable degree exercised that power—to shape the world as we chose. In the next century, that will not be possible.

Japan is destined to play a larger and larger role on the world scene, exercising greater economic and political power and, one hopes, assuming greater economic and political responsibility. The same can be said of Western Europe, which in 1993 took a major step toward economic integration. Greater political unity is bound to follow (despite opposition to the Maastricht Treaty), and it will strengthen Europe's power in world politics.

And by the middle of the next century, several of the countries of what in the past we have termed the Third World will have grown so dramatically in population and economic power as to become major forces in international relations. India is likely to have a population of 1.6 billion; Nigeria, 400 million; Brazil, 300 million. If China achieves its ambitious economic goals for the year 2000, and maintains satisfactory but not spectacular growth rates for the next fifty years, its 1.6 billion people will have the income—the affluence—of Western Europeans in the mid-twentieth century. Its total gross domestic product will exceed that of the United States, Western Europe, Japan, or Russia. It will indeed be a power to be reckoned with. These figures are highly speculative, of course, but I cite them to emphasize the magnitude of the changes that lie ahead.

While remaining the world's strongest nation, the United States will live in a multipolar world, and its foreign policy and defense programs must be adjusted to this emerging reality. In such a world, a need clearly exists for developing new relationships both among the Great Powers—of which there will be at least five: China, Europe, Japan, Russia, and the United States—and between the Great Powers and other nations.

Many political theorists—in particular, those classified as "realists"—predict a return to traditional power politics. They argue that the disappearance of ideological competition between East and West will trigger a reversion to traditional relationships based on territorial and economic imperatives: that the United States, Russia, Western Europe, China, Japan, and India will seek to assert themselves in their own regions while still competing for dominance in other areas of the world where conditions are fluid. This view has been expressed, for example, by Harvard Professor Michael Sandel: "The end of the Cold War does not mean an end of global competition between the Superpowers. Once the ideological dimension fades, what you are left with is not peace and harmony, but old-fashioned global politics based on dominant powers competing for influence and pursuing their internal interests."[2]

Henry Kissinger, also a member of the realist school, has expressed a similar conclusion:

> Victory in the Cold War has propelled America into a world which bears many similarities to the European state system of the eighteenth and nineteenth centuries. . . . The absence of both an overriding ideological or strategic threat frees nations to pursue foreign policies based increasingly on their immediate national interest. In an international system characterized by perhaps five or six major powers and a multiplicity of smaller states, order will have to emerge much as it did in past centuries from a reconciliation and balancing of competing national interests.[3]

Kissinger's and Sandel's conceptions of relations among nations in the post–Cold War world are historically well founded, but I would argue that they are inconsistent with our increasingly interdependent world. No nation, not even the United States, can stand alone in a world in which nations are inextricably entwined with one another economically, environmentally, and with regard to security. The United Nations charter offers a far more appropriate framework for international relations in such a world than does the doctrine of power politics.

I am not alone in this view. Carl Kaysen, former director of the Institute for Advanced Study at Princeton, has argued: "The international system that relies on the national use of military force as the ultimate guarantor of security, and the threat of its use as the basis of order, is not the only possible one. To seek a different system [based on collective security] . . . is no longer the pursuit of an illusion, but a necessary effort toward a necessary goal."[4]

And George F. Kennan, at a celebration in honor of his ninetieth birthday held at the Council on Foreign Relations on February 15, 1994, observed that for the first time in centuries, no prospective Great Power conflicts threaten the peace of the world. It is this peace among the Great Powers—at least for the near term—that makes it truly possible both to pursue my vision of the post–Cold War world and, at the same time, to hedge against failure by maintaining the capacity to protect ourselves and our interests should the world experience a return to Great Power rivalry.

Maintaining that capacity does not mean that defense spending should remain at its current exorbitant level. In the United States, for example, defense expenditures during fiscal year 1993 totaled $291 billion—25 percent more in inflation-adjusted dollars than in 1980. Moreover, President Clinton's five-year defense program for fiscal years 1995–1999 projects only a very gradual decline in expenditures from 1993 levels. Defense outlays in 1999, in inflation-adjusted dollars, are estimated to be only 3 percent less than under President Nixon, in the midst of the Cold War.[5] The United States spends almost as much for national security as the rest of the world combined.

Such a defense program is not consistent with my view of the post–Cold War world—or the financing of domestic programs equally vital for our security. It assumes that in conflicts outside the NATO area—for instance, in Iraq, Iran, or the Korean peninsula—we will act unilaterally and without military support from other Great Powers. And it assumes that we must be prepared to undertake two such confrontations simultaneously. These are assumptions I find debatable at best.

Before nations can respond in an optimum manner to the end of the Cold War, they need a vision—a conceptual framework—of a world that would not be dominated by the East-West rivalry that shaped foreign and defense programs across the globe for more than forty years. In that new world, I believe relationships among nations should be directed toward five goals: They should

1. Provide all states guarantees against external aggression—frontiers should not be changed by force
2. Codify the rights of minorities and ethnic groups within states—the Kurds in Iran, Iraq, and Turkey, for instance—and provide them a means to redress their grievances without resort to violence

3. Establish a mechanism for resolving regional conflicts and conflicts within nations without unilateral action by the Great Powers

4. Increase the flow of technical and financial assistance to developing nations to help them accelerate their rates of social and economic advance

5. Assure preservation of the global environment as a basis of sustainable development for all

In sum, we should strive to create a world in which relations among nations would be based on the rule of law, a world in which national security would be supported by a system of collective security. The conflict prevention, conflict resolution, and peace-keeping functions necessary to accomplish these objectives would be performed by multilateral institutions, a reorganized and strengthened United Nations together with new and expanded regional organizations.

That is my vision of the post–Cold War world.*

Such a vision is easier to articulate than to achieve. The goal is clear; how to get there is not. I have no magic formula, no simple road map to success. I do know that such a vision will not be achieved in a month, a year, or even a decade. It will be achieved slowly and through small steps, by leaders of dedication and persistence. So I urge that we move now in that direction.

The post–Cold War world, seeking to deal with the conflicts that will inevitably arise within and among nations, while minimizing the risk of the use of military force and holding casualties resulting from its application to the lowest possible level, will need leaders. The leadership role may shift among nations depending on the issue at hand. Often, it will be filled by the United States. But in a system of collective security, the United States must accept collective decision making—and that will be very difficult for us. Correspondingly, if the system is to survive, other nations (in particular

---

*The Brookings Institution has recently published a study—Janne E. Nolan, ed., *Global Engagement: Cooperation and Security in the Twenty-first Century* (1994)—in which twenty policy makers and scholars explore a geopolitical system quite similar to what I propose here.

Germany and Japan) must accept a sharing of risks and costs—the political risks, the financial costs, and the risk of casualties and bloodshed—and that will be very difficult for them.

Had the United States and other major powers made clear their commitment to such a system of collective security, and had they stated they would protect nations against attack, the 1990 Iraqi invasion of Kuwait might well have been deterred. Similarly, had the United Nations or NATO taken action when conflict in the former Yugoslavia erupted in the early 1990s, the ensuing slaughter of tens of thousands of innocent victims might have been prevented. But today I fear Bosnia falls in the category of problems for which there is no recognizable solution—or at least no military solution.

In the post–Cold War world, the United States should be clear about where, and how, it would apply military force. This requires a precise statement of U.S. foreign policy objectives. For forty years our objective remained clear: to contain an expansionist Soviet Union. But that can no longer be the focus of our efforts; we have lost our enemy. What will we put in its place? President Clinton told the U.N. General Assembly on September 27, 1993: "Our overriding purpose must be to expand and strengthen the world's community of market-based democracies." Anthony Lake, the national security adviser, echoed this when, during the same week, he stated that "the successor to a doctrine of containment must be a strategy of enlargement—enlargement of the world's free community of market democracies."[6] Such a general formulation of our objectives is not sufficient.

The United States clearly cannot and should not intervene in every conflict arising from a nation's attempt to move toward capitalist democracy—for example, we were surely correct not to support with military force Eduard Shevardnadze's attempt to install democracy in Georgia. Nor can we be expected to try to stop by military force every instance of the slaughter of innocent civilians. More than a dozen wars currently rage throughout the world: in Bosnia, Burundi, Georgia, Iraq, Kashmir, Rwanda, Sudan, and Yemen to name only a few. And serious conflicts may soon break out in Kosovo, Lesotho, Macedonia, and Zaire. Where, if at all, should we be involved? Neither the United States nor any other Great Power has a clear answer to that question. The answers can be developed only through intense debate, over a period of years, within our own nation, among the Great Powers, and in the councils of international organizations.

We must establish well-defined criteria for the use of military force by our own and other nations. The rules governing response to aggression across national borders can be relatively simple and clear. But those relating to attempts to maintain or restore political order and to prevent wholesale slaughter within nations—as, for instance, within Rwanda in 1994—are far less so.

Several crucial questions must be faced: To what degree of human suffering should we respond? Under a U.N. convention, formalized in a global treaty that became our national law in 1989, the United States agreed to join in stopping genocide. But what constitutes genocide? In June 1994, the U.S. government, while recognizing the killing of over 200,000 Rwandans as "acts of genocide," refused to state that the killing fell under the treaty's provisions.[7] And would there not be other cases, short of genocide, that would also justify intervention? At what point should we intervene—as preventive diplomacy fails and killing appears likely, or only when the slaughter is increasing? How should we respond when nations involved in such conflicts—as was the case in the former Yugoslavia—claim that outside intervention clearly infringes on their sovereignty? We have seen the Organization of African Unity and the Organization of American States time and time again fail to support such intervention.

Above all else, the criteria governing intervention should recognize that, as we learned in Vietnam, military force has only a limited capacity to facilitate the process of nation building. Military force, by itself, cannot rebuild a "failed state."

It should be made clear to the American people that such questions will, at best, require years to answer. But we should force the debate within our own nation and within international forums.

Some of the issues may never be resolved; there may be times when we must recognize that we cannot right all wrongs. Our judgments about the appropriateness of using force to maintain order in such an imperfect world cannot be certain. They must be checked, therefore, against the willingness of other nations with comparable interests to join in the decision, to assist in its implementation, and to share in its costs—another lesson of Vietnam.

At times U.S. military intervention will be justified not on humanitarian or peacekeeping grounds but on the basis of national security. Clearly, if a direct threat to this nation emerges, we should and will act unilaterally—after appropriate consultation with Congress and the American people. If the threat is less direct but still potentially serious—for example, strife in Kosovo or Macedonia that could trigger a larger Balkan conflict involving Greece, Turkey, and perhaps Italy—how should we respond? I strongly urge that we act *only* in a multilateral decision-making and burden-sharing context— another lesson of Vietnam.

The wars we fight in the post–Cold War world are likely more often than not to be "limited wars," like Vietnam. General West-moreland made a comment about Vietnam at an LBJ Library Conference in March 1991 that is relevant here. Referring to the constraints that kept the Vietnam War "limited," he said: "At the time I felt that our hands were tied," but "we have to give President Johnson credit for *not* allowing the war to expand geographically [emphasis in original]."[8] Certainly Vietnam taught us how immensely difficult it is to fight limited wars leading to U.S. casualties over long periods of time. But circumstances will arise where limited war is far preferable to unlimited war. Before engaging in such conflicts, the American people must understand the difficulties we will face; the American military must know and accept the constraints under which they will operate; and our leaders—and our people—must be prepared to cut our losses and withdraw if it appears our limited objectives cannot be achieved at acceptable risks or costs.

We must learn from Vietnam how to manage limited wars effectively. A major cause of the debacle there lay in our failure to establish an organization of top civilian and military officials capable of directing the task. Over and over again, as my story of the decision-making process makes shockingly clear, we failed to address fundamental issues; our failure to identify them was not recognized; and deep-seated disagreements among the president's advisers about how to proceed were neither surfaced nor resolved.

As I have suggested, this resulted in part from our failure to organize properly. No senior person in Washington dealt *solely* with Vietnam. With the president, the secretaries of state and defense, the national security adviser, the chairman of the Joint Chiefs, and their associates dividing their attention over a host of complex and demanding issues, some of our shortcomings—in particular, our failure to debate systemically the most fundamental issues—could have been predicted. To avoid these, we should have established a full-time team at the highest level—what Churchill called a War Cabinet—focused on Vietnam and nothing else. At a minimum, it should have included deputies of the secretaries of state and defense, the national security adviser, the chairman of the Joint Chiefs, and the CIA director. It should have met weekly with the president at prescribed times for long, uninterrupted discussions. The weekly meetings should have been expanded monthly to include the U.S. ambassador and U.S. military commander in Vietnam. The meetings should have been characterized by the openness and candor of Executive Committee deliberations during the Cuban Missile Crisis—which contributed to the avoidance of a catastrophe. Similar organizational arrangements should be established to direct all future military operations.

Finally, we must recognize that the consequences of large-scale military operations—particularly in this age of highly sophisticated and destructive weapons—are inherently difficult to predict and to control. Therefore, they must be avoided, excepting only when our nation's security is clearly and directly threatened. These are the lessons of Vietnam. Pray God we learn them.

I want to add a final word on Vietnam.

Let me be simple and direct—I want to be clearly understood: the United States of America fought in Vietnam for eight years for what it believed to be good and honest reasons. By such action, administrations of both parties sought to protect our security, prevent the spread of totalitarian Communism, and promote individual freedom and political democracy. The Kennedy, Johnson, and Nixon administrations made their decisions and by those decisions demanded sacrifices and, yes, inflicted terrible suffering in light of those goals and values.

Their hindsight was better than their foresight. The adage echoes down the corridors of time, applying to many individuals, in many situations, in many ages. People are human; they are fallible. I concede with painful candor and a heavy heart that the adage applies to me and to my generation of American leadership regarding Vietnam. Although we sought to do the right thing—and believed we were doing the right thing—in my judgment, hindsight proves us wrong. We both overestimated the effect of South Vietnam's loss on the security of the West and failed to adhere to the fundamental principle that, in the final analysis, if the South Vietnamese were to be saved, they had to win the war themselves. Straying from this central truth, we built a progressively more massive effort on an inherently unstable foundation. External military force cannot substitute for the political order and stability that must be forged *by* a people *for* themselves.

In the end, we must confront the fate of those Americans who served in Vietnam and never returned. Does the unwisdom of our intervention nullify their effort and their loss? I think not. They did not make the decisions. They answered their nation's call to service. They went in harm's way on its behalf. And they gave their lives for their country and its ideals. That our effort in Vietnam proved unwise does not make their sacrifice less noble. It endures for all to see. Let us learn from their sacrifice and, by doing so, validate and honor it.

As I end this book, I am reminded of lines from Rudyard

Kipling's poem "The Palace." I first read it nearly sixty years ago. Kipling's words have assumed greater meaning over my lifetime. Today they are haunting.

When I was a King and a Mason—a Master proven and skilled—
I cleared me ground for a Palace such as a King should build.
I decreed and dug down to my levels. Presently, under the silt,
I came on the wreck of a Palace such as a King had built.

There was no worth in the fashion—there was no wit in the plan—
Hither and thither, aimless, the ruined footings ran—
Masonry, brute, mishandled, but carven on every stone:
"After me cometh a Builder. Tell him, I too have known."

Swift to my use in my trenches, where my well-planned groundworks grew;
I tumbled his quoins and his ashlars, and cut and reset them anew.
Lime I milled of his marbles; burned it, slacked it, and spread;
Taking and leaving at pleasure the gifts of the humble dead.

Yet I despised not nor gloried; yet, as we wrenched them apart,
I read in the razed foundations the heart of that builder's heart.
As he had risen and pleaded, so did I understand
The form of the dream he had followed in the face of the thing he had planned.

★★★

When I was a King and a Mason—in the open noon of my pride,
They sent me a Word from the Darkness. They whispered and called me aside.
They said—"The end is forbidden." They said—"Thy use is fulfilled.
"Thy Palace shall stand as that other's—the spoil of a King who shall build."

I called my men from my trenches, my quarries, my wharves, and my sheers.
All I had wrought I abandoned to the faith of the faithless years.
Only I cut on the timber—only I carved on the stone:
"After me cometh a Builder. Tell him, I too have known!"

Each human being lives with unrealized dreams and unfulfilled objectives. Certainly I have. But now, as a century of bloody conflict comes to a close, we have an opportunity to view the future with new hope: The Cold War has ended. We have the lessons of Vietnam before us—they can be learned and applied. We should see more clearly the dangers of a world armed with thousands of nuclear weapons, and we can take steps to avoid nuclear catastrophe. We have a better understanding of the potential—and limitations—of multilateral institutions for minimizing and alleviating disputes within and among nations. Do we not have reason, therefore, to believe that the twenty-first century, while not a century of tranquillity, need not witness the killing of another 160 million people by war? Surely that must be not only our hope, not only our dream, but our steadfast objective. Some may consider such a statement so naive, so simplistic, and so idealistic as to be quixotic. But as human beings, citizens of a great nation with the power to influence events in the world, can we be at peace with ourselves if we strive for less?

Appendix:
The Nuclear Risks of the 1960s
and Their Lessons for the Twenty-first
Century

W e—and all other inhabitants of our globe—continue to live
with the risk of nuclear destruction. The United States's war
plans today provide for contingent use of nuclear weapons just as
they did in the 1960s.[1] But the average American does not recognize
this fact. No doubt, he or she was surprised and pleased by the
announcement by Presidents Bush and Yeltsin in June 1992 that
they had agreed to reduce dramatically U.S. and Russian nuclear
weapons stockpiles. Today, there are 40,000–50,000 nuclear warheads in the world, with a total destructive power more than one
million times greater than that of the bomb that flattened Hiro-
shima. Assuming the reductions called for by the START 1 Treaty
are achieved, the total weapons inventory will be reduced to
approximately 20,000. Bush and Yeltsin agreed to further reductions
that would leave the five declared nuclear powers with a total of
about 12,000 warheads in 2003. It was a highly desirable move, but
even if the U.S. Senate and the Russian Parliament ratify the
agreement—and that is not at all certain—the risk of destruction of
societies across the globe while somewhat reduced, is far from eliminated. I doubt a survivor—if there was one—could perceive much

difference between a world in which 12,000 nuclear warheads had been exploded and one subject to attack by 40,000. Can we not go further? Surely the answer must be *yes*.

The end of the Cold War, along with the growing understanding of the lack of utility of nuclear weapons and the high risk associated with their continued existence, points to both the opportunity and the urgency with which the five declared nuclear powers (the United States, Russia, France, the United Kingdom, and China) should reexamine their long-term nuclear force objectives. We should begin with a broad public debate over three alternative nuclear strategies, which I will outline. I believe such a debate would support the conclusion that, insofar as achievable—and I underline that phrase—we should move back to a nonnuclear world.

In support of my position, I will make three points:

1. The experience of the Cuban Missile Crisis in 1962—and, in particular, what has been learned about it recently—makes clear that so long as we and other Great Powers possess large inventories of nuclear weapons, we will face the risk of their use.
2. That risk is no longer—if it ever was—justifiable on military grounds.
3. In recent years, there has been a dramatic change in the thinking of leading Western security experts regarding the military utility of nuclear weapons. More and more of them—although certainly not yet a majority—are expressing views similar to those I have stated.

First, let us look at the Cuban Missile Crisis. It is now widely recognized that the actions of the Soviet Union, Cuba, and the United States in October 1962 brought the three nations to the verge of war. But what was not known then, and is not widely recognized today, was how close the world came to the brink of nuclear disaster. None of the three nations involved intended to create such risks.

The crisis began when the Soviets moved nuclear missiles and bombers to Cuba—secretly and with the clear intent to deceive—in the summer and early fall of 1962. The missiles and bombers were to be targeted against cities along America's East Coast. Photographs taken by a U-2 reconnaissance aircraft on Sunday, October 14, 1962, brought the deployments to President Kennedy's attention. He and his military and civilian security advisers recognized that the Soviets' action posed a threat to the West. President Kennedy therefore authorized a naval quarantine of Cuba, a blockade, to be effective on Wednesday, October 24. Preparations also began for air strikes and an amphibious invasion. The contingency plans called for a first-day air attack of 1,080 sorties. An invasion force totaling 180,000 troops was assembled in southeastern U.S. ports. The crisis came to a head on Saturday, October 27, and Sunday, October 28. Had Khrushchev not publicly announced on Sunday, October 28, that he was removing the missiles, on Monday, October 29, a majority of Kennedy's military and civilian advisers would have recommended launching the attacks.

To understand what caused the crisis—and how to avoid similar ones in the future—high-ranking Soviet, Cuban, and American participants in the decisions relating to it have met in five conferences extending over five years. A meeting chaired by Fidel Castro in Havana, Cuba, in January 1992 was the last. By the conclusion of the third meeting in Moscow in January 1989, it had become clear that the decisions of all three nations, before and during the crisis, had been distorted by misinformation, misjudgment, and miscalculation.

I shall cite only four of many examples:

1. Before Soviet missiles were introduced into Cuba in the summer of 1962, the Soviet Union and Cuba believed the United States intended to invade the island in order to overthrow Castro and remove his government. We had no such intention.
2. The United States believed the Soviets would never base nuclear warheads outside the Soviet Union, but they did. In

Moscow, we learned that by October 1962, although the CIA at the time was reporting no nuclear weapons on the island, Soviet nuclear missile warheads had, indeed, been delivered to Cuba and were to be targeted on U.S. cities.

3. The Soviets believed that nuclear weapons could be introduced into Cuba secretly, without detection and that the United States would not respond when their presence was disclosed. Here, too, they were in error.

4. Finally, those who were prepared to urge President Kennedy to destroy the missiles by a U.S. air attack, which, in all likelihood, would have been followed by an amphibious invasion, were almost certainly mistaken in their belief that the Soviets would not have responded militarily. At the time, the CIA reported 10,000 Soviet troops in Cuba. At the Moscow conference, participants learned there were in fact 43,000 Soviet troops on the island, along with 270,000 well-armed Cuban troops. Both forces, in the words of their commanders, were determined to "fight to the death." The Cuban officials estimated they would have suffered 100,000 casualties. The Soviets—including longtime Foreign Minister Andrei Gromyko and former ambassador to the United States Anatoly Dobrynin—expressed utter disbelief that we would have thought that, in the face of such a catastrophic defeat, they would not have responded militarily somewhere in the world. Very probably the result would have been uncontrollable escalation.

By the end of our meeting in Moscow, we had agreed we could draw two major lessons from our discussion: (1) in this age of high-technology weapons, crisis management is inherently dangerous, difficult, and uncertain; and (2) because of misinformation, misjudgment, and miscalculation of the kind I have just enumerated, it is not possible to predict with confidence the consequences of military action between Great Powers. Therefore, we must direct our attention and energies to crisis avoidance.

In 1962, during the crisis, some of us—particularly President Kennedy and I—believed the United States faced great danger. The Moscow meeting confirmed that judgment. But during the Havana conference, we learned that both of us—and certainly others—had seriously underestimated those dangers. We were told by the former Warsaw Pact chief of staff, Gen. Anatoly Gribkov, that in 1962 Soviet forces in Cuba possessed not only nuclear warheads for the intermediate-range missiles but nuclear bombs and tactical nuclear warheads as well. The tactical warheads were to be used against U.S. invasion forces. At the time, as I mentioned, the CIA was reporting no warheads on the island.

In November 1992, we learned still more. An article in the Russian press stated that, at the height of the crisis, Soviet forces in Cuba possessed a total of 162 nuclear warheads, including at least 90 tactical warheads. Moreover, it was reported that on October 26, 1962—a moment of great tension—warheads were moved from their storage sites to positions closer to their delivery vehicles in anticipation of a U.S. invasion.* The next day, Soviet Defense Minister Rodion Malinovsky received a cable from General Issa Pliyev, the Soviet commander in Cuba, informing him of this action. Malinovsky sent it to Khrushchev. Khrushchev returned it with "Approved" scrawled across its face. Clearly, there was a high risk that, in the face of a U.S. attack—which, as I have said, many in the U.S. government, military and civilian alike, were prepared to recommend to President Kennedy—the Soviet forces in Cuba would have decided to use their nuclear weapons rather than lose them.[2]

We need not speculate about what would have happened in that event. We can predict the results with certainty.

Although a U.S. invasion force would not have been equipped with tactical nuclear warheads—the president and I specifically prohibited that—no one should believe that, had American troops been attacked with nuclear weapons, the United States would have refrained from a nuclear response. And where would it have ended? In utter disaster. Not only would our casualties in Cuba have been

---

*General Gribkov elaborated on these points at a Wilson Center meeting in Washington, D.C., on April 5, 1994, which I attended.

devastating, and the island destroyed, but there would have been a high risk of the nuclear exchange extending beyond Cuba as well.

The point I wish to emphasize is this: human beings are fallible. We all make mistakes. In our daily lives, they are costly but we try to learn from them. In conventional war, they cost lives, sometimes thousands of lives. But if mistakes were to affect decisions relating to the use of nuclear forces, they would result in the destruction of whole societies. Thus, the indefinite combination of human fallibility and nuclear weapons carries a high risk of a potential catastrophe.

Is there a military justification for continuing to accept that risk? The answer is no.

In "Nuclear Weapons After the Cold War," Carl Kaysen, George W. Rathjens, and I pointed out that proponents of nuclear weapons "have produced only one plausible scenario for their use: a situation where there is no prospect of retaliation, either against a non-nuclear state or against one so weakly armed as to permit the user to have full confidence in his nuclear forces' capability to achieve a totally disarming first strike." We added that "even such circumstances have not, in fact, provided a sufficient basis for the use of nuclear weapons in war. For example, although American forces were in desperate straits twice during the Korean War—first immediately following the North Korean attack in 1950 and then when the Chinese crossed the Yalu—the United States did not use nuclear weapons. At that time, North Korea and China had no nuclear capability and the Soviet Union only a negligible one." Our argument leads to the conclusion that the military utility of nuclear weapons is limited to deterring one's opponent from their use. Therefore, if our opponent has no nuclear weapons, there is no need for us to possess them.[3]

———

Partly because of our increased understanding of how close we came to disaster during the missile crisis, but also because of a growing recognition of the lack of military utility of the weapons, there has been a revolutionary change in thinking about the role of nuclear forces. Much of this change has occurred in the last three years. Many U.S. military leaders—including two former chairmen of the Joint Chiefs of Staff, a former supreme commander of Allied Forces in Europe, and a senior air force officer currently on active duty— are now prepared to go far beyond the Bush-Yeltsin agreement. Some go as far as to state, as I have, that the long-term objective should be a return, insofar as practical, to a non-nuclear world.

That is, however, a very controversial proposition. A majority of Western security experts—both military and civilian—continue to believe that the threat of nuclear weapons prevents war. Zbigniew Brzezinski, President Carter's national security adviser, has argued that a plan for eliminating nuclear weapons "is a plan for making the world safe for conventional warfare. I am therefore not enthusiastic about it." A report of an advisory committee appointed by former Defense Secretary Richard Cheney and chaired by former Air Force Secretary Thomas Reed made essentially the same point. The current administration appears to support that position.[4] However, even if one accepts this argument, it must be recognized that its deterrent to conventional force aggression carries a very high long-term cost: the risk of a nuclear exchange.

Unbeknownst to most people, John Foster Dulles, President Eisenhower's secretary of state, recognized this problem in the mid-1950s. In a highly secret memorandum to the president, declassified only a few years ago, Dulles went so far as to state, "Atomic power was too vast a power to be left for the military use of any one country." He proposed, therefore, to "universalize the capacity of atomic thermonuclear weapons to deter aggression" by transferring control of nuclear forces to a vetoless U.N. Security Council.[5]

Dulles's concern has been echoed in recent years by other prominent security experts, although I doubt that the public is aware of their views. They have been reflected in three reports and numerous unclassified but not widely disseminated statements.

The three reports have all been published since 1990:

1. In 1991, a committee of the U.S. National Academy of Sciences, in a report signed by retired Joint Chiefs of Staff Chairman Gen. David C. Jones, stated: "Nuclear weapons should serve no purpose beyond the deterrence of . . . nuclear attack by others." The committee believed U.S. and Russian nuclear forces could be reduced to 1,000–2,000 warheads.[6]

2. The Spring 1993 issue of *Foreign Affairs* carried an article coauthored by another retired chairman of the Joint Chiefs of Staff, Adm. William J. Crowe, Jr., which concluded that by the year 2000 the United States and Russia could reduce strategic nuclear forces to 1,000–1,500 warheads each. The article, later expanded into a book, added: "Nor is 1,000–1,500 the lowest level obtainable by the early twenty-first-century."[7]

3. And in August 1993, Gen. Andrew J. Goodpaster, former supreme allied commander of NATO Forces in Europe, published a report in which he said the five existing nuclear powers should be able to reduce nuclear weapons stockpiles to "no more than 200 each" and "the ultimate would be a *zero level*" [emphasis in original]."[8]

These three reports should not come as surprises. For nearly twenty years, more and more Western military and civilian security experts have expressed doubts about the military utility of nuclear weapons. This is what they have said:

- By 1982, five of the seven retired chiefs of the British Defence Staff had expressed their belief that initiating the use of nuclear weapons, in accordance with NATO policy, would lead to disaster. Lord Louis Mountbatten, chief of staff from 1959 to 1965, said a few months before he was murdered in 1979: "As a military man I can see no use for any nuclear weapons." And Field Marshall Lord Carver, chief of staff from 1973 to 1976, wrote in 1982 that he was totally opposed to NATO ever initiating the use of nuclear weapons.[9]

- Henry Kissinger, President Nixon's national security adviser and secretary of state, speaking in Brussels in 1979, made quite clear he believed the United States would never initiate a nuclear strike against the Soviet Union, no matter what the provocation. "Our European allies," he said, "should not keep asking

us to multiply strategic assurances that we cannot possibly mean
or if we do mean, we should not execute because if we execute
we risk the destruction of civilization."[10]

- Admiral Noel Gayler, former commander in chief of U.S. air,
  ground, and sea forces in the Pacific, remarked in 1981: "There
  is no sensible military use of any of our nuclear forces. The only
  reasonable use is to deter our opponents from using his nuclear
  forces."[11]

- Former West German Chancellor Helmut Schmidt stated in a
  1987 BBC interview: "Flexible response [NATO's strategy
  calling for the use of nuclear weapons in response to a Warsaw
  Pact attack by nonnuclear forces] is nonsense. Not out of date,
  but nonsense. . . . The Western idea, which was created in the
  1950's, that we should be willing to use nuclear weapons first,
  in order to make up for our so-called conventional deficiency,
  has never convinced me."[12]

- Melvin Laird, President Nixon's first secretary of defense, was
  reported in *The Washington Post* of April 12, 1982, as saying:
  "A worldwide zero nuclear option with adequate verification
  should now be our goal. . . . These weapons . . . are useless for
  military purposes."[13]

- General Larry Welch, former U.S. Air Force chief of staff and
  previously commander of the Strategic Air Command, recently
  put the same thought in these words: "Nuclear deterrence
  depended on someone believing that you would commit an act
  totally irrational if done."[14]

- And in July 1994, Gen. Charles A. Horner, chief of staff of the
  U.S. Space Command, stated: "The nuclear weapon is obsolete.
  I want to get rid of them all."[15]

In the early 1960s, I had reached conclusions similar to these. In
long private conversations, first with President Kennedy and then
with President Johnson, I had recommended, without qualification,
that they never, under any circumstances, initiate the use of nuclear
weapons. I believe they accepted my recommendations.[16] But
neither they nor I could discuss our position publicly because it was
contrary to established NATO policy.

Today, given the totally contradictory views regarding the role of nuclear weapons by the administration and the Brzezinskis and Reeds on the one hand, and Goodpasters, Lairds, and Schmidts on the other—but with the recognition by all that initiating the use of nuclear weapons against a nuclear-equipped opponent would lead to disaster—should we not begin immediately to debate the merits of alternative long-term objectives for the five declared nuclear powers?

We could choose from three options:

1. A continuation of the present strategy of "extended deterrence." This would mean limiting the United States and Russia to approximately 3,500 strategic warheads each, the figure agreed upon by Presidents Bush and Yeltsin.
2. A minimum deterrent force—as recommended by a U.S. National Academy of Sciences committee and supported by General Jones and Admiral Crowe—with the two major nuclear powers retaining no more than 1,000–2,000 warheads each.
3. As General Goodpaster and I strongly advocate, a return, by all five nuclear powers, insofar as practicable, to a nonnuclear world.*

If we dare break out of the mind-set that has guided the nuclear strategy of the nuclear powers for over four decades, I believe we can indeed "put the genie back in the bottle." If we do not, there is a substantial risk that the twenty-first century will witness a nuclear tragedy.

Andrei Sakharov said: "Reducing the risk of annihilating humanity in a nuclear war carries an absolute priority over all other considerations."[17] He was right.

---

*"Insofar as practicable" refers to the necessity of maintaining protection against "breakout" or acquisition of weapons by terrorists. The movement toward the elimination of nuclear weapons could be accomplished in a series of steps, as both General Goodpaster and I have suggested.

Appendix to
the Vintage Edition

A s I said in the Preface to this edition, *In Retrospect*'s publication sparked both harsh criticism and warm praise. I have included samples of each in this Appendix.

The selections begin with strong criticism in a *New York Times* editorial, apparently written by Editorial Page editor Howell Raines, and in a book review by David Halberstam published in the *Los Angeles Times*.* These are followed by Theodore Draper's two reviews in the *New York Review of Books*. Draper apparently wrote the first review before he had an opportunity to read the *Times* editorial. His second review addresses several of the issues raised by Raines, as does a letter to the *Times* by Robert McAfee Brown, and an article by George Melloan in the *Wall Street Journal*. These are followed by long-time *Washington Post* columnist Richard Harwood's article challenging many of Raines' and Halberstam's assertions.

Recently, Louis G. Sarris, a former State Department analyst,

---

*Although Vintage Books and I requested Mr. Halberstam's permission to reproduce the review, Mr. Halberstam declined to give it just as this edition went to press.

published an essay in the *New York Times* disputing several statements in my book. I include it, along with my reply, also printed in the *Times*.

Favorable reactions are illustrated in reviews by the *Wall Street Journal*'s Lee Lescaze and the widely syndicated columnist Molly Ivins, and by comments of John Kenneth Galbraith, professor of economics emeritus at Harvard.

Jonathan Alter, writing in *Newsweek,* and David Shribman, in the *Boston Globe,* combine reviews of the book with extracts of interviews with me.

It is too early for most scholars to have rendered judgment on the book. However, a few have already spoken and I include several of their reactions: from Ernest May, professor of history at Harvard; W. W. Rostow, professor of economics at the University of Texas; and James Galbraith, professor at the LBJ School of Public Affairs, University of Texas.

Finally, on a more personal note, I include the statement of Richard Rusk, co-author of his father Dean Rusk's autobiography.

Appendix to
the Vintage Edition

Contents

Comes now Robert McNamara with the announcement that he has in the fullness of time grasped realities that seemed readily apparent to millions of Americans throughout the Vietnam War. At the time, he appeared to be helping an obsessed President prosecute a war of no real consequence to the security of the United States. Millions of loyal citizens concluded that the war was a militarily unnecessary and politically futile effort to prop up a corrupt Government that could neither reform nor defend itself.

Through all the bloody years, those were the facts as they appeared on the surface. Therefore, only one argument could be advanced to clear President Johnson and Mr. McNamara, his Secretary of Defense, of the charge of wasting lives atrociously. That was the theory that they possessed superior knowledge, not available to the public, that the collapse of South Vietnam would lead to regional and perhaps world domination by the Communists; and moreover, that their superior knowledge was so compelling it rendered unreliable and untrue the apparent facts available to even the most expert opponents of the war.

With a few throwaway lines in his new book, "In Retrospect," Mr. McNamara admits that such knowledge never existed. Indeed, as they made the fateful first steps toward heavier fighting in late 1963 and 1964, Mr. Johnson and his Cabinet "had not truly investigated what was essentially at stake and important to us." As for testing their public position that only a wider war would avail in the circumstances, "We never stopped to explore fully whether there were other routes to our destination."

Such sentences break the heart while making clear that Mr. McNamara must not escape the lasting moral condemnation of his countrymen.

Mr. McNamara wants us to know that he, too, realized by 1967 that the dissidents were right, that the war had to be stopped to avoid "a major national disaster." Even so, he wants us to grant that his delicate sense of protocol excused him from any obligation to join the national debate over whether American troops should continue to die at the rate of hundreds per week in a war he knew to be futile. Mr. McNamara believes that retired Cabinet members should not criticize the Presidents they served no matter how much the American people need to know the truth. In Mr. McNamara's view, the President can never become so steeped in a misguided war that patriotic duty would compel a statement.

Perhaps the only value of "In Retrospect" is to remind us never to forget that these were men who in the full hubristic glow of their power would not listen to logical warning or ethical appeal. When senior figures talked sense to Mr. Johnson and Mr. McNamara, they were ignored or dismissed from government. When young people in the ranks brought that message, they were court-martialed. When young people in the streets shouted it, they were hounded from the country.

It is important to remember how fate dispensed rewards and punishment for Mr. McNamara's thousands of days of error. Three million Vietnamese died. Fifty-eight thousand Americans got to come home in body bags. Mr. McNamara, while tormented by his role in the war, got a sinecure at the World Bank and summers at the Vineyard.

So much has changed since those horrendous times. The nation has belatedly recognized the heroism of the American troops who served in good faith because they, in their innocence, could not fathom the mendacity of their elders. But another set of heroes—the thousands of students who returned the nation to sanity by chanting, "Hell, no, we won't go"—is under renewed attack from a band of politicians who sat out the war on student or family deferments. In that sense we are still living in the wreckage created by the Cabinet on which Mr. McNamara served.

His regret cannot be huge enough to balance the books for our dead soldiers. The ghosts of those unlived lives circle close around Mr. McNamara. Surely he must in every quiet and prosperous moment hear the ceaseless whispers of those poor boys in the infantry, dying in the tall grass, platoon by platoon, for no purpose. What he took from them cannot be repaid by prime-time apology and stale tears, three decades late.

Mr. McNamara says he weeps easily and has strong feelings when he visits the Vietnam Memorial. But he says he will not speak of those feelings. Yet someone must, for that black wall is wide with the names of people who died in a war that he did not, at first, carefully research nor, in the end, believe to be necessary.

"McNamara's Peace"
by Theodore Draper
The New York Review of Books
May 11, 1995

Former Secretary of Defense Robert S. McNamara has written a "Now It Can Be Told" book about the Vietnam War. He does not tell us all we need to know about the war: he has little to say about the battles on the ground and the local situation in South Vietnam, except as they bear on his main subject. McNamara deals almost entirely with how decisions were made at the top of the American command structure in Washington and what they were. We could not wish for a more highly placed witness, except for the presidents whom McNamara served. John F. Kennedy and Lyndon B. Johnson, neither of whom left us anything comparable. Though McNamara has produced a personal testament, it is largely based on documentation, some of it unpublished, from the Kennedy and Johnson libraries and government files.

This book commands our attention because the Vietnam War is still with us. It was with us in Somalia where again we tried—and failed politically—to understand and change a people strange to us. It is with us in Bosnia-Herzegovina, where we have not ventured, because we are afraid to get into another quagmire in a place we do not understand and do not dare to try to change. It will take longer than a quarter of a century for us to put the Vietnam War behind us and act as if it had never happened.

The key decisions of these wars and near wars were made in Washington, where in the last analysis the president decides. This is why McNamara's portrait of the presidents he served and their inner circles has much to teach us, because the problems have not changed all that much.

––––––

McNamara himself was a most unlikely secretary of defense. He was an Irish American, born in 1916 in San Francisco to parents who had never gone to college; his father did not go beyond the eighth grade. He graduated from high school in 1933 at the bottom of the Depression and went to the University of California at Berkeley, because it was the only first-rate university he could afford. Then came the Harvard Graduate School of Business Administration, three years teaching a statistical control system in World War II, and soon after the war a job with the Ford Motor Company in Detroit. A few years later, he was head of the Ford Division, the company's largest unit, and in 1960, president of the entire Ford Motor Company. He made his reputation as a hard-driving executive at Ford and nowhere else.

When the newly elected President Kennedy offered him the post of secretary of defense in December 1960, soon after he became president of Ford, McNamara's reply was, "I am not qualified." McNamara knew so little of Washington's ways that, as he says, he did not know the difference between "off the record" and "on background." He confesses: "I had entered the Pentagon with a limited grasp of military affairs and even less grasp of covert operations." He knew nothing about Vietnam—but, as he points out, neither did President Kennedy, National Security Adviser McGeorge Bundy, military adviser General Maxwell Taylor, and many others. Nevertheless, Kennedy told him that there were no schools for defense secretaries—or for presidents. At the age of forty-four, McNamara was the youngest secretary of defense ever, a year older than Kennedy. McNamara's background may help explain why he was more likely to break away from the official line than others with more bureaucratic experience. In any case, he was the odd man out in the later Johnson years.

The great merit of McNamara's book is that it enables us to see how and to what extent the Vietnam War was fought and lost in Washington.

The self-inflicted ordeal in Washington began with Kennedy's predecessor, Dwight D. Eisenhower. On January 19, 1961, Eisenhower's last day in office, he and his chief associates met with Kennedy and his chief designated nominees for office, including McNamara. Eisenhower told Kennedy's group that the loss of Laos—and by implication South Vietnam—to the Communists meant the loss of all of Southeast Asia.[1] Yet Eisenhower had refused to intervene in Vietnam to rescue the French in 1954. Later that year, Eisenhower had put forward his " 'falling domino' principle," according to which "You have a row of dominoes set up, you knock over the first one, and what will happen to the last one is a certainty that it will go over very quickly." He specifically applied it to Indochina and Southeast Asia. His advice to Kennedy in 1961 was based on the same assumption.

The falling-domino "principle" haunted the United States throughout the Vietnam War and beyond. It is one of the most insidious ideas in the repertoire of foreign policy. It is a mechanistic theory, because it assumes a necessary succession from an initial starting point to a fore-ordained end. It inflates the importance of any single loss by making it apply to an entire region or even the world. A relatively minor part of the world can be made into a

---

[1]This was the gist of several memoranda about the meeting written by participants, including McNamara, now in the Kennedy Library. Eisenhower touched on the meeting in his autobiography, *Waging Peace*, but tells little about what he actually said. Kennedy was an ardent believer in the domino theory. In September 1963, he was asked whether he had "any reason to doubt this so-called 'domino theory,' that if South Vietnam falls, the rest of Southeast Asia will go with it?" He replied: "No, I believe it. I believe it." (NBC interview, September 9, 1963.) The most ardent believer in the domino "principle" was Richard Nixon. If Vietnam fell, he prophesied, Laos, Cambodia, Thailand, Burma, and Indonesia had to be written off: we would have to fight a major war to save the Philippines, the Pacific would become a "red sea," and the United States would have to face up to Chinese Communist aggression as far as Australia in only four or five years (*Congressional Record,* January 31, 1966, pp. 21928–21930). That there were deep differences between the Chinese and Vietnamese never seems to have been seriously considered by any of these leaders.

major disaster by theoretically adding any number of other countries to it. But the future is never that determined: the loss of Vietnam did not bring about the Communist takeover of all Southeast Asia. One lost domino *may* bring down other dominoes, but it may also spread an alarm that will save other dominoes. By its simplicity and fatalism, the domino "principle" makes further thought unnecessary and actually represents a form of abdication as well as a call to arms.

In any case, the Kennedy novices in power were overly impressed by Eisenhower's authority, even though during his administration he had not shown what to do about Vietnam. In June 1965, President Johnson sent an emissary to get more of Eisenhower's advice, and he again replied that "we have got to win" and recommended increasing the number of U.S. forces in Vietnam.

Yet Eisenhower believed in something else which undercut his domino principle. He had been convinced that the French could not win the war in Vietnam, because the internal political situation in Vietnam was "weak and confused."[2] Thus he made strong and clear internal Vietnamese political leadership a condition of victory. Later, Kennedy expressed this view as meaning that the South Vietnamese "are the ones who have to win it or lose it."[3] Johnson reiterated that "the South Vietnamese have the basic responsibility for the defense of their own freedom."[4]

These two beliefs were incompatible. If the South Vietnamese were incapable of winning a war which only they could win, that war had to be given up for lost. But if the price of defeat was so great that it could not be tolerated, a Vietnam failure was unthinkable and whatever the cost the United States had to take over the war.

McNamara's treatment of this contradiction, which bedeviled all the presidents during the Vietnam War, tells much about his book. For much of his tenure McNamara went along with the prevailing wisdom; not for nothing was it once called "McNamara's war." It

[2] Dwight D. Eisenhower, *Mandate for Change, 1953–1956* (Doubleday, 1963), p. 372.
[3] Interview with Walter Cronkite, September 2, 1963.
[4] August 12, 1964.

took him time to get his bearings and lose his respect for the bitter-end generals. His book is retrospective and does not always represent fully what he thought or did during his period in office.

In effect, McNamara set himself two tasks—to report on what was happening in Washington during the Vietnam war and to say *mea culpa* for the mistakes that were made. In both cases, he is richly worth attending to.

_____

The critical episode in Kennedy's period was the plot to get rid of the Vietnamese leader, Ngo Dinh Diem. He had been the prime minister of South Vietnam for almost ten years when his regime seemed to disintegrate as a result of internal disruption by Buddhists, students, and others opposed to him. Raids on the Buddhist pagodas in August 1963 brought his rule to the breaking point. The Americans did not seem to dislike Diem so much as they detested his brother, Ngo Dinh Nhu, head of South Vietnam's security forces, and his wife, Madame Nhu, both of whom were considered irrational and uncontrollable.

_____

McNamara goes into the Diem affair in detail, and it is worth the effort. Diem's downfall may have been the decisive moment of the entire war, and, above all, it showed how Washington acted at cross purposes and did not know how to handle a Vietnamese crisis.

McNamara holds the United States directly responsible for the anti-Diem coup. On August 24, 1963, he says, "Before the day was out, the United States had set in motion a military coup, which I believe was one of the truly pivotal decisions concerning Vietnam made during the Kennedy and Johnson Administrations." In September, he adds, the Americans were "already in the process of initiating" a coup. The initiative, according to McNamara, was taken by Roger Hilsman, the Assistant Secretary of State for Far Eastern Affairs. He was aided by Averell Harriman, the Under Secretary of State for Political Affairs, and Michael Forrestal of the National

Security Council staff. Hilsman drafted a cable to Saigon which said that if Diem remained "obdurate" about removing the Nhus, "we are prepared to accept the obvious implication that we can no longer support Diem." Hilsman, Harriman, and Forrestal were allegedly determined to send the cable that same day—and did.

Unfortunately, none of the highest officials was present in Washington at that time. President Kennedy was on Cape Cod. Dean Rusk, the secretary of state, was in New York, McNamara was on vacation. The new U.S. ambassador to South Vietnam, Henry Cabot Lodge, had been in Saigon for only two days and had not yet had a serious talk with Diem. As a result, the three so-called schemers succeeded in getting approval of the cable by getting most high-level officials, including Kennedy, to think that others had already accepted it. Lodge immediately sent the CIA station chief to two leading Vietnamese generals to tell them that the Nhus had to go but left the generals to decide whether Diem also had to leave.

Within two days, second thoughts began to trouble Washington. Kennedy regretted his approval. Kennedy's military adviser, General Maxwell Taylor, was shocked at the move. McNamara merely wanted Diem to alter his policies. Almost everyone but Hilsman changed his mind or could not make it up. Kennedy sent a secret cable to Lodge telling him that the President reserved "a contingent right to change course and reverse previous instructions."

This, in brief, is McNamara's story. But, almost twenty years ago, Hilsman gave a much longer and more detailed version of the same episode, and it disagrees with McNamara in some crucial respects. One of the most important is that McNamara had the United States "set in motion" the military coup; Hilsman says that two Vietnamese generals first "contacted American officials" to find out what the attitude of the United States would be if they "felt compelled" to move against Nhu and the regime. The generals said they needed to know quickly. Hilsman also says that he did not draft the cable alone: Under-Secretary of State George

Ball, Harriman, and Hilsman allegedly participated in the drafting. Hilsman is as critical of McNamara as McNamara is of Hilsman.[5]

There is a third version of some interest. George Ball says that the allegedly fatal wire of August 24, 1963, was composed by Harriman and Hilsman and that they showed it to him on a golf course. After Ball essentially approved the message, he got in touch with Kennedy in Hyannisport, who went along with it on condition that Rusk and Roswell Gilpatric, McNamara's deputy, agreed. Ball also pleads that he "signed off" on the telegram because Harriman and Hilsman said that Ambassador Lodge needed a prompt answer.[6]

In any case, all these versions attest to the almost chaotic state of the leading circles in Washington. Subordinate figures snowballed their superiors by telling them that someone else had gone along with the scheme. Ball's story of how he got Kennedy to agree is the most troublesome: the President put the responsibility on two others. Yet it is hard to see how the United States could have "set in motion" the coup if Kennedy and others regretted it two days later and held it up. No coup came soon after August 24; it did not come until November 1, 1963, over two months later.[7] Diem and Nhu were murdered after they were captured. "When President Kennedy received the news, he literally blanched," McNamara recalls. "I had never seen him so moved."

The Vietnamese coup was clearly less simple than McNamara makes it. It may not have been initiated by Hilsman, but by Vietnamese generals, and it was certainly not "set in motion" on August

---

[5]Roger Hilsman, *To Move A Nation: The Politics of Foreign Policy in the Administration of John F. Kennedy* (Doubleday, 1967), pp. 484–487, 507.

[6]George W. Ball, *The Past Has Another Pattern: Memoirs* (Norton, 1982), pp. 371–372.

[7]Earlier versions play variations on these themes. Arthur M. Schlesinger, Jr., also names Harriman, Hilsman, and Forrestal as the chief wire-pullers against Diem but calls them "the Harriman group." Schlesinger attributes the first intimations of the coming coup to the Vietnamese generals; Kennedy felt that "he had been pressed too hard and fast" and soon drew back; the coup took place when Lodge and Diem seemed to be reaching some understanding. "It is important to state clearly that the coup of November 1, 1963, was entirely planned and carried out by the Vietnamese." (*A Thousand Days,* Houghton Mifflin, 1965, pp. 990–997.)

24, 1963. McNamara himself says that Kennedy soon regretted it and held it up. When the coup came, over two months later, it was carried out by the Vietnamese generals, who went off on their own. No doubt the generals knew that the Americans had been thinking about it, but that is not the same as "setting in motion" or "in the process of initiating" a coup. On the other hand, those who made the United States altogether innocent of responsibility for the coup have gone too far, because the August 24, 1963, cable was made known to the Vietnamese generals, even if it was regretted soon afterward. George Ball, the opposite pole from McNamara, thought that the cable was a "damp squib" and had little to do with the coup.[8]

The entire incident still needs to be cleared up, because McNamara's version is not altogether satisfactory. But something is more important than the details of the coup. Policy-making in Washington was chaotic. Kennedy and his top advisers first made a hasty decision to threaten to overthrow Diem if he did not get rid of the Nhus and then dithered for over two months until the Vietnamese generals took matters into their own bloody hands, to the surprise of the Americans. Those Americans who had opposed toppling Diem—McNamara among them—had done so not out of sympathy with Diem but because they did not believe there was a suitable successor to him among the Vietnamese generals. And they were proven right. One Vietnamese government after another collapsed after Diem's fall. Though Diem had virtually no defenders in the American government, what made the Americans hesitate was that they considered everyone else worse.

Theodore C. Sorensen says that Kennedy did not want to bring Diem down. "Kennedy's advisers were more deeply divided on the internal situation in Saigon than on any previous issue. . . . Whichever way he turned—continuing to support Diem or interfering in his internal affairs—Kennedy foresaw the United States losing respect in the eyes of many Vietnamese. [The coup] received no assistance from the United States, nor did this country do anything to prevent or defeat it." (*Kennedy,* Harper and Row, 1965, pp. 659–660.)

Both these versions conflict sharply with Hilsman's and McNamara's.
[8]George Ball, *The Past Has Another Pattern,* pp. 373–374.

Here we come to the nub of the question. Every president from Eisenhower to Johnson said that the war could be won only by the Vietnamese themselves. McNamara comes back again and again to this principle:

> Throughout the Kennedy years, we operated on two premises that ultimately proved contradictory. One was that the fall of South Vietnam to Communism would threaten the security of the United States and the Western world. The other was that only the South Vietnamese could defend their nation, and that America should limit its role to providing training and logistical support.

> If there is a strong South Vietnamese effort, [U.S. combat troops] may not be needed; if there is not such an effort, U.S. forces could not accomplish their mission in the midst of an apathetic or hostile population.

> The cardinal question had never gone away: If the South Vietnamese government, such as it was, could not gain and keep its people's support and defeat the insurgents, could we do it for them?

Thus the coup against Diem and the demoralization of the Vietnamese regimes after him presented the Americans with a fundamental choice—either to give up the Vietnam War as a bad bargain or to assume full responsibility for it in place of the Vietnamese. Kennedy himself spoke out of both sides of his mouth. On one occasion, he made the South Vietnamese responsible for their own fate; on another, he embraced the domino theory and said, "We should not withdraw." McNamara thinks that Kennedy, if he had lived, would have pulled us out of Vietnam. It is, in my opinion, doubtful because Kennedy did not have the prestige in foreign affairs to take a step which would have marked him as the president who had lost a war even before the United States had made every effort to avoid such a historic loss.

Forever after in the Vietnam War, the fundamental clash of policy was between the domino theory and the only-the-Vietnamese-can-win-the-war premise. In part, the confusion of U.S. policy resulted because the presidents professed to believe in both, and in a pinch chose the domino theory. The choice underlies the crises that beset the entire war.

———

Lyndon Johnson had opposed the coup against Diem. His own national security team—including a reformed George Ball and an unreconstructed Dean Rusk—was also deeply split. "Johnson," according to McNamara, "inherited a god-awful mess eminently more dangerous than the one Kennedy had inherited from Eisenhower." Johnson was more convinced than Kennedy that the takeover of South Vietnam was a step in the direction of Soviet and Chinese world hegemony. Johnson "wanted to win the war."

Thus McNamara introduces Johnson into the Vietnam War. In the early years of the Johnson administration and to the end of 1965, McNamara himself backed the prosecution of the war. He agreed to send more troops to Vietnam but had increasingly less hope that they could prevail.

Johnson's Rubicon was the Tonkin Gulf Resolution of September 1964. Again the details are less important in themselves than in what they signify. McNamara reveals that Johnson had contemplated getting a congressional resolution in support of the war as early as May 1964.[9] But two alleged attacks by North Vietnamese patrol boats against the U.S. destroyer *Maddox* took place, the first on August 2 and the second on August 4, 1964. Johnson did not react to the first one but added another destroyer, the *C. Turner Joy* to the patrol. The second attack was dubious, if not fictitious: even the commander of the *Maddox* sent word that it was at least

---

[9]McNamara says that a small group under George Ball submitted a draft resolution to the National Security Council on May 24, 1964, that it was discussed at a meeting in Honolulu on June 1, 1964, and that it was decided to present it to Congress in September. Ball says nothing of this draft resolution.

"doubtful." Nevertheless, with McNamara concurring, Johnson ordered sixty-four bombing missions against North Vietnamese PT bases and an oil complex in retaliation.

———

These were not the only circumstances of the incident. In January 1964, the CIA was authorized to support South Vietnamese covert operations against North Vietnam, known as Plan 34A. Another operation, the DESOTO patrols, carried out electronic reconnaissance of North Vietnam using the *Maddox* and other U.S. vessels: they stayed more than twenty-five miles off the North Vietnamese coast to protect themselves from attack. On July 30, 1964, a 34A mission by South Vietnamese patrol boats attacked two North Vietnamese islands in the Tonkin Gulf. Both Plan 34A and the DESOTO patrols were engaged in acts of war during a war: it is questionable how much the North Vietnamese could be expected to distinguish between the South Vietnamese and U.S. roles in these operations. Whether or not the second North Vietnamese attack against the U.S. ships had actually occurred, the U.S. retaliated forcibly; the *C. Turner Joy* sank three PT boats and the *Maddox* one or two.

But Johnson was not satisfied with this score. He seized the opportunity to press his congressional resolution, which he later claimed gave him a "blank check" in Vietnam.[10] McNamara has little patience with this subterfuge. Congress, he says, "did not conceive of it as a declaration of war and did not intend it to be used, as it was, as authorization for an enormous expansion of U.S. forces in Vietnam—from 16,000 military advisers to 550,000 combat troops." He also admits that he was wrong to tell senators that the *Maddox* did not know of the South Vietnamese attack on the two North Vietnamese islands.

———

[10]It was passed in the Senate by 88 to 2, with Senators Wayne Morse of Oregon and Ernest Gruening of Alaska opposed, and in the House by 416 to 0. The Senate floor leader was Senator J. William Fulbright of Arkansas, who at the time said that it did not authorize the landing of large American armies in Vietnam (*Congressional Record*, August 5, 1964, p. 18403).

Nevertheless, McNamara labors to defend the Johnson administration from the charge of having deliberately deceived Congress with the Tonkin Gulf Resolution. But he admits that Congress was "misled" and that "Congress did *not* intend to authorize without further, full consultation the expansion of U.S. forces in Vietnam from 16,000 to 550,000 men." He seems to rest his case on the proposition that "the problem was not that Congress did not grasp the resolution's potential but that it did not grasp the war's potential and how the administration would respond in the face of it."

It is hard to take this reasoning seriously. If Congress did not intend to authorize the immense expansion of the war, it did not have to grasp the war's potential. Whatever that potential, it should still have been necessary for the Johnson administration to come back to Congress for further authorization to expand the U.S. forces in the war. Congressional approval of appropriations bills for the armed forces is no substitute for congressional approval of a large-scale war.

McNamara gives the text of a telephone conversation with Johnson on July 14, 1965, months later, in which Johnson said: "We know, ourselves, in our own conscience, that when we asked for this Tonkin Gulf Resolution, we had no intention of committing this many . . . ground troops." Johnson added: "And we're doin' so now and we know it's goin' to be bad, and the question [is]: do we just want to do it out on a limb by ourselves?" Thus Johnson knew that he was going out "on a limb" constitutionally by resting on the Tonkin Gulf Resolution. In fact, both the President and Congress acted cravenly during the Vietnam War.

———

The most unmitigated warriors were the Joint Chiefs of Staff. All they wanted was more troops and more bombing in Vietnam. They put on the main pressure to get Johnson to send more and more forces to Vietnam. For them the domino theory was sacrosanct; when one of their representatives was asked how badly the loss of South Vietnam would shake the faith and resolve of other non-

Communist nations, he answered: "Disastrously or worse." As a result of this view, McNamara writes, more bombs were dropped on Vietnam than on all of Europe during World War II.

McNamara reveals that the Joint Chiefs even contemplated the use of nuclear weapons to avoid defeat. On March 2, 1964, they sent a long memorandum to McNamara in which they reiterated "the overriding importance to the security interests of the United States of preventing the loss of South Vietnam." The United States should be prepared to destroy military and industrial targets in North Vietnam, mine its harbors, and undertake a naval blockade. China might intervene militarily, but a non-nuclear U.S. response might not be able to force China to stop. They added that "nuclear attacks would have a far greater probability of" doing so, without claiming that even then they could prevent the loss of South Vietnam. McNamara comments:

> It was clear: the chiefs recognized that their program involved a change in U.S. policy—including the possible use of nuclear weapons—but they nonetheless urged that it be adopted.

The possible use of nuclear weapons was also mentioned in November 1964 by a "Working Group" made up of senior civilian officials. "The president and I," says McNamara, "were shocked by the almost cavalier way in which the chiefs and their associates, on this and other occasions, referred to, and accepted the risk of, the possible use of nuclear weapons." Again, on June 30, 1965, McGeorge Bundy, the national security adviser, referred to nuclear weapons in a way that implied to McNamara that we should consider threatening their use. In 1966, the Joint Chiefs put forward a program which would require "utilizing the nation's full military capability, including the possible use of nuclear weapons." And on May 20, 1967, the Joint Chiefs sent McNamara another memorandum that it might become necessary to use nuclear weapons in southern China.

These references to the possible use of nuclear weapons in the

Vietnam War have never before been made public and, in fact, have been denied. In his magisterial work, *Danger and Survival,* McGeorge Bundy stated that from 1965 to 1975 "the nuclear forces always at the president's command were kept out of it." He seems to be right that none of the three presidents in the war "ever came close to using a nuclear weapon," but he may have gone too far in suggesting that no one else in the administrations ever thought of their possible use. The temptation was there, even if it never got far enough to command the President's attention.[11]

————

McNamara's fall from grace came as he gave up hope for a U.S. military victory in Vietnam. Until then, he had gone along with the U.S. escalation, even if sometimes with misgivings. As the United States poured more troops into South Vietnam, so did the North Vietnamese, with the result that nothing seemed to be gained militarily by merely increasing the numbers. The Americans never understood that the North Vietnamese were willing to fight to the last man, and for this reason were not amenable to ordinary diplomatic bargaining, except on their own terms.

On November 23, 1965, McNamara received a "shattering blow" from the U.S. commander in South Vietnam. General William Westmoreland called for 200,000 more troops in 1966, bringing the total by the end of 1966 to 410,000 instead of the 275,000 previously estimated. Another 200,000 was considered possible in 1967. McNamara flew to Saigon to see for himself; he discovered that "the U.S. presence rested on a bowl of jelly: political instability had increased; pacification had stalled; South Vietnamese Army desertions had skyrocketed."

On November 30, 1965, McNamara gave Johnson his latest appreciation of the war. He called it a "bleak choice" between a "compromise solution" or Westmoreland's escalation. By a compromise he meant accepting "less than our objective of an inde-

[11]McGeorge Bundy, *Danger and Survival* (Random House, 1988), p. 536.

pendent, non-Communist South Vietnam." Just what was less he did not say. This choice received no serious attention. From this point on, McNamara was torn between a political compromise and an increased military offensive. The more he gave up the idea of a military victory, the more he veered over to a "diplomatic solution." While others in the administration were still optimistic, he was progressively pessimistic. Gradually he estranged himself from the Joint Chiefs of Staff and most of Johnson's senior advisers.

Finally, on May 19, 1967, he submitted a critical memorandum to Johnson. It virtually gave up on the South Vietnamese. It admitted that the North Vietnamese "seem uninterested in a political set-tlement and determined to match U.S. military expansion of the conflict." It raised the specter of nuclear and chemical weapons: "The use of tactical nuclear and area-denial-radiological-bacterio-logical-chemical weapons would probably be suggested at some point if the Chinese entered the war in Vietnam or Korea or if U.S. losses were running high while conventional efforts were not producing desired results." It showed that McNamara was vul-nerable to the antiwar movement mounting in the U.S.: "The Vietnam war is unpopular in this country." It took into consid-eration the broader view of the war in the world: "The picture of the world's greatest superpower killing or seriously injuring 1000 noncombatants a week, while trying to pound a tiny backward nation into submission on an issue whose merits are hotly disputed, is not a pretty one."

McNamara urged that U.S. policy be based on two principles:

(1) Our commitment is only to see that the people of South Vietnam are permitted to determine their own future.
(2) This commitment ceases if the country ceases to help itself.

Since McNamara had long believed that South Vietnam would not or could not help itself, he implied that the U.S. commitment had ceased. In practice, however, he did not go that far. McNamara proposed "a politico-military strategy that raised the possibility of compromise." This strategy entailed more restricted bombing and "a more flexible bargaining position while actively seeking a political settlement." He recognized the dangers in such an approach but believed that the military option "could lead to a major national disaster."

The Joint Chiefs reacted with fury. McNamara's civilian associates were no less wrathful. His position as secretary of defense became increasingly untenable. In June 1967, McNamara asked John McNaughton, his Assistant Secretary for International Security Affairs, to collect documents on the war for the use of future scholars; this project resulted in what came to be known as the "Pentagon Papers." In July 1967, Johnson asked McNamara to visit Vietnam again: General Westmoreland still thought the war was being won but asked for 200,000 more U.S. troops. McNamara himself was momentarily persuaded that progress was being made. In Washington, however, the main issue was whether to increase the bombing of North Vietnam. McNamara argued that no amount of bombing could prevent the North from reinforcing its troops in the South, and that anyway most of its war supplies were coming from the Soviet Union and China.

In the war of words between McNamara and the Joint Chiefs, McNamara did not stand a chance. On November 1, 1967, he gave Johnson another memorandum, in which he recommended stabilizing the fronts, halting the bombing of North Vietnam, and seeking to bring about negotiations. Virtually no one else liked it. This memorandum brought the agony of Robert S. McNamara to an end. Johnson found a way of getting rid of him by sending him to the World Bank as its president.

———

In retrospect, McNamara is not happy with his record in the Vietnam War. Unlike other books by leading participants, McNamara's is full of regrets and remorse. He regrets that the most critical questions about the war were never adequately analyzed. He lists the five most basic questions that were never asked: "Was it true that the fall of South Vietnam would trigger the fall of all Southeast Asia? Would that constitute a grave threat to the West's security? What kind of war—conventional or guerrilla—might develop? Could we win it with U.S. troops fighting alongside the South Vietnamese? Should we not know the answers to all these questions before deciding whether to commit troops?"

One reason these questions were not asked is that the Americans knew so little about the country and region to which they were sending hundreds of thousands of their troops. The Pentagon and State Department had no senior officials with intimate knowledge of Southeast Asia, because the top East Asian and China experts in the State Department had been driven out during the McCarthy years of the 1950s. "How were we to know," McNamara asks piteously, "when we were moving in an alien environment, alongside a people whose language and culture we did not understand and whose history, values, and political traditions differed profoundly from our own?" The American officers long maintained an attitude of optimism, because they were receiving false information from the Vietnamese. CIA Director John McCone later admitted that "the province and district chiefs felt obliged to 'create statistics' which would meet the approbation of the Central Government." The Americans on the spot, without knowing the language or the customs, passed on the same figures to their superiors in Saigon who passed them on to their superiors in Washington.

Nevertheless, McNamara made an effort to cut short the war without a military victory. His problem was that he was willing to go so far and no further. He never advised getting out of the war; the nearest he came to it was to recommend a "compromise" or "political solution," which he once implied meant a "coalition government." But this idea was never taken up and probably had no future. He now sees that his memorandum of May 19, 1967, should have called for U.S. withdrawal from South Vietnam "through either negotiation or direct action." But it did not.

———

The Vietnam War peculiarly demanded a hardheaded assessment of what it was worth in the national interest of the United States. By itself, Vietnam was a fairly small, remote country, with which the United States had little in common. For this reason, the domino theory was so important in order to make it worth more than it was. The real test of American leadership was to see Vietnam as it was and not as it was multiplied by a theoretical formula. If we were to cut our losses and get out, it was clearly easier and better to do so sooner rather than later. The ideal time would have been after the coup against Diem, when it was shown, as McNamara puts it, that "political stability did not exist and was unlikely ever to be achieved; and the South Vietnamese, even with our training assistance and logistical support, were incapable of defending themselves."

In retrospect, McNamara now believes that we should have withdrawn from South Vietnam either in later 1963, following Diem's assassination, or in late 1964 or early 1965, when it became clear that South Vietnam's political and military weakness could not be remedied. If we had done so, our losses could not have been greater than they were seven or eight years later, and undoubtedly would have been much less. How difficult it was to go from recognizing that a military victory was a mirage to calling for a timely withdrawal was shown by McNamara himself.

McNamara now writes that "we were wrong, terribly wrong. We owe it to future generations to explain why." With this book, he has paid his debt.

"The Abuse of McNamara"
by Theodore Draper
The New York Review of Books
May 25, 1995

The vitriolic and protracted campaign in *The New York Times* against former Secretary of Defense Robert S. McNamara and his new book, *In Retrospect,* is largely based on a false premise, one that can be best demonstrated by *The New York Times* of over twenty years ago.

On April 12, the lead editorial stated: "Mr. McNamara wants us to know that he, too, realized by 1967 that the dissidents were right, that the war had to be stopped to avoid 'a major national disaster.' " Then it goes on: "Even so, he wants us to grant that his delicate sense of protocol excused him from any obligation to join the national debate over whether American troops should continue to die at the rate of hundreds per week in a war he knew to be futile."

On April 16, the lead review in *The New York Times Book Review* by Max Frankel begins: "In his 79th year, Robert S. McNamara at long last offers the public a glimpse of his aching conscience. The most willful Vietnam warrior in the Kennedy and Johnson Administrations, he was also the first at the top to admit defeat, in private." The words "in private" should be emphasized. Later, Frankel convicts McNamara of refusing "once out of office, to share his policy disagreements with the country."

Also on April 16, Frank Rich joined in the attack on McNamara who, Rich wrote, "took his charts to Washington, where he used them to prolong a war whose body count totaled 58,000 American and some 3 million Vietnamese lives," as if McNamara alone had prolonged the entire war.

On April 17, the why-didn't-he-speak-up-sooner line of attack on McNamara was made even more explicitly by Anthony Lewis. For him, McNamara's "greater wrong" was in "failing to speak the truth then, when it mattered." After summarizing McNamara's thoughts on the war in 1965, 1966, and 1967, Lewis claims: "But Mr. McNamara said none of that in public at the time." Finally, Lewis charges: "Many have noted that 58,000 Americans and more than 3 million Vietnamese died in that war while Robert McNamara and many others swallowed their doubts."

Again on April 17, the theme was picked up by Robert MacNeil on *The MacNeil/Lehrer Newshour* during an interview with McNamara: "Many people are saying, reviewers, television interviewers, others, that you should have aired your doubts twenty-seven years ago." McNamara answered: "What should I have said that would not have brought aid and comfort to the enemy?" He might also have answered that his doubts had been aired twenty-four years ago.

———

In short, the case against McNamara largely hinges on the premise that he did not express his doubts about the Vietnam War while it was going on and that he waited until 1995 to make known his views on "whether American troops should continue to die."

As I tried to show in my review of McNamara's book in the last issue of *The New York Review,* it is open to criticism on various counts. But one thing that cannot be held against McNamara is that no one knew about his views on the war during the war. Anyone who read *The New York Times* in 1971 knew. In fact, McNamara's book is not notable for any revelations about the course of the war. Its main interest is in McNamara's repeated expressions of regret and remorse for what the Kennedy and Johnson administrations did and did not do.

McNamara did not have much new to tell about his disillusionment with the war, because it had already been told in detail in the Pentagon Papers. He was responsible for collecting them in the first place. In July 1967, McNamara asked John McNaughton, his Assistant Secretary for International Security Affairs, to collect documents on the war for the use of future scholars. This collection was leaked to *The New York Times,* which courageously fought off a government attempt to stop it from publishing the documents.

The oddest thing about the highly censorious references to McNamara's book is the fact that the *Times* published the Pentagon Papers with McNamara's knowledge and approval. The *Times* writers could have read McNamara's account in his book of how he knew of and approved publication. McNamara tells how the *Times*'s then Washington bureau chief, James ("Scotty") Reston, was dining at McNamara's home on June 14, 1971. A telephone call came for Reston, telling him that Attorney General John Mitchell was trying to prevent publication of the papers. Reston asked McNamara what he thought. "I said," McNamara writes, "the *Times* should continue printing them but should hedge its position by making clear it would obey any order issued by the Supreme Court."[1] Thus McNamara knew in advance that he was going "to share his policy disagreements with the country" (Frankel) and that he was not one of those who "swallowed their doubts" (Lewis).

The New York Times had begun publishing the Pentagon Papers on June 13, 1971. The Vietnam War was still on; the U.S. phase of the war lasted two more years. After publication in *The New York Times* the entire series came out in book form in July 1971. The book is more easily available to interested readers than the newspaper and is best cited here.[2]

Chapter 9 is headed: "Secretary McNamara's Disenchantment:

---

[1] *In Retrospect* (Times Books, 1995), p. 281.
[2] A cloth edition was published by Quadrangle and a paperback by Bantam. A five-volume edition of the complete papers was issued by Beacon in 1971.

October, 1966–May, 1967." It is divided into a summary by Hedrick Smith, followed by a section of supporting documents. Smith noted: "Mr. McNamara's disillusionment with the war has been reported previously, but the depth of his dissent from established policy is documented for the first time in the Pentagon study, which he commissioned on June 17, 1967." After summarizing McNamara's efforts to scale down the U.S. effort in the war, Smith states: "The Pentagon study underscores the significance of Mr. McNamara's break with policy." McNamara's failure to sway Johnson is conveyed in these words: "But in a series of decisions on the air war during July and August [1968], the President adopted a course that differed markedly from the strategy of de-escalation that Secretary McNamara had urged on him."

The documents in the Pentagon Papers are almost exactly the same as those given in McNamara's book. McNamara's first misgivings appear in a memorandum to Johnson of November 30, 1965. This was only four months after the announcement by President Johnson escalating the U.S. role in the war. In his memo, McNamara said that the United States faced a "choice" between accepting a "compromise solution" or increasing the U.S. forces in Vietnam as requested by General William Westmoreland.[3]

On October 14, 1966, McNamara sent Johnson a memorandum in which he struck a note that is a central theme in his book. "This important war," he declared, "must be fought and won by the Vietnamese themselves. We have known this from the beginning. But the discouraging truth is that, as was the case in 1961 and 1963 and 1965, we have not found the formula, the catalyst, for training and inspiring them into effective action." Nevertheless, he still expressed hope that some way might be found to turn the Vietnamese factor around.

---

[3]The memorandum of November 30, 1965, did not spell out what McNamara meant by a "compromise solution." In his book, McNamara says that it entailed "less than our objective of an independent, non-Communist South Vietnam" (p. 222). Even this formula shows that McNamara was vaguely groping for an alternative to escalation and was merely starting to question the goal of a military victory by increasing U.S. ground forces and bombing.

Finally, on May 19, 1967, McNamara sent Johnson a crucial memorandum, parts of which cover seven pages in the Pentagon Papers. In effect, it virtually gave up on the South Vietnamese and recommended "a politico-military strategy that raised the possibility of compromise." Some of its passages reveal the tenor of McNamara's thoughts and feelings at the time:

The Vietnam war is unpopular in this country. It is becoming increasingly unpopular as it escalates—causing more American casualties, more fear of its growing into wider war, more privation of the domestic sector, and more distress at the amount of suffering being visited on the noncombatants in Vietnam, South and North. Most Americans do not know how we got where we are, and most, without knowing why, but taking advantage of hindsight, are convinced that somehow we should not have gotten this deeply in. All want the war ended and expect their President to end it. Successfully, or else.

The use of tactical nuclear and area-denial-radiological-bacteriological-chemical weapons would probably be suggested at some point if the Chinese entered the war in Vietnam or Korea or if U.S. losses were running high while conventional efforts were not producing desired results.

There may be a limit beyond which many Americans and much of the world will not permit the United States [bombing] to go. The picture of the world's greatest superpower killing or seriously injuring 1000 noncombatants a week, while trying to pound a tiny backward nation into submission on an issue whose merits are hotly disputed, is not a pretty one.

(1) Our commitment is only to see that the people of South Vietnam are permitted to determine their own future.
(2) This commitment ceases if the country ceases to help itself.[4]

---

[4]These passages are quoted from McNamara's book, pp. 266–270. Only the third of them appears in *The New York Times* edition of the Pentagon Papers. Nevertheless, Hedrick Smith commented, "Let there be no mistake, these were radical positions for a senior U.S. policy official within the Johnson administration to take."

On November 1, 1967, another McNamara memorandum proposed stabilizing the fronts, halting the bombing of North Vietnam, and seeking to bring about negotiations. It was McNamara's last word on Vietnam to Johnson.

———

All this and more has been known since 1971. It is true that McNamara never made his views of 1965–1967 known before publishing his recent book; the fact is, however, that they were made known for him in the Pentagon Papers. Much in his book is merely a recapitulation of those documents. Once he concluded that the United States could not win militarily in Vietnam, he sought for two years, with growing conviction and without success, to persuade the President and his colleagues to pull back from escalating the war and to seek some way out of it by trying to negotiate a compromise. In 1967, he was almost the only voice within the top echelons of the administration to give up the goal of military victory and to seek some way out of the war by negotiation.

McNamara never went so far as to call for withdrawal from the war. He regrets it now. But it is unfair to accuse him of not sharing his policy disagreements with the country, of swallowing his doubts while millions of Americans and Vietnamese died, or to make him the scapegoat for prolonging the entire war. *The New York Times* enabled him to share his policy disagreements with the country, to reveal his doubts, and to show that he made some effort not to prolong the war.

McNamara's behavior reflected the political culture of the United States. In this tradition, a cabinet officer is not an elected official and serves at the behest of the President. If he disagrees with the President and decides to leave office, he is expected to do so quietly and with a minimum of fuss. This was the course taken by Dean Acheson in the 1930s and by Cyrus Vance in the late 1970s. For McNamara to have acted differently and to have declared political war on Lyndon Johnson in the midst of the Vietnam War would have represented a breach with the American political culture. He did not take that step for at least two reasons. For one thing, McNamara's doubts about the war were still not fully developed; they were enough to make him a pariah to the military leaders but far from fully formed enough to send him into the streets. For another thing, he was obviously shaken by his experiences in the Johnson administration and could not shift from supporting the war to actively opposing it.

Whatever McNamara's shortcomings, it is bizarre to attack him now for the wrong reasons. McNamara was not the arch-villain of the war, and he deserves credit for trying to make amends for the damage that he and his colleagues in the administration did thirty years ago.[5]

---

[5]The reader may wonder why I have written this note. I do not know McNamara and have no connection with him. I happen to have been one of the earliest critics and opponents of the Vietnam War. I contributed articles against the war to *The New York Review of Books* and *Commentary* (in its pre-neoconservative phase) in 1966 and 1967, and brought out a book critical of the war. *Abuse of Power,* in 1967 (Viking). One of its readers was Robert Kennedy, who told his first biographer, Jack Newfield, that *Abuse of Power* "was one of the very best about Vietnam, even though it isn't too kind to me and my friends" (*Robert Kennedy,* Dutton, 1969, p. 132). My sole reason is that I have been dismayed by the abuse of Robert McNamara.

"We Can All Learn from McNamara's Remorse"
by Robert McAfee Brown
"Editorials/Letters"
The New York Times
April 13, 1995

To the Editor:

——

In a strong attack on Robert S. McNamara's account of the Vietnam years, "In Retrospect," your April 12 lead editorial, "Mr. McNamara's War," insists that "Mr. McNamara must not escape the lasting moral condemnation of his countrymen."

Let it also be noted, however, that it is a great and almost unprecedented moral achievement for a man in public life to have offered such an honest accounting of how people like himself, with initially good intentions, became enmeshed in structures of their own creation from which it was finally impossible to escape. Most public servants' memoirs turn out to be self-serving exercises in which their political decisions are retrospectively interpreted in the best possible light.

Not so with Robert McNamara, who makes clear that his own activities in the public sphere were activities for which he now feels deep remorse.

"What we did," he concludes, "was terribly, terribly wrong."

His intention is not to justify his political decisions but to expose them at whatever personal cost, to let the record hang out publicly, hoping that the lessons learned too late in the Vietnamese struggle can be appropriated to avoid similar mistakes in the future. All honor, therefore, to Mr. McNamara for having set a pattern virtually unknown in our nation's public life.

We are left with the question: What can be done with our mistakes? In some cases, overt punishment follows, and an individual is held to have paid his debt to society. In many cases, including Robert McNamara's, the punishment is covert, self-inflicted and lacerating to a degree no one else can ever measure; whatever evils have been done cannot be undone, nor can the dead be returned to us.

But there is something else that can be done with past mistakes, and that is to use them in such a way that the errors of the past do not become the temptations of the future. We can at least learn what not to do next time, and that is a specific moral gain.

This is clearly what motivated Robert McNamara to bare his soul in such unprecedented fashion. His own words are important:

"I want Americans to understand why we made the mistakes we did and to learn from them. I hope to say, 'Here is something we can take away from Vietnam that is constructive and applicable to the world of today and tomorrow.' that is the only way our nation can ever hope to leave the past behind."

Like many others, I disagreed at the time with almost every position Mr. McNamara held, and have my own residual share of deep anger as a legacy of those years. But I see nothing to be gained, and much to be lost, by reinforcing such resentment in the present, as you urge us to do. The lessons Mr. McNamara has learned are lessons we all need to learn, and we owe him thanks for that.

"McNamara's War? You've Got to Be Kidding"
by George Melloan
Wall Street Journal
April 17, 1995

Some inner need for approval apparently compelled Robert S. McNamara to overcome his reluctance to write a memoir of the Vietnam War. He wanted to tell the world that at age 78 he has come to believe that those who opposed "McNamara's War" were right.

"I believe we could and should have withdrawn from South Vietnam either in late 1963 amid the turmoil following Diem's assassination or in late 1964 or early 1965 in the face of increasing political and military weakness in South Vietnam," he writes in his just-published "In Retrospect." Since some of his doubts were at least hinted at when he stepped down as Secretary of Defense in 1967, they hardly come as earth-shaking news today.

But such was the remarkable career of Bob McNamara that even in old age he is to be denied peace and tranquility. His confession has not won him benisons from those whose opinions he seems to value. Quite the opposite. It was greeted by a vicious editorial in *The New York Times*, which for reasons not clear considers itself the repository of all wisdom on Vietnam. Just to make sure Mr. McNamara has bad dreams, the *Times* wound up by giving him almost the entire blame for the 58,000 body bags that came home from Vietnam.

This, of course, is utterly ridiculous. Vietnam was not Bob McNamara's war. Its management was a group effort led by a string of presidents. He simply became the lightning rod for attacks from both right and left because he was never quite a card-carrying liberal or a true-blue conservative. Both sides eventually were looking for someone to punch when the whole enterprise was going sour. The patrician left and the ingrown Washington press were from the beginning suspicious of a self-made man who had ascended from the San Francisco docks to that most disdained of all jobs, auto company executive. The Goldwater right couldn't understand how such a man could so greatly admire so many of those same patricians, such as John Kenneth Galbraith and the Kennedys, and be such a complex combination of tough-guy executive and social philosopher.

The rancor that both sides eventually directed at Mr. McNamara no doubt stemmed in part from frustration that a man of such personal presence and intellectual capacity could not win the war for America. He was a man that Henry Ford II, John F. Kennedy and Lyndon B. Johnson had each in turn sought out as a strong and loyal adjutant, capable of remarkable feats of organization and problem solving.

But for all his special qualities, Mr. McNamara was only a player in a long-running drama. History, not any individual, was the author. The Vietnam War, as with much of the political drama of the last 50 years, began with a post-World War II policy— vigorously supported by all but the American far left—that set containment of communism as the country's highest international priority. John F. Kennedy's eloquent inaugural address rearticulated this policy and he handed Bob McNamara one of the leading roles in carrying it out. Mr. McNamara started out by reorganizing the Pentagon, which was a good and necessary piece of work.

What the defense secretary could not do was instill much order in JFK's conduct of foreign policy. He remains too loyal to the young president's memory today to explicitly criticize the indecisiveness that led to the first big mistake in Vietnam, inciting a coup against South Vietnam's leader, Ngo Dinh Diem. But as his memoir unfolds the sad tale of how the President let the headstrong and arrogant Roger Hilsman Jr. and Henry Cabot Lodge Jr. run out of control in their quest to destroy Diem, that conclusion is inescapable. Mr. Kennedy, for all his leadership skills, had trouble sorting out advice. In this case, the right advice was coming from Secretary McNamara, among others. With Diem went any semblance of popular government in South Vietnam and the anticommunist war effort started downhill.

Quite possibly the *Times*'s sensitivity to the McNamara book is not unrelated to its own dubious opinions on this issue at the time. It helped arouse anti-Diem sentiment with its coverage of Diem's handling of Buddhist riots, some of which were later found to have been incited by Hanoi.

The millions of words that have been written about Vietnam have hashed over these and all the other wrong turns many times. The merit of the McNamara book is that it offers an insider's glimpse of the confusion and moral uncertainty that attended such matters as the handling of the Diem affair.

As Mr. McNamara and many other public officials have reminded us over the years, hindsight is always better than the information available when decisions actually have to be made. But it is clear as well that an American president must have a good compass of his own. Even if the men and women who surround him are said to be the "best and the brightest," his success or failure will ultimately rest on the quality of his own judgments. Every administration is, in some sense, a Tower of Babel.

But there is another point to be made about the McNamara memoir. In the light of the sad outcome of the war, many people will choose to accept the former defense secretary's judgment that the U.S. should have pulled out in the mid-1960s. It is offered in typical McNamara style, as a problem-solving matrix of the type that he and others pioneered in the 1950s. But there is one flaw in any such postmortem: No one really knows what might have been had the drama not played out the way it did.

The best strategists of the Cold War, men like Dean Acheson and Dwight Eisenhower, were convinced that the U.S. must wage this great historic struggle against communism. There was indeed little dissent in the U.S. foreign policy establishment, and why should there have been? It was easily evident by the 1960s to thinking people that communism was merely a carryover from that prewar era when a contagion of totalitarianism had spread across Europe, resulting in horrible atrocities in Germany and the Soviet Union. Ronald Reagan would later describe the Soviet Union as an "evil empire," a description that shocked some effete ears in the West but made perfect sense to those who had to live under communist regimes.

The U.S. lost the Vietnam battle in this long Cold War struggle and without doubt managed the whole affair badly. But because Americans did not allow this defeat to permanently shake their confidence in freedom and democracy they ultimately prevailed. The U.S. may have looked like a loser in 1975, but today it is Vietnam that is the loser, a victim of the very system it fought so hard to promulgate. That's the real lesson of Vietnam and Mr. McNamara deserves far more honor than he is accorded for doing his best with the cards he was dealt.

"As Wrong as McNamara"
by Richard Harwood
Washington Post
April 19, 1995

The punishment of Robert McNamara for his role in the Vietnam War has begun anew with the publication of his apologetic memoirs. "We were wrong, terribly wrong," he tells us now.

On the talk shows the "war criminal" charge is heard. In other quarters "moral condemnation" is proposed. *The New York Times*, in a scathing editorial, "Mr. McNamara's War," writes of "how fate dispensed rewards and punishment for [his] thousand days of error. Three million Vietnamese died. Fifty-eight thousand Americans got to come home in body bags. Mr. McNamara . . . got a sinecure at the World Bank and summers at the Vineyard." Mickey Kaus in the New Republic asks: "Has any single American of this century done more harm than Robert McNamara?"

On the promotional tour for his book he has taken to weeping. The lesson, I suppose, is that what goes around comes around.

That may be fair. But to lay all of this heavy burden on McNamara's frail shoulders too easily lets a lot of us, both living and dead, off the hook. He did not single-handedly make the war. It was the American Establishment—political, military, journalistic and academic—that wrote the script: the "best and the brightest" as David Halberstam, years later, put it. A virtually unanimous consensus supported the judgment that the war had to be fought. That judgment was strongly supported by a very substantial majority of the American people as well.

It is fashionable these days to argue that the people were (and are) sheep-like dupes, misled and betrayed by rose-colored lies from their leaders, McNamara included: The devil made me do it. But that is not true. Lies, deliberate or unknowing, may have been told. But the people knew what was happening. They could read the casualty reports and were not blinded by lights at the end of the tunnel.

By mid-1967 a plurality of Americans had concluded without any help from Washington that "the U.S. made a mistake in sending troops to fight in Vietnam." A year later a clear majority shared that view. Nevertheless, public support for a precipitous withdrawal was thin—10 percent in late 1967, 13 percent in September 1968, 29 percent in June 1969. (These numbers come from John Mueller's classic study, *War, Presidents and Public Opinion*, published in 1985.)

There is an explanation (not Mueller's) for the apparent inconsistency in American opinion at that time. It involves the press.

The *Times* said in its editorial last week that McNamara finally has "grasped realities that seemed readily apparent to millions of Americans throughout the Vietnam War."

But *The New York Times* was not among those prescient millions, nor the *Washington Post*, nor virtually every other major American newspaper, the *Chicago Tribune* excepted. The *Times* hailed the Tonkin Gulf resolution in 1964 as proof of "our united determination to support the cause of freedom in Southeast Asia . . . [against] the mad adventure by the North Vietnamese Communists. . . . United States determination to assure the independence of South Vietnam, if ever doubted before, can not be doubted now by the Communists to the north or their allies."

Halberstam, the *Times* correspondent in Vietnam, published a few months later his well-received book, *The Making of a Quagmire*. He opposed any American abandonment of South Vietnam:

"It would mean that those Vietnamese who committed themselves fully to the United States will suffer the most under a Communist government. . . . It means a drab, lifeless and controlled society for a people who deserve better. Withdrawal also means that the United States' prestige will be lowered throughout the world and it means that the pressure of Communism on the rest of Southeast Asia will intensify. Lastly, withdrawal means that throughout the world the enemies of the West will be encouraged to try insurgencies like the one in Vietnam."

Halberstam was apprehensive about a major U.S. military involvement. But it may come to that, he warned, because Vietnam "is a legitimate part of [America's] global commitment. A strategic country in a key area, it is perhaps one of only five or six nations in the world that is truly vital to U.S. interests."

For years, beginning in the 1950s and long before McNamara came on the scene, this was an insistent theme in the media's coverage of Vietnam and was the subject of a major study in 1970 by Susan Welch, a political scientist at the University of Illinois. It was a theme that helped set in concrete in the American mind the "issues" in Indochina. It helped ensure, Welch concluded, "that the reading public would view the war as a struggle between Communism and the Free World, vital to the preservation of all of Southeast Asia and perhaps all of Asia." Finally, she wrote, our major newspapers propagated a view that "the only way out of the crisis which could result in a satisfactory solution for the West was a military victory over the forces of Ho Chi Minh." These assumptions were not abandoned or seriously challenged by the mainstream press until the late 1960s.

The public had earlier begun arriving at the conclusion that the war was a mistake but, having been indoctrinated for so many years about our "vital interests" in Vietnam, were nevertheless reluctant to give in.

The *Times* now can say of McNamara: "His regret cannot be huge enough to balance the books for our dead soldiers. The ghosts of those unlived lives circle close around Mr. McNamara. Surely he must in every quiet and prosperous moment hear the ceaseless whispers of those poor boys in the infantry, dying in the tall grass, platoon by platoon, for no purpose. What he took from them cannot be repaid by prime-time apology and stale tears, three decades later."

A lot of us in the press, if we are honest with ourselves, will hear those whispers, too. We do not balance the books or cleanse our own record with glib and self-serving revisionism in these prosperous times. We could begin by acknowledging that McNamara's vision was no more flawed than our own.

"McNamara's War, and Mine"
by Louis G. Sarris
"Op-Ed"
The New York Times
September 5, 1995

For years, I have been silent about my long involvement in Vietnamese affairs as an analyst for the State Department in the 1960s. But the publication of Robert S. McNamara's book on Vietnam, in which he acknowledges his mistakes and those of other American leaders, has reawakened old and painful memories.

In his memoir, *In Retrospect: The Tragedy and Lessons of Vietnam*, McNamara claims there was a lack of reliable information about Vietnam upon which to make correct decisions in the crucial early 1960s. "Our government lacked experts for us to consult," he writes.

This statement is untrue. In fact, there was, from the earliest days of our involvement in Vietnam, a number of reliable analyses in the State Department, the C.I.A. and even the Defense Intelligence Agency, let alone information from American officials and journalists in the field and academic military experts.

David Halberstam and Neil Sheehan among others have chronicled cases in which respected officers in Washington and in the field warned, or tried to warn, the top brass about the dangers of military involvement, but they were ignored, silenced or reprimanded. When Lieut. Col. John Paul Vann, for example, came back to Washington and gave a sobering account of the situation, he was not allowed to brief the Joint Chiefs of Staff.

The basic problem was the unwillingness of McNamara and other top policy makers to accept the relevance of information with which they personally disagreed.

For me, these memories, and their lessons for today, resurface every time I look at two memorandums that have been hanging in my study for many years. The first is a handwritten note from McNamara to Secretary of State Dean Rusk, dated Nov. 6, 1963. The second is Rusk's reply.

McNamara's memo was provoked by a critical analysis of the military situation in Vietnam that I wrote on Oct. 22, 1963, in what was a fairly routine assignment in the State Department.

Here is what McNamara wrote to Secretary Rusk:

Dean, Attached is the State memo re the war in Vietnam. Below it are the comments of the Chiefs. If you were to tell me that it is not the policy of the State Department to issue military appraisals without seeking the views of the Defense Department, the matter will die, Bob.

The response from Rusk came two days later:

. . . . It is not the policy of the State Department to issue military appraisals without seeking the views of the Defense Department. I have requested that any memoranda given interdepartmental circulation which include military appraisals be coordinated with your Department. Cordially yours, Dean Rusk.

Rusk's reply makes clear that the State Department would acquiesce in the military's demand that State stop issuing independent assessments of the overall military situation in Vietnam. This gave the Pentagon the overwhelming role in producing such analyses and denied top officials data and appraisals that might call the military's official position into question.

Many of those involved in pursuing the war for the Kennedy, Johnson and Nixon Administrations, including McNamara, have since acknowledged that the almost willful dependence on Pentagon military assessments during this period was a factor which entangled us in the war.

The origin of my critical report was a briefing I gave to Roger Hilsman, then Assistant Secretary of State for East Asia, in early October. He was worried that the accelerating political crisis in South Vietnam would hurt the military effort by the Government of Ngo Dinh Diem against the Viet Cong.

Hilsman reminded me that the Pentagon was stating privately and publicly that, notwithstanding the political turmoil there, the military effort against the Viet Cong was going quite well. A few days after the meeting, my boss, Thomas Hughes, the State Department's director of intelligence and research, asked me to write an analysis of the military situation in South Vietnam.

This was a pivotal time, just before the assassination of President John Kennedy, when the groundwork was being laid for our tragic escalation of the war. The White House was greatly concerned that growing unrest by Vietnamese Buddhists aimed at Diem and his powerful Roman Catholic family was threatening the stability of the Saigon Government. A harsh crackdown by Diem only fueled the Buddhist movement, and its influence spread even into the ranks of the South Vietnamese army.

In early September, I had prepared a separate assessment that warned of the possibility such disaffection could "erode the resistance to Communist attacks and subversion."

My October assessment went to Secretary Rusk, through Thomas Hughes. It concluded that available statistics "indicate an unfavorable shift in the military balance, and that Viet Cong casualties, weapons losses and defections were down while their armed attacks were increasing."

The paper further concluded, "On the basis of available statistical trends, there appears to have been a number of significant and unfavorable changes in the military situation in South Vietnam."

I noted that the data used, while not thoroughly trustworthy, were from the Defense Intelligence Agency; the Pentagon's Office of the Special Assistant for Counterinsurgency and Special Activities, then headed by Gen. Victor Krulak; and from field reports submitted by the U.S. military mission in South Vietnam.

According to standard practice, the report was distributed throughout the State Department, and to the Pentagon, Central Intelligence Agency and the White House.

About two weeks later, I received some private forewarning of the Pentagon's displeasure. Col. John Arthur of General Krulak's staff called to tell me that the general was "extremely agitated" over it and felt the State Department had overstepped itself in making judgments on military matters.

Colonel Arthur also said that Gen. Maxwell Taylor, chairman of the Joint Chiefs, had "hit the ceiling" over the report and told General Krulak to prepare a memorandum to Secretary McNamara advising him to take the matter up with Rusk. McNamara was to make clear that the State Department should not undertake military assessments. (My only other experience with Maxwell Taylor had been similarly distant. I was a corporal in Taylor's 101st Airborne Division at the Battle of the Bulge in 1944.)

(In Halberstam's book, *The Best and the Brightest*, he wrote that my assessment was a threat to the Pentagon because "it showed that the war effort was slipping away.")

The official rumble began one Friday afternoon a few days after Colonel Arthur's call. Thomas Hughes summoned me to his office and stated that Rusk wanted to talk to us right away. He opened by saying that Secretary McNamara and the Joint Chiefs were very upset and had called a meeting to discuss my report.

Rusk asked why my report had not been cleared with his personal staff before being circulated outside the State Department. Hughes told him the report indeed had been cleared.

In any case, Rusk said McNamara was "very upset" and had sent him his memorandum. Attached to McNamara's note was a rather lengthy critique of my report by the Joint Chiefs, dated Nov. 6. The Pentagon had cabled my report to the United States military mission in South Vietnam and the Pacific Military Command in Hawaii to ask for their views. Rusk ordered Hughes and me to prepare a response to Secretary McNamara, and I worked through the weekend.

On Monday morning I had a memorandum on Hughes' desk, to be sent to Secretary Rusk. It was only two pages long, since that is all it took to rebut the lengthy Defense Department comments.

The Pentagon had claimed, for example, that the confidence and fighting efficiency of the South Vietnamese armed forces had improved. I pointed out that the U.S. military attaché in Saigon had recently reported that a Vietnamese military official had described mass desertions, possibly as high as 80 percent in his own region. My rebuttal concluded by noting that a C.I.A. report, independently prepared after my own, had used essentially the same statistical indicators, had covered the same time period, and had concurred with my findings.

My memorandum was signed off by Rusk and, I was told, sent to McNamara and the Joint Chiefs. I heard of no immediate reaction.

But early in 1964, after the American-backed military coup which overthrew Diem, I learned I was widely referred to in the Pentagon as the "coup plotter," and my analysis was known as the "coup report," suggesting that it was the final straw influencing Washington's decision to support the South Vietnamese military's ouster of Diem.

I take strong exception to this inference. It may be that some Pentagon officials opposed to American support of the coup conveniently used my paper to fix responsibility for our policy on the State Department's inaccurate (to their mind) analysis of the military situation under Diem.

So what did all this mean? As a result of this incident so early in our involvement in Vietnam, the State Department no longer routinely issued its own overall appraisals of the progress of the conflict. If we were to do so, we had to obtain the views of the Defense Department, which in effect meant its concurrence.

We could continue to analyze to our hearts' content such subjects as Viet Cong and North Vietnamese strength, strategy, tactics and infiltration. I believe we did this with a substantial degree of accuracy. But overall appraisals of the war were off limits, and in most cases our reports were kept within the department.

Things went on this way for four years, and the storm seemed to have settled. In 1967, however, I violated the Rusk-McNamara agreement. That spring, Gen. William Westmoreland, the commander in Vietnam, delivered an address to a joint session of Congress in which he applauded the great progress being made in the war.

I had just returned from Vietnam myself, and my discussions, primarily with middle-level American military and civilian officials, revealed a strikingly different view. Even a senior general, Frederick C. Weyand, had told me during a two-hour lunch that the Viet Cong could hit him anywhere in his sector with little or no warning. I was therefore amazed at General Westmoreland's confidence.

So I wrote another report, published just before the Tet Offensive, noting the potential for an imminent large-scale attack by Communist forces. I waited for the storm to break out, but there was no reaction from Rusk or McNamara. Perhaps it was an oversight on Rusk's part. Or perhaps the Defense Secretary had by that time changed his mind about the war, as he now claims he had.

In any event, this report escaped controversy. It also apparently escaped attention, since we were taken by surprise by the Tet Offensive early in 1968.

Robert McNamara's Reply to Mr. Sarris:
A Letter to the Editor of
*The New York Times**

To the Editor:

_____

I should like to respond to Louis G. Sarris' statement, referring to my book *In Retrospect*, which was printed in the Op-Ed section of the *Times,* September 5.

1. On page 32 I wrote "When the Berlin crisis occurred in 1961, and during the Cuban Missile Crisis in 1962, President Kennedy was able to turn to senior people like Llewellyn Thompson, Charles Bohlen and George Kennan, who knew the Soviets intimately. There were no senior officials in the Pentagon or State Department with comparable knowledge of Southeast Asia." Mr. Sarris writes, "this statement is untrue." But it is he who is incorrect. Thompson, Bohlen and Kennan had studied Soviet history, culture and politics for decades, and had associated both socially and professionally with the top Russian leaders, including Khrushchev. As a result, at critical moments in U.S.-Soviet relations they could interpret for the President, Secretary of State Dean Rusk, National Security Advisor McGeorge Bundy, and me the intent of Soviet actions

**The New York Times* printed an abbreviated version of my letter (cut by about 502 words) on September 14, 1995.

and suggest how to respond. We had no counterparts with respect to South Vietnam, North Vietnam, or China. As a result, during the particular period Mr. Sarris refers—the time just before and after the overthrow of President Diem—we were flying blind. President Kennedy had laid down two conditions for U.S. involvement in Vietnam: there must be a stable political base in the South and the South Vietnamese must recognize it was their war which only they could win— our support was to be limited to training and logistics. A Thompson, Bohlen or Kennan counterpart could have told the President that neither of these conditions could be met. The erroneous decisions were ours and we must accept the responsibility for them, but the absence of experienced senior advisors helps to explain the basis for the errors.

2. Mr. Sarris states: "The basic problem was the unwillingness of McNamara and other top policymakers to accept the relevance of information with which they disagreed." I don't believe the record supports that judgment. On the contrary, the President, Dean Rusk, Mac Bundy, Bill Bundy, the Assistant Secretary of Defense for International Security Affairs, and I were all skeptical of much of the information we received, not because we questioned the integrity of the originators of the reports, but because we doubted their ability to penetrate and understand the extraordinarily complex political, economic, social, and military environment and actions they were reporting. Sarris misinterprets a note I sent to Dean (the note said "The State Department [should not] issue military appraisals without seeking the views of the Defense Department" as "denying top officials data and appraisals that might call the military's official position into question." On the contrary, what I was saying, and what I believe Dean clearly understood me to say, was that no one of our departments should develop appraisals and judgments without taking account of the views of the others. Where differences existed they should be surfaced and debated and where they could not be resolved the divergent views should be presented to the principles. We did all too little of that. However, I did so want to check the military reports of our progress—or lack of it— that I later asked President Johnson to permit me to request Dick Helms, the director of the CIA, to set up a special

department to assess independently military operations. This was done. Moreover, on my trips to South Vietnam, I asked State Department, National Security Council, and CIA representatives to accompany me so that they could make their own judgments of the problems we faced.

3. Mr. Sarris states that just before the assassination of President Kennedy, "the groundwork was being laid for our tragic escalation of the war." I believe the record shows that far from planning an escalation, President Kennedy had decided—and publicly announced on October 2, 1963—that the United States would plan to withdraw its military forces by the end of 1965 and would start by withdrawing 1,000 (of our 16,000 men) by the end of 1963. Sarris is correct in stating there were many U.S. military officials who were overly optimistic about progress. But others held opposite views. I state on page 79 that the debate in the National Security Council "reflected a total lack of consensus over where we stood in meeting our objectives." But the President nonetheless authorized the beginning of withdrawal, believing that either our training and logistical support had led to the progress claimed or, if it had not, additional training would not change the situation and, in either case, we should plan to withdraw.

4. With respect to the coup which overthrew Diem, Sarris appears to be saying that some Pentagon officials fixed responsibility on the State Department and, in particular, on his analysis. That may have been the view of some Defense officials, but it was not and is not mine. I do believe U.S. support of the overthrow of Diem was a mistake, but I hold the senior officials—the President, Dean Rusk, and me—responsible, not Mr. Sarris.

ROBERT S. McNAMARA
September 12, 1995

"My Vietnam Policy Was a Terrible Mistake"
by Lee Lescaze
Wall Street Journal
April 14, 1995

Like chess, the Vietnam War supports a huge body of analysis. The very impossibility of knowing all the right moves only adds to the fascination of the puzzle.

One piece, though, has been famously missing. For more than 25 years Robert S. McNamara, defense secretary from January 1961 until after the Tet offensive of January 1968, angered those who hated the policies he had devised and disappointed those war proponents who would have liked his support by refusing to discuss the subject.

In Retrospect: The Tragedy and Lessons of Vietnam (Times Books, 414 pages, $27.50) ends Mr. McNamara's silence. He wastes no time letting readers know what he thinks of U.S. policy. He and other officials "were wrong, terribly wrong," he writes in his preface.

Mr. McNamara might well have written these words when they would have had political impact. But protest isn't his style.

Nevertheless, even at this date, Mr. McNamara's is a refreshing approach. Unlike so many other former officials who helped make Vietnam decisions during the Kennedy, Johnson and Nixon administrations, Mr. McNamara is unsparing of himself. He isn't out to make excuses, defend his talents or save his reputation by clever argument.

The spirit of *In Retrospect* is the spirit of confession. What he confesses is that "the best and the brightest"—and all those who followed them—never addressed the fundamental alternatives open to them on Vietnam because they were ignorant of Indochina's history and, equally, were overly concerned about "the domino theory," which held that a U.S. withdrawal from Vietnam would encourage communist expansion throughout Asia.

Mr. McNamara knows that men like Walt Rostow, who was President Johnson's second White House chief of staff, and Lee Kwan Yew, Singapore's prime minister from 1959 to 1990, believe that the U.S. war effort, despite its ultimate failure, bolstered freedom throughout the region by allowing Vietnam's neighbors to grow stronger during the war years.

He questions that judgment and makes clear that, whatever might have been gained, the cost—in lives on both sides and in social disruption for Americans—was too high. The U.S. should have withdrawn as soon as it became evident that South Vietnam was unable to achieve political stability and incapable of defending itself. He cites five dates when, with hindsight, that decision could have been made.

By the first of them, November 1963, when President Ngo Dinh Diem was overthrown (with U.S. approval), 78 Americans had been killed in action. By the last, December 1967, when it already had been announced that Mr. McNamara was to leave the Pentagon for the presidency of the World Bank, 15,979 Americans had been killed.

Because Mr. McNamara's confessional choice is to shoulder blame himself but not point fingers at others, he avoids making a political point of the fact that the majority of the total 58,191 U.S. combat deaths came on someone else's watch—indeed, almost 50% under the Nixon administration, which entered office seeking not to win the war but to end it.

Mr. McNamara is interested in writing the history of policy making, not in offering the personal detail of a memoirist. Still, there are telling private moments. In one, his horror at the suicide of Quaker Norman Morrison, who burned himself 40 feet from Mr. McNamara's Pentagon window, led him to stop discussing Vietnam outside the office—even with his wife and children, who he knew shared some of Morrison's views. This repression of his feelings, Mr. McNamara writes, was a grave mistake.

He adds to the record some recently declassified papers, including a September 1967 private memo from Central Intelligence Agency Director Richard Helms to President Johnson analyzing the impact of U.S. failure in Vietnam and finding that the domino effect would be less than most officials expected. LBJ never showed the memo to anyone.

Mr. McNamara's book will be disliked by those Americans who think that the U.S. could have scored a victory in Vietnam if it had "done things right." But it is a clear, concise and extremely interesting look at a crucial period of U.S. decision making. It deserves to be widely read by people who lived through the war, but its value will be greater if it finds a large audience of young Americans—too many of whom can think of the war only as ancient history. Mr. McNamara argues that military operations cannot build political stability (Somalia, Bosnia, Haiti come to mind) and that, absent stability, a country cannot successfully fight a war.

He admits that he came to government believing that every problem had a solution. Vietnam convinced him otherwise. He also observes that government leaders—in all administrations—are handling so many problems that they often don't have time to think straight. Bad enough when American soldiers aren't being killed as a result.

" 'We Were Wrong, Terribly Wrong' in Vietnam"
by Molly Ivins
San Francisco Chronicle
April 12, 1995

> *"We were wrong, terribly wrong.*
> *We owe it to future generations to explain why."*
> —Robert S. McNamara, former secretary of defense,
> speaking of the Vietnam War

THERE IT IS. Thank you, Mr. McNamara. "Stop the presses!" is the way we in the newspaper bidness say, "This is REALLY important." I wish there were some way to stop all the presses—to get all the spin doctors and O.J. media hypesters and smug Republicans and back-pedaling Democrats and busy moms and teens who read only about Madonna to sit down, be quiet and listen to Robert McNamara for a little while.

Odd but appropriate that as we celebrate the 50th anniversary of our victory in the Good War, we should also be reminded of the one we mucked up. Important, so important, for everyone holding public office, everyone, to consider the possibility that 20 years hence they too may have to sit down and write: "We were wrong, terribly wrong." And for those of us who were outside the Pentagon, on the other side of all those fences and police lines, trying to scream truth to power, we, too, have something to learn from McNamara's confession.

Much as I like to make fun of the Decline of Absolutely

Everything Gang, it does worry me that "history," in contemporary American usage, is a synonym for "toast." Because unless we understand how we got from the end of World War II to the end of the Vietnam War, then we cannot understand how we got from the end of 'Nam to where we are now. All this distrust and dislike that Americans now have for one another—all this cynicism. How did we get from GI Joe to fragging? From raising the flag at Iwo Jima to My Lai! How many lies did our government tell us before no one believed it anymore?

No one person can wholly understand a tragedy like Vietnam, but I plan to put McNamara's book on the small shelf of indispensable books, along with Michael Herr's *Dispatches* and Neil Sheehan's *A Bright Shining Lie*. McNamara offers us Reasons 1 Through 11, rather in the style of H&R Block, for why millions of people died in vain. Lying is one of them. Anything new? Wrong time, wrong place, wrong side equal wrong war. McNamara says John F. Kennedy was ready, in the fall of 1963, "to bug out," as Lyndon B. Johnson later put it. There was a lot on the line in Dallas that November 22.

McNamara's subtitle is "Tragedy and Lessons of Vietnam." Funny—people have been writing, and living, tragedies at least since the ancient Greeks, but are the lessons ever really new?

McNamara painfully details all the times they could have listened, should have listened to those who disagreed. John Kenneth Galbraith, whose dissenting opinions on Vietnam got him labeled "not useful," believes McNamara's book is one of the most important of our time.

What are we to learn, then, aside from the modest assessment I made years ago: You cannot prop up a government that does not have the support of its own people. McNamara concurs.

Part of the poison of Vietnam is that we ended it as badly as we fought it, and for that, I blame Richard Nixon and Henry Kissinger. Lies, lies, lies, right through the end. It has taken us years, while the poison has spread, to lance the wound and let the pus out. By now, we believe all politicians are liars. Last week in Washington, speaking to a group of journalists, I vigorously insisted that it is a far more important obligation of ours to root out official lies than it is to report on the private behavior of public officials. Came the question: "Do you really think lying is worse than adultery? Than breaking a vow made before God and company!"

I don't know. I do know that it ain't my job to know. All a journalist can do is cover the public realm; judgment of private lives is left to biographers, spouses and God. In the public realm, lying is the original sin. And the only antidote for it is the truth told as unsparingly as Robert McNamara has done. God knows, we certainly need still more of it; all the files of the CIA, the most hubris-driven organization on Earth, must be made public.

So our lessons are: Don't lie. Certitude is the enemy. Self-doubt is good. Particularly difficult lessons in a nervous age, when the search for certainty compels so many. This column is dedicated to one of the 58,000-plus names on The Wall.

Comments by Professor John Kenneth Galbraith at the John F. Kennedy School of Government, Harvard University
April 25, 1995*

PROFESSOR GALBRAITH: This [observation] is enormously and sadly in conflict with my normally retiring nature. (Laughter.)

I do think, however, I perhaps can claim that I have some anti-Vietnam credentials of the safer sort. I was sent to Vietnam in 1961, after I had expressed to the President strong objections to what was at that time the rather famous Rostow-Taylor report, saying that we should send troops into the Vietnam Delta disguised as flood control workers.

I protested the idea of sending troops, even in disguise, and Kennedy said, "Well, you go to Vietnam." His impression was that I didn't have an open mind. I didn't disappoint him. (Laughter.) I came back with a report and a series of letters that are being published by the Harvard University Press later this year and will undoubtedly outsell McNamara. (Laughter.) All of them entered objection to our involvement there on several grounds.

First, I had the sense that I had from India, that we were involved as enemies of Vietnam nationalism, something that they understood from the ancient experience with the Chinese, and later the French and their very recent Japanese experience. They understood the intervention of a seeming colonial power much better than they

*Transcribed from tape.

understood the difference between Communism and democracy.

I was particularly impressed, as I've often told, on a Sunday, going with an armed escort many miles north of Saigon. That Sunday was a very strongly educational experience because I saw the enormous difficulty of telling a Communist jungle from a democratic jungle. You would be astonished at how alike they were.

I went on to argue inside the administration, from a distance—I don't want to exaggerate my role—and then publicly within the anti-war movement. I was one of the leaders of Gene McCarthy's campaign, seconded his nomination at the great Chicago convention of 1968, was his floor manager under circumstances in which it was not evident that anybody in that particular gathering was taking my management. (Laughter.) And so I think that even the most energetic and motivated people here this wonderful evening will forgive me.

But I want to, on the basis of that record, say a word about Robert McNamara. During all of this time, he was the one person to whom we had access. He was the one person who would talk, and we hoped on occasion could persuade. He was open to persuasion, which came, not from me, but from others similarly motivated.

And we see this evening a remarkable man who has gone back over that period with care. We must also emphasize the extraordinary research that has already been mentioned by my colleagues, the good writing and the compelling lesson.

I was particularly struck, Bob, by the seemingly narrow margin that we sometimes were facing on the use of nuclear weapons. This, to an extraordinary extent, was new to me from your book.

So I want, with many others here this evening, to add my word of admiration for this remarkable piece of research. And again the extraordinarily good writing and the compelling lesson which it conveys. I do that partly in response to an old friend, but partly in response to the criticism that Bob McNamara could have avoided if, like so many others, he had opted for silence.

(Applause.)

"Confessing the Sins of Vietnam"
by Jonathan Alter
Newsweek
April 17, 1995*

The "S" in Robert S. McNamara stands for "Strange," his mother's maiden name, but during the war in Vietnam this was the mildest of the epithets flung at him. "Murderer." "War criminal." From the other side: "Peacenik." "Made the military fight with one hand tied behind its back." For Americans of a certain generation, the passions are dimmer but still visible in the elephant grass, halfway back across their lives. The war— "McNamara's War," it was sometimes called—ended 20 years ago this month. McNamara left office as secretary of defense more than 27 years ago. And finally, in his 79th year, after cross-country skiing to the top of Colorado's Continental Divide, he has finally broken his long pained silence in a book studded with mea culpas and plaintive pleas that the lessons of Vietnam be learned. No confession can bring back the dead or absolve guilt. But his public remorse took some guts, even now.

For a major public official to admit profound error is extraordinarily rare, perhaps unprecedented, in American history. Of course, losing a war was unprecedented for the United States, too. But even failed efforts rarely yield apology. In his memoirs, Jefferson Davis could not bring himself to acknowledge major error

Newsweek granted me permission to reproduce the review subject to the condition that I also include in this Appendix my interview with Jonathan Alter. I am happy to do so.

by the Confederacy. And Richard Nixon and Henry Kissinger, who could have exited Vietnam in 1969 on the same terms they obtained in 1973 (more than 19,000 American lives later), never expressed the slightest contrition over their choices. McNamara is different.

He was always the most complex of the Kennedy men David Halberstam immortalized as the "Best and the Brightest." As one of the legendary Whiz Kids, he helped resuscitate the Ford Motor Company in the 1940s and 1950s; the quintessential Organization Man. And the link was soon drawn between his deep faith in numbers and the perverse "body count" of Viet Cong dead. The standard biographic cliché continued: After leaving government, the brainiac with the slicked-back hair and reputation as a cool bureaucratic in-fighter became an emotional do-gooder—helping feed millions through the green revolution as president of the World Bank, preaching nuclear disarmament, weeping easily, shattered by Vietnam.

McNamara himself says gamely that he has not changed. "People today are seeing a different side of me because it wasn't appropriate for me to be talking this way then," he said in an interview last week, addressing the issue publicly for the first time (page 52). "Why did I go to the World Bank? Some people say it was for atonement, expiation. That's garbage. I went there because I was fascinated by the development problem and wanted to accelerate the rate of social and economic advances of the billions of poor people in the world."

The expiation theory robs McNamara of his subtlety—the weave of ambition, idealism, manipulation, duty. His friends say it doesn't account for certain facts of his years at Ford, when he rejected the conventional corporate culture and pushed safety, or his early efforts within the Pentagon to teach thousands of military recruits how to read. Same do-gooder he always was, they say. His critics—often agreeing that he never really changed—point to the mechanical, memo-heavy quality of much of the new book. Same bureaucrat he always was, they say.

But the notion that he never underwent a transformation collapses under the weight of the war years and the almost Shakespearean torment. Anyone predicting in 1961 that Bob McNamara would one day cry publicly while admitting colossal error would have been laughed out of Washington. And the release he now feels can't but be genuine. His research associate, Brian VanDeMark, a history professor at the U.S. Naval Academy, says that in writing the book McNamara "has been liberated from that monkey on his back." He adds: "You know that old saying—'he just doesn't get it.' Well, he *did* get it, and it makes him a little more relaxed."

Halberstam doesn't believe McNamara gets it at all. "The book is shallow and deeply disingenuous. For him to say, 'We couldn't get information' borders on a felony, because he was the creator of the lying machine that gave him that information. The point was to make a flawed policy look better. It's almost a time warp: He sees Mac Bundy as the best national-security adviser ever and Maxwell Taylor as a soldier statesman. Taylor actually hammered anyone who told the truth and said the war wasn't going well."

Without refighting the war, it's clear Halberstam is right on one point: McNamara can't come fully to terms with the mistakes of Vietnam without criticizing other policymakers more vigorously. (The barbs directed at the late Henry Cabot Lodge are an exception.) That was an unavoidable trap: if McNamara were to trash others, he would look defensive and cheap. But because he doesn't really single out his colleagues, the book doesn't provide a full accounting. While he adds the human dimension in describing the toll on his family, he fails to convey the tangled personal motivations of the players, including himself. He can't, for instance, plainly admit that the 1964 Gulf of Tonkin incident was convenient for their aim of winning greater leeway from Congress.

McNamara is not finished wrestling with his Vietnam ghosts. Lonely after the death of his wife 14 years ago, he is constantly jetting off to conferences. The one he yearns for now would be with the Vietnamese, modeled after the meetings he participated in with former U.S., Soviet and Cuban policymakers to discuss the Cuban Missile Crisis. The Council on Foreign Relations is trying to arrange this historic exchange, though nothing has been finalized with Vietnam. Bob McNamara's old adversaries would find him strangely energetic to relive the horrors they shared.

———

Robert S. McNamara sat down last week in his Washington, D.C., office with *Newsweek*'s Jonathan Alter:

Was there a moment that gave you the most anguish?
What gives me the most anguish today—and I think then—was the recognition of the errors we made, that the course we were on was not going to achieve our objective. I couldn't seem to get us off that course and achieve the objective at less cost of human life. That was the stress.

One of the most moving moments involved your son . . .
He [Craig McNamara, now a farmer in California] was at Stanford and was eligible for a college deferment, but he decided not to request it. He felt that the war was wrong but that it was immoral for him to get one, because others in his age group didn't qualify. So he wrote the draft board and asked for a medical exam. He was classified 1-A. But he did have then—and had in the past—an ulcer, for which he was treated at Johns Hopkins Hospital, and eventually he was classified 4-F. I said, "What would you have done if you weren't 4-F?" Well, he said, "I consider it immoral to fight in Vietnam and kill people. But I would have to go, because as a citizen I felt I had to accept the instructions of my elected government." I tell you, that was a pretty damn hard thing to talk about.

The fact that it's your son who might be involved may bring it closer to home, but most of them [other policymakers] and I were just as concerned about the names on the Vietnam memorial, which is why it was such an emotional feeling to visit there. But I'm not going to discuss those feelings.

What would you say to the argument that you put your loyalty to Lyndon Johnson over your loyalty to the American people?

I don't think that's the case. We are not a parliamentary government, where ministers can overthrow the prime minister. A minister in our government is there *solely* as the representative of the president. Therefore, every cabinet officer must do as the president says, or get the hell out. And if he gets out, my view is that he cannot attack the president from outside the cabinet, essentially using the power given to him by the president. I recognize this is not a widely accepted view, but I believe it's the correct view—grounded in the Constitution and shared by such former cabinet officers as Dean Acheson.

But when you weigh that constitutional view against thousands of lives . . .

Well, as I say in the book, from May of '67 until Feb. 29, 1968 [my last day in office], I fought against sending 200,000 more troops. I stayed because I thought I was effective.

And after you left office, did you do all you could to end the war?

I was willing to quit my job [as president of the World Bank]. If I thought I could have helped stop the war—responsibly—I surely would have done it. But I didn't know of any way to do it. At that point my voice wouldn't have made any difference.

Really? If you had written this book then?

I wasn't capable of it. I wasn't as wise.

When you were working on the book—deep into Vietnam—did you dream about it?

No, but I sure sweated blood at night about it. I was obsessed by it, and I kept a pen and pad by my bed, and I'd turn the light on three or four times in the middle of the night and jot down ideas.

You cry easily, don't you?

I do cry easily, but one of the reasons is, I have deep-seated emotions. They're deep-seated today, and they were deep-seated then.

Did you cry in the '60s?

I think so, sure. Just because [others] didn't doesn't mean they weren't tormented. Crying is an external manifestation, and I don't like seeing it in myself. I always thought it was just me and Hubert Humphrey who succumbed to that weakness.

Weren't you working through some of the anguish you felt for the war?

Absolutely not. If my friends think I behave differently after Vietnam, they haven't read yet what I write in the book about my days at the Ford Motor Co. At Ford, they basically thought I was an oddball. This guy lived in Ann Arbor, not Grosse Pointe or Bloomfield Hills. He didn't go to Henry Ford's daughter's wedding. He didn't give contributions to the Republican Party. But the deal was, I could live my life as I wanted to so long as I made money for the company, which I did. I was pushing safety, seat belts, environmental considerations, gas economy, which the industry didn't really care about.

Were you arrogant then? You were known for taking people apart in meetings sometimes.

I wouldn't call it arrogant. I was single-minded, determined, forceful. And I haven't changed. I catch myself sometimes today. I am much too brutal—or what appears to be brutal. I don't mean to be that way, but I come on strong, and that's not good. But that's not arrogance, it's conviction.

Did you rely too heavily on the body count and other numbers?

The answer is no, but that is the wrong question. The right question is, did you rely on the wrong *strategy*—conventional military tactics instead of winning the hearts and minds of the people—and the answer to that is yes. It was totally wrong.

I'm not arguing that we measured progress right. My point is, I have no apologies that we tried to measure progress. You must set objectives and evaluate your strategy or plan. If you're committing people to war—risking their lives to achieve a national objective—and you're not going to measure progress, I don't want to have anything to do with you. But we measured the progress very, very poorly. We misjudged how the enemy would react.

Newt Gingrich said that his views on government were shaped partly by reading in *The Best and the Brightest* that Johnson said the problem was that none of the Harvard boys had ever run for sheriff.

Gingrich is wrong. Johnson didn't have to keep the Harvard boys. He *wanted* them. And he's wrong that political leaders shouldn't use intelligence and education. But what Gingrich is saying—there's something to it. If I could live my life over again, I would try to become one [a politician]. Run for "sheriff." In that sense, I lacked experience. I never met a political payroll.

What do you say to the argument that if we had unleashed the military, we could have won?

Johnson and I held the lid on unleashing the military. One of the reasons was we didn't want war with China and the Soviet Union. The chiefs recommended action that they said might lead to a military confrontation with the Soviets and Chinese, in which case we might have to resort to the use of nuclear weapons. We were just totally opposed to that. If we had invaded North Vietnam, I can't believe they [Chinese or Soviets] wouldn't have gotten in. We would either have confronted an escalating conflict with the Great Powers or been bogged down in a hostile environment for years. It's analogous to "Should we go after Saddam Hussein in Baghdad?" Bush and Powell were absolutely right not to.

The Vietnamese are now estimating that they suffered 3 million fatalities. If we'd occupied North Vietnam, they would have just gone to the hills. Should we have carried out Nixon's '72 bombing in '66? The chiefs didn't recommend it then, and it wouldn't have worked anyway. I was in the Marianas during World War II, and we killed 100,000 people in Tokyo in *one day* in 1945 with [conventional] bombing. It didn't change Japanese behavior. Short of genocide, it is unlikely that you can break a nation's will by bombing. I know of no thoughtful analysis of the war that says we would have won if we had "unleashed" our military. The military scholars don't say it.

In the end, what are the two or three most important lessons of Vietnam?

The concluding chapter of the book focuses on this subject. Put very simply: don't misjudge the nature of the conflict. Don't underestimate the power of nationalism. Many conflicts of the future will be about nationalism. Don't overestimate what outside military forces can accomplish—they can't reconstruct a "failed" state. And don't act unilaterally unless the security of our country is directly threatened.

"Robert McNamara's Inner War"
by David M. Shribman
Boston Globe
April 17, 1995

WASHINGTON—Thirty years on, and Robert S. McNamara is still consumed—with Vietnam, with moral issues, with controversy.

Now he is 78 years old, holding forth in a well-appointed suite in an elegant office building a few blocks from the White House. He speaks with precision, passion and pain. The Cold War and the communist threat have long since passed, and yet the fires of Vietnam burn again, in part because McNamara has broken his silence and, in doing so, has broken the nation's domestic peace.

"This was a long time ago," he is saying. It is early in the evening, and the mandarins of Bill Clinton's Washington—many of them still scarred by the war former Defense Secretary McNamara prosecuted—are rushing home in the gathering dusk. But McNamara is speaking slowly, measuring each word, getting it exactly right. "To me it was yesterday. I can see it. I can see the March on the Pentagon. It's so vividly in my mind."

It is there, in the mind of the Ford whiz kid that John Kennedy brought to Washington in 1961, a long time ago, and now it is in the mind of the whole country. The wounds, almost healed, are being rubbed raw again. The architect of the war has committed an explosive act. He has written a book.

Robert Strange McNamara is in the center of the storm again.

On any level, McNamara's book, *In Retrospect*, is an extraordinary event. One of the principal figures in that convulsive war is explaining himself, saying he was wrong and saying he is sorry.

"There is no precedent for his position," said Stephen Ambrose, a University of New Orleans historian and biographer of Dwight Eisenhower and Richard Nixon. "A lot of people lose wars, and there have been culpable people in every one of them, and people who were privately opposed to these wars. But they never wrote a book about it. None of the guys in the dock at Nuremburg did that, none of the Japanese leaders did that, and no one in the Confederacy did that."

McNamara said he did not do it for himself. He said he did it for the country.

"I didn't write it for cathartic purposes," McNamara said, opening the conversation. "I wrote it because I had come to the conclusion we had made serious mistakes. I began with the judgment that the mistakes weren't as easy to see in the '60s as they are today—and that we would draw some lessons for the future."

―――――

But many of those who saw those "mistakes" in the 1960s—who argued against McNamara and the president who escalated the war, Lyndon Johnson—are not taking yes for an answer. Once they were angry about the war, and they focused their anger against McNamara. Now they are angry with McNamara again.

"I've gone through two stages on this," said former Democratic Sen. George S. McGovern, whose antiwar presidential campaign lost 49 states in 1972. "At first I said, 'Gee, isn't that great?' Then about two days later I thought: 'My God, he has been silent all these days.' My feeling of gratitude has turned to outrage."

And so a book designed, at least in part, to put the war behind us, has put it in front of us again, with all its savage emotions. Once again the call goes out for reason.

"I really wish people would read the book instead of the debate over why it took him so long," said McGeorge Bundy, the special assistant for national security affairs for Presidents Kennedy and

Johnson. "This is a very important and, I think, a very good book. It helps to explain how we came to be so wrong. It will need to be taken account of by historians of this and the next generation."

McNamara's thesis is that he and the military and diplomatic leaders of the time got things wrong because they underestimated the force of nationalism in Southeast Asia; lacked understanding of the history, language, culture and values of the region; misunderstood the nature and threats of the Cold War; misguidedly transformed South Vietnam's fight into America's fight; and made political and military blunders at every turn.

"We of the Kennedy and Johnson administrations who participated in the decisions on Vietnam acted according to what we thought were the principles and traditions of this nation," McNamara writes. "We made our decisions in light of those values. Yet we were wrong, terribly wrong."

———

None of these men had been accustomed to being wrong. David Halberstam's epic 1972 chronology of the Vietnam era has lent a phrase "the best and the brightest" to the political lexicon, and nothing so aptly describes McNamara's pedigree. He was elected to Phi Beta Kappa at the end of his sophomore year at the University of California. He took an MBA from the Harvard business school, later teaching there. He was the president of the Ford Motor Co. at a time when the power, pride and prerogatives of the big domestic automakers were unassailable.

Now McNamara is a different man—like so many, bent, if not broken, by the war. He went off to be president of the World Bank for 13 years, a period of great personal growth and fulfillment for him but often described with a single cold word—"penance"—by his critics. His wife, Marg, died 14 years ago.

"McNamara has had this long time alone," said Horace W. Busby, a longtime Johnson aide. "He's gone through a vast change as a man. He's facing a world that's not the kind of world he grew up in. He's talking about himself, and you can't step on a guy who is talking about himself."

The motivations of men like McNamara were geopolitical, to be sure, but they were also moral. Their martyred president, Kennedy, had talked of the fight at the ramparts of liberty, of bearing any burden and fighting any fight to assure the survival of freedom. Vietnam was where America's will was being tested.

———

Now a moral imperative of a different sort has led McNamara to his book, and to this comment, made softly in conversation:

"In this century, we the human race will have killed 160 million people. It's an unbelievable thought to me to think that we did this. Some of them were killed in Vietnam. This has been the bloodiest century in history. Are we going to let that happen again?"

McNamara said that he and the administration were wrong almost from the start.

"We exaggerated the risks," he said. "I believe that the situation in Vietnam and in Indochina was not as dangerous a threat to the security of the West as we thought. But the world was a very dangerous place.

"People," he continued, clapping his fist into his palm, punctuating every word, "don't . . . understand . . . that . . . at . . . all . . . anymore."

Here is the situation as he remembers it:

"In my seven years in Defense—and this is not at all recognized any more—the Soviets sought to take West Berlin from the West, Khruschev introduced nuclear weapons into Cuba, the Egyptians were determined to destroy Israel, the Chinese were saying the U.S. was a 'paper tiger' and that they were going to fight 'wars of liberation' to turn the developing world communist. I mention this only to recreate the environment we were in."

But, McNamara said, the threat was not as great as the nation's leaders said it was.

"Vietnam fell to the Communists. The other dominoes— Malaysia, Thailand, Indonesia, India—didn't fall with the loss of Vietnam. Even if this had been as great a threat as many believed, the strategy and tactics we tried weren't appropriate to the threat."

Much of this book is an answer to the questions the protesters asked McNamara during the war. Some of those questions, probably the most painful, came in his own family. His three children at various times were associated with war protests.

"I lived in the world of protests," he said. "I understand the protesters: the immorality of the action, the killing of human beings. But they hadn't lived in the period we had, and they didn't understand what we thought was the threat to the West. It was very hard to bridge."

His intimacy with the antiwar movement forced him to look again at the old verities.

"Other people turned their backs on young people," said Michael Klare, a one-time Vietnam protester who now is a military specialist at Hampshire College. "McNamara wasn't able to do that because his children were there. He's saying the young people were right."

McNamara has faced a firestorm for his mea culpa; the nation's papers have been filled with letters to the editor, and some of them are piled neatly on the desk he took with him from the World Bank. There is resentment everywhere. With Vietnam, even contrition brings criticism.

"The man bores me," Irving Kristol, the neoconservative theorist, said in an interview.

"He looks bad, real bad," said Jack Christ, director of the leadership program at Ripon College in Wisconsin. "He was caught in a bad situation trying to be a good soldier. But when you hold him up against the heroes of history—Martin Luther King and all the civil-disobedience people—you expect more out of him."

"This is foolish and even pathetic," said Wolfgang J. Lehmann, who was U.S. consul general in the Mekong Delta before becoming the last deputy chief of the U.S. mission in Saigon. "We did not misjudge the geopolitical goals of our adversaries. And, of course, there was nationalism, but there was nationalism in the South, not just in the North."

And yet there are words of comfort, sometimes from the least likely places. The Vietnamese Foreign Ministry said that McNamara's book represents "a judgment suitable with the reality." There are others.

At first Busby, LBJ's aide, suspected that Johnson—who was exceedingly agitated by the publication of the Pentagon Papers in 1971—would feel betrayed by McNamara. "But so much time has passed," Busby said. "Johnson might be on the other side right now and be opposed to himself."

"People have been a little harsh," said William Sloane Coffin, one of the leading voices of protest in the Vietnam era. "They've allowed their natural feelings of resentment to take them over. The appropriate emotion is a gratitude: At last someone of his stature has made this apology. But the sad thing is that we could have used this kind of confession in 1968."

At base these discussions really aren't about Vietnam, or about Robert McNamara, at all. They are about leadership and responsibility, and on these subjects McNamara perhaps makes his most piercing points:

"The press, public and Congress throughout the time I was there all supported the war. Damn it, the leaders of this country aren't elected to respond to polls and the press and to follow solely the views of Congress. The leaders are elected to lead, and we led wrong.

"That was our responsibility," Robert S. McNamara said, "and we led in the wrong direction."

Comments by Professor Ernest R. May
at the John F. Kennedy School of Government,
Harvard University
April 25, 1995

PROFESSOR MAY: Thank you, Graham.* I want to make three quick points following the eloquent comments of my colleague, Tam Tai.

The first is a quite academic point. It is a criticism of Secretary McNamara's book. Though on the whole an excellent book, it involves too much clinical and rational retrospect. As he looks back and explains mistakes in judgment and policy, he fails adequately to re-create the frame of mind in which those mistakes were made.

Take the transition from the Eisenhower to the Kennedy administrations, which is described in some detail in the book. Here are the best and the brightest, not only of the Kennedy administration but of the Eisenhower administration, and they sit there and *believe*—they say to each other and *believe*—that the fate at least of Southeast Asia and perhaps of the civilized world hinges on what happens in Laos, a landlocked country of mountain hamlets, with three million people who, according to their own king, devoted themselves primarily to singing songs, making love, and raising opium.

There was a theology at the time, or at least a set of beliefs, that the book does not recapture. This makes it a little like a memoir by

---

*Professor May had been asked by Professor Graham Allison, chairman of the meeting at which I spoke, to comment on *In Retrospect*.

a crusader who cannot remember why he particularly cared about the fate of Jerusalem. That is a weakness in what is generally a splendid book.

My second point is an observation that the book is unique. I have tried to think of counterparts and cannot do so. No other memoir I know combines the two striking features of this one. The first such feature is the thoroughness of its research base. In some ways it is more a history than a memoir. It draws very heavily on documents. Where there is a document, Secretary McNamara will rely on that in preference to his memory. The scholarly character of the book is quite extraordinary.

The second striking feature of the book is the extent to which it confesses error. There are many memoirs in which people try to justify themselves and to explain what they did, but I do not know any other memoir devoted so fully and frankly to saying what was done wrongly. These features in combination—depth of research and forthrightness in describing mistakes—make this memoir like no other.

Lastly, I want to say that I think *In Retrospect* an extraordinarily useful and wise book. Many lessons have been drawn from Vietnam. They began to be drawn while the war was still going on. Many different lessons are drawn from many different perspectives. Someone once did a list of twenty-nine different lessons of Vietnam in wide circulation. Some contradict others. Some of those not necessarily consistent lessons remain powerful. They affected our debates about the Gulf War. They affect our debates about Bosnia. But most of the lessons prescribe what ought to be done or not done on an assumption that circumstances in the Gulf or in Bosnia or some other place are like circumstances in Vietnam. So we have a lesson that, if we intervene in the Gulf, we must do so in great force and get out very quickly. For Bosnia, we hear the lesson that we should not intervene in what can be characterized as a civil war. Such prescriptions may be right or wrong. Their wisdom depends on the circumstances in which they are applied.

But the lessons that Secretary McNamara draws in this book are lessons of broad application. They are not prescriptions that depend on circumstances. They are universally applicable lessons about how to think about public policy problems.

I would boil down his eleven precepts into two. The first is a precept that, in thinking about any foreign area or any government or organized force in the world that has a different history and a different culture, we need to think about its history and culture and not assume that thought and behavior will be like ours. We have to think about people in their own contexts.

The second precept is that, when we think about doing something in the world, we should always very closely inspect our own premises. Secretary McNamara says that, regarding Vietnam, premises were left unanalyzed. The proposition that this should never be allowed to happen is one of universal validity. It is not brand new. Oliver Cromwell made the same point vividly when he wrote the General Assembly of the Church of Scotland in 1650, "I beseech you in the bowels of Christ to consider that you may be wrong." It is nevertheless a point of tremendous importance yet constantly forgotten.

There is another lesson in the book, which is not among the eleven. It is, however, as important as any of these, especially because of the extent to which it runs against the conventional wisdom that is taught in this university and around the world about international relations. As I read Secretary McNamara's memoir, he says that his painful voyage through the Vietnam War was a voyage of discovery about the nature of government. He says or at least implies that the conduct of foreign policy and even of war is not primarily the conduct of relations with other governments; it is above all a matter of domestic leadership. That may be the most valuable lesson that this book conveys to readers both now and in generations to come. Thanks.

———

(Applause.)
(End of speech.)

"The Case for the War"
by W. W. Rostow
Times Literary Supplement (London)
June 9, 1995

For seven years, Robert McNamara and I were colleagues in the Kennedy and Johnson administrations. It is difficult to describe the ties that were formed as a result of our facing together the series of crises that confronted the United States in the 1960s. On occasion, my advice to the President differed from McNamara's, most notably on Vietnam and on policy towards Southeast Asia. Such differences among colleagues were inevitable and proper, however, and now, thirty years after we worked together, I continue to hold McNamara's devoted service in high regard.

In Retrospect: The Tragedy and Lessons of Vietnam begins with a dozen or so interesting but terse pages on the author's background: his schooling; his meeting, and marriage to, Margaret McKinstry Craig, to whose memory the book is dedicated; his war-time service as an air corps statistical control officer; and his post-war service with the Ford Motor Company. He had been president of that company for only seven weeks when John Kennedy made him Secretary of Defense in 1961. The problems of Vietnam from 1961 to early 1968 occupy virtually the rest of the book. Although the war lasted some eight more years, the story ends with McNamara's translation to the World Bank in 1968, as the Tet offensive begins.

In the period 1965–7, Robert McNamara came to believe that Vietnam was "a problem with no solution." This is the theme of his book. His frustration arose because the war was fought under five rules, which, as he saw it, proved incompatible with victory. These rules were: (1) that Southeast Asia as a whole must be kept from Communist control; (2) that U.S. troops should not be sent outside the borders of South Vietnam; (3) that the South Vietnamese should achieve political stability and—with U.S. tutelage and military aid—learn to defend themselves; (4) that the United States under no circumstances should initiate the use of nuclear weapons; and (5) that the enemy operated under the assumption that it could win "a long inconclusive war." In the face of these rules, McNamara came to believe that the United States should withdraw from Vietnam, because Rule 3 proved impossible of attainment, and the costs of withdrawal (Rule 1) would be tolerable. To a degree impossible to determine, his conclusion, by his own account, was influenced also by the anti-war sentiment in the country which extended to his immediate family.

As far as the South Vietnamese were concerned, McNamara found President Ngo Dinh Diem inscrutable; was much disturbed by the assassination of Diem and his brother and close collaborator, Ngo Diem Nhu; was rendered almost hopeless by the subsequent period, when one impotent government followed another; and quoted with approval a characterization by an American official that President Nguyen Van Thieu and Vice-President Nguyen Cao Ky were "the bottom of the barrel, absolutely the bottom of the barrel."

On the tolerability of pulling out American forces from Vietnam, McNamara relies heavily in arguing his conclusion, already arrived at, on a private memorandum to the President of September 12, 1967, from Richard Helms. This memorandum was recently declassified and released. Written by "an experienced intelligence analyst" in the CIA, it addressed the question, "Implications of an Unfavorable Outcome in Vietnam." The general conclusion of a thirty-three-page analysis was that the risks of withdrawal "are probably more limited and controllable than most previous argument has indicated." The specific conclusion about Southeast Asia was that "The most direct and immediate [implications] would be in the region of Southeast Asia itself." The key country would prove to be Thailand, where the situation would be "perilous and complicated."

On the U.S. domestic scene, the memorandum said:

The worst potential damage would be of the self-inflicted kind: internal dissension which would limit our future ability to use our power and resources wisely and to full effect, and lead to a loss of confidence by others in the American capacity for leadership.

Having concluded, then, that the South Vietnamese would be unable to defend themselves in any time that would not overstretch the patience of American public opinion, and that the costs of pulling out were tolerable, McNamara in retrospect feels we ought to have withdrawn our forces "either in late 1963 amid the turmoil following Diem's assassination or in late 1964 or early 1965 in the face of increasing political weakness in South Vietnam." He adds three other dates when a pull-out would have been possible and desirable: July 1965, December 1965 and December 1967.

At the end of the book, McNamara offers a list of eleven major failures in Vietnam policy, which follow closely his point of view in hindsight. There are also eight pages of reflection on post-Cold War military policy and a final word on Vietnam, the heart of which is:

Although we sought to do the right thing—and believed we were doing the right thing—in my judgment, hindsight proves us wrong. We both overestimated the effect of South Vietnam's loss on the security of the West and failed to adhere to the fundamental principle that, in the final analysis, if the South Vietnamese were to be saved, they had to win the war themselves.

This is as accurate a statement as I can muster of the author's present position.

McNamara's argument depends heavily on his view of the importance of Asia to the United States and the extent to which withdrawal from Vietnam would affect the balance of power in

Asia. At one point, referring to the human and material costs of the war, he asks:

Were such high costs justified?

Dean Rusk, Walt Rostow, Lee Kwan Yew and many other geo-politicians across the globe to this day answer yes. They conclude that without U.S. intervention in Vietnam, Communist hegemony—both Soviet and Chinese—would have spread farther through South and East Asia to include control of Indonesia, Thailand, and possibly India. Some would go further and say that the U.S.SR would have been led to take greater risks to extend its influence elsewhere in the world particularly in the Middle East, where it might well have sought control of the oil-producing nations. They might be correct, but I seriously question such judgments.

What these "geopoliticians" thought did not matter to the outcome. What Dwight Eisenhower, John Kennedy and Lyndon Johnson thought did matter. Each, from a different experience and per-spective, had thought deeply about Asia; and they had arrived at similar conclusions about the balance of power in that continent.

Eisenhower had served in the Philippines on General MacArthur's staff. His job required him to think about the strategic shape of Asia. It was he who mounted in 1954 the South-East Asia Treaty Organization (SEATO) as a bipartisan effort in the wake of the Korean War, designed to hold the balance of power in Southeast Asia as it was held in Northeast Asia by the outcome of the Korean War. It was he who first applied the phrase "domino theory" to the American engagement in what was French Indo-China. The day before Kennedy's Inaugural, he laid before the new President and his major aides (Rusk, McNamara and Dillon) the two serious problems he most wished them to understand: the balance of payments issue and Laos. Although there are several versions of what Eisenhower said about Laos, the evidence, on balance, is that he thought it likely that Kennedy would have to invoke the SEATO

Treaty and put troops into Laos: if possible, with others, if necessary, alone. Eisenhower, from 1961 to 1968, gave unfailing support to Presidents Kennedy and Johnson on Southeast Asia.

Kennedy's experience of Asia was quite different, although it brought him to similar conclusions. As a member of Congress, in the immediate aftermath of the Second World War, he was focused on the Soviet threat in Europe, and a repetition by Stalin of Hitler's attack on Western Europe. He did not vote for Truman's Point Four technical assistance program for the developing countries.

In 1951, when it was clear that the Communist attack in Korea was not a feint for an attack on Western Europe, and the truce negotiations had begun at Panmunjom, Kennedy went with members of his family on a tour of the Middle East, India and the Far East, including Vietnam. He returned convinced that the Communist threat would come mainly in the underdeveloped regions. He told his colleagues in the House of Representatives that he had been wrong on Point Four and subsequently supported it. And, in time, he believed China would succeed the Soviet Union as the main threat. He led support in the Senate during 1958 for the Indian Second Five-Year Plan with Senator John Sherman Cooper, a Republican Senator from Kentucky, who had also been Ambassador in India. At the time of the Cuban Missile Crisis, he created a special team to work in support of India over the concurrent clash in Ladakh, saying that in the long run this conflict might well be more important than the confrontation with the Soviet Union in the Caribbean.

All this background bears on the much debated question of whether or not Kennedy would have ended U.S. military involvement in Vietnam. He was clearly frustrated by the political performance of Diem and Nhu. On the other hand, he was against American encouragement of a coup, and was appalled when Diem and Nhu were killed in the coup that took place. That the two were killed in an American-made armored troop-carrier added to his unhappiness.

McNamara writes that it is "highly probable" that Kennedy

would have pulled U.S. forces out of Vietnam. But in the autumn of 1963, Kennedy said this to Walter Cronkite, harking back to his Asian trip of 1951:

> Our best judgment is that he [Diem] can't be successful on this basis. We hope that he comes to see that, but in the final analysis it is the people and the government [of South Vietnam] itself who have to win or lose this struggle. All we can do is help, and we are making it very clear, but I don't agree with those who say we should withdraw. That would be a great mistake. I know people don't like Americans to be engaged in this kind of an effort. Forty-seven Americans have been killed in combat with the enemy, but this is a very important struggle even though it is far away.

> We . . . made this effort to defend Europe. Now Europe is quite secure. We also have to participate—we may not like it—in the defense of Asia.

A week later, in a similar interview with David Brinkley, he was asked:

> "Mr. President, have you had any reason to doubt this so-called 'domino theory,' that if South Vietnam falls, the rest of Southeast Asia will go behind it?"

> "No, I believe it. I believe it. I think that the struggle is close enough. China is so large, looms so high just beyond the frontiers, that if South Viet-Nam went, it would not only give them an improved geographic position for a guerrilla assault on Malaya, but would also give the impression that the wave of the future in Southeast Asia was China and the communists. So I believe it."

The main weight of the war fell, of course, on President Johnson. His view of Asia came out of a quite different background. He had been briefly in Australia during the Second World War; and this experience led to a life-long sympathy and affection for that country. In the late 1950s, his view of Asia as a whole crystallized. The turning-point was the question of statehood for Hawaii. Johnson spoke of this matter during a speech at the East-West Center in Honolulu on October 18, 1966:

> My forebears came from Britain, Ireland, and Germany. People in my section of the country regarded Asia as totally alien in spirit as well as nationality. . . . We therefore looked away from the Pacific, away from its hopes as well as away from its great crises. Even the wars that many of us fought here were often [fought] with left overs of preparedness, and they did not heal our blindness. . . . One consequence of that blindness was that Hawaii was denied its rightful part in our Union of States for many, many years. Frankly, for two decades I opposed its admission as a State, until at last the undeniable evidence of history, as well as the irresistible persuasiveness of Jack Burns [the non-voting Hawaiian delegate to the Congress], removed the scales from my eyes. Then I began to work and fight for Hawaiian statehood. And I hold that to be one of the proudest achievements of my twenty-five years in Congress.

Later in the speech, he referred to Hawaii as "a model of how men and women of different races and different cultures can come and live and work together; to respect each other in freedom and in hope." The period of an intense and ultimately successful struggle for Hawaiian statehood (achieved in 1959) coincided with the emergence of Johnson as an effective civil rights leader in the Senate—with his critical role in the passage of the 1957 legislation, the first formal civil rights action by the Congress since the Civil War. The link in his mind between his positions on civil rights and on Asia remained throughout his life.

In May 1961, Johnson, as Vice President, was plunged still more deeply into the Asian scene. At Kennedy's request, he visited South Vietnam, Thailand, the Philippines, Taiwan, India and Pakistan. Johnson's recommendation to Kennedy was to create an organization of the free nations of the Pacific and Asia which would not only deal with defence issues but issues of social justice, housing, land reform: "the greatest danger Southeast Asia offers to nations like the United States is not the momentary threat of Communism itself, rather that danger stems from hunger, ignorance, poverty, and disease." It was this line of thought which led Johnson as President to deliver on April 7, 1965, his speech at Johns Hopkins University, from which the Asian Development Bank arose.

But a great deal was going on in Asia in 1964–5 which McNamara does not detail. Sukarno left the United Nations on January 7, 1965, and allied with Hanoi and Peking. Within Indonesia, he worked closely with Aidit, head of that country's Communist party. He launched the confrontation with Malaysia just as the first North Vietnamese regulars infiltrated South Vietnam. Some eighty ships of the British Commonwealth were mobilized to defend Malaysia. As McNamara said in a joint memorandum to the President with McGeorge Bundy on January 27, 1965: "The underlying difficulties in Saigon arise from the spreading conviction that the future is without hope for anti-communists." From one end of Asia to the other, the local people knew that a dangerous crisis was taking place in 1965 which could go one way or the other.

This was the setting in which McNamara and Bundy wrote their famous "Fork in the Road" memorandum at the end of January 1965. This memorandum told President Johnson that he had to choose between sending more troops to Vietnam or "negotiations aimed at salvaging what little can be preserved with no further addition to our present military risk." Both favored the first course. The memorandum played a significant role in President Johnson's reluctant decision in early 1965 to commit a substantial number of American troops to South Vietnam. It was a late and painful decision to match the escalating activity of the North Vietnamese regulars and Sukarno, an escalation which was, in turn, an opportunistic but understandable response to the disarray of South Vietnamese politics in the wake of the assassination of Diem and Nhu.

Is it credible that the United States would have withdrawn in the aftermath of a coup and assassination which were seen by the world to have been carried out with its acquiescence? Is it credible that any U.S. President would not respond to the Communist "nutcracker" of 1965; the simultaneous entrance of North Vietnamese regulars into South Vietnam and the enterprise of Sukarno in joining the supposed Communist wave of the future in Asia? I think not.

———

And so in Vietnam, General Westmoreland set about the slow work of building up an adequate logistical base, dealing with the Communist forces as he found them and as they were introduced and supplied via the Ho Chi Minh Trails in Laos. By the end of 1965, he had achieved a stalemate: about a million men, women and children in 1966 were added to those under the protection of the Vietnamese government. And this positive trend continued for most of 1967. The plan for the Tet offensive of 1968, hatched in the summer months of 1967, was Hanoi's reaction to the slowly eroding position in the South.

On September 29, 1967, President Johnson replied in San Antonio both to McNamara and to the "experienced intelligence analyst" who had written the memorandum sent to him a few weeks earlier by Richard Helms, the memorandum whose latter-day release made such a profound impression on McNamara:

> I cannot tell you tonight as your president—with certainty—that a Communist conquest of South Vietnam would be followed by a Communist conquest of Southeast Asia. But I do know there are North Vietnamese troops in Laos. I do know that there are North Vietnamese trained guerrillas tonight in Northeast Thailand. I do know that there are Communist-supported guerrilla forces operating in Burma. And a Communist coup was barely averted in Indonesia, the fifth largest nation in the world.
>
> So your American President cannot tell you with certainty that a Southeast Asia dominated by Communist power would bring a

third world war much closer to terrible reality. One could hope that this would not be so.

But all that we have learned in this tragic century strongly suggests to me that it would be so. As President of the United States, I am not prepared to gamble on the chance that it is not so. I am not prepared to risk the security—indeed, the survival of this American Nation on mere hope and wishful thinking. I am convinced that by seeing this struggle through now, we are greatly reducing the chances of a much larger war—perhaps a nuclear war. I would rather stand in Vietnam, in our time, and by meeting this danger now, and facing up to it, thereby reduce the danger for our children and for our grandchildren.

There is no doubt President Johnson was frustrated by his inability to bring the war to a quick conclusion. But he was heartened by the progress of the rest of Asia behind the barrier created by South Vietnam and her allies who were "holding aggression at bay."

From the beginning to the end of his time as President, Johnson was governed by the conclusion he had reached in the late 1950s: namely, that Asia—all of Asia—mattered greatly to the future of America and was worth fighting for and nurturing. When he went through Asia for three weeks at the end of 1966, he spoke at least 90 per cent of the time about the need for Asia to unite and organize, not about the struggle in Vietnam.

In the end, Johnson left for his successor a good post-Tet situation in the field, both military and political; but a difficult political situation at home. He met Thieu in Honolulu after he had announced, on March 31, that he would not run in 1968. He refused Thieu's offer to put in the joint communique that American forces would be reduced over the next year. He chose to leave that decision to his successor.

The Malaysian foreign minister, speaking retrospectively in Boston on November 11, 1981, first recalled the early days of the Association of South-East Asian Nations (ASEAN) between 1968 and 1975:

They were very useful years to further bind the member countries together. . . . In 1975 North Vietnamese tanks rolled past Danang, Cam Ranh Bay, and Ton Son Nut into Saigon. The United States withdrew their last soldiers from Vietnam, and the worst of ASEAN's fears which underscored the Bangkok Declaration of 1967 came to pass. But ASEAN by then had seven solid years of living in neighborly cooperation. Call it foresight, or what you will, the fact remains that with ASEAN solidarity there were no falling dominoes in Southeast Asia following the fall of Saigon to the Communists, and the United States withdrawal from Southeast Asia.

Both the NICs (Newly Industrialized Countries) and the ASEAN members roughly quadrupled their real GNP between 1960 and 1981. They were, socially and politically as well as economically, quite different countries to what they had been when Southeast Asia went through the crisis of 1965. McNamara does not deal with the importance of Southeast Asia or its dynamics in these critical years.

Another weakness of McNamara's book is his failure to discuss systematically the gift of sanctuary which rendered the war inevitably "long and inconclusive." There have been no examples in which a guerrilla war (or a war dependent on external supply) has been won in which one side was granted sanctuary by the other. The guerrilla wars in the Philippines under Magsaysay and the British effort in Malaysia were successful because one was a group of islands, while the other had a narrow neck of land to the north and sea supply for the guerrillas in Malaysia was denied. On the other hand, Napoleon met his first setback in the Peninsular War when the British helped the guerrillas; the guerrillas in Algeria were helped through Morocco and Tunisia; and the United States and others helped the Afghan defenders against the Russians through Pakistan.

South Vietnam was explicitly protected, by the Laos Accords of 1962, from the North Vietnamese transiting of Laos and Cambodia, via the Ho Chi Minh Trails and the Cambodian ports. This was not an understanding whispered in the corridors of the Palais des Nations, but a formal agreement between Ambassador Pushkin of the Soviet Union and Averell Harriman, who negotiated the treaty. It called for the Soviet Union to guarantee that no third party be transited by Hanoi in supply to the guerrillas in the South.

The North Vietnamese did not obey the Laos Accords for a single day after they came into force in early October 1962, nor did the Soviet government ever act on its freely taken responsibilities. October 1962 was the month of the Cuban missile crisis; and it led to a visit to Washington by Anastas Mikoyan, fresh from a rather miserable experience in Havana. There were those who urged President Kennedy to confront the Soviet Union immediately over its failure to act on its Laos Treaty commitments. They were turned down. It was not difficult to explain President Kennedy's reluctance to act in the wake of the traumatic confrontation in the Caribbean; but the alternative put to President Kennedy was to act decisively now or face a crisis "in a waning situation."

General Maxwell Taylor had all this in mind when he sent a long cable at the end of 1964 that included this passage:

> It [Hanoi] enjoys the priceless asset of a protected logistic sanctuary in the DRV and in Laos. I do not recall in history a successful anti-guerrilla campaign with less than a 10 to 1 numerical superiority over the guerrillas and without the elimination of assistance from outside the country.

Senator John Stennis echoed this point in August 1967: "The question is growing in the Congress as to whether it is wise to send more men if we are going to just leave them at the mercy of the guerrilla war without trying to cut off the enemy's supplies more effectively."

And McNamara himself quotes General DuPuy, General Westmoreland's planner, in a 1986 interview: ". . . it turned out that it [search and destroy] was a faulty concept, given the sanctuaries, given the fact that the Ho Chi Minh Trail was never closed. It was a losing concept of operation." Thus, the sanctuary granted Hanoi was historically incompatible with American and South Vietnamese victory in a time-span consistent with American patience as a nation; and the bombing of the supply trails or other devices to reduce the flow from North Vietnam were demonstrably inadequate.

Those who advocated blocking the trails on the ground believed that action would force a concentration of North Vietnamese troops to keep the trails open, and two or three reinforced U.S. divisions together with air supremacy could deal with them. This happened, incidentally, at Khe Sanh, where Hanoi concentrated during the Tet offensive several divisions (some think five) which were defeated by some 6,000 U.S. and Vietnamese forces plus air power intelligently directed by General Momyer. This reversed at Khe Sanh the normal proportions of guerrillas versus the defending force.

———

This proposal was definitively turned down on April 27, 1967, by President Johnson and Secretaries Rusk and McNamara, presumably on the grounds that any movement of American troops to block infiltration on the trails would bring the Russians and Chinese into the war.

On this matter General William Westmoreland (whom McNamara quotes) may have the last word:

> . . . the geographic restraints on the ground war were very real, and understandable.

> Yet if you'll look at the situation as it's turned out, we basically attained our strategic objectives. We stopped the flow of communism. . . . I conclude that by strength, awkwardness, and good luck, most of our strategic objectives have been reached. I also say that we have to give President Johnson credit for not allowing the war to expand geographically . . . he was quite fearful that this was going to escalate into a world war. One of his main strategic objectives was to confine the war. He did not want it to spread. . . . Having said that, that's not the way I felt at the time. I felt that our hands were tied.

Historians will have to decide in the light of President Johnson's conclusion at San Antonio whether that price was worth paying. Clearly, if the alternative might have been a larger war or the risk of nuclear war, it was worth paying. In any case, Johnson was following the rules governing the policy of containment: block the extension of Communist rule while minimizing the likelihood of nuclear war. McNamara refers to, but does not discuss, this central issue.

Considering that he is writing in the 1990s, McNamara's view of the Vietnamese is remarkably static. It stops in early 1968, if not earlier. In fact, the whole period 1954–75 was highly dynamic in South Vietnam. Vietnam was an underdeveloped, post-colonial country. Like Syngman Rhee in Korea, its first nationalist ruler earned his legitimacy by having nothing to do with the occupying power. Diem was also a mandarin to whom the sharing of power outside the family was extremely awkward. Each president was followed by a series of weak rulers and then their countries found relative stability with men of the next generation—in Korea under Park, in Vietnam under Thieu and Ky from 1965.

Starting in September 1966, a political process was started. A Constituent Assembly was elected to draft a constitution. Despite Communist intimidation, 81 percent of the population voted, out of 5.3 million registered. On September 3, 1967, a well-inspected presidential election was held. The Thieu-Ky ticket won with 34.8 percent of the votes. Typical of an underdeveloped country, there were ten civilian candidates. Registration had increased 11 percent since the vote of the previous year. Fifty-seven percent of the population of the country of voting age took part. Ambassador Dobrynin of the Soviet Union was almost precisely accurate when he said before the election that the Popular Front candidate commended by the Communists would get 16 percent of the vote. The rest were explicitly anti-Communist.

———

The Tet offensive is not dealt with in McNamara's book, except for one reference at the end to the attack on the U.S. Embassy compound. Thieu was in the Delta when the Tet offensive struck late in January 1968: but Ky and Robert Komer, Westmoreland's deputy for civilian affairs, led in the clean-up of Saigon, where many refugees congregated. American and Vietnamese marines cleared Hue, where the North Vietnamese had established a foothold in the Citadel. And most remarkable of all, it was the local police and militia that picked up the Communist forces which attacked thirty-four of the forty-four provincial capitals, five of the six autonomous cities, seventy-one of 242 district capitals, and fifty hamlets. Thus the Communists failed to produce the uprising they expected. Thieu mobilized an additional 122,000 men for the armed forces in the first half of 1968. The South Vietnamese remained steady. Tet was an utter military and political defeat for the Communists in Vietnam, yet a political disaster in the United States. The conventional American view was that the South Vietnamese government's military, economic and social program was set back by some years.

This program had resulted in a revolution in education, where school enrollment increased massively, for example, from 410,000 to 2.7 million in primary education, starting in 1954. There were similar advances made over the same period in agriculture, trade and industry. The South Vietnam of 1969 was not the same country it was in 1954, 1961 or even 1967. I have no doubt that it would have followed the development path of South Korea if it had not been caught up in a difficult war and then Communist rule.

As for the military, it is essential to understand that neither North nor South Vietnam produced any armaments at all. Essentially, however, the war was fought with weapons imported into Vietnam by their respective allies. As time passed, the average skill of the Vietnamese divisions improved, although they continued to vary greatly according to their commanding officers. This uneven but improving force, under General Abram's tutelage, was tested by the battle with the North Vietnamese of 1972. American ground forces had been withdrawn, leaving only air and naval units in support of the South Vietnamese. The North Vietnamese were generously supported by Soviet tanks and artillery superior to those available to the South Vietnamese, as well as many anti-aircraft guns. It was in the context of this battle that President Nixon used B-52s against Hanoi, mined the harbor at Haiphong and attacked the railway lines leading to China from Hanoi. The upshot was a military victory on the ground for the South Vietnamese.

In 1973, an accord was negotiated between North and South Vietnam. The North licked its wounds, paved the supply trails through Laos, and watched the American air and naval units withdraw on President Nixon's promise of $2.2 billion dollars in military aid to complete the process of Vietnamization of the South Vietnam military.

Lee Kwan Yew of Singapore was a kind of Greek chorus for the Asians throughout this period. In 1965, when all of Southeast Asia was menaced, he had remarked that "We may all go through the mincing machine." In 1966, he said to a group of students after noting that the Americans were buying time for a united Asia to emerge: "If we just sit down and believe people are going to buy time forever after for us, then we deserve to perish." In 1967, ASEAN was founded. In April 1973, at the National Press Club, Lee Kwan Yew laid out the alternatives in the following terms:

At the risk of being proved wrong, there are three scenarios I envisage as a result of the Paris agreement. First, . . . the provisions are in the main honored. . . . In this case, the contest will become primarily political. The South Vietnamese government stands a very fair chance in such a contest. Second, an all-out offensive by both the North Vietnamese and the Vietcong as soon as they believe they are strong enough to overwhelm the armed forces of the South Vietnamese government. . . . Third, the North Vietnamese, to avoid unnecessary risks, ostensibly honor the Paris agreement. However, they will leave it to the Vietcong, with North Vietnamese infiltrators and fresh military supplies to augment their strength, to make a bid for power in the South. . . . But, if the worst does happen, and the Vietcong, with the help of the North Vietnamese, do gain control over the South in the middle 1970s, it does not necessarily follow that the rest of

Southeast Asia will go communist. The morale of the other peoples of Southeast Asia is now very different from what it was after Dien Bien Phu in 1954. The Thais are now more prepared psychologically to face up to such a situation. . . . A crucial factor is whether they believe they can depend on American military and economic aid, as spelled out under the Guam doctrine.

For reasons which no one could have predicted in the spring of 1973, before Watergate had progressively undermined Nixon's authority and legitimacy, it was Lee's second scenario that came to pass in the mid-1970s. The simple fact is that, as of April 1975, the American public, with the China *détente* established, was prepared to end its involvement with Vietnam; and Southeast Asia was prepared to stand on its own feet. Second, the South Vietnamese did all that could be expected of them in the post-Diem period; and as time passes, they will deserve better of history than McNamara allows.

One returns to the wild card in this story: the manner in which the United States, including McNamara's own family, were driven into painful controversy over the war. And that is a part of the equation that all Americans must weigh for themselves. In fact, only McNamara can weigh all the factors which have driven him into the position that, whatever the cost, the United States should have withdrawn its troops from Vietnam.

With the exception of the Second World War, every conflict in which Americans have been engaged has involved public controversy. And this is to their credit; for who wants war? In the Revolutionary War, perhaps one-third of the people wanted independence; one third were pro-British; and one-third were simply out to make a fast buck by selling supplies to the Continental army. In the war of 1812, the New England states, after the Hartford Convention, passed a resolution calling for withdrawal from the union rather than joining in the war against Canada. The Mexican War stirred great controversy in the United States. The Civil War split the nation from top to bottom. The Spanish-American War was followed by the unpopular conflict with the Philippine guerrillas. The First World War, like the Civil War, touched off draft riots. The Korean War left Truman more unpopular than either Nixon at the nadir of his fortunes, or Lyndon Johnson at his lowest point in the polls.

No one has promised that American independence itself, or America's role as a bastion for those who believe deeply in democracy, could be achieved without pain or loss or controversy. The pain, loss and controversy resulting from Vietnam were accepted for ten years by the American people. That acceptance held the line so that a free Asia could survive and grow; for, in the end, the war and the treaty which led to it were about who would control the balance of power in Asia, an issue which was evidently at stake in the Asian crisis of 1965 and thereafter. Those who died or were wounded in Vietnam or are veterans of that conflict were not involved in a pointless war.

"McNamara's War In Retrospect"
by James Galbraith
Texas Observer
August 10, 1995

Not many of the thousand people who crowded to hear Robert McNamara at the LBJ Library in Austin on May 1 could have yet read his book. None, of course, had missed the torrent of invective that accompanied its publication.

McNamara's assailants had come from all sides. *The New York Times* trotted out that old catch-phrase "the best and the brightest," recasting itself as the voice of the sixties war critics, though it was no such thing. On the left, commentators treated that spectacle with contempt; "War Criminal says Sorry, Sobs" was the headline on Alexander Cockburn's *Times*-bashing column in *The Nation*. Among McNamara's few defenders, CIA veteran and whistleblower John Stockwell wondered whether this might be the last time a senior policymaker admits to error on such a subject.

At the Library, McNamara engaged mainly in that rare but important psycho-social spectacle: the high official who accepts responsibility. No doubt this is the chief legacy of *In Retrospect*. Though equally galling to old colleagues (who disagree) and old war critics (who knew it all along), McNamara's statement that the Vietnam war was "terribly, terribly wrong" was a landmark, the kind of thing that history books twenty and thirty years from now will not be able to ignore.

But there is another dimension to McNamara and his book. What contribution do they make to history? Here the critics have been equally harsh, and yet they have so far entirely overlooked an issue on which McNamara's position stands at odds with almost everything yet written about Vietnam. This issue surfaces in Chapter Three, "The Fateful Fall of 1963," which McNamara summarizes in these words:

> "A pivotal period of U.S. involvement in Vietnam, punctuated by three important events: the overthrow and assassination of South Vietnam's president Ngo Dinh Diem; President Kennedy's decision on October 2 to begin the withdrawal of U.S. forces; and his assassination fifty days later."

This issue came up at the Library, in a question sent up from the audience and read by Austin TV newscaster Neal Spelce. If Kennedy did intend eventually to withdraw the combat advisers then in Vietnam, Spelce asked, why did the withdrawal not occur?

It was a reasonable question, which McNamara did *not* answer. Instead, he jumped straight to a description of the "very important" National Security Council meeting of October 2, 1963, at which, McNamara told the audience, as indeed he stipulates in the book, President Kennedy *decided* three things. They were (1) a complete withdrawal of U.S. forces from Vietnam "by December 31, 1965"; (2) a first-phase withdrawal of 1,000 troops "by the end of 1963"; and (3) a public announcement, to put the decision "in concrete."

How did McNamara know (or confirm his memory) that Kennedy had "decided" these things? Answer: there is a tape of this meeting, recorded on Kennedy's White House taping system, "just like Nixon's," McNamara said. The tape resides in the Kennedy Presidential Library in Boston. It is accessible, McNamara said, only through the Kennedy family, which granted access to McNamara and his coauthor Brian VanDeMark.

Why is the issue important? Because virtually *none* of the dozens of books on Vietnam decision-making in thirty years includes the story of Kennedy's decision to withdraw, nor the logically implied story of why that decision was not put into effect. It is not in David Halberstam's *The Best and the Brightest,* not in Stanley Karnow's

Vietnam, not in Richard Reeves' *President Kennedy,* not in any of the scholarly volumes.

Instead, *all* of the previous sources, except three, maintain that Kennedy's policy was one of unbroken commitment to Vietnam, and that Lyndon Johnson's policy was a smooth continuation of JFK's. An early dissent, Peter Dale Scott's 1972 *The War Conspiracy,* disappeared long ago. Arthur Schlesinger's 1978 *Robert Kennedy and His Times* tells the story, but in brief. And there is John M. Newman's 1992 *JFK and Vietnam,* a book of compelling scholarship that was prominently reviewed and vigorously attacked when it appeared, prompting among other things a whole book of rebuttal from no less than Noam Chomsky. Incredibly, Newman's book is already out of print.

Now comes McNamara, with confirmation of Newman's argument and the flat statement that there exists a tape as proof. McNamara's book spells out the story of the October 2 meeting (including direct quotation referenced to the tape). He omits mention of the NSC meeting of October 5, which formalized the October 2 decision, and of National Security Action Memorandum 263, issued on October 11 and available since 1971 in the Gravel edition of the *Pentagon Papers,* which codified it. Details of this chronology are, however, laid out carefully by Newman. And McNamara himself is on record as far back as July 1986, confirming Kennedy's decision to withdraw, in an oral history closely held since then by the Kennedy Library, but released by McNamara to Newman in 1993. McNamara's oral history makes plain, though his book fudges the issue, that Kennedy's decision was based on McNamara's own recommendation to withdraw *in spite of the fact that the U.S. was losing the war.*

So, to Spelce's question: why did the withdrawal not occur? To this, McNamara only said, "it's in the book." And it is. Lyndon Johnson, in line with the military and intelligence chiefs, had other ideas. On November 24, 1963, he told Ambassador Cabot Lodge that his priority was to "win the war." On November 26, he signed NSAM 273, which (as McNamara also confirms) was the authorization for direct, U.S.-controlled covert operations against North

Vietnam, known as OPLAN 34A. The proposal for such operations was as McNamara writes "first raised [to the Cabinet] at the November 20, 1963 Honolulu conference"—a proposal (by whom?) for escalation at a moment when presidential policy was formally committed to phased withdrawal, and would be for another six days.

McNamara himself has no evident axe to grind in presenting these facts. He nowhere tries to exculpate himself, nor to lift Kennedy above Johnson, nor to disparage his colleagues in either administration. He makes reference to none of the established history from which he departs so sharply. And the facts he presents are oddly incongruous with the larger psycho-social posture that he strikes—for they show that at the crucial moment McNamara himself, along with Kennedy, had decided to end the war.

All of this creates problems for those, especially one might say on the left, who continue to hold to the established version of history (according to which the reservations Kennedy expressed about Vietnam, to his staff and to Senators such as Mike Mansfield and Wayne Morse, were never reflected in presidential action). If McNamara were making things up, things which can now easily be checked against his citations, what could possibly be his motive?

McNamara's narrative thus calls into question the integrity of our history on this issue of high policy, longstanding myth and deep suspicion. It calls attention to the fact that issues which touch deeply on the reputations of American political leaders—especially the once-magical image of John F. Kennedy—remain unresolved.

Will professional historians now correct the incomplete or, in some cases, flawed record left to us by themselves and (often as part of otherwise admirable books) by the pioneering journalists such as Halberstam, Karnow and Reeves? Will the journalists who have written on McNamara and his book now revisit the "Fateful Fall of 1963" and take account of what McNamara actually says about it? Will textbook writers do the same?

More important, will the government now release *all* of the still-classified records surrounding Vietnam and other military decision-making, including nuclear policy, in the fall of 1963, including *all* records of the Honolulu conference of November 20–21, and *all* tapes from the Kennedy and Johnson White Houses? Can there be any justification for withholding such documents and transcripts now that McNamara has provided direct quotation from them?

· "Did He Help With the Healing?"
by Richard Rusk
Washington Post
April 26, 1995

Two decades after the American withdrawal from Vietnam, 27 years since my father, former secretary of state Dean Rusk, left office, the Vietnam War explodes again in the national consciousness, thanks to Robert McNamara's new book.

"This is the book I planned never to write," wrote McNamara in *In Retrospect: The Tragedy and Lessons of Vietnam*. But at age 79, he changed his mind. "We must tell the American people why their government and its leader behaved as we did." He implores us all "to learn from that experience."

I first met Robert McNamara in January 1961 at the swearing-in ceremony for John Kennedy's new Cabinet. I was a squirt-faced kid of fourteen. I met him again in 1985 at his office in Washington, D.C., while researching my dad's memoirs, published under the title *As I Saw It*.

Our paths crossed once more last Sunday night, this time on a radio talk show in Sacramento, California. Bob McNamara wasn't on the air, but Ron Kovic was. On Christmas Eve in 1964, Ron and I rode a Greyhound bus from boot camp to Washington, D.C., two young Marines going home for the holidays.

I had forgotten the bus ride and Ron Kovic. He wasn't yet famous. Ron hadn't yet gone to Nam, been horribly wounded or written *Born on the Fourth of July*.

"Hey, Ron," I asked last Sunday. "What's it like having Oliver Stone and Tom Cruise make a movie about your life?"

"Incredible!" said Kovic.

That was the easy question. The tough one was asked by radio host Phil Angeles:

"Does it help with the healing?" Angeles queried us. "Should McNamara have written this book?"

McNamara's published mea culpa—"we were wrong, terribly wrong"—has gut-punched many Americans, especially Vietnam vets.

"Why now?" demand his critics. "Why didn't McNamara do anything about the war while in office?"

I can't speak for Bob McNamara beyond restating his written views. But I know something about my father's views. He too was an "architect" of the Vietnam War. Critics dubbed it "Dean Rusk's War" as much as "Robert McNamara's War."

"It was 'Ho Chi Minh's War,' " my father always insisted.

My dad remembered Ron Kovic and his Vietnam Veterans Against the War. They had hurled their medals from the steps of the Capitol in angry and bitter protest. It was a searing moment.

"They compelled our attention," my dad said.

But they didn't change his mind about Vietnam.

Years later I asked my father point-blank:

"Pop, why didn't you change your mind about the war?"

It was a central question of *As I Saw It* and a riddle for me. In five years of research and long hours talking with my dad, I never heard his "mea culpa" about Vietnam. He went to his grave last Dec. 20 with no public apologies and no confessions. There were no private ones either.

"I believed in those decisions at the time they were made," explained my father. "There is nothing I can say now that would diminish my share of responsibility. I live with that, and others can make of it what they will."

"We all made decisions we came to regret," he added. "But I

feel that I owe my primary allegiance to my two presidents, to the men and women we sent to South Vietnam, and to the cause they tried their best to serve."

My dad's staunchness won him grudging respect as the years went by. But somehow, failing to change his mind became a kind of virtue. And in this same curious alchemy, changing one's mind—i.e., Bob McNamara—became a vice. For me, my dad's resoluteness in supporting a doomed cause was neither good nor bad, just part of the continuing tragedy of Vietnam.

As much as I loved my father and revere his memory, honesty compels me to say more.

I have no secret wisdom with which to unravel these mysteries. But in this son's perspective, one thing was never acknowledged by my father, McNamara, McGeorge Bundy, Clark Clifford, George Ball or any of those with whom I talked.

Let's call it the "psychology of command decision-making."

By the mid and late '60s, Americans by the thousands were dying in Vietnam. My dad and Bob McNamara made decisions that sent young men to their deaths. They had the blood of thousands on their consciences.

Once American troops were committed, there would be no turning back, goes the syndrome. And thus began the process by which "one dead American begets another dead American," wrote David Halberstam.

From a son's perspective, I often wondered: What choice did my dad have, once the buildup had begun and the coffins started coming home to small towns all across America? What choice did he have, this decent, humane father of mine to whom the sanctity of human life was all-important?

His taciturn nature, which served him well in negotiating with heads of state, ill prepared him for the wrenching, introspective, soul-shattering journey that a true reappraisal of Vietnam policy would have involved.

For all my father's strength and courage and intelligence, changing his mind on Vietnam was something he just couldn't do.

Although trained for high office, he was unprepared for such a journey, for admitting that thousands of lives might have been lost in vain.

He couldn't do it. He just couldn't do it. That is how I saw it.

And that is what I read to him in our final draft.

"That's bull——!" my father roared. In our 48 years together I had never heard him use the phrase.

It may well have been. And maybe I was practicing "pop psychology" as Pop suggested.

———

But the fact remains: Of that small circle who made Vietnam policy in the '60s, only one was able to stare into the abyss, challenge his own assumptions and confront that horrible question:

"What if I am wrong?"

That man was Robert McNamara.

He may have been weak in conversion, irresolute in pressing his doubts. But a shattered Bob McNamara did try to change policy. He lost that argument within the administration, out of public view, and resigned—or was fired—in 1967.

There was another panelist on Sunday's talk show who thought McNamara had done right—a former Marine who also knows something about sin and confession and courage—and laying bare one's soul. Thirty-one years ago, we rode a Greyhound bus together.

Ron Kovic.

"Over the long run," Ron said, "McNamara's book and his comments will promote healing.

"As Americans, we must all embrace McNamara.

"We must all welcome him home."

Personae

DEAN ACHESON Secretary of state in the Truman administration, 1949–1953; thereafter, an influential member of the nation's foreign policy elite until his death in 1969. Counseled President Johnson on Vietnam as a member of the Wise Men, 1965–1968.

RAYMOND AUBRAC French left-wing Socialist, former Resistance member, and longtime friend of Ho Chi Minh who, along with Herbert Marcovich, served as intermediaries to North Vietnam during the Pennsylvania peace initiative, July–October 1967.

GEORGE W. BALL Undersecretary of state in the Kennedy and Johnson administrations, 1961–1966. Former legal counsel to the French government. Believed U.S. interests in Europe far overshadowed those in Asia.

ERNEST R. BREECH Executive vice president of Ford Motor Company, 1946–1960.

DAVID K. E. BRUCE One of the most senior U.S. foreign policy officials of the 1960s. Ambassador to Great Britain during the Kennedy and Johnson administrations.

MCGEORGE BUNDY Harvard professor and dean who served as national security adviser to Presidents Kennedy and Johnson, 1961–1966.

Remained an outside adviser to LBJ and a member of the Wise Men, 1966–1968.

WILLIAM P. BUNDY Elder brother of McGeorge Bundy. Heavily involved in Vietnam policy making as assistant secretary of defense for international security affairs during the Kennedy administration and assistant secretary of state for Far Eastern affairs during the Johnson administration.

ELLSWORTH BUNKER American businessman and diplomat who served as U.S. ambassador to South Vietnam under Presidents Johnson and Nixon, 1967–1973.

GEORGE A. CARVER, JR. CIA intelligence analyst on Southeast Asia during the 1960s. Frequently briefed senior advisers and the Wise Men on the Vietnam situation.

CLARK M. CLIFFORD Washington attorney and adviser to Democratic presidents since Truman. Counseled LBJ on Vietnam as an outside adviser and member of the Wise Men, 1965–1967. Appointed secretary of defense in March 1968.

WILLIAM E. COLBY CIA station chief in Saigon, 1959–1962. Became the agency's leading expert on Vietnam and directed its counterguerrilla program in the South. Later served as director of the CIA in the Nixon and Ford administrations.

JOHN B. CONNALLY, JR. Political associate of Lyndon Johnson who became secretary of the navy in the Kennedy administration, 1961–1962. Later served as governor of Texas and treasury secretary in the Nixon administration.

CHARLES DE GAULLE Leader of Free French forces during World War II and postwar leader of France. Favored neutralization of Vietnam and criticized America's deepening military involvement in Indochina during the 1960s.

EVERETT M. DIRKSEN Republican senator from Illinois and senate minority leader during the 1960s. Supported the Johnson administration's policy on Vietnam.

BERNARD B. FALL Widely respected French-born Indochina scholar and commentator. Initially supported U.S. policy in Vietnam, but grew increasingly skeptical and critical. Killed while reporting in South Vietnam in 1967.

HENRY FORD II Grandson of automotive pioneer Henry Ford and chairman of the board of Ford Motor Company, 1945–1987. Hired McNamara and the other Whiz Kids after World War II.

MICHAEL V. FORRESTAL Son of the first secretary of defense, James V. Forrestal, aide to W. Averell Harriman, and NSC staff member, 1962–1965. Favored ouster of the Ngo brothers from power in South Vietnam.

ABE FORTAS Washington lawyer, Supreme Court justice (1965–1969), and member of LBJ's Kitchen Cabinet. Advised Johnson on Vietnam and other matters.

J. WILLIAM FULBRIGHT Democratic senator from Arkansas, 1945–1975, and chairman of the Senate Foreign Relations Committee. Shepherded the Tonkin Gulf Resolution through Congress in 1964. Later turned against the war and held hearings criticizing it.

ROSWELL L. GILPATRIC Wall Street lawyer and former Truman administration official who served as deputy secretary of defense, 1961–1964. Headed an interagency review of Vietnam policy in spring of 1961.

ARTHUR J. GOLDBERG Secretary of labor (1961–1962), Supreme Court Justice (1962–1965), and U.S. ambassador to the United Nations (1965–1968). Pushed for negotiations with North Vietnam.

BARRY GOLDWATER Conservative senator from Arizona and Republican candidate for president in 1964, who campaigned on a stridently anti-Communist platform; resoundingly defeated by Lyndon Johnson. Heatedly criticized restraints on U.S. military operations in Vietnam.

ANDREW J. GOODPASTER Military assistant to President Eisenhower, member of the Joint Staff during the Johnson administration, and later supreme allied commander in Europe. Led a study of American military operations in Vietnam in the summer of 1965.

WALLACE M. GREENE, JR. Commandant of U.S. Marine Corps, 1964–1968.

PAUL D. HARKINS Commander, U.S. Military Assistance Command, Vietnam, 1962–1964. Opposed the coup against Diem. Consistently optimistic about progress in the war against the Vietcong.

W. AVERELL HARRIMAN Assistant secretary of state for Far Eastern affairs and undersecretary of state for political affairs under President Kennedy and special ambassador under President Johnson. Headed U.S. delegations to Geneva Conference on Laos (1962) and Paris peace talks on Vietnam (1968). Supported the overthrow of Diem.

RICHARD HELMS Deputy director for plans of CIA (1962–1965), director of the CIA (1966–1973). Advised the president on the political and military situation in South Vietnam and the effectiveness of bombing against North Vietnam.

ROGER HILSMAN, JR. Harriman's successor as assistant secretary of state for Far Eastern affairs, 1963–1964. Played a key role in promoting the coup against Diem.

HO CHI MINH Communist leader of the modern Vietnamese independence movement. Led the Vietminh in war against France, 1946–1954, and North Vietnam and the Vietcong in the war against South Vietnam and the United States from 1954 until his death in 1969.

HAROLD K. JOHNSON U.S. Army chief of staff, 1964–1968. Questioned bombing's effectiveness in debates with other chiefs. Favored rapid ground buildup in Vietnam.

LYNDON BAINES JOHNSON Thirty-sixth president of the United States, 1963–1969. Opposed the coup against Diem as vice president under Kennedy; deepened U.S. military involvement in Vietnam as president. A domestic reformer whose political consensus was shattered by the war.

U. ALEXIS JOHNSON Career ambassador who served as deputy ambassador to South Vietnam under Maxwell Taylor in 1964–1965.

NICHOLAS DEB. KATZENBACH Acting attorney general (1964–1965) and undersecretary of state (1966–1969). Defended President Johnson's right to commit U.S. forces to Vietnam under the Tonkin Gulf Resolution. Advocated a negotiated solution to the war.

GEORGE F. KENNAN Head of the State Department's Policy Planning Staff in the late 1940s who conceived the strategy of containment to block Soviet expansion. This strategy became the basis of Western security during the Cold War. Later ambassador to the Soviet Union (1952) and Yugoslavia (1961–1963).

JOHN F. KENNEDY Born 1917. Thirty-fifth president of the United States, 1961–1963. Presided over U.S. policy during the era of mounting guerrilla activity in South Vietnam and the deterioration of Diem regime. Assassinated November 22, 1963—three weeks after the death of Diem.

ROBERT F. KENNEDY Born 1925. Attorney general (1961–1964) and Democratic senator from New York (1965–1968). JFK's closest adviser. Became increasingly critical of U.S. involvement in Vietnam. Assassinated while seeking the Democratic nomination for president in June 1968.

NIKITA S. KHRUSHCHEV Leader of the Soviet Union, 1958–1964. Supported "national liberation" wars in the Third World. Confronted the United States during the Cuban Missile Crisis in October 1962.

HENRY A. KISSINGER Harvard professor who served as the U.S. intermediary in the Pennsylvania peace initiative in 1967. Appointed national security adviser by President Nixon, in which capacity he negotiated the 1973 Paris Accords, ending U.S. involvement in the Vietnam War. Secretary of state in the Nixon and Ford administrations.

ROBERT W. KOMER NSC staff member (1960–1965), special assistant to President Johnson (1965–1966), and director of the U.S. pacification program in South Vietnam (1967–1968).

ALEXEI KOSYGIN Premier of the Soviet Union, 1964–1980. Served with British Prime Minister Harold Wilson as intermediary between the United States and North Vietnam in 1967. Met with American officials at Glassboro, New Jersey, in June 1967 to discuss limiting the strategic arms race.

LEE KWAN YEW Prime minister of Singapore, 1965–1990. Supported U.S. intervention in Vietnam, viewing it as a necessary check to Communist expansion in South and East Asia.

CURTIS E. LEMAY U.S. Air Force chief of staff (1961–1965) and George Wallace's vice presidential running mate in 1968. Pressed for unrestricted air attacks against North Vietnam.

LIN BIAO Chinese defense minister during the Vietnam War. Delivered a major speech in September 1965 urging guerrilla wars throughout the Third World. Died in a mysterious airplane crash in 1971.

HENRY CABOT LODGE, JR. Former Republican senator and vice presidential candidate who served two tours as U.S. ambassador to South Vietnam—the first, 1963–1964; the second, 1965–1967. Played a key role in the overthrow of the Diem regime.

ROBERT A. LOVETT Assistant secretary of war for air during World War II—including direction of the unit of which McNamara was a part—undersecretary of state (1947–1949), and secretary of defense during the Korean War (1951–1953). Counseled Presidents Kennedy and Johnson on national security issues, including Vietnam. Member of the Wise Men, 1965–1968.

MAI VAN BO North Vietnamese diplomatic official in Paris during the 1960s. Served as Hanoi's contact with the United States in various negotiating initiatives, including those involving Henry Kissinger in 1967.

MIKE MANSFIELD Democratic senator from Montana (1945–1977) and Senate majority leader (1961–1977). Early supporter of Diem. Later turned against the war.

MAO ZEDONG Leader of Communist China, 1949–1976. Provided political and logistical assistance to North Vietnam during the Vietnam War. Plunged China into the Cultural Revolution, 1966–1976.

HERBERT MARCOVICH French scientist and Pugwash member who, along with Raymond Aubrac, worked as an intermediary to North Vietnam during the 1967 Pennsylvania project.

JOHN J. MCCLOY Assistant secretary of war under FDR; president of the World Bank and American proconsul in occupied Germany under Truman. Advised LBJ on Vietnam as one of the Wise Men.

JOHN A. MCCONE California industrialist, Atomic Energy Commission official during the Eisenhower administration, and CIA director under Presidents Kennedy and Johnson, 1961–1965.

DAVID L. MCDONALD U.S. chief of naval operations, 1963–1967. Favored air strikes against North Vietnam in 1964, supported U.S. intervention in the ground war.

JOHN T. MCNAUGHTON Pentagon general counsel (1962–1964) and assistant secretary of defense for international security affairs (1964–1967). Deeply involved in Vietnam policy making. Grew increasingly skeptical about the war.

THOMAS H. MOORER U.S. Pacific fleet commander, 1964–1965, and later chief of naval operations. Set schedules for DESOTO patrols in the Tonkin Gulf.

WAYNE MORSE Senator from Oregon, 1943–1969, and leading congressional critic of U.S. involvement in the Vietnam War. Cast one of two Senate votes against the 1964 Tonkin Gulf Resolution.

BILL MOYERS Longtime political associate of Lyndon Johnson who served as a Peace Corps official during the Kennedy administration and press secretary to President Johnson, 1965–1966.

NGO DINH DIEM Leader of South Vietnam, 1954–1963. Overthrown and assassinated in November 1963 coup, which ushered in a long era of political instability in South Vietnam.

NGO DINH NHU Brother of Ngo Dinh Diem and head of South Vietnam's security forces. His repression of Buddhist protesters sparked the November 1963 coup, in which he was also killed.

NGUYEN CAO KY Born 1930. Air force commander (1964–1965), prime minister (1965–1967), and vice president (1967–1971) of South Vietnam. Member of the junior officer corps—the "Young Turks"—who came to power after Diem's death.

NGUYEN KHANH Born 1927. A senior figure in the anti-Diem coup. Leader of South Vietnam, 1964–1965. Initially opposed and later favored U.S. military action against North Vietnam.

NGUYEN VAN THIEU Born 1929. General who became the leader of South Vietnam in 1965. Rose to power in the aftermath of the anti-Diem coup. Held the presidency until the fall of South Vietnam in the spring of 1975.

MADAME NHU Outspoken wife of Ngo Dinh Nhu. Her inflammatory statements in the summer and fall of 1963 angered South Vietnamese Buddhists and alienated the United States from the Diem regime.

PAUL H. NITZE Assistant secretary of defense (1961–1963), Navy secretary (1963–1967), and deputy secretary of defense (1967–1969). Supported U.S. military escalation in 1965; later came to question the strategic wisdom of American involvement in Vietnam.

FREDERICK E. NOLTING, JR. Career Foreign Service officer who served as U.S. ambassador to South Vietnam, 1961–1963. Opposed the overthrow of the Diem regime.

BRUCE B. PALMER, JR. Deputy commanding general, U.S. Army, Vietnam (1967) and U.S. Army vice chief of staff (1968–1973). Later criticized the attrition strategy pursued in Vietnam.

PHAM VAN DONG Founder, along with Ho Chi Minh, of the Vietminh movement and premier of North Vietnam, 1950–1986. Frequent diplomatic spokesman for Hanoi during the Vietnam War.

STANLEY RESOR Secretary of the army, 1964–1969.

WALT W. ROSTOW NSC staff member (1961), State Department policy planning director (1961–1966), and national security adviser to President Johnson (1966–1969). Advocated forceful military action against North Vietnam.

DEAN RUSK Secretary of state in the Kennedy and Johnson administrations, 1961–1969. Consistently favored strong U.S. involvement in Vietnam, believing Communist aggression had to be stopped.

RICHARD B. RUSSELL, JR. Democratic senator from Georgia, 1933–1971, and chairman of the Senate Armed Services Committee during the 1950s and 1960s. A powerful and influential voice in military affairs. Questioned the wisdom of U.S. military intervention in Vietnam but supported the war once that commitment was made.

U.S. GRANT SHARP, JR. Commander in chief, Pacific, 1964–1968. In charge of U.S. air operations during the Vietnam War. Frequently pressed for more intensive bombing of North Vietnam.

DAVID M. SHOUP World War II Medal of Honor recipient and commandant of the U.S. Marine Corps, 1959–1963. After retirement emerged as a prominent critic of the Vietnam War.

JOHN C. STENNIS Democratic senator from Mississippi and influential member of the Senate Armed Services Committee during the Vietnam War. Became a hard-line critic of restraints on U.S. military action in Vietnam during the Johnson administration.

ADLAI E. STEVENSON III Democratic nominee for president in 1952 and 1956 and U.S. ambassador to the United Nations, 1961–1965. Favored negotiations with North Vietnam shortly before his death in 1965.

SUKARNO Leader of Indonesia, 1949–1965. His tilt toward China's orbit provoked an army coup in the fall of 1965 that led to his downfall.

MAXWELL D. TAYLOR Special military adviser to President Kennedy (1961–1962), chairman of the Joint Chiefs of Staff (1962–1964), U.S. ambassador to South Vietnam (1964–1965), and special Vietnam adviser to President Johnson (1965–1968).

U THANT Burmese diplomat and U.N. secretary-general, 1961–1971. Urged a negotiated settlement of the Vietnam conflict and occasionally played a role in attempting to broker such a settlement.

LLEWELLYN THOMPSON Career ambassador and a leading Soviet specialist during the 1960s. Advised the Kennedy and Johnson administrations on Russian motivation and behavior during the Cuban Missile Crisis and the Vietnam War.

SIR ROBERT THOMPSON British military officer who, after directing counterinsurgency efforts in Malaya in 1950s, served as an adviser to the U.S. government and Military Assistance Command, Vietnam, beginning in 1961.

CHARLES B. "TEX" THORNTON Leader of the Army Air Corps statistical control program during World War II and organizer of the Whiz Kids. Negotiated their employment with Ford Motor Company in November 1945.

STROM THURMOND Dixiecrat (later Republican) senator from South Carolina since 1954. Vocal right-wing critic of the Johnson administration's policy in Vietnam. Favored unrestrained use of U.S. military force.

CYRUS R. VANCE Pentagon general counsel (1961–1962), secretary of the army (1962–1964), deputy defense secretary (1964–1967), and Paris peace negotiator (1968). Later secretary of state in the Carter administration.

VO NGUYEN GIAP Commander of Vietminh forces during the war against France and North Vietnamese defense minister during the war against South Vietnam and United States. Stressed political and diplomatic dimensions of guerrilla fighting.

PAUL C. WARNKE Washington lawyer who joined the Defense Department as general counsel in 1966 and served as assistant secretary of defense for international security affairs, 1967–1969.

WILLIAM C. WESTMORELAND Commander, U.S. Military Assistance Command, Vietnam (1964–1968) and U.S. Army chief of staff (1968–1972). Led U.S. ground forces during the first part of the Vietnam War. Pursued an attrition strategy through search-and-destroy operations.

EARLE G. "BUS" WHEELER Chairman of the Joint Chiefs of Staff, 1964–1970. Principal military figure in Washington overseeing the Vietnam War.

HAROLD WILSON Labor Party prime minister of Great Britain, 1964–1970, who served with Soviet Premier Alexei Kosygin as intermediaries in a failed negotiating initiative between the United States and North Vietnam in early 1967.

EUGENE ZUCKERT Secretary of the air force, 1961–1965.

Notes

1. My Journey to Washington

1. John A. Byrne, *The Whiz Kids* (New York: Doubleday, 1993), p. 98.

2. The Early Years

1. *Public Papers of the Presidents of the United States* (hereafter cited as *Public Papers*), *John F. Kennedy, 1961* (Washington: U.S. Government Printing Office, 1962), pp. 1–3.

2. *Department of State Bulletin,* February 13, 1950, p. 244.

3. *Public Papers, Dwight D. Eisenhower, 1954* (Washington: U.S. Government Printing Office, 1960), pp. 382–384.

4. John F. Kennedy, "America's Stake in Vietnam," *Vital Speeches,* August 1, 1956, pp. 617–619.

5. Clark Clifford to President Kennedy, Memorandum on Conference between President Eisenhower and President-elect Kennedy and Their Chief Advisers on January 19, 1961, January 24, 1961, "Eisenhower, Dwight D., January 17–December 9, 1961," President's Office Files, John

F. Kennedy Papers, John Fitzgerald Kennedy Library (hereafter cited as JFKL).

6. See Dean Rusk as told to Richard Rusk, *As I Saw It* (New York: Norton, 1990), p. 428.

7. Memorandum to the President, January 24, 1961, reprinted in *Journal of American History,* June 1993, p. 363.

8. Quoted in Fred I. Greenstein and Richard H. Immerman, "What Did Eisenhower Tell Kennedy About Indochina? The Politics of Misperception," *Journal of American History,* September 1992, p. 583.

9. John S. D. Eisenhower's Memorandum of a Conference with the President, December 31, 1960, "Staff Notes–December 1960," Eisenhower Diary Series, Whitman File, Dwight D. Eisenhower Library.

10. See Memorandum of Conversation, Meeting in the Cabinet Room on August 29, 1961, to Discuss Southeast Asia, "Meetings with the President, General, 7/61–8/61," National Security File (hereafter cited as NSF), Box 317, JFKL.

11. Taylor Mission Report, November 3, 1961, U.S. Department of State, *Foreign Relations of the United States* (hereafter cited as *FRUS*), *1961–1963,* vol. 1, *Vietnam, 1961* (Washington: U.S. Government Printing Office, 1988), pp. 477–532.

12. Memorandum to the President, November 8, 1961, ibid., pp. 559–561.

13. House Committee on Armed Services, *United States–Vietnam Relations, 1945–1967* (Washington: U.S. Government Printing Office, 1971), bk. 11, pp. 359–366.

14. See Notes of Meeting, White House, Washington, November 11, 1961, 12:10 P.M., *FRUS, 1961–1963,* vol. 1, pp. 577–578.

15. See Notes of National Security Council (NSC) Meeting, Washington, November 15, 1961, 12:10 A.M., ibid., pp. 607–610.

16. See Telegram to Commander in Chief, Pacific (Felt) and Chief, Military Assistance Advisory Group, Vietnam (McGarr), November 28, 1961, ibid., pp. 679–680; Maj. Gen. T. W. Parker to Gen. Lyman L. Lemnitzer, December 18, 1961, ibid., pp. 740–741; and Edwin W. Martin to Sterling J. Cottrell, December 18, 1961, ibid., pp. 742–744.

17. Joint Chiefs of Staff (JCS) Memorandum 33-62 to the Secretary of Defense, January 13, 1962, *The Pentagon Papers: The Defense Department History of United States Decisionmaking on Vietnam* (hereafter cited as *PP*), Senator Gravel ed. (Boston: Beacon Press, 1971), vol. 2, pp. 663–666; and Memorandum for the President, January 27, 1962, ibid., p. 662.

18. See Gen. Tran Van Don's insights, reported in CIA telegram

0265, Saigon Station to Agency, August 24, 1963, *FRUS, 1961–1963,* vol. 3, *Vietnam, January–August 1963* (Washington: U.S. Government Printing Office, 1991), p. 615.

19. Ernest K. Lindley, "An Ally Worth Having," *Newsweek,* June 29, 1959, p. 31; and Hearings on Foreign Operations Appropriations for 1964, House Appropriations Committee, 88th Cong., 1st sess., May 15, 1963 (Washington: U.S. Government Printing Office, 1963), p. 90.

20. Press conference, The Pentagon, February 5, 1962, *Public Statements of Robert S. McNamara, Secretary of Defense* (hereafter cited as *PSRSM*), *1962,* vol. 2, pp. 735–736.

21. News Release, Camp H. M. Smith, Hawaii, July 23, 1962, ibid., vol. 4, p. 1589.

22. Remarks to the Press, Andrews Air Force Base, Maryland, October 9, 1962, ibid., p. 182.

23. Record of Sixth Secretary of Defense Conference, Camp H. M. Smith, Hawaii, July 23, 1962, *FRUS, 1961–1963,* vol. 2, *Vietnam, 1962* (Washington: U.S. Government Printing Office, 1990), pp. 546–556.

24. John McCone to Dean Rusk, January 7, 1964, *FRUS, 1964–1968,* vol. 1, *Vietnam, 1964* (Washington: U.S. Government Printing Office, 1992), p. 5.

25. See note 23.

26. See Memorandum of Conversation, Department of State, Washington, April 1, 1963, *FRUS, 1961–1963,* vol. 3, pp. 193–195.

27. See Memorandum for the Record of the Secretary of Defense Conference, Honolulu, May 6, 1963, ibid., pp. 265–270.

28. See JCS Memorandum 629-630 to the Secretary of Defense, August 20, 1963, ibid., pp. 590–591.

3. The Fateful Fall of 1963

1. See *FRUS, 1961–1963,* vol. 4, *Vietnam, August–December 1963* (Washington, D.C.: U.S. Government Printing Office, 1991), pp. 89–90, p. 55 n. 7; and Ellen J. Hammer, *A Death in November: America in Vietnam, 1963* (New York: Dutton, 1987; reprint ed., New York: Oxford University Press, 1988), pp. 224–230.

2. State Department telegram (hereafter cited as Deptel) 243, Ball to Lodge, August 24, 1963, *FRUS, 1961–1963,* vol. 3, pp. 628–629.

3. CAP 63460, Michael Forrestal to the President, August 24, 1963, ibid., p. 627.

4. Maxwell D. Taylor, *Swords and Plowshares* (New York: Norton, 1972), p. 292.

5. Robert F. Kennedy Oral History, February 29, 1964, p. 122, JFKL.

6. See Michael Charlton and Anthony Moncrieff, *Many Reasons Why: The American Involvement in Vietnam* (New York: Hill and Wang, 1978), pp. 95-96; and Saigon Embassy telegram (hereafter Embtel) 375, Lodge to Rusk, August 29, 1963, *FRUS, 1961-1963,* vol. 4, *Vietnam, August–December 1963,* p. 21.

7. See CIA Saigon Station to Agency, August 26, 1963, *FRUS, 1961-1963,* vol. 3, p. 642.

8. This quotation is drawn from Presidential Recordings in the Kennedy Library (hereafter cited as PR, JFKL). Because no transcripts exist, I requested access to the recordings, took verbatim notes on them, and obtained the NSC's clearance to quote the verbatim notes in this book.

9. Memorandum for the Record of a Meeting at the White House, August 26, 1963, *FRUS, 1961-1963,* vol. 3, pp. 638-641; and PR, JFKL.

10. See Memorandum of a Conference with the President, August 27, 1963, *FRUS, 1961-1963,* vol. 3, pp. 659-665.

11. See Memorandum of a Conference with the President, August 28, 1963, *FRUS, 1961-1963,* vol. 4, pp. 1-6.

12. See Memorandum of a Conversation, August 28, 1963, 6:00 P.M., ibid., pp. 12-14.

13. PR, JKFL.

14. Memorandum of a Conference with the President, August 29, 1963, *FRUS, 1961-1963,* vol. 4, pp. 26-31; and CAP 63465, President to Lodge, August 29, 1963, ibid., pp. 35-36.

15. See Memorandum of a Conversation, Department of State, August 31, 1963, ibid., pp. 69-74.

16. *Public Papers, John F. Kennedy, 1963* (Washington: U.S. Government Printing Office, 1964), p. 652.

17. See Memorandum of a Conference with the President, September 3, 1963, *FRUS, 1961-1963,* vol. 4, pp. 100-103.

18. See Memorandum of a Conference with the President, September 6, 1963, ibid., pp. 117-120.

19. *Public Papers, John F. Kennedy, 1963,* p. 659.

20. See Memorandum of a Conversation, Department of State, September 10, 1963, *FRUS, 1961-1963,* vol. 4, pp. 169-171.

21. Embtel 478, Lodge to Rusk, September 11, 1963, ibid., pp.

171–174; and Memorandum of a Telephone Conversation Between the Secretary of State and the President's Special Assistant for National Security Affairs, September 11, 1963, ibid., p. 176.

22. See Memorandum for the Record of a Meeting at the Department of State, September 16, 1963, ibid., pp. 217–220.

23. CAP 63516, President to Lodge, September 17, 1963, ibid., pp. 252–254.

24. Memorandum of Telephone Conversation between Harriman and Forrestal, September 17, 1963, ibid., p. 251.

25. See Embtel 536, Lodge to the President, September 18, 1963, ibid., p. 255.

26. Telephone Conversation between McGeorge Bundy and Rusk, ibid., n. 3; and Deptel 431, President to Lodge, September 18, 1963, ibid., pp. 256–257.

27. Memorandum from the President to the Secretary of Defense, September 21, 1963, ibid., pp. 278–279; and Memorandum for the Record of a Meeting, September 23, 1963, ibid., pp. 280–282.

28. Letter, Hilsman to Lodge, September 23, 1963, ibid., pp. 282–283.

29. David Halberstam, *The Making of a Quagmire* (New York: Random House, 1965), p. 315.

30. *CBS Reports,* "McNamara and the Pentagon," September 25, 1963, *PSRSM, 1963,* vol. 5, pp. 2315–16.

31. See Memorandum for the Record, September 23, 1963, *FRUS, 1961–1963,* vol. 4, pp. 284–287.

32. See Report by the Secretary of Defense, September 26, 1963, ibid., pp. 293–295.

33. See Memorandum of a Conversation by the Secretary of Defense, Saigon, September 30, 1963, ibid., pp. 323–325.

34. Report by the Secretary of Defense, ibid., pp. 301–303.

35. Letter from the Chairman of the Joint Chiefs of Staff to President Diem, October 1, 1963, ibid., pp. 328–330.

36. Memorandum of a Conversation, Gia Long Palace, September 29, 1963, ibid., pp. 310–321.

37. See Memorandum from the Chairman of the Joint Chiefs of Staff and the Secretary of Defense to the President, October 2, 1963, ibid., pp. 336–346.

38. PR, JFKL.

39. Ibid.

40. Summary Record of the 519th Meeting of the National Security

Council, October 2, 1963, ibid., pp. 350–352; White House Press Release, 6:52 P.M., October 2, 1963, "NSC Meetings, 1963," NSF, Box 314, JFKL; and PR, JFKL.

41. See Memorandum for the Files of a Conference with the President, October 5, 1963, *FRUS, 1961–1963,* vol. 4, pp. 368–370.

42. Lodge to McGeorge Bundy, October 25, 1963, ibid., pp. 434–436; and McGeorge Bundy to Lodge, October 25, 1963, ibid., p. 437.

43. See Memorandum of a Conference with the President, October 29, 1963, 4:20 P.M., ibid., pp. 468–471; McCone quotation is in Senate Select Committee to Study Governmental Operations, *Alleged Assassination Plots Involving Foreign Leaders* (Washington: U.S. Government Printing Office, 1975), p. 221.

44. See Memorandum of a Conference with the President, October 29, 1963, 6:00 P.M., *FRUS, 1961–1963,* vol. 4, pp. 472–473; and McGeorge Bundy to Lodge, October 29, 1963, ibid., pp. 473–475.

45. MACV 2028, Harkins to Taylor, October 30, 1963, ibid., pp. 479–482; CIA station telegram 2063, Lodge to Rusk, October 30, 1963, ibid., pp. 484–488; and McGeorge Bundy to Lodge, October 30, 1963, ibid., pp. 500–502.

46. Embtel 841, Lodge to Rusk, November 1, 1963, ibid., pp. 516–517.

47. CIA station telegram 22, DTG 020410Z, November 2, 1963, ibid., p. 527, n. 2.

48. Quotations are in Tran Van Don, *Our Endless War* (San Rafael: Presidio Press, 1978), p. 111; and Marguerite Higgins, *Our Vietnam Nightmare* (New York: Harper & Row, 1965), p. 215.

49. Forrestal interview in *NBC White Paper,* "Death of Diem," December 22, 1971; and Arthur M. Schlesinger, Jr., *A Thousand Days: John F. Kennedy in the White House* (Boston: Houghton Mifflin, 1965), pp. 997–998.

50. See Memorandum of Conference with the President, November 2, 1963, NSF, JFKL.

51. See *Sunday Times* (London), February 14, 1965.

52. Embtel 917, Lodge to Rusk, November 4, 1963, *FRUS, 1961–1963,* vol. 4, pp. 560–562.

53. See Memoranda for the Record of Discussions at November 13 and November 22, 1963, Daily White House Staff Meetings, ibid., pp. 593–594 and 625–626.

54. *Public Papers, John F. Kennedy, 1963,* pp. 846, 848.

55. Ibid., pp. 652, 660.

4. A Time of Transition

1. See Memorandum for Gen. Maxwell Taylor, April 26, 1961, "Cuba—Subjects, Paramilitary Study Group, Taylor Report Part III, Annex 18," Box 61A, NSF, JFKL.

2. See Transcript of Cuban Missile Crisis Meeting, October 27, 1962 passim, Papers of John F. Kennedy, Presidential Papers, President's Office Files, JFKL.

3. Bill Moyers, "Flashbacks," *Newsweek,* February 10, 1975, p. 76.

4. See Memorandum for the Record of a Meeting, Executive Office Building, November 24, 1963, *FRUS, 1961–1963,* vol. 4, pp. 635–637.

5. NSAM 273, November 26, 1963, ibid., pp. 637–640. See Chapter 5 for more details on Plan 34A.

6. See Memorandum of a Telephone Conversation Between the Secretary of State and the Secretary of Defense, December 7, 1963, 12:40 P.M., ibid., p. 690; and DIASO-34783-63, Telegram from the Secretary of Defense to the Ambassador in Vietnam, December 12, 1963, ibid., pp. 702–703.

7. See Memorandum from the Director of the Defense Intelligence Agency to the Secretary of Defense, December 13, 1963, ibid., pp. 707–710.

8. See John McCone letter to the President, December 23, 1963, ibid., p. 737.

9. See Memorandum for the Record by the Under Secretary of State for Political Affairs, Special Assistant, December 21, 1963, ibid., pp. 728–731; Memorandum from the President's Special Assistant for National Security Affairs to the President, January 7, 1964, *FRUS, 1964–1968,* vol. 1, pp. 4–5.

10. Remarks at the White House, December 21, 1963, *PSRSM, 1963,* vol. 6, p. 2792.

11. Memorandum to the President, December 21, 1963, *FRUS 1961–1963,* vol. 4, pp. 732–735.

12. See Memorandum from Sen. Mike Mansfield to the President, January 6, 1964, *FRUS, 1964–1968,* vol. 1, pp. 2–3; and Memorandum from the President's Special Assistant for National Security Affairs to the President, January 9, 1964, ibid., pp. 8–9.

13. Memorandum to the President, January 7, 1964, ibid., pp. 12–13.

14. JCS Memorandum 46–64 to the Secretary of Defense, January 22, 1964, *PP,* vol. 3, pp. 496–499.

15. Bruce Palmer, Jr., *The Twenty-five-year War: America's Military Role in Vietnam* (Lexington: University Press of Kentucky, 1984), p. 46.

16. See note 14.

17. JCS Memorandum 174–64 to the Secretary of Defense, March 2, 1964, *FRUS, 1964–1968,* vol. 1, pp. 112–118.

18. Hearings Before House Appropriations Committee, Defense Appropriations Subcommittee, February 17, 1964, *PSRSM, 1964,* vol. 2, p. 698; and Hearings Before Senate Appropriations Committee, July 22, 1964, ibid., vol. 3, p. 1423.

19. Deptel 1281, President to Lodge, February 21, 1964, *FRUS, 1964–1968,* vol. 1, p. 96.

20. Memorandum to the Chairman of the Joint Chiefs of Staff, February 21, 1964, ibid., pp. 97–99.

21. See note 17.

22. Remarks to the Press, Hickam Air Force Base, Hawaii, March 9, 1964, *PSRSM, 1964,* vol. 3, p. 970.

23. See Summary Record of the 528th Meeting of the National Security Council, April 22, 1964, *FRUS, 1964–1968,* vol. 1, p. 258.

24. Memorandum to the President, March 16, 1964, ibid., pp. 153–167.

25. General Greene's comments are in JCS 2343/346-1, March 17, 1964, and General LeMay's are in CSAFM-263-64 to JCS, March 14, 1964; as quoted in Historical Division, Joint Secretariat, Joint Chiefs of Staff, *History of the Joint Chiefs of Staff: The Joint Chiefs of Staff and the War in Vietnam, 1960–1968* (hereafter cited as *HJCS*) (1970), pt. 1, ch. 9, pp. 18–19. I thank the Office of the Secretary of Defense Historian's Office for sharing this heretofore unavailable study with me, and the JCS Historical Division for declassifying relevant portions of it for use in this book.

26. See Memorandum from Michael V. Forrestal to the President's Special Assistant for National Security Affairs, March 18, 1964, *FRUS, 1964–1968,* vol. 1, pp. 174–175.

27. *Congressional Record,* vol. 110, pp. 6227–32.

28. Speech before the James Forrestal Memorial Awards Dinner of the National Security Industrial Association, Sheraton Park Hotel, Washington, D.C., March 26, 1964.

29. Interview with Peter Hackes, NBC-TV *Sunday Show,* March 29, 1964.

30. See Embtel 2203, Lodge to Rusk, May 14, 1964, *FRUS, 1964–1968,* vol. 1, pp. 315–321.

31. Notes for Report to the President, May 14, 1964, ibid., pp. 322–327.

32. News Conference, the Pentagon, April 24, 1964, *PSRSM, 1964,* vol. 3, p. 1210.

33. Memorandum prepared by Directorate of Intelligence, Central Intelligence Agency, May 15, 1964, *FRUS, 1964–1968,* vol. 1, p. 336.

34. JCS Memorandum 426–64 to the Secretary of Defense, May 19, 1964, ibid., pp. 338–340.

35. See Summary Record of the National Security Council Executive Committee Meeting, May 24, 1964, ibid., pp. 369–374.

36. Special National Intelligence Estimate 50-2-64, May 25, 1964, ibid., pp. 378–380.

37. See Summary Record of Meeting, Honolulu, June 1, 1964, 8:30 A.M.–12:30 P.M., ibid., pp. 412–422; Summary Record of a Meeting, Honolulu, June 1, 1964, 2:15–6:15 P.M., ibid., pp. 422–428; Summary Record of Meetings, June 2, 1964, ibid., pp. 428–433; and William Bundy, Vietnam Manuscript (hereafter cited as WB, VNMS), ch. 13, p. 19.

38. JCS Memorandum 471–64 to the Secretary of Defense, June 2, 1964, *FRUS, 1964–1968,* vol. 1, pp. 437–440.

39. Taylor Memorandum to the Secretary of Defense, CM-1451-64, June 5, 1964, ibid., pp. 457–458.

40. Board of National Estimates Memorandum to CIA Director McCone, June 9, 1964, ibid., pp. 484–487.

5. The Tonkin Gulf Resolution

1. See Edward J. Marolda and Oscar P. Fitzgerald, *The United States Navy and the Vietnam Conflict,* vol. 2, *From Military Assistance to Combat, 1959–1965* (Washington: Naval Historical Center, 1986), pp. 396 and 411.

2. See Socialist Republic of Vietnam, *Vietnam: The Anti-U.S. Resistance War,* p. 60; and Marolda and Fitzgerald, *U.S. Navy and the Vietnam Conflict,* p. 415.

3. See William Conrad Gibbons, *The U.S. Government and the Vietnam War: Executive and Legislative Roles and Relationships,* pt. 3, *January–July 1965* (Princeton: Princeton University Press, 1989), p. 10.

4. Embtel 282, Taylor to Rusk, August 3, 1964, *FRUS, 1964–1968,* vol. 1, pp. 593–594.

5. 041727Z, Department of State, Central Files, POL 27 VIET S., cited in ibid., p. 609.

6. A Recording—Admiral Sharp to General Burchinal at 2:08 P.M. EDT, August 4, Transcript of Telephone Conversations, August 4–5, p. 31; and 041848Z, both in "Gulf of Tonkin (Miscellaneous)," Country File, Vietnam (hereafter cited as CF, VN), Box 228, NSF, LBJL.

7. 4:08 P.M. Telephone Conversation between Secretary McNamara and Admiral Sharp, ibid.

8. A Recording—Admiral Sharp to General Burchinal at 5:23 P.M. EDT, August 4, ibid.

9. See Summary Notes of the 538th Meeting of the National Security Council, August 4, 1964, *FRUS, 1964–1968,* vol. 1, pp. 611–612.

10. See Notes of the Leadership Meeting, August 4, 1964, ibid., pp. 615–621.

11. See *U.S. News & World Report,* July 23, 1984, pp. 63–64; and James Bond Stockdale and Sybil B. Stockdale, *In Love and War* (New York: Harper & Row, 1984), pp. 21, 23.

12. *Joint Hearing on Southeast Asia Resolution before the Senate Foreign Relations and Armed Services Committees,* 88th Cong., 2d sess., August 6, 1964 (Washington: U.S. Government Printing Office, 1966); and *Executive Sessions of the Senate Foreign Relations and Armed Services Committees (Historical Series),* 88th Cong., 2d sess., 1964 (Washington: U.S. Government Printing Office, 1988), pp. 291–299.

13. Senate debate is in *Congressional Record,* vol. 110, pp. 18399–471.

14. Michael Charlton and Anthony Moncrieff, *Many Reasons Why: The American Involvement in Vietnam* (New York: Hill & Wang, 1978), p. 108.

15. Ibid., p. 117; and WB, VNMS, p. 14A-36.

16. WB, VNMS, pp. 14A-38, 14A-40.

17. Senate Report 90-797 (1967), pp. 21–22.

18. Senate Foreign Relations Committee, *The Gulf of Tonkin, The 1964 Incidents,* Hearing on February 20, 1968, 90th Cong., 2d sess. (Washington: U.S. Government Printing Office, 1968), pp. 82–87 and 106.

6. The 1964 Election and Its Aftermath

1. See Theodore H. White, *The Making of the President, 1964* (New York: Atheneum, 1965), pp. 132–133.

2. Remarks in New York City Before the American Bar Association, August 12, 1964, *Public Papers, Lyndon B. Johnson, 1963–1964,* p. 952.

3. Ibid., p. 953.

4. Barry Goldwater, *Where I Stand* (New York: McGraw-Hill, 1964), p. 67.

5. Ernest R. Breech to Frank Middleton, Finance Coordinator, Goldwater Campaign Headquarters, April 5, 1964. Robert S. McNamara Papers (hereafter cited as RSMP).

6. McGeorge Bundy to the President, August 13, 1964, *FRUS, 1964–1968,* vol. 1, pp. 672–679.

7. See JCSM-701-64, Joint Chiefs of Staff to the Secretary of Defense, August 14, 1964, ibid., pp. 681–682.

8. CSAM-472-64 to JCS, September 4, 1964, JMF 9155.3, cited in *History of the Joint Chiefs,* pt. 1, ch. 12, pp. 14–16.

9. Sigma II-64 Final Report, LBJL, pp. D-14, D-15.

10. Embtel 768 (Saigon), Taylor to Rusk, September 6, 1964, *FRUS, 1964–1968,* vol. 1, pp. 733–736; and SNIE 53–64, "Chances for a Stable Government in South Vietnam," September 8, 1964, ibid., pp. 742–746.

11. Deptel 654, Rusk to Taylor, September 6, 1964, ibid., pp. 766–767; CINCPAC 25, Sharp to Wheeler, September 25, 1964, *PP,* vol. 3, pp. 569–570; and CIA Paper, "Deterioration in South Vietnam," September 28, 1964, *FRUS, 1964–1968,* vol. 1, p. 801, n. 6. See also SNIE 53-2-64, October 1, 1964, ibid., pp. 806–811.

12. George W. Ball, "Top Secret: The Prophecy the President Rejected," *Atlantic Monthly,* July 1972, p. 45.

13. Ibid., p. 49.

14. JCSM-902-64, Wheeler to McNamara, October 27, 1964, *FRUS, 1964–1968,* vol. 1, pp. 847–857.

15. Notes of Meeting with General Wheeler, November 1, 1964, Robert S. McNamara Papers, Department of Defense; Embtel 251 (Saigon), Taylor to McNamara, November 3, 1964, *FRUS, 1964–1968,* vol. 1, pp. 882–884; and MACV 5532, Westmoreland to Wheeler, October 17, 1964, ibid., pp. 838–839.

16. Vice Admiral Mustin to William Bundy, November 10, 1964, *PP,* vol. 3, pp. 621–628; and JCSM-955-64, Wheeler to McNamara, November 14, 1964, *FRUS, 1964–1968,* vol. 1, pp. 1057–59.

17. CIA Intelligence Assessment: The Situation in Vietnam, November 24, 1964, *PP,* vol. 3, pp. 651–656.

18. Quotations are from John McNaughton's and McGeorge Bundy's handwritten notes of this meeting, in Box 1, Meeting Notes File (hereafter cited as MNF), LBJL; and Papers of McGeorge Bundy, ibid.

19. Embtel 2010 (Saigon), Taylor to Rusk, December 31, 1964, NSF, LBJL.

20. CAP-64375, President Johnson to Taylor, December 30, 1964, *FRUS, 1964–1968,* vol. 1, pp. 1057–59.

21. Embtels 2052–2058 (Saigon), Taylor to President Johnson, January 6, 1965, "Deployment of Major U.S. Forces to Vietnam, July 1965" (hereafter cited as "Deployment"), vol. 1, tabs 1–10, National Security Council History (hereafter cited as NSCH), Box 40, NSF, LBJL.

22. McGeorge Bundy to President Johnson, January 27, 1965, "Memos to the President," vol. 8, 1/1–2/28/65," Aides Files, McGeorge Bundy, Box 2, NSF, LBJL.

7. The Decision to Escalate

1. Bundy's comments are in Bromley Smith to the President, February 4, 1965, "Trip, McGeorge Bundy—Saigon, Vol. 1, 2/4/65," International Meetings and Travel File, Box 28/29, NSF, LBJL.

2. Summary Notes of 545th NSC Meeting (by Bromley Smith), February 6, 1965, Box 1, MNF, LBJL.

3. McGeorge Bundy to the President, February 7, 1965, "Vol. 3, Tab 29, 2/8/65, Situation in Vietnam, Tab B," NSC Meetings File (hereafter cited as NSCMF), Box 1, NSF, LBJL; and Annex A, "A Policy of Sustained Reprisal" (drafted by McNaughton for Bundy), "McGeorge Bundy—Memos to the President, vol. 8, 1/1–2/28/65," Aides Files, McGeorge Bundy, Box 2, ibid.

4. Summary Notes of 547th NSC Meeting, February 8, 1965, "Vol. 3, Tab 29, 2/8/65, Situation in Vietnam," NSCMF, Box 1, ibid.

5. Memorandum of Meeting with the President, 17 February 1965 (by Goodpaster), "February 17, 1965—10 A.M. Meeting with General Eisenhower and Others," Box 1, MNF, ibid.

6. Dean Rusk to the President, February 23, 1965, "Deployment," vol. 2, tabs 61–87, NSCH, Box 40, NSF, LBJL.

7. See George Gallup, "Viet-Nam Air Strikes Get 67% U.S. Approval," *Washington Post.* February 16, 1965.

8. See George Ball to the President, February 13, 1965, "Deployment," vol. 1, tabs 42–60, NSCH, Box 40, NSF, LBJL.

9. Quotation is in Marvin Kalb and Elie Abel, *Roots of Involvement: The United States in Asia* (New York: Norton, 1971), p. 184.

10. George C. Herring argued this point in a paper delivered at the LBJ Library's Vietnam Symposium in October 1993.

11. See John Schlight, ed., *The Second Indochina War* (Washington: U.S. Government Printing Office, 1986), p. 154; and Interview with Gen. Bruce Palmer, Jr., 1975, Senior Officer Oral History Program, U.S. Army Military History Institute, Carlisle Barracks, Pa.

12. Congressional Research Service (hereafter cited as CRS) Interview with Gen. William C. Westmoreland, November 15, 1978.

13. CRS Interview with Gen. Andrew Goodpaster, November 16, 1978.

14. See CINCPAC 192207Z and JCS Memorandum 204-65, cited in *PP*, vol. 3, p. 406.

15. See McGeorge Bundy's notes of this April 1, 1965, meeting in Papers of McGeorge Bundy, LBJL.

16. See "Summary of NSC Meeting on April 2, 1965," drafted by Chester Cooper on April 5, "Vol. 3, Tab 33, 4/2/65, Situation in South Vietnam," NSCMF, Box 1, NSF, LBJL; and McCone to Rusk et al., April 2, 1965, "Deployment," vol. 2, tabs 120–140, NSCH, Box 40, LBJL.

17. See NSAM 328, April 6, 1965, reprinted in *PP*, vol. 3, pp. 702–703.

18. McGeorge Bundy to the President, March 6, 1965, "Memos to the President, vol. 9, Mar.–Apr. 14, 1965," Aides Files, McGeorge Bundy, Box 3, NSF, LBJL.

19. Address at Johns Hopkins University: "Peace Without Conquest," April 7, 1965, *Public Papers: Lyndon B. Johnson, 1965,* bk. 1, pp. 394–399.

20. Embtel 3248 (Saigon), Taylor to Rusk, April 7, 1965, "Vol. 32," CF, VN, Box 16, NSF, LBJL.

21. See John McNaughton, "Minutes of April 20, 1965, Honolulu Meeting," in "McNaughton XV—Miscellaneous, 1964–66," John McNaughton Files, Papers of Paul Warnke (hereafter cited as PPW), Box 7, LBJL.

22. Memorandum for the President, April 21, 1965, "Vietnam 2EE, 1965–67," CF, VN, Box 74/75, NSF, LBJL.

23. See draft of Rusk to Taylor, April 22, 1965, "Vol. 32," CF, VN, Box 16, NSF, LBJL; the final, amended version, Deptel 2397, Rusk to Taylor, April 22, 1965, "NODIS-LOR, Vol. 2(B)," CF, VN, Box 45/46, NSF, LBJL; and President's News Conference, April 27, 1965, *Public Papers: London B. Johnson, 1965,* bk. 1, pp. 448–456.

24. Johnson quotation is in George W. Ball, *The Past Has Another Pattern: Memoirs* (New York: Norton, 1982), p. 393.

25. Ball to Johnson, April 21, 1965, "Political Track Papers, 4/65," CF, VN, Box 213, NSF, LBJL.

26. See George C. Herring, ed., *The Secret Diplomacy of the Vietnam*

War: The Negotiating Volumes of the Pentagon Papers (Austin: University of Texas Press, 1983), pp. 57–58.

27. Ky interview with Brian Moynahan, published in *Sunday Mirror* (London), July 4, 1965, p. 9; and transcript, William Bundy Oral History Interview, May 29, 1969, by Paige E. Mulholland, tape 2, p. 30, LBJL.

28. Embtel 4035 (Saigon), Taylor to Rusk, June 3, 1965, "Vol. 2 (A), 3/65–9/65," CF, VN, Box 45/46, NSF, LBJL.

29. Embtel 4074 (Saigon), Taylor to Rusk, June 5, 1965, "Deployment," vol. 4, tabs 258–280, NSCH, Box 41, NSF, LBJL.

30. See Papers of McGeorge Bundy, LBJL; and WB, VNMS, ch. 26, pp. 3–6.

31. MACV 19118, Westmoreland to Sharp and Wheeler, June 7, 1965, "Deployment," vol. 4, tabs 258–280, NSCH, Box 41, NSF, LBJL.

32. Papers of McGeorge Bundy, LBJL.

33. Ibid.

34. June 10, 1965, 6:40 P.M., Tape 6506.02, Program Number (hereafter PNO) 8, PR, LBJL.

35. News Conference, the Pentagon, June 16, 1965, *PSRSM, 1965,* vol. 5, pp. 1794 and 1800.

36. See A. J. Goodpaster, "Memorandum of Meeting with General Eisenhower, June 16, 1965, President Eisenhower," Name File, Box 3, NSF, LBJL; and confidential Louis Harris surveys in Hayes Redmon to the President, June 17, 1965, "ND 19/CO 312 VIETNAM (Situation in 1964–1965)," Confidential File, Box 80, NSF, LBJL.

37. June 21, 1965, 12:15 P.M., Tape 6506.04, PNO 18, PR, LBJL.

38. Quotations are in Henry F. Graff, "How Johnson Makes Foreign Policy," *New York Times Magazine,* July 4, 1965, pp. 18–20; and *The Tuesday Cabinet: Deliberation and Decision on Peace and War Under Lyndon B. Johnson* (Englewood Cliffs: Prentice Hall, 1970), pp. 53–55.

39. President's News Conference, June 17, 1965, *Public Papers, Lyndon B. Johnson, 1965,* bk. 2, pp. 669–685.

40. See WB, VNMS, ch. 26, pp. 22–23.

41. Draft Memorandum for the President, June 26, 1965, "Vol. 3, Tab 35, 7/27/65, Deployment of Additional U.S. Troops in Vietnam," NSCMF, Box 1, NSF, LBJL.

42. McGeorge Bundy to McNamara, June 30, 1965, "Deployment," vol. 6, tabs 341–356, NSCH, Box 43, NSF, LBJL.

43. Rusk to the President, July 1, 1965, ibid., tabs 357–383.

44. McGeorge Bundy to Johnson, July 1, 1965, ibid.

45. See WB, VNMS, ch. 27, p. 13.

46. See William Bundy, "Vietnam Panel" (drafted July 10, 1965), "Deployment," vol. 7, tabs 401–420, NSCH, Box 43, NSF, LBJL; WB, VNMS, ch. 27, pp. 15–21; Acheson to Truman, July 10, 1965, "Acheson Correspondence (1964–1971)," Post Presidential Name File, Harry S Truman Library; and Walter Isaacson and Evan Thomas, *The Wise Men: Six Men and the World They Made* (New York: Simon & Schuster, 1986), pp. 650–652.

47. Quotation is in *U.S. News & World Report,* July 26, 1965, p. 45.

48. James Cannon and Charles Roberts interview with the president, July 14, 1965, reprinted in *Newsweek,* August 2, 1965, pp. 20–21.

49. July 14, 1965, 6:15 P.M., Tape 6507.02, PNO 22, PR, LBJL.

50. "Record of Questions and Answers at Meeting Between Secretary McNamara and His Party, Ambassador Taylor and His Staff, and COMUSMACV and His Staff, 16 [and 17] July 1965," Westmoreland–CBS Papers, National Archives.

51. "Intensification of the Military Operations in Vietnam, Concept and Appraisal," pp. ii, and J-1, CF, VN, LBJL.

52. Memorandum for the President, July 20, 1965 (submitted July 21), "Vietnam 2EE, 1965–67," CF, VN, Box 74/75, NSF, LBJL.

53. Cater to the President, July 10, 1965, White House Aides Files, Office Files of Douglass Cater, LBJL.

8. The Christmas Bombing Pause

1. See *Washington Post,* August 27 and September 12, 1965.

2. See Summary Notes of 554th NSC Meeting, August 5, 1965, 6:00 P.M., NSF, LBJL.

3. Sigma II-65 Final Report, pp. D-4 and D-5, LBJL.

4. See "Periscope," *Newsweek,* September 27, 1965; and "The Realist," *Newsweek,* October 11, 1965, p. 2. See also Bernard Fall, "Vietnam Blitz," *New Republic,* October 9, 1965, pp. 17–21, and November 13, 1965, pp. 33–34.

5. USMACV, "Concept of Operations in the Republic of Vietnam," September 1, 1965, Papers of the Capital Legal Foundation, Box 58F, LBJL.

6. Andrew F. Krepinevich, *The Army and Vietnam* (Baltimore: Johns Hopkins University Press, 1986), pp. 164, 196, and 259.

7. CRS Interview with Gen. William E. DePuy, August 1, 1988, quoted in Gibbons, *U.S. Government,* pt. 4, *July 1966–January 1968* (Washington: U.S. Government Printing Office, 1994), p. 50.

8. Palmer, *Twenty-five-Year War,* pp. 45–46.

9. See WB, VNMS, ch. 31, pp. 31–32.

10. JCSM-670-65, Wheeler to McNamara, September 2, 1965, described in *PP,* vol. 4, p. 29; and McNamara to Wheeler, "Air Strikes Against North Vietnam," September 15, 1965, Record Group 330, National Archives.

11. See Thompson Report, Department of State, Lot File 85, D 240 (William Bundy Papers).

12. Quoted in *The Vietnam Hearings* (New York: Vintage Books, 1966), p. 140.

13. *New York Times,* November 3, 1965, p. 1.

14. See *New York Times,* November 29, 1965.

15. *PSRSM, 1965.*

16. "Courses of Action in Vietnam," First Rough Draft, November 3, 1965, sent to the president on November 7, RSMP.

17. See Lyndon Baines Johnson, *The Vantage Point; Perspectives on the Presidency, 1963–1969* (New York: Holt, Rinehart and Winston, 1971), p. 234.

18. William C. Westmoreland, *A Soldier Reports* (Garden City: Doubleday, 1976; New York: Da Capo, 1989), p. 154; and Memorandum for the President, November 30, 1965, RSMP.

19. MACV 41485, Westmoreland to CINCPAC, November 23, 1965, LBJL.

20. Remarks to the Press Upon Departing Saigon, November 29, 1965.

21. Memorandum for the President, November 30, 1965, RSMP.

22. See Eric Sevareid, "The Final Troubled Hours of Adlai Stevenson," *Look,* November 1965, pp. 81–86.

23. See WB, VNMS, ch. 33, p. 18.

24. December 2, 1965, 12:15 P.M., Tape 6512.01, PNO 5, PR, LBJL.

25. See McGeorge Bundy's notes of December 7, 1965, meeting in Papers of McGeorge Bundy, LBJL.

26. See Jack Valenti's notes of December 17 and 18, 1965, meetings in MNF, LBJL.

27. See JCSM16-66, Wheeler to McNamara, January 8, 1966; and Jack Valenti's notes of January 3, 1966, White House meeting, in MNF, LBJL.

28. See Jack Valenti's notes of January 10, 1966, Cabinet Room meeting, 1:10 P.M., ibid.

29. CINCPAC 120205Z, Sharp to Joint Chiefs of Staff, January 12, 1966; and CSM-41-66, Wheeler to McNamara, January 18, 1966, LBJL.

30. Office of Air Force History, Bolling Air Force Base, Washington, D.C.

31. See John T. McNaughton, "Some Observations about Bombing North Vietnam," January 18, 1966, in PPW, LBJL; BNE Special Memorandum, cited in Gibbons, *U.S. Government,* pt. 4, p. 153; and Jack Valenti's notes of January 22, 1966, White House meeting, in MNF, LBJL.

32. *Newsweek,* January 17, 1966; and *Congressional Record,* January 24, 1966, vol. 112, pp. 965–966.

33. January 17, 1966, 9:15 A.M., Tape M6601.01, PNO 1, PR, LBJL.

34. See Jack Valenti's notes of January 28, 1966, "Wise Men" meeting, MNF, LBJL; Bromley Smith's Notes of 556th NSC meeting, January 30, 1966, NSCMF; NSF, LBJL; and *Washington Post,* January 31, 1966.

35. Chester L. Cooper, *The Lost Crusade: America in Vietnam* (New York: Dodd, Mead, 1970), p. 296.

36. See Hanoi VNA International Service in English, January 4, 1966, reprinted in Herring, p. 133; and Embtel 394 (Rangoon), Byroade to Rusk, January 31, 1966, reprinted in ibid., pp. 141–142.

9. Troubles Deepen

1. George C. Herring, *LBJ and Vietnam: A Different Kind of War* (Austin: University of Texas Press, 1994), p. 11.

2. See Ted Gittinger, ed., *The Johnson Years: A Vietnam Roundtable* (Austin: LBJL, 1993), pp. 126–128, 163–176.

3. Memorandum for the President, Subject: The Military Outlook in Vietnam, January 24, 1966, RSMP.

4. CIA Memorandum SC No. 01399/67, May 23, 1967, "The Situation in Vietnam: An Analysis and Estimate," pp. 1–2; "CIA 80-82 (Vietcong Order of Battle Documents, May 1967)," Papers of the Capital Legal Foundation, Box 3, LBJL.

5. See Don Kowet, *A Matter of Honor* (New York: Macmillan, 1984), pp. 100–101, 276–282.

6. Handwritten note from General Wheeler, April 23, 1966, Robert S. McNamara Papers, Department of Defense.

7. George C. Herring, *America's Longest War: The United States and Vietnam, 1950–1975,* 2d ed. (New York: Knopf, 1986), p. 151.

8. See R. W. Komer Memorandum for the President, September 13,

1966, NSF, LBJL; and Memorandum for the President, Subject: Actions Recommended for Vietnam, October 14, 1966, RSMP.

9. Herring, *America's Longest War,* p. 146.

10. Ibid., p. 149.

11. Hearings before the Senate Armed Services and Appropriations committees on Supplemental Defense Appropriations and Authorizations for Fiscal Year 1967, January 23, 1967, p. 70.

12. See Herring, *Secret Diplomacy,* p. 160.

13. Embtel 5840 (Saigon), Lodge to Rusk, June 29, 1966, excerpted in ibid., pp. 231–239.

14. See text of Goldberg's September 22 address in *New York Times,* September 23, 1966.

15. Memorandum of Conversation between McNaughton and Minister Zinchuk, January 3, 1967, Memos to the President—Walt Rostow, NSF, LBJL.

16. See Wilson quotation in *Washington Post,* July 26, 1969; and Embtel 5015 (Moscow), Thompson to Rusk, May 19, 1967, NSF, LBJL.

17. *Washington Post,* February 28, 1966.

18. Charlton and Moncrieff, *Many Reasons Why,* p. 115; and diary entry, January 5, 1967, Lady Bird Johnson, *A White House Diary* (New York: Holt, Rinehart and Winston, 1970), p. 469.

19. Commencement Address at Chatham College, May 22, 1966, *PSRSM, 1966,* vol. 7, p. 2333.

20. Folder "M," Personal Correspondence Files.

21. Robert Kennedy reported this episode to me. See also Arthur M. Schlesinger, Jr., *Robert Kennedy and His Times* (Boston: Houghton Mifflin, 1978), pp. 768–769.

22. *Journals of David Lilienthal* (New York: Harper & Row, 1964–1983), vol. 6, p. 418; Rusk, *As I Saw It,* p. 417.

23. Draft Memorandum for the President, May 19, 1967, p. 19, RSMP.

24. Attachment (dated April 5, 1966) to "Some Thoughts About Vietnam," April 4, 1966, State Department, Lot File 70 D 207.

25. See Jack Valenti's notes of April 2, 1966, meeting in MNF, LBJL.

26. Rusk, Memorandum of Conversation with South Vietnamese Foreign Minister Tran Van Do, June 28, 1966, State Department, Central File, Pol 27 Viet S; Rostow Memorandum to the President, June 25, 1966, Memos to the President, NSF, LBJL; Embtel 5830 (Saigon), Lodge to Rusk, June 29, 1966, State Department, Central File, Pol 27 Viet S; Komer Memorandum to the President, July 1, 1966, PPW, LBJL; and

Harriman Postscript to Memorandum of Conversation with Secretary McNamara, June 23, 1966, W. Averell Harriman Papers, Manuscript Division, Library of Congress.

27. Lodge memorandum, October 3, 1966, Henry Cabot Lodge, Jr. Papers, Massachusetts Historical Society; and "COMUSMACV Policy Points," October 3, 1966, Westmoreland Papers, U.S. Army Center of Military History.

28. See note 8.

29. George A. Carver, Jr., to Richard Helms, October 15, 1966, Subject: Comments on Secretary McNamara's Trip Report, "McNaughton VIII—Late Vietnam . . . (2)," PPW, Box 3, LBJL: *PP*, vol. 4, p. 356; and JCSM-672-66, Wheeler to McNamara, October 14, 1966, "Vietnam, JCS Memos, Vol. II," CF, VN, Box 193, NSF, LBJL.

30. See Rostow's notes of Meeting with the President, Friday, December 17, 1966, Austin, Texas (dated December 19, 1966), Files of Walt W. Rostow, Box 3, NSF, LBJL; Attachment to Summary Notes of 568th NSC Meeting, February 8, 1966, NSCMF, LBJL; and COMUSMACV 09101 to CINCPAC, "Force Requirements," March 18, 1967, PPW, LBJL.

31. Quotation is in Westmoreland, *Soldier Reports,* p. 299; Westy's estimate and Johnson's comment are in John McNaughton's "Notes on Discussions with the President, 27 April 1967," PPW, LBJL.

32. Memorandum to the President, Subject: Proposed Bombing Program Against North Vietnam, May 9, 1967; William Bundy, "Bombing Strategy Options for the Rest of 1967," May 9, 1967; McGeorge Bundy to the President, Memorandum on Vietnam Policy, May 3, 1967; CIA Intelligence Memorandum 0642/67, "The Current State of Morale in North Vietnam," May 12, 1967; CIA Intelligence Report 0643/67, "Bomb Damage Inflicted on North Vietnam Through April 1967," May 12, 1967; and CIA Intelligence Memorandum 0649/67, May 23, 1967, all in CF, VN, NSF, LBJL.

33. Draft Memorandum for the President, Subject: Future Actions in Vietnam, May 19, 1967, RSMP.

34. Walt Rostow Memorandum to the President, May 19, 1967, CF, VN, NSF, LBJL.

10. Estrangement and Departure

1. *PP,* vol. 4, p. 177.

2. See *FRUS, 1964–1968,* vol. 1, pp. 172–173 and 153–167.

3. See JCSM-286-67, Memorandum for the Secretary of Defense, Subject: Operations Against North Vietnam, May 20, 1967; and JSCM-288-67, Memorandum to the Secretary of Defense, Subject: Worldwide US Military Posture, May 20, 1967, CF, VN, NSF, LBJL.

4. Richard Helms to Robert S. McNamara, June 1, 1967, and Attachment, CIA Memorandum 196752/67, Subject: Evaluation of Alternative Programs for Bombing North Vietnam, June 1, 1967, ibid.

5. Eugene J. Carroll, Jr., Rear Admiral, USN (Ret.), to Jeanne Moore, September 24, 1993, and Attachment, RSMP.

6. Draft Memoranda for the President, Subjects: Summary and Alternative Military Actions Against North Vietnam, June 12, 1967, CF, VN, NSF, LBJL.

7. Quoted in Sanford J. Ungar, *The Papers and the Papers: An Account of the Legal and Political Battle over the Pentagon Papers* (New York: Dutton, 1972), pp. 20–21.

8. Westmoreland, "Vietnam Sec Def Briefings, 7–8 July 1967— COMUSMACV Assessment," Department of State, Lot File 70 D 48; and Bunker, CF, VN, NSF, LBJL.

9. Harry Middleton, *LBJ: The White House Years* (New York: Abrams, 1990), p. 178; and Notes of July 12, 1967, meeting, Tom Johnson's Notes of Meetings, LBJL.

10. *New York Times,* May 17, 1967.

11. Notes of October 17, 1967, Tuesday Lunch, Tom Johnson's Notes of Meetings, LBJL.

12. Notes of August 8, 1967, Tuesday Lunch, LBJL.

13. See *PP,* vol. 4, p. 199.

14. See, for example, CIA/DIA Memorandum S-2408/AP4AS, An Appraisal of the Bombing of North Vietnam (through July 18, 1967), July 1967, p. 2, CF, VN, NSF, LBJL.

15. Testimony of Robert S. McNamara, Secretary of Defense, August 25, 1967, "Air War Against North Vietnam," *Hearings Before the Preparedness Investigating Subcommittee of the U.S. Senate Armed Services Committee* (Washington: U.S. Government Printing Office, 1967), pp. 280–281.

16. Ibid., pp. 304–305.

17. Ibid., p. 297.

18. Ibid., p. 282.

19. News Release by John Stennis, Chairman, Preparedness Investigating Subcommittee, Senate Armed Services Committee, August 31, 1967.

20. See Mark Perry, *Four Stars* (Boston: Houghton Mifflin, 1989), pp. 163–166.

21. Richard Helms Memorandum for the President, Subject: Effects of the Intensified Air War Against North Vietnam, August 29, 1967; and Attachment, Walt W. Rostow to the President, August 29, 1967, 5:55 P.M., NSF, LBJL.

22. Richard Helms, Memorandum for the President, September 12, 1967, CF, VN, Box 259/260, NSF, LBJL.

23. "Implications of an Unfavorable Outcome in Vietnam," September 11, 1967, ibid.

24. Barry Goldwater, "Is McNamara Less Popular?" *Atlanta Constitution,* September 7, 1967.

25. See Chester L. Cooper Memorandum for the Negotiations Committee, August 2, 1967, in Herring, *Secret Diplomacy,* pp. 717–725, esp. p. 720.

26. Notes of August 8, 1967, meeting, Tom Johnson's Notes of Meetings, LBJL.

27. Cooper, *Lost Crusade,* p. 379.

28. Herring, ed., *Secret Diplomacy,* p. 745.

29. Embtel 3070 and 3097 (Paris), excerpted in ibid., pp. 736–738.

30. Embtel 3143 (Paris), Text of Message from Kissinger, September 11, 1967, Files of Walt W. Rostow, NSF, LBJL.

31. Memorandum of Conversation with Secretary McNamara, August 22, 1967, W. Averell Harriman Papers, Manuscript Division, Library of Congress.

32. Jim Jones's Notes of Weekly Luncheon, September 12, 1967, MNF, LBJL; and Embtel 3242 (Paris), from Kissinger, September 13, 1967, Files of Walt W. Rostow, NSF, LBJL.

33. Notes of September 26, 1967, Weekly Luncheon, Tom Johnson's Notes of Meetings, LBJL.

34. Nicholas deB. Katzenbach, Memorandum for the President, Subject: Negotiations with North Vietnam, September 26, 1967, Files of Walt W. Rostow, NSF, LBJL.

35. See Herbert Marcovich to Henry Kissinger, October 2, 1967, NSF, LBJL.

36. Notes of October 18, 1967, Cabinet Room meeting, Tom Johnson's Notes of Meetings, LBJL.

37. See Embtel 5545 (Paris), October 20, 1967, in Herring, *Secret Diplomacy,* p. 769.

38. David E. McGiffert, Memorandum for the Chief of Staff, U.S.

Army, October 20, 1967, Anti-Vietnam Demonstrations," Papers of Warren Christopher, Box 8, LBJL.

39. Jimmy Breslin, "Quiet Rally Turns Vicious," *Washington Post,* October 22, 1967, pp. A-1 and A-10.

40. Richard Harwood, "Restraint Works for the Army," ibid.

41. McGeorge Bundy, Memorandum for the President, Subject: Vietnam—October 1967, October 17, 1967, NSF, LBJL.

42. Memorandum for the President, Subject: A Fifteen Month Program for Military Operations in Southeast Asia, November 1, 1967, RSMP.

43. See Jim Jones's summary and notes of the President's Meeting with Foreign Policy Advisers, Thursday, November 2, 1967, MNF, LBJL.

44. Abe Fortas, Comments, November 5, 1967, NSF, LBJL.

45. Clark Clifford, Memorandum, November 7, 1967, ibid.

46. McGeorge Bundy, Memorandum for the President, Subject: A Commentary on the Vietnam Discussion of November 2, November 10, 1967, President's Appointments File, November 2, 1967, LBJL.

47. Letter to the President, "McNamara, Robert," White House Famous Names File, Box 6, LBJL.

48. LBJ to Margie McNamara, February 7, 1968, "McNamara, Robert S.," Name File, White House Central File, Box 318, LBJL.

11. The Lessons of Vietnam

1. Robert S. McNamara, "The Post–Cold War World and Its Implications for Military Expenditures in the Developing Countries," World Bank Conference on Development Economics, Washington, D.C., April 25, 1991, p. 33.

2. Quoted in *New York Times,* December 31, 1989.

3. Henry Kissinger, *Diplomacy* (New York: Simon & Schuster, 1994), p. 805.

4. Carl Kaysen, "Is War Obsolete?" *International Security,* vol. 14, no. 4 (Spring 1990), p. 63.

5. *Budget of the United States: Historical Tables FY 1995* (Washington: U.S. Government Printing Office, 1994), p. 86.

6. Bill Clinton, "Confronting the Challenge of a Broader World," U.N. General Assembly, New York, September 27, 1993; and Anthony Lake, "From Containment to Enlargement," Johns Hopkins University School of Advanced International Studies, Washington, D.C., September 21, 1993.

7. See *Washington Post,* June 11, 1994, p. A1.

8. Quoted in Gittinger, *Johnson Years,* p. 76.

Appendix

1. See William Perry's statement to the Stimson Center, September 20, 1994; and Department of Defense press briefing, September 22, 1994.

2. See Anatoly Dokochaev, "Afterword to Sensational 100 Day Nuclear Cruise," *Krasnaya Zvezda,* November 6, 1992, p. 2; and V. Badurkin interview with Dimitri Volkogonov in "Operation Anadyr," *Trud,* October 27, 1992, p. 3.

3. See *Foreign Affairs,* Fall 1991, p. 95.

4. See John J. Fialks and Frederick Kemps, "U.S. Welcomes Soviet Arms Plan, but Dismisses Pact as Propaganda," *Wall Street Journal,* January 17, 1986; Thomas C. Reed and Michael O. Wheeler, "The Role of Nuclear Weapons in the New World Order," December 1991; and note 1.

5. See Richard H. Immerman, ed., *John Foster Dulles and the Diplomacy of the Cold War* (Princeton: Princeton University Press, 1990), pp. 47–48.

6. National Academy of Sciences, "The Future of the U.S.-Soviet Nuclear Relationship" (Washington, D.C., 1991), p. 3.

7. McGeorge Bundy, William J. Crowe, Jr., and Sidney O. Drell, *Reducing Nuclear Danger: The Road away from the Brink:* (New York: Council on Foreign Relations Press, 1993), p. 100.

8. Andrew J. Goodpaster, "Further Reins on Nuclear Arms: Next Steps by Nuclear Powers," Atlantic Council, Washington, D.C., August 1993.

9. See Solly Zuckerman, *Nuclear Illusions and Reality* (New York: Viking, 1982), p. 70; and *Sunday Times* (London), February 21, 1982.

10. Henry Kissinger, "NATO Defense and the Soviet Threat," *Survival,* November–December 1979, p. 266.

11. Quoted in *Congressional Record,* July 1, 1981.

12. BBC Radio interview with Stuart Simon, July 16, 1987.

13. See *Washington Post,* April 12, 1982.

14. Larry Welch to Adam Scheinman, March 21, 1994.

15. *Boston Globe,* July 16, 1994.

16. Robert S. McNamara, "The Military Role of Nuclear Weapons," *Foreign Affairs,* Fall 1983, p. 79.

17. See Secretary Perry's statement to Stimson Center.

Select Bibliography
of Published Works

Adler, Renata. *Reckless Disregard: Westmoreland v. CBS et al.: Sharon v. Time.* New York: Knopf, 1986.

Ball, George W. *The Past Has Another Pattern: Memoirs.* New York: Norton, 1982.

Berman, Larry. *Lyndon Johnson's War: The Road to Stalemate in Vietnam.* New York: Norton, 1989.

————. *Planning a Tragedy: The Americanization of the War in Vietnam.* New York: Norton, 1982.

Beschloss, Michael R. *The Crisis Years: Kennedy and Khrushchev, 1960–1963.* New York: HarperCollins, 1991.

Brewin, Bob, and Sydney Shaw. *Vietnam on Trial.* New York: Atheneum, 1987.

Califano, Joseph A., Jr. *The Triumph and Tragedy of Lyndon Johnson: The White House Years.* New York: Simon & Schuster, 1991.

Charlton, Michael, and Anthony Moncrieff. *Many Reasons Why: The American Involvement in Vietnam.* New York: Hill & Wang, 1978.

Clarke, Jeffrey J. *United States Army in Vietnam,* vol. 3, *Advice and Support: The Final Years, 1965–1973.* Washington: U.S. Army Center of Military History, 1988.

Clifford, Clark, with Richard Holbrooke. *Counsel to the President: A Memoir.* New York: Random House, 1991.

Clodfelter, Mark. *The Limits of Air Power: The American Bombing of North Vietnam.* New York: Free Press, 1989.

Cooper, Chester L. *The Lost Crusade: America in Vietnam.* New York: Dodd, Mead, 1970.

Enthoven, Alain C., and K. Wayne Smith. *How Much Is Enough?: Shaping the Defense Program, 1961–1969.* New York: Harper & Row, 1971.

Gelb, Leslie H., with Richard K. Betts. *The Irony of Vietnam: The System Worked.* Washington: Brookings Institution, 1979.

Gibbons, William Conrad. *The U.S. Government and the Vietnam War: Executive and Legislative Roles and Relationships,* pt. 2, *1961–1964.* Washington: U.S. Government Printing Office, 1985.

———. *The U.S. Government and the Vietnam War: Executive and Legislative Roles and Relationships,* pt. 3, *January–July 1965.* Washington: U.S. Government Printing Office, 1988.

———. *The U.S. Government and the Vietnam War: Executive and Legislative Roles and Relationships,* pt. 4, *July 1965–January 1968.* Washington: U.S. Government Printing Office, 1994.

Gittinger, Ted, ed. *The Johnson Years: A Vietnam Roundtable.* Austin: Lyndon Baines Johnson Library, 1993.

Goulding, Phil G. *Confirm or Deny: Informing the People on National Security.* New York: Harper & Row, 1970.

Graff, Henry F. *The Tuesday Cabinet: Deliberation and Decision on Peace and War Under Lyndon B. Johnson.* Englewood Cliffs: Prentice Hall, 1970.

Halberstam, David. *The Best and the Brightest.* New York: Random House, 1972.

———. *The Making of a Quagmire.* New York: Random House, 1965.

Hammer, Ellen J. *A Death in November: America in Vietnam, 1963.* New York: Dutton, 1987.

Hammond, William M. *United States Army in Vietnam, Public Affairs: The Military and the Media, 1962–1968.* Washington: U.S. Army Center of Military History, 1988.

Herring, George C. *America's Longest War: The United States and Vietnam, 1950–1975.* 2d ed. New York: Knopf, 1986.

———. *LBJ and Vietnam: A Different Kind of War.* Austin: University of Texas Press, 1994.

———, ed. *The Secret Diplomacy of the Vietnam War: The Negotiating Volumes of the Pentagon Papers.* Austin: University of Texas Press, 1983.

Hilsman, Roger. *To Move a Nation: The Politics of Foreign Policy in the Administration of John F. Kennedy.* Garden City: Doubleday, 1967.

Hoopes, Townsend. *The Limits of Intervention: An Inside Account of How the*

Johnson Policy of Escalation in Vietnam Was Reversed. New York: McKay, 1969.

Isaacson, Walter. *Kissinger: A Biography.* New York: Simon & Schuster, 1992.

Johnson, Lyndon Baines. *The Vantage Point: Perspectives on the Presidency, 1963–1969.* New York: Holt, Rinehart and Winston, 1971.

Karnow, Stanley. *Vietnam: A History.* 2d ed. New York: Viking, 1991.

Kaufmann, William W. *The McNamara Strategy.* New York: Harper & Row, 1964.

Kearns, Doris. *Lyndon Johnson and the American Dream.* New York: Harper & Row, 1976.

Kissinger, Henry. *Diplomacy.* New York: Simon & Schuster, 1994.

Kowet, Don. *A Matter of Honor.* New York: Macmillan, 1984.

Kraslow, David, and Stuart H. Loory. *The Secret Search for Peace in Vietnam.* New York: Random House, 1968.

Krepinevich, Andrew F., Jr. *The Army and Vietnam.* Baltimore: Johns Hopkins University Press, 1986.

Lake, Anthony, ed. *The Legacy of Vietnam.* New York: New York University Press, 1976.

Lewy, Guenter. *American in Vietnam.* New York: Oxford University Press, 1978.

Littauer, Raphael, and Norman Uphoff, eds. *The Air War in Indochina.* Rev ed. Boston: Beacon Press, 1972.

Marolda, Edward J., and Oscar P. Fitzgerald. *The United States Navy and the Vietnam Conflict,* vol. 2, *From Military Assistance to Combat, 1959–1965.* Washington: Naval Historical Center, 1986.

McCloud, Bill, ed. *What Should We Tell Our Children About Vietnam?* Norman: University of Oklahoma Press, 1989.

McNamara, Robert S. *The Essence of Security: Reflections in Office.* New York: Harper & Row, 1968.

Momyer, William M. *Air Power in Three Wars.* Washington: U.S. Government Printing Office, 1978.

Nolan, Janne E., ed. *Global Engagement: Cooperation and Security in the Twenty-first Century.* Washington: Brookings Institution, 1994.

Nolting, Frederick. *From Trust to Tragedy: The Political Memoirs of Frederick Nolting, Kennedy's Ambassador to Diem's Vietnam.* New York: Praeger, 1988.

Palmer, Bruce, Jr. *The Twenty-five Year War: America's Military Role in Vietnam.* Lexington: University Press of Kentucky, 1984.

The Pentagon Papers: The Defense Department History of United States Deci-

sionmaking on Vietnam, Senator Gravel ed. 5 vols. Boston: Beacon Press, 1971.

Perry, Mark. *Four Stars.* Boston: Houghton Mifflin, 1989.

Pfeffer, Richard M., ed. *No More Vietnams?: The War and the Future of American Foreign Policy.* New York: Harper & Row, 1968.

Reeves, Richard. *President Kennedy: Profile of Power.* New York: Simon & Schuster, 1993.

Reston, James. *Deadline: A Memoir.* New York: Random House, 1991.

Rostow, W. W. *The Diffusion of Power: An Essay in Recent History.* New York: Macmillan, 1972.

Rusk, Dean, as told to Richard Rusk. *As I Saw It.* New York: Norton, 1990.

Rust, William J. *Kennedy in Vietnam.* New York: Scribner, 1985.

Schandler, Herbert Y. *The Unmaking of a President: Lyndon Johnson and Vietnam.* Princeton: Princeton University Press, 1977.

Schlesinger, Arthur M., Jr. *Robert Kennedy and His Times.* Boston: Houghton Mifflin, 1978.

————. *A Thousand Days: John F. Kennedy in the White House.* Boston: Houghton Mifflin, 1965.

Schlight, John. *The United States Air Force in Southeast Asia, The War in South Vietnam: The Years of the Offensive, 1965–1968.* Washington: Office of Air Force History, 1988.

Shaplen, Robert. *The Lost Revolution: The U.S. in Vietnam.* New York: Harper & Row, 1965.

Shapley, Deborah. *Promise and Power: The Life and Times of Robert McNamara.* Boston: Little, Brown, 1993.

Sharp, U. S. Grant. *Strategy for Defeat: Vietnam in Retrospect.* Novato: Presidio Press, 1978.

Sharp, U. S. Grant, and W. C. Westmoreland. *Report on the War in Vietnam, 1964–1968.* Washington: U.S. Government Printing Office, 1968.

Sheehan, Neil. *A Bright Shining Lie: John Paul Vann and America in Vietnam.* New York: Random House, 1988.

Shulimson, Jack. *U.S. Marines in Vietnam: An Expanding War, 1966.* Washington: U.S. Marine Corps History and Museums Division, 1982.

Shulimson, Jack, and Charles M. Johnson. *U.S. Marines in Vietnam: The Landing and the Buildup, 1965.* Washington: U.S. Marine Corps History and Museums Division, 1978.

Sorensen, Theodore C. *Kennedy.* New York: Harper & Row, 1965.

Taylor, Maxwell D. *Swords and Plowshares*. New York: Norton, 1972.

Trewhitt, Henry L. *McNamara*. New York: Harper & Row, 1971.

Ungar, Sanford J. *The Papers and the Papers: An Account of the Legal and Political Battle over the Pentagon Papers*. New York: Dutton, 1972.

U.S. Congress. Senate. Committee on Armed Services. *Air War Against North Vietnam: Hearings Before the Preparedness Investigating Subcommittee, August 9–29, 1967*. 90th Cong., 1st sess., 1967. Committee Print.

U.S. Department of State. *Foreign Relations of the United States, 1961–1963*, vol. 1, *Vietnam, 1961*. Washington: U.S. Government Printing Office, 1988.

———. *Foreign Relations of the United States, 1961–1963*, vol. 2, *Vietnam, 1962*. Washington: U.S. Government Printing Office, 1990.

———. *Foreign Relations of the United States, 1961–1963*, vol. 3, *Vietnam, January–August 1963*. Washington: U.S. Government Printing Office, 1991.

———. *Foreign Relations of the United States, 1961–1963*, vol. 4, *Vietnam, August–December 1963*. Washington: U.S. Government Printing Office, 1991.

———. *Foreign Relations of the United States, 1964–1968*, vol. 1, *Vietnam, 1964*. Washington: U.S. Government Printing Office, 1992.

VanDeMark, Brian. *Into the Quagmire: Lyndon Johnson and the Escalation of the Vietnam War*. New York: Oxford University Press, 1991.

The Vietnam Hearings. Introduction by J. William Fulbright. New York: Vintage Books, 1966.

Westmoreland, William C. *A Soldier Reports*. Garden City: Doubleday, 1976.

Acknowledgments

I am deeply indebted to many individuals and institutions for their help in the completion of this work. But none more than to Brian VanDeMark.

During my seven years as secretary of defense, I kept no diary, and, when I left the Pentagon, I took no records with me other than one three-ring binder of highly classified memoranda to Presidents Kennedy and Johnson. I would never have undertaken the task of writing this book had not Brian—a young professor of history at the U.S. Naval Academy, Annapolis; author of his own work on Vietnam, *Into the Quagmire;* and associate of Richard Holbrooke in the writing of Clark Clifford's autobiography—offered to help me. Above all else, his assignment was to ensure that, insofar as humanly possible, I remained true to the contemporaneous written, and taped, record—that where it ran contrary to my memory, I remained bound by the record. He performed that task to perfection.

But he did much, much more. We began by dividing my seven years of association with Vietnam into a series of time periods. For each he searched for and extracted documents from the Kennedy and Johnson presidential libraries, the Defense Department archives, the National Archives, and other public sources. To these were added material from personal interviews, oral histories, replies to written questions, and published articles and books. From all these sources, Brian provided me with a "file"—literally hundreds—of documents for each period. Based on these, I wrote the first draft of each chapter. Brian then reviewed my text for historical accuracy. In the process, he added to the balance and clarity of my writing. It is literally correct to say I could not have written this book without his collaboration.

Many others generously, and graciously, aided me in the preparation of the text.

I thank those who shared their own writings with me, in particular Raymond Aubrac, McGeorge Bundy, William Bundy, Roswell Gilpatric, Nicholas Katzenbach, Rear Adm. Eugene Carroll and Gene R. LaRocque, USN (Retired), Paul Warnke, and Adam Yarmolinsky.

I benefited greatly from the numerous people who read the manuscript carefully and critically, in whole or in part: McGeorge Bundy, William Bundy, Douglass Cater, Chester Cooper, Ben Eisman, Clayton Fritchey, David Ginsburg, Marion and Vernon Goodin, Phil Goulding, David Hamburg, Nicholas Katzenbach, Ernest May, Blanche Moore, Richard Neustadt, Robert Pastor, Walter Pincus, Lt. Gen. Robert Pursley, USAF (Retired), Elliot Richardson, Thomas Schelling, Arthur Schlesinger, Jr., Paul Warnke, Thomas Winship, and Adam Yarmolinsky. I did not accept all their suggestions—some offered alternative points of view or disagreed with my judgments—but I considered (and appreciated) every one of them.

Still more people helped in other ways.

William Gibbons and George Herring, two well-known Vietnam scholars, generously shared manuscripts of their latest monographs before publication. Nicole Ball researched the number of people killed by wars in the twentieth century. Martin Kaplan facilitated my correspondence with Raymond Aubrac. Blanche

Moore helped with translations and photographs. John Newman brought intelligence documents to my attention.

I chose Random House from among four publishers who bid for the book because of Peter Osnos, head of its Times Books division. Peter proved a marvelous editor, wise and involved from the beginning. He pushed me at the right moments—and supported me on the occasions when I was ready to give up. He and his editorial associate Geoffrey Shandler greatly improved the structure and flow of the narrative. The other Random House personnel who assisted in the book's publication—copy editor Susan M.S. Brown, designer Naomi Osnos, production and promotion staff—all worked with enthusiasm and efficiency.

Every step of the way, I relied on the good judgment and counsel of my literary agent, Sterling Lord, who bolstered the project with enthusiasm from concept to completion.

My endeavor has been greatly facilitated by the Defense Department's assistance. Alfred Goldberg, historian of the Office of the Secretary of Defense, and his associates Stuart Rochester, Lawrence Kaplan, Ronald Landa, and Steven Rearden read the manuscript both for factual errors and to question interpretive judgments. They offered many useful suggestions. The Pentagon's longtime director of administration and management, "Doc" Cooke, handled my access and clearance requests with dispatch. Harold Neeley, records administrator in the OSD, together with Brian Kinney and Sandra Meagher of its Declassification and Historical Research Branch, performed a variety of helpful chores. The Joint Chiefs of Staff Historical Division processed classified notes expeditiously.

Four government officials took time away from busy schedules to expedite access to records under their jurisdiction in my papers at the Pentagon and the National Archives: former Secretary of Defense Les Aspin; Secretary of State Warren Christopher; National Security Adviser Anthony Lake; and former CIA Director James Woolsey. I thank them all.

Previously restricted or unavailable records—used here for the first time—proved especially valuable in preparing my text: the Joint Chiefs of Staff's classified *History of the JCS and the War in Vietnam;* President Kennedy's recordings of White House meetings on Vietnam in the fall of 1963; and President Johnson's recorded telephone conversations, 1963–1968. I thank Gen. John Shalikashvili, Burke Marshall, and Harry Middleton, respectively, for arranging access to these important records.

Various institutions tendered much-needed and timely help, and I wish to acknowledge their contributions here: John Fitzgerald Kennedy Library, Boston, Massachusetts: Charles Daly, Bradley Gerratt, Suzanne Forbes, Mary Boluch, Stuart Culy, Allan Goodrich, William Johnson, June Payne, Maura Porter, and Ron Whealan; Lyndon Baines Johnson Library, Austin, Texas: Harry Middleton, Regina Greenwell, John Wilson, Claudia Anderson, Jacquie Demsky, Jeremy Duval, Ted Gittinger, Linda Hanson, Tina Houston, Mary Knill, Irene Parra, Philip Scott, and Jennifer Warner; State Department Historical Office: William Zlany, David Humphrey, and Glenn LaFantasie; Army Center of Military History: Vincent Demma; Office of Air Force History: Wayne Thompson; National Security Council Information Management and Disclosure Office: Nancy Menan and David Van Tassel; National Archives' Office of Presidential Libraries: John Fawcett and Edie Price.

Miss Jeanne Moore, my never-complaining secretary, worked nights and weekends through innumerable drafts and changes to produce the final text.

Index

Permissions Acknowledgments